Services Marketing

Services Marketing: Principles and Practice

Adrian Palmer
De Montfort University

Catherine Cole
University of Iowa

Prentice-Hall, Englewood Cliffs, New Jersey 07632

Library of Congress Cataloging-in-Publication Data

Palmer Adrian
    Services marketing: principles and practice / Adrian Palmer,
Catherine Cole
      p.   cm.
    Includes bibliographical references and index.
    ISBN 0-02-390563-8
    1. Service industries—Marketing.   I. Cole, Catherine.
II. Title.
HD9980.5.P26   1995
658.8—dc20   94–36242
                                  CIP

Editorial/Production Supervision: Ruttle, Shaw & Wetherill, Inc.
Acquisitions Editor: David Borkowsky
Assistant Editor: Melissa Steffens
Editorial Assistant: Aviva Rosenberg
Cover Designer: Bruce Kenselaar
Buyer: Marie McNamara

© 1995 by Prentice-Hall, Inc.
A Simon & Schuster Company
Englewood Cliffs, New Jersey 07632

Printed in the United States of America
10 9 8 7 6 5 4 3 2 1

ISBN 0-02-390563-8

Prentice-Hall International (UK) Limited, *London*
Prentice-Hall of Australia Pty. Limited, *Sydney*
Prentice-Hall Canada Inc. *Toronto*
Prentice-Hall Hispanoamericana, S.A., *Mexico*
Prentice-Hall of India Private Limited, *New Delhi*
Prentice-Hall of Japan, Inc., *Tokyo*
Simon & Schuster Asia Pte. Ltd., *Singapore*
Editora Prentice-Hall do Brasil, Ltda., *Rio de Janeiro*

Contents

Preface

The service sector today occupies a preeminent position in the economies of most Western countries. In the United States, more people now work in services industries than in manufacturing and agriculture combined. Not only are we producing and consuming more services than ever before, the markets in which they are provided are becoming much more competitive. Service producers have to be increasingly sure that they are producing the right services, in the right way, in the right places, for the right people, at the right time, for the right price. In short, marketing is more important in the service sector than it has ever been.

Many of the familiar principles of marketing were first developed when the fast-moving consumer goods markets experienced great growth in competitive activity. This legacy has been handed down to marketers who are engaged in the current growth in services marketing. Yet, it is now widely recognized that services can be quite different from goods in how they should be marketed. Some of the tried and tested frameworks for analysis cannot sensibly be stretched to cover services. The intangibility and inseparability of the service offer are just two factors that call for new approaches, for example, in understanding the ways in which buyers evaluate a service offer. Services are processes that usually involve customers in their production, calling for a whole new framework of analyzing producer–consumer interaction during the service encounter.

This book provides the student with a framework for understanding the key issues of services marketing. Readers who have developed their marketing skills in the context of goods marketing may find the contrasts presented in this book a revelation. For the student who needs reminding of some of the basic principles of marketing, Chapter 1 provides a brief overview.

It could be argued that in a truly market-oriented service organization, marketing is so fundamental that it cannot be separated from the other basic functions of a business. Indeed, many have argued that services marketing can be sensibly understood only as the bringing together of the principles of marketing, human resource management, and operations management. This is acknowledged in this book, where emphasis is placed on the management of personnel as a vital element of marketing a service offer. Similarly, the importance of operations management is recognized in tackling such problems as the peaked pattern of demand that faces many service organizations.

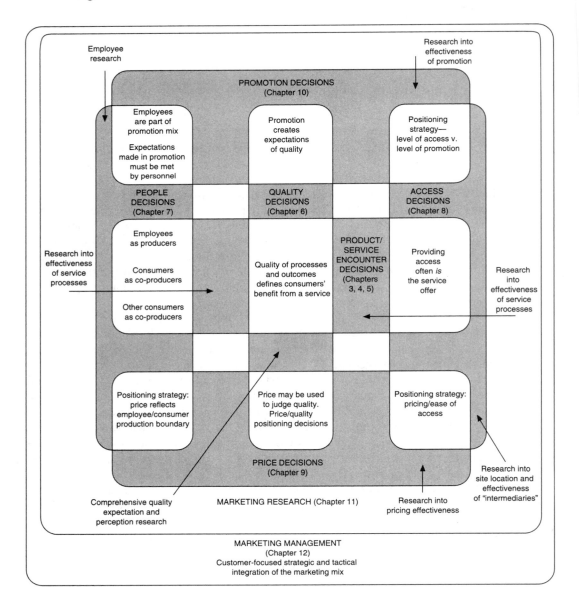

As with most marketing books, the arrangement of the chapters in this book is to some extent arbitrary, with many important overlaps between chapter topics. The first two chapters set the scene by trying to define the nature of services and basic marketing principles. Subsequent chapters examine aspects of marketing mix planning. Some of these chapters are based loosely on the traditional "4 Ps," but that concept is supplemented by analysis of issues that are quite unique to the service sector. In this respect, particular attention is paid to analyzing service encounters, the importance of service quality, and the topical subject of developing relationships with customers. The traditional "P" for place is redefined in terms of accessibility to services, and a fifth "P" for people is added. Finally, problems and opportunities in the internationalization of services are discussed.

Some indication of the organization of the book, and the interrelationships between chapters, is shown in the diagram.

Each chapter contains case studies that illustrate some of the principles discussed in the chapter. The cases are followed by review questions. To encourage further study of each topic, suggestions are made for further reading.

About the Authors

Adrian Palmer teaches in Services Marketing at De Montfort University, Leicester, United Kingdom. He previously worked in the travel and tourism industry, in which he continues to pursue an active research interest. He has written for numerous publications on that subject and has also published widely on the topic of relationship marketing. His teaching and research experience includes a period as Visiting Professor of Marketing at the University of North Carolina at Wilmington.

Catherine Cole is Assistant Professor of Marketing at The University of Iowa. She has taught services marketing to undergraduates, full-time executives, and off-campus MBA students. Her primary research involves studying how the purchasing habits of older consumers differ from those of their younger counterparts. In addition, she is interested in problems related to the development of promotional strategy for goods and services.

Acknowledgments

The authors gratefully acknowledge contributions from a number of specialists in their field:

Tony Conway, University College, Salford, United Kingdom (promotion of services);

Ian Clark, De Montfort University, United Kingdom (human resource management within the service sector);

Gary Gaeth, University of Iowa, Iowa City (services marketing);

Jasmine Williams, University of Plymouth Business School, United Kingdom (marketing research for services).

The authors would also like to acknowledge the contributions of many fine manuscript reviewers whose comprehensive suggestions were used to refine and develop *Services Marketing: Principles and Practice:*

David Bejou, University of North Carolina at Wilmington

Richard R. Brand, Florida State University

Craig A. Kelley, California State University at Sacramento

Gary McCain, Boise State University

Daryl McKee, Louisiana State University

Services Marketing

1

What Is Marketing?

CHAPTER OBJECTIVES

After reading this chapter, you should be able to understand

- the importance of marketing as a fundamental business philosophy in competitive services environments

- the nature of needs, wants, and exchanges in market-based distribution systems

- the tools by which marketing management responds to customer needs in the form of the marketing mix, and the appropriateness of these tools to the marketing of services

- the nature of a service organization's marketing environment, and frameworks for its analysis

- the nature of internal marketing and network marketing, and the importance attached to developing relationships with customers

1.1 INTRODUCTION

Marketing as a business discipline is becoming all embracing in Western economies, being adopted by large sections of both the private and the public sector. There are many definitions of marketing, and two typical definitions are presented here:

Marketing consists of "the anticipation, management, and satisfaction of demand through the exchange process."[1]

Marketing is the process of planning and executing the conception, pricing, promotion and distribution of ideas, goods and services to create exchange relationships and satisfy individual and organizational objectives.[2]

Most definitions of marketing revolve around the primacy of customers as part of an exchange process. Customers' needs are seen as the starting point for all marketing activity. Marketing managers try to identify these needs and then develop products that will satisfy customers' needs through an exchange process. While customers may drive the activities of a marketing-oriented organization, organizational factors constrain the extent to which an organization is actually able to cater to identified customer needs. Most private sector organizations operate under some kind of profit-related objectives, and if an adequate level of profits cannot be earned from a particular group of customers, a firm will not normally wish to meet those needs. In general, though, the closer an organization comes to meeting customers' needs, the greater is its ability to gain an advantage over its competitors and thereby sell a higher volume and/or at a higher price than its competitors. Consequently, it is also more likely to be able to meet its profit objectives.

Within the not-for-profit sectors, financial objectives are often qualified by nonfinancial social objectives. An organization's desire to meet individual customers' needs must be further constrained by its requirement to meet these wider social objectives. In this way a public library may set an objective of providing the public with a range of materials that help to develop the knowledge and skills of the population it serves. Therefore, the "quality press" may be the only type of newspapers purchased, although customers may request popular entertainment newspapers. This apparently centrally planned approach is not incompatible with a marketing philosophy—the library may work within its objectives of developing knowledge and skills by seeking to maximize the number of people reading its high-quality newspapers. Marketing strategies that might be employed to achieve this could include a promotional campaign, convenient hours, and a staff with a friendly, welcoming attitude.

The purpose of this chapter is to explore some of the key concepts of marketing that are of relevance to services, within both the private and the not-for-profit sectors. Readers who are familiar with marketing concepts can skip rapidly through this chapter and proceed to Chapter 2, which focuses on the distinctive characteristics of services. Many items introduced in this chapter are returned to for a more detailed analysis in subsequent chapters.

1.2 THE EMERGENCE OF MARKETING SUPREMACY

As the earlier example of the public library illustrates, it can sometimes be difficult to define the circumstances in which marketing is considered to be either desirable or feasible. This is particularly true of many services provided by the government, which are being exposed to increasing levels of competition. Before examining what marketing is in more detail, it would be useful to examine some alternative philosophies by which services have been delivered to the consumer, from both the private and the not-for-profit sectors. Despite its increasing importance as a business discipline, marketing neither is universal nor has been with us at all times.

Today, the needs of consumers assume primary importance in the provision of most services. However, in some circumstances, organizations have been driven by a desire more to reduce costs than to maximize the benefit received by consumers of their output. Organizations providing services on this basis are said to be operating in a production-oriented environment. At other times, the business environment has been dominated by the need for aggressive selling of an organization's output. This has been described as a philosophy of sales orientation (Figure 1.1).

1.2.1 Production Orientation

Marketing as a business discipline has much less significance where goods or services are scarce and considerable unsatisfied demand exists. If an organization is operating in a stable environment in which it can sell all that it can produce, why bother spending time and money trying to understand precisely what benefit a customer seeks from buying a product? If the market is stable, why take time trying to anticipate future requirements? Furthermore, if a company has significant monopoly power, it may have little interest in being more efficient in meeting customer requirements. The state monopolies of Eastern Europe are frequently cited as examples of organizations that produced what they imagined consumers wanted. Planning for full utilization of capital equipment was often seen as more important than ensuring that the equipment was used to provide goods and services that people actually wanted.

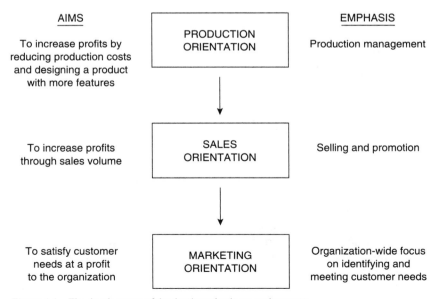

Figure 1.1   The development of the dominant business environment

Production-oriented firms aim for efficiency in production rather than effectiveness in meeting customers' needs.

In the United States, it has been argued that a production orientation was common until the 1920s, when a general shortage of goods relative to demand for them, and a lack of competition, resulted in a sellers' market. In the case of many goods markets, the world depression of the 1920s and 1930s had the effect of tilting the balance of supply and demand more in favor of buyers. As a result, sellers had to address the needs of increasingly selective customers more seriously. Services markets in most countries have tended to retain a production orientation longer than most goods markets. This reflected the fact that many key services—such as postal services, telecommunications, electricity, gas, and water supply—were dominated by state or private monopolies, which gave consumers very little if any choice of supplier. If consumers did not like the service they received from their electricity supplier, they could not switch their business to another electricity company. Management in these circumstances had greater freedom to satisfy their own interests rather than those of the consumer and could increase financial returns to their organization more effectively by keeping production costs down rather than by applying effort and possibly taking greater risk through developing new services based on consumers' needs.

A production orientation sometimes returns to services operating in an otherwise competitive market during periods of shortage. The shortage may come about through supply limitations caused by strikes or bad weather, or it may be the result of a sudden increase in demand relative to supply. For example, during a public transportation strike, taxi operators may realize that there is a temporary massive excess of demand relative to supply and so may be tempted to lower their standards of service to casual customers (e.g., by allowing longer waiting times and overlooking many of the operational courtesies that they would ordinarily provide).

1.2.2 Sales Orientation

Faced with an increasingly competitive market, the natural reaction of some organizations was to shout louder to attract customers to buy their products. No thought had yet gone into examining precisely what benefits customers sought from buying a product—product policy was driven by the desire to produce products that the company felt it was good at producing. However, in order to increase throughput, the focal point of the business moved away from the production manager to the sales manager. The company sought to increase effective demand by the use of various sales techniques. Advertising, sales promotion, and personal selling were increasingly used to emphasize product differentiation and branding.

A sales orientation was a move away from a strict product orientation, but it still did not focus on satisfying customer needs. Little effort was made to research customer needs and devise new offerings that were customer led rather than production led.

A sales orientation has been evident in a number of service sectors. Supermarkets have often grown by heavy advertising of their competitive price advantage, supported by aggressive sales promotion techniques within their stores. There are signs that this sales-led approach is now being replaced by a greater analysis of the diverse needs that customers seek to satisfy in a supermarket visit, such as the range of goods available, the atmosphere of the store, the speed of check-outs, and the quality of after-sales service. For example, Dominick's Finer Foods, a supermarket chain in the Chicago area, recently added a food court to one of its supermarkets. It plans to continue adding food courts in as many as a quarter of its eighty-six stores. These food courts serve food typically found in white-tablecloth restaurants: Caesar salad, Thai dishes, and twice-baked potatoes. The chain is trying to win back some of the food dollars that have increasingly gone to takeout eateries.[3]

If a company accurately identifies consumer needs and provides a product offering that satisfies these needs, then consumers should want to buy the product, and the company should not have to rely on intensive sales techniques. Thus, in the example just given, if the in-store food court meets genuine consumer needs, Dominick's should not have to rely on extensive couponing and discounting to generate customers and profit at the food courts.

In the words of Peter Drucker,

> The aim of marketing is to make selling superfluous. The aim of marketing is to know and understand the customer so well that the product or service fits him and sells itself. Ideally, marketing should result in a customer who is ready to buy. All that should be needed is to make the product or service available.[4]

1.2.3 Marketing Orientation

Marketing orientation as the dominant business discipline came about as increasingly competitive markets turned in favor of the buyers. It was no longer good enough for a company to simply produce what it was good at or to sell its products more aggressively than its competitors.

Some of the elements of marketing orientation can be traced far back to the ancient Greeks, the Phoenicians, and the Venetian traders. In modern times, a marketing orientation became important in the relatively affluent countries, among products where competition between suppliers had emerged most strongly. It became an important discipline in the United States from the 1950s and has since become dominant around the world. In a marketing-oriented business environment, an organization will survive in the long term only if it ascertains the needs of clearly defined groups in society and produces goods and services that satisfy their requirements. The emphasis is put on the customer's wanting to buy rather than the producer's needing to sell.

Many people have tried to define just what is meant by marketing orientation. Recent work by Narver and Slater[5] has attempted to define and measure the extent of a company's marketing orientation. Their analysis identifies three important components:

- *Customer orientation,* meaning that an organization understands its target buyers well enough to create superior value for them. This comes about through increasing the benefits to the buyer in relation to the buyer's costs or by decreasing the buyer's costs in relation to the buyer's benefits. A customer orientation requires that the organization understands value to the customer not only as it is today but also as it will evolve over time.

- *Competitor orientation,* defined as an organization's understanding of the short-term strengths and weaknesses and long-term capabilities and strategies of current and potential competitors.

- *Interfunctional coordination,* referring to the manner in which an organization uses its resources to create superior value for target customers. Many individuals within an organization, not just marketing staff, have responsibility for creating value. A marketing orientation requires that the organization draws upon and integrates its human and physical resources effectively and adapts them to meet customers' needs.

Marketing orientation is used to describe both the basic philosophy of an organization and the techniques it uses.

As a *business philosophy,* marketing puts the customer at the center of all the organization's considerations. Basic values, such as the requirement to understand and respond to customer needs and the necessity to constantly search for new market opportunities, are instilled in all members of a truly marketing-oriented organization. For a fast-food retailer, the training of serving staff would emphasize aspects such as the standard of dress and speed of service that research had found to be particularly valued by existing and potential customers. The personnel manager would have a selection policy that sought to recruit staff who could fulfill the needs of customers rather than simply minimizing the wage bill. The accountant would investigate the effects on customers before deciding to save money by cutting inventory levels, thereby possibly reducing customer choice. It is not sufficient for an organization to merely appoint a marketing manager or set up a marketing department. Viewed as a philosophy, marketing, like Total Quality Management, is an attitude that pervades the whole organization.

A marketing orientation is associated with a range of *techniques.* As an example, market research is a technique for finding out about customer needs, and advertising is a technique to communicate the service offer to potential customers. However, these techniques lose much of their value if they are conducted by an organization that has not fully embraced the philosophy of marketing. The techniques of marketing also include—among other things—pricing, the design of channels of distribution, and new product development. Within the services sector, it is now widely accepted that the motivation and control of service personnel are important marketing techniques. Application of these techniques to the services sector is described in later chapters.

CASE STUDY

WE'RE NOT DELTA—BUT WE'RE TRYING TO FLY!

"We want to be like Delta!" proclaimed Anatoly Brylov, Chief Executive of the Russian airline Aeroflot. That's quite an easy thing to say, but it poses an enormous challenge for an airline that is only just coming to terms with marketing. Delta has grown steadily from its 1920s origins as a Southern crop-spraying company to its present status as the number 3 airline in the United States. By all accounts, it is popular with its customers. It has to be, for most of its routes are operated in competition with other airlines (Figure 1.2). Aeroflot, by contrast, has been associated with everything that is anathema to the management of Delta. Travel on

They speak it in England, France and Germany. It sounds the same in the U.S., Hong Kong and Tokyo. It's the international language of business. And at Delta Air Lines, we understand how important it is for you to be a part of the conversation. That's why we offer you a schedule with more than 4,900 flights every day to over 300 cities in 34 countries around the world. And along the way, we'll provide a level of personal service so extraordinary, you won't have to say a word to be understood. So join us on your next business trip. We think you'll love the way we fly.

Wherever The International Language Of Business Is Spoken, We'll Make Sure You Don't Miss A Word.

▲DELTA AIR LINES
YOU'LL LOVE THE WAY WE FLY™

Based on cities served by Delta and the Delta Connection.® Delta Connection flights operate with Delta flight numbers 3000-5999 and 7000-7999. ©1994 Delta Air Lines, Inc.

Figure 1.2   Delta—an airline that has successfully grown by putting customers at the center of its efforts. Source: Delta Air Lines.

Aeroflot has been so haphazard and unpleasant that the airline—disparagingly referred to as "Aeroflop"—has often been described as the world's worst airline.

The contrast between Delta and Aeroflot can be explained in terms of the extent to which the two airlines have adopted a marketing orientation. Delta has had to fully embrace the principles and practices of marketing because if it didn't, competitors who did would soon win over customers. Aeroflot, on the other hand, has had little need for marketing. It operated in a centrally planned economy, where consumer sovereignty had little meaning. A passenger who wanted to fly somewhere usually had no choice but to fly with Aeroflot. Aeroflot's managers were not really concerned with attracting more passengers or making life better for their existing passengers. They saw themselves as government bureaucrats charged with implementing a centrally planned economic program. As long as they met very loosely defined targets, they were OK. The targets themselves weren't marketing targets at all but operational targets referring to the number of flights operated or the fuel consumption of aircraft. There was little concern for whether the flights were going to the right places at the right times, or with the right level of facilities before, during, and after the flight.

In a communist centrally planned economy, it was not surprising to find Aeroflot adopting a production orientation for its business. Operational considerations came first; passengers came second. Stories abound about what this actually meant for passengers. Planes were known to leave late because members of the crew were drunk. Baggage was routinely stolen by ground staff. The ticketing and reservations systems were corrupt and inefficient. It was commonplace for passengers to bribe flight attendants to be allowed onto an aircraft, even when all seats were full. As for in-flight services, there weren't any, unless warm water in plastic cups is counted.

The breakup of the former Soviet Union and the rapid disintegration of the centrally planned economy propelled Aeroflot into a new era in which marketing took on significance for the first time. The spur to marketing was the withdrawal of the heavy subsidies that the airline received from the government. The airline now had to earn all its income from fares paid by passengers—and those passengers were able to exercise increasing choice as the domestic civil aviation market was opened to competition for the first time.

The first thing the new management did was to repaint its fleet of aircraft with a new name: Aeroflot Russian International Airlines. That was a skin-deep change; to achieve a true marketing orientation, the airline had to embark on much more fundamental change. Part of that fundamental change was to impress upon staff that passengers were important people whose needs had to be satisfied rather than nuisances to be brushed aside. Staff had to be made aware that more than seventy new regional airlines had appeared on the scene, many of them competing with Aeroflot for passengers' business. One of these carriers—Uzbekistan Air—had already acquired modern Western-built aircraft and put its crews through a customer care program that even Delta might have approved of. The management structure also had to change from a monolithic, authoritarian structure to one that was able to integrate operational and marketing functions, in order to allow new opportunities to be profitably exploited.

Despite the enormity of the airline's task, some changes have already been put in place. The aircraft fleet is being modernized, and five European Airbuses have been leased. This should help allay potential customers' fears over the safety record of Aeroflot's primitive Tupolev and Illuyshin aircraft, many of which will be scrapped. Locally prepared in-flight meals have been replaced with products made in the West. Flight attendants have been attending politeness seminars, often run in conjunction with Western consultants. Several key executives have been enrolled in Western-run marketing and management courses. Fares are now determined with due regard to market considerations, rather than being set according to a central plan. Marketing research is now taken very seriously to monitor customers' reactions to the airlines' service levels. In short, "passengers" have become "customers" whose business can no longer be taken for granted.

Is Delta worried by the regeneration of Aeroflot? At the moment, there is very little direct competition between the two airlines, but over the longer term, Aeroflot has expressed its desire to become a global airline. It has already signed an agreement with British Airways, which will help it expand beyond its Russian base. Global success would have seemed preposterous to an observer of Delta back in 1924. But by putting customers first and adopting the principles and practices of marketing, Delta has achieved its current enviable position. With the same attitude and determination, Aeroflot could just do the same.

CASE STUDY REVIEW QUESTIONS

1. What do you consider to be Aeroflot's principal problems in its attempts to introduce a marketing orientation to its business?
2. Discuss how airlines in the United States have segmented the air travel market. Compare the marketing efforts of Delta Air Lines with those of a discount airline such as Kiwi Air Lines or MarkAir (operating out of Chicago's Midway airport) in reaching these different segments.
3. How should Aeroflot go about analyzing the needs of its potential customers? How could Aeroflot make effective use of market segmentation and other marketing techniques in the light of increasing competition in the Russian air travel market?

1.3 KEY MARKETING CONCEPTS

Marketing activity in any organization has no beginning or end—marketing-oriented organizations continually monitor their operating environments and respond by adapting their output to meet changing needs. Some of the key elements of the marketing process are presented here and will be returned to in more detail in later chapters.

Needs

The starting point for all marketing activity is the complex set of needs that consumers seek to satisfy. We no longer live in a society in which the main motive of individuals is to satisfy the basic needs for food and drink. Maslow [6] recognized that once individuals have satisfied these basic physiological needs, they may seek to satisfy social needs—for example, the need to have fruitful interaction with peers. More complex still, Western cultures see increasing numbers of people seeking to satisfy essentially internal needs for self-satisfaction (Figure 1.3). Services therefore satisfy increasingly complex needs. Food is no longer seen as a basic necessity to be purchased and cooked for one's own consumption. With growing prosperity, people have attempted to satisfy social needs by eating out with friends or family. With further prosperity still, the need to simply eat out with friends becomes satisfied, and a higher-order need emerges to experience different types of meals. Thus, the great growth in eating out that occurred during the 1970s and 1980s has been followed by a growing diversity of restaurants that cater to peoples' need for variety and curiosity,

Figure 1.3   Needs, wants, demand, and exchange

and the emergence in many American towns of restaurant styles as diverse as Spanish, Japanese, Malaysian, and Australian. With the fulfillment of basic needs, consumers develop higher expectations of services.

Need refers to something that is rooted deeply in an individual's personality. How individuals seek to satisfy needs will be conditioned by the society of which they are members. Thus, the need for team-based competitive physical exercise may express itself in the United States in a desire to play basketball, whereas in Britain it is more likely to be met by playing soccer. Wants, culturally conditioned by the society in which an individual lives, are referred to as expressed wants rather than needs. Wants subsequently become effective demand for a product when there is both a willingness and an ability to pay for the product.

While this analysis reflects the needs likely to be felt by private buyers of services, it must not be forgotten that commercial buyers of services have complex needs they also attempt to satisfy. Greater complexity occurs when the economic needs of the organization may not be entirely the same as the personal needs of individuals within the organization. For example, a business traveler may prefer to fly Delta Air Lines because of a mileage club membership, but her employer may want the employee to fly the least expensive carrier.

Exchange

Goods and services can be acquired in many ways. One primitive way is by hunting for food. Another, for some people in some societies, is by begging. In socialist economies—and for many public services in Western economies—goods and services are acquired as a result of centrally planned decisions. For organizations operating in a marketing environment, goods are acquired—and needs satisfied—on the basis of exchange. Exchange implies that each party gives something of value to the other party. There is a presumption that each party can decide whether or not to enter into an exchange with the other party and can choose between several alternative potential partners. In the usual form of exchange, a product is exchanged for money; however, in some trading systems goods and services are exchanged through barter. In some cases, the value that potential customers place on a product is below the cost to an organization of producing it; therefore, in the case of profit-motivated organizations, no exchange of value normally takes place over the longer term.

Marketers have debated whether exchange is an essential element of marketing. The restricted view that marketing is based on a series of discrete exchanges has been refined, adapted, and extended by many writers in the attempt to incorporate the concept of external benefits provided by some producers (usually in the not-for-profit sectors) when it is neither possible nor desirable to charge the recipient for the benefits received. In this sense, it has been argued that the payment of taxes to the government in return for the provision of social services is a form of social marketing exchange, although it is difficult to identify what sovereignty consumers of government services have in determining the manner or source of their delivery.[7] Others have tried to move the defining characteristic of marketing away from the concept of exchange to one of matching.[8] More recently, marketers have attempted to move the analysis of exchange transactions away from a series of discrete exchanges toward ongoing relationships, as will be discussed.

Value

In an exchange between an organization and its customers, one party generally expects to receive something that it values from the other party, in return for which it gives something that the other party values. For the service supplier, value may be represented by payment received; for some not-for-profit services, by more qualitative factors such as the SAT scores of incoming students to a university. For customers, value is represented by the ratio of perceived benefits to price paid. Customers will evaluate benefits according to the extent to which a service allows their needs to be satisfied. Customers also evaluate how well the service benefits add to their own wellbeing in comparison with competitors' offerings.

The value consumers place on an offer may be quite different from the value as perceived by the service producer. Service organizations succeed by adding value at a faster rate than they add to their own production costs. Value can be added by specifying the service offer in accordance with customers' expectations of its attributes—for example, by providing easy access to the service or the reassurance of after-sales service.

Customers

Customers provide payment to an organization in return for the delivery of goods and services and therefore form a focal point for an organization's marketing activity. The customer is generally understood to be the person who makes the decision to purchase a service and/or the one who pays for it. In fact, services—like goods—are often bought by one person for consumption by another; therefore, the customer and the consumer need not be the same person. For example, colleges must market themselves not only to high school seniors, but also to the parents, guidance counselors, alumni, and employers. In these circumstances it can indeed be difficult to identify whom an organization's marketing effort should be focused upon.

The nature of the relationship between customers and producers often differs between the manufactured goods and services sectors in two significant ways. First, suppliers of services are often in a position of trust in relation to their customers, something not so commonly found in the brief transactions that generally occur when goods are sold from a company to its customers. The professional nature of the relationship is often reflected in the names used to describe customers: *patient* implies a caring relationship, *passenger* implies an ongoing responsibility for the safety of the customer, and *client* implies that the relationship is governed by a formal or informal code of ethics. Second, many publicly supplied services differ from goods in that society as a whole, not just the immediate customer, benefits from their consumption. In education, it can be naive to regard the student as the customer, or even their parents or sponsors. In fact, society as a whole can be regarded as the customer, because we all benefit from having a more highly trained and literate work force.

Markets

The term *market* has traditionally referred to a place where buyers and sellers gather to exchange goods and services. Economists refined this definition to include the abstract concept of the interaction between buyers and sellers, so that we can talk about the insurance market as referring to the aggregate level of transactions between all buyers and sellers of insurance, regardless of the existence of a formal marketplace. Marketers more commonly confine the term *market* to describe characteristics of consumers rather than producers. The hotel market is defined in terms of those people who have the need and want to stay in a hotel and have the willingness and ability to pay for it.

Different customers within a market have different needs they seek to satisfy. To be fully marketing oriented, a company would have to adapt its offering to meet the needs of each individual. In fact, very few firms can justify aiming to meet the needs of each specific individual; instead, they aim to meet the needs of small subgroups within the market. These subgroups are referred to as segments. A segment represents a subsection of a market where people share similar needs, to which a company responds with a product offering designed to meet these specific needs. People or firms within a market can be segmented according to various criteria. An example of how a market can be broken down into segments is shown in Figure 1.4, where a three-dimensional criterion for segmenting a market in terms of sex, income level, and environmental awareness results in twenty-seven different segments, only some of which are likely be of interest to an organization.

A target market is the segment toward which a business directs its strategies. The development of segmentation and target marketing reflects the movement away from production orientation toward marketing orientation. When the supply of services is scarce relative to demand, organizations may attempt to minimize production costs by producing one homogeneous product that satisfies the needs of the whole population. Over time, increasing affluence has increased customers' expectations. Affluent customers are no longer satisfied with a basic bank checking account. Instead, they are able to demand one that satisfies an increasingly wide range of needs—not just for money transfer, but for security, ease of operation, and status associations. Furthermore, society has become much more fragmented and the "average" consumer has become much more of a myth as incomes, attitudes, and lifestyles have diverged. For the purpose of market analysis, consumers of services can be segmented on the basis of socioeconomic, geodemographic, and behavioral factors. The bases for identifying market segments are considered in more detail in Chapter 5.

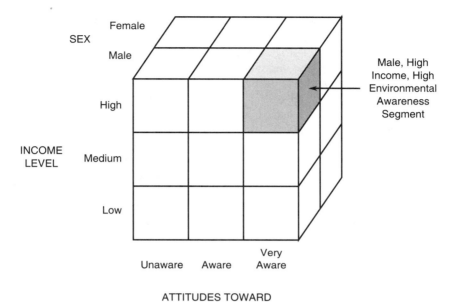

Figure 1.4   Hypothetical segmentation of a population by income, sex, and attitudes toward environmental issues

Alongside the greater fragmentation of society, technology is increasingly allowing highly specialized services to be tailored to ever smaller market segments. Using computerized databases, insurance companies need no longer aim their policies at broad market segments but can allow individual customers to put together elements of coverage that most effectively meet their needs.

1.4   THE MARKETING MIX

The marketing mix is the set of tools available to the marketing manager and used to shape the nature of the service offered to consumers. The tools can be used to develop both long-term strategies and short-term tactical programs. A marketing manager can be seen as someone who mixes a set of ingredients to achieve a desired outcome, much as a cook mixes ingredients for a cake. Two cooks may meet a common objective of baking an edible cake by the end of the day, but they may use very different sets of ingredients to achieve their objective. Marketing managers can similarly be seen as mixers of many ingredients that may differ in content but achieve similar objectives. The mixing of ingredients in both cases is a combination of a science—learning by a logical process from what has proved effective in the past—and an art form, in that both the cook and the marketing manager frequently encounter situations in which they have no direct experience to draw upon and must make a creative decision.

The concept of the marketing mix was given prominence by Borden, who described the marketing executive as "a mixer of ingredients, one who is constantly engaged in fashioning creatively a mix of marketing procedures and policies in his efforts to produce a profitable enterprise."[9]

Identifying the ingredients of the marketing mix has led to some debate. Borden initially identified twelve elements of the marketing mix of manufacturers, although these were later simplified by other authors. The framework that has endured reduced the marketing mix to four elements: the familiar "4 Ps" of Product, Price, Promotion, and Place.[10] Each of these elements in turn has its own mix of ingredients. Thus the Promotion element involves the mixing of various combinations of advertising, sales promotion, personal selling, and public relations.

Borden's initial analysis of marketing mix elements was based on a study of the manufacturing industry at a time when the importance of services to the economy was considered to be relatively unimportant. More recently, the "4 Ps" of the marketing mix have been found to be too limited in their application to services. Some particular problems can be identified:

- The intangible nature of services is overlooked in most analyses of the mix. For example, the product mix is frequently analyzed in terms of tangible design properties, which may not be relevant to a service. Likewise, physical distribution management may not be an important element of place mix decisions.
- The price element overlooks the fact that many services are provided by the not-for-profit sectors and a price is not charged to the final consumer.
- The promotion mix of the traditional "4 Ps" fails to recognize the promotion of services that takes place at the point of consumption by production personnel. This is in contrast to the situation with most fast-moving consumer goods, which are normally produced away from the consumer, resulting in no direct opportunities for production personnel to be involved in promotion to the final consumer. For a bank clerk, hairdresser, or singer, the manner in which a service is produced is an important element of the total promotion of the service.

As well as throwing up ambiguities about the meaning of some of these four elements of the marketing mix, this simple list also fails to recognize several key factors that marketing managers in the service sector use to design their service output. Particular problems focus on these issues:

- The difficulty in defining the concept of quality for intangible services and of identifying and measuring the mix elements that can be managed in order to create a quality service
- The importance of people as an element of the service product, both as coproducers and as coconsumers
- The oversimplification of the elements of distribution that are of relevance to strategic services distribution decisions

To compensate for these weaknesses, analysts have redefined the marketing mix in a manner that is more applicable to the service sector. While many have attempted to refine the marketing mix for general application[11,12,13] the expansions by Booms and

Bitner[14] and Christopher, Payne, and Ballantyne[15] provide useful frameworks for analysis, even though they are not empirically proven theories of services marketing. In addition to the four traditional elements of the marketing mix, both frameworks add the elements of People and Process. In addition, Booms and Bitner talk about Physical Evidence making up a seventh "P," while Christopher et al. add Customer Service as another element.

The principle of the extended marketing mix (as indeed with the traditional marketing mix) is to break a service offering down into component parts and to arrange them into manageable subject areas for making strategic decisions. Decisions on one element of the mix can be made only by reference to other elements of the mix in order to give a sustainable product positioning (see Chapter 12). The importance attached to each element of the extended marketing mix will vary between services—in a highly automated service such as vending machine dispensing, the people element will be a less important element of the mix than in a people-intensive business such as a restaurant.

A brief overview of these extended marketing mix elements is given here; fuller discussion will follow in the subsequent chapters.

Products.   Products are the means by which organizations seek to satisfy consumer needs. A product in this sense is anything an organization offers to potential customers that might satisfy a need, whether tangible or intangible. After initial hesitation, most marketing managers are now happy to talk about an intangible service as a product. Bank accounts, insurance policies, vacations, rock stars, and even politicians are frequently referred to as products, sometimes to the amusement of nonmarketers.

Product mix decisions facing a services marketer can be very different from those dealing with goods. Most fundamentally, pure services can be defined only by using process descriptions rather than tangible descriptions of outcomes. Quality becomes a key element defining the product. Other elements of the product mix, such as design, reliability, brand image, and product range, may sound familiar to a goods marketer but assume different roles, as discussed in Chapter 3. Another significant difference from goods is that new service developments cannot be easily protected by patent.

Pricing.   Price mix decisions include strategic and tactical decisions about the average level of prices to be charged, discount structures, terms of payment, and the extent to which price discrimination between different groups of customers is to take place. These are very similar to the issues facing a goods marketer. Differences do occur, however, when the intangible nature of a service can mean that price itself can become a very significant indicator of quality. The personal and nontransferrable nature of many services presents additional opportunities for price discrimination within service markets, while the fact that many services are marketed by the public sector at a subsidized price, or at no price, can complicate price setting.

Promotion.   The traditional promotion mix includes various methods of communicating the benefits of a service to potential consumers. The mix is traditionally broken down into four elements: advertising, sales promotion, public relations, and personal selling. While the promotion mix for goods may appear similar to the mix for services, the promotion of services often needs to place particular emphasis on increasing the apparent tangibility of a service. Also, in the case of services marketing, production personnel can themselves become an important element of the promotion mix.

Place.   Place decisions refer to the ease of access that potential customers have to a service. Place decisions can therefore involve physical location decisions (as in deciding where to place a hotel), decisions about which intermediaries to use in making a service accessible to a consumer (e.g., whether a tour operator uses travel agents or sells its vacations direct to customers), and nonlocational decisions used to make services available (e.g., the use of telephone delivery systems). For pure services, decisions about how to physically move goods are of little strategic relevance. However, most services involve movement of some form of goods. These may be materials necessary to produce a service (such as travel brochures and fast-food packaging material), or the service can have as its whole purpose the movement of goods (e.g., freight forwarders, plant rental).

People.   For most services, people are a vital element of the marketing mix. Where production can be separated from consumption—as is the case with most manufactured goods—management can usually take measures to reduce the direct effect of people on the final output as received by customers. Therefore, how a car is made is of relatively minor interest to the person who buys it. He or she is not concerned about whether a production worker dresses untidily, uses bad language at work, or turns up for work late, as long as there are quality control measures that reject the results of lax behavior before they reach the customer. In service industries, everybody can be described as a "part-time marketer"[16] in that their actions have a much more direct effect on the output received by customers.

While the importance attached to people management in improving quality within manufacturing companies is increasing—for example, through the development of quality circles—people planning assumes much greater importance within the service sector. This is especially true in services whose staff members have a high level of contact with customers. For this reason, it is essential that services organizations clearly specify what is expected from personnel in their interaction with customers. To achieve the specified standard, methods of recruiting, training, motivating, and rewarding staff cannot be regarded as purely personnel decisions—they are important marketing mix decisions.

People planning within the marketing mix also involves developing a pattern of interaction between customers themselves, which can assume great importance where service consumption takes place in public. An important means by which diners judge a restaurant might be the kind of people who frequent it. Casual dress standards might make it difficult for the restaurant to develop an upscale image. As well as planning the human input to its own production, marketing management must also develop strategies for producing favorable interaction between its customers—for example, by excluding certain groups and developing a physical environment that affects customers' behavior.

Physical evidence. The intangible nature of most services means that potential customers are unable to judge a service before it is consumed, increasing the riskiness inherent in a purchase decision. An important part of marketing mix strategy, therefore, is to reduce this level of perceived risk by offering tangible evidence about the nature of the service. This evidence can take various forms. At its simplest, a brochure can describe and give pictures of important elements of the service product—a vacation brochure gives pictorial evidence of hotels and resorts for this purpose. The appearance of staff can give evidence about the nature of a service—a tidily dressed ticket clerk for an airline gives some evidence that the airline operation as a whole is run with care and attention. Buildings are frequently used to give evidence of service nature. A clean, bright environment used in a service outlet can help reassure potential customers at the point where they make a service purchase decision. For this reason, fast-food and photo processing outlets often use red and yellow color schemes to convey an image of speedy service.

Process. Services are best defined in terms of their production processes rather than their tangible outcomes. Whereas the process of production is usually of little concern to the consumer of manufactured goods, it is often of critical concern to the consumer of "high contact" services where the customer can be seen as a co-producer of the service. A customer of a restaurant is deeply affected by the manner in which staff serve them and the amount of waiting that is involved during the production process. Issues arise as to the boundary between the producer and consumer in terms of the allocation of production functions—for example, a restaurant might require customers to collect their meals from a counter, or to throw away their own trash. With services, a clear distinction cannot be made between marketing and operations management.

Customer service. The meaning of customer service varies from one organization to another. Within the service sector, it can best be described as the total quality of the service process as perceived by the customer. Managing the level of service quality becomes an important feature of the marketing mix for services, and responsibility for defining, delivering, and monitoring service quality levels cannot be isolated within a narrowly defined customer services department. It becomes a concern of all production personnel, both those directly employed by the organization and those employed by its suppliers. Service quality decisions are closely linked to decisions on the related marketing mix elements of product design and personnel.

The definition of the elements of the marketing mix is not scientific—it is largely intuitive and semantic. In addition to the four traditional "Ps", this book recognizes the importance of the fifth "P" of people and devotes a chapter to this element. The importance of service production processes is reflected in the attention given to encounters between producers and consumers, and a chapter is therefore devoted to analyzing buyer-seller consumption-production processes. The importance of quality in customers' perception of service is reflected in a chapter on the conceptualization and measurement of service quality. The importance of tangible evidence is recognized in a number of chapters; for example, it is recognized as an important element in the product design and promotional elements.

1.5 THE MARKETING ENVIRONMENT

A marketing orientation requires organizations to monitor their environments and to adjust their offering so that consumer needs are fulfilled, thereby facilitating the organization in meeting its own objectives. An organization's marketing environment can be defined as

> . . . the actors and forces external to the marketing management function of the firm that impinge on the marketing management's ability to develop and maintain successful transactions with its customers.[17]

Here, marketing has to look both into its organization and to the outside world. Within the organization, the structure and politics of an organization affect the manner in which it responds to changing consumer needs. An organization that assigns marketing responsibilities to a narrow group of people may in fact create tensions within the organization, which make it less effective at responding to changing consumer needs than one in which marketing responsibilities are disseminated widely.

The external environment comprises all those uncontrollable events outside the organization that impinge on its activities. Some of these events impinge directly on the firm's activities and can be described as the immediate external environment. Other events, which are beyond the immediate environment, nevertheless affect the organization and can be described as the indirect external environment (Figure 1.5).

The immediate external environment of an organization includes suppliers and distributors. It may deal directly with some of these, while others exist with whom there is currently no direct contact but who could nevertheless influence its policies.

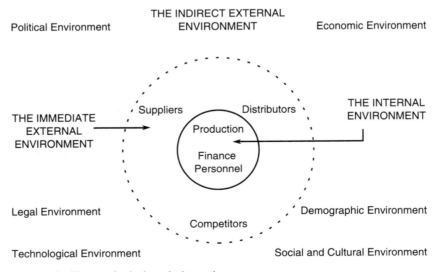

Figure 1.5   The organization's marketing environment

Similarly, an organization's competitors could have a direct effect on its market position and form part of its immediate external environment.

Beyond this immediate external environment is the indirect external environment, which comprises a whole set of factors that can indirectly affect an organization's relationship to its markets. The organization may have no direct relationships with legislators as it does with suppliers, yet their actions in passing new legislation may have profound effects on the markets the organization seeks to serve and may also affect its production costs. The indirect environmental factors cover a wide range of nebulous phenomena. They represent general forces and pressures rather than institutions that the organization relates directly to. There are various methods of describing these factors, some of which are described briefly here.

The economic environment.   The development of services markets tends to be closely related to the rate of economic growth, with the proportion of Gross Domestic Product (GDP) consumed by services tending to increase as total GDP per capita rises. Throughout the economic cycle, service consumption tends to increase during the boom period and to decline during recessionary periods. The difficulty in forecasting the level of demand for a service activity is therefore often quite closely linked to the difficulty of forecasting future economic prosperity. This difficulty is compounded by the problem of understanding the relationship between economic factors and the state of demand. Most services are positively related to total available income, but some—such as bus services and bankruptcy lawyers—are negatively related. Furthermore, while aggregate changes in spending power may indicate a likely increase for services in general, the actual distribution of spending power among the population will influence the pattern of demand for a specific service. In addition to measurable economic prosperity, the level of perceived wealth and confidence in the future can be important determinants of demand for some high-value services.

An analysis of the economic environment will also indicate the level of competitor activity: an oversupply of services in a market sector normally results in a downward pressure on prices and profitability. Competition for resources could also affect the production costs of an organization, which in turn will affect its production possibilities and pricing decisions. Rising unemployment may put downward pressure on wage rates, favoring service providers who offer a labor-intensive service.

The political environment.   Politicians are instrumental in shaping the general nature of the external environment as well as being responsible for passing legislation that affects specific service providers. At a national level, government is responsible for the nature of the economic environment (through its monetary and fiscal policy) and for the distribution of income and wealth between the public sector, the company sector, and individuals and also between different groups of individuals. Federal and state governments pass legislation that can affect market and production possibilities for individual firms, including the competitive framework within which service providers operate.

The political environment includes supranational organizations that can directly or indirectly affect service providers. These can be highly specific in their effects on an industry (e.g., the International Civil Aviation Organization is an international quasigovernmental body concerned with setting international standards in civil aviation), or they can be general multilateral agreements between governments (e.g., the General Agreement on Tariffs and Trade affects access to overseas markets for many services industries).

The social and cultural environment.   Attitudes to specific services change over time and between different groups at any one time. As an example, attitudes toward healthy living have changed from representing values held by a small fanatical minority to those which now represent mainstream cultural values. Marketers who monitored this emerging value system have been able to respond with a wide range of services, such as fitness clubs and low-fat items on restaurant menus. The dominant cultural attitude toward the role of women has similarly changed, presenting many new challenges for services marketers. The increased acceptability for young mothers to continue working has given rise to a large childcare and home-care service sector. New challenges for the marketing of services are posed by the diverse cultural traditions of ethnic minorities, as is seen by the growth of travel agencies catering to families wishing to visit relatives or go on religious pilgrimages.

The demographic environment.   Changes in the size and age structure of the population are critical to many services organizations, for predicting both the demand for service output and the availability of service personnel required for production. Analysis of the demographic environment raises many issues that are important to services organizations. Although the total population of most Western countries is stable, their composition is changing. Most countries are experiencing an increase in the proportion of elderly people. Organizations have monitored this growth and responded with the development of residential homes, cruise holidays, and financial portfolio management services aimed at meeting the needs of this growing group (Figure 1.6). At the other end of the age spectrum, the birth rate of most countries is cyclical. The decline in the birth rate in the United States in the late 1970s initially had a profound effect on those services providing for the very young, such as maternity wards in hospitals and kindergartens. Organizations who monitored the progress of this diminished cohort were prepared for the early 1990s, when there were fewer teenagers requiring high schools or wanting to buy music from record shops. Service providers who had relied in the early 1980s on the over supply of teenage labor to provide a cheap input to their service production process could have reacted to the downturn in numbers by replacing quantity of staff with quality and by mechanizing many jobs previously performed by the teenagers.

Other aspects of the demographic environment that service providers need to monitor include the changing geographical distribution of the population (between different regions of the country and between urban and rural areas), the changing composition of households (especially the service requirements of the growing num-

Figure 1.6   More affluent elderly consumers make for new market opportunities. Source: 1993 Sharon Brooks & Associates for Classic Residence by Hyatt.

ber of single-person households), and the effects of the growing cultural diversity of the population.

The technological environment.   To the services marketer, technological developments must be monitored for their effects in four related areas:

- Technological development allows new services to be offered to consumers: telephone chatlines, karaoke bars, and fax bureaus, for example.
- New technology can allow existing services to be produced more cheaply, thereby lowering their price and widening their markets. In this way, more efficient aircraft have allowed new markets for air travel to develop.
- Technological development allows for new methods of distributing services. Bank ATM machines allow many banking services to be made available at times and places that were previously not economically possible, while modern technology-based control systems allow home shopping services to be made more widely available.
- New opportunities for service providers to communicate with their target customers

have emerged. Many financial services organizations have used information technology to develop databases to target potential customers and to maintain a dialogue with established customers.

1.6 DISTINCTIVE CHARACTERISTICS OF NOT-FOR-PROFIT MARKETING

Organizations operating in the not-for-profit sector now account for about 20 percent of all economic activity in the United States. Many types of organizations operate in this sector, which can be classified as cultural (e.g., museums, art galleries, orchestras), knowledge-oriented (colleges, schools, research organizations), public (city, state, federal government, and quasigovernmental services such as the U.S. Postal Service), philanthropic (charities, welfare organizations), social causes (environmental and consumer groups), and religious (churches and religious associations).

Over time, marketing has become an important activity for not-for-profit organizations, reflecting an increasingly competitive environment in which many of them operate. Many organizations, such as museums and recreational facilities, are being given clearly defined business objectives that make it much more difficult for them to continue doing what they like doing rather than what the public they serve wants. Marketing orientation has been most rapidly adopted by those not-for-profit organizations that provide marketable goods and services, such as urban public transportation services. An organization that is a monopoly provider of a statutory service and that cannot be subjected to the test of market forces—a police force or a fire service, for example—finds it much more difficult to fully adopt the marketing philosophy.

Although the not-for-profit sector covers a wide range of services operating in diverse environments, a few generalizations can be made about the ways in which their marketing differs from that provided by the private sector:

- The aim of most private sector organizations is to earn profits for the owners of the organization. In contrast to these quantifiable objectives, not-for-profit organizations operate with relatively diverse and unquantified objectives. For example, a museum may have qualitative scholarly objectives in addition to relatively quantifiable objectives, such as maximizing revenue or the number of visitors.

- The private sector is usually able to monitor the results of its marketing activity, as the benefits are usually internal to the organization. By contrast, many aims that not-for-profit organizations attempt to achieve are external. A profit-and-loss statement cannot be produced in the way that is possible with a private sector organization operating under narrow internal financial goals.

- The degree of discretion given to a private sector marketing manager is usually greater than that given to a counterpart in the not-for-profit sector. The checks and balances imposed on many of the latter reflect the fact that their organizations are accountable to a wider constituency of interests than the typical private sector organization.

- Many of the marketing mix elements that private sector organizations can tailor to meet the needs of specific groups of users are often not open to the not-for-profit marketer. For public services that are not traded, price—if it is used at all—is a reflection of centrally determined social values rather than of the value placed on a service by consumers.

- Not-for-profit organizations are frequently involved in supplying publicly beneficial services in which it can be difficult to identify just who the customer is. Should the customer of a school be regarded as the student, the parents, or society as a whole, which is investing in the trained workforce of tomorrow?

- Just as the users of some public services may have no choice in who supplies their service, so too the suppliers may have no choice in who they can provide services to. Within the not-for-profit sectors, organizations may be constrained by their constitutions from providing services beyond specified groups of users. On the other hand, some not-for-profits may be required by law to supply service to specific groups, even though a market-led decision may lead them not to supply.

CASE STUDY

U.S. POSTAL SERVICE TRIES TO DELIVER BETTER SERVICE WITH MARKETING

Historically, governments have been eager to have a monopoly on mail services in their countries. At first, some might have seen control of the mail as a means of controlling communication between possibly critical groups in society. While this motivation for a monopoly has all but passed, governments have recognized that a good postal service is an essential part of the social and economic infrastructure of a country. Like good roads and education facilities, a postal service is vital to secure social and economic development. In the early history of the United States, a nationwide postal organization was seen as important in facilitating communication to the farthest reaches of the expanding union. Had it been left to private market forces, there was a danger that postal service would have been provided by a series of local carriers who concentrated on the trunk routes, possibly to the detriment of remote parts of the Union.

The federal government, therefore, became a carrier of last resort—its postal service was required to carry mail for anybody to any place, as long as the sender was able to pay a postage charge in accordance with a standard scale of charges. Like many public services, the U.S. Mail became a very rigid bureaucracy, in which individuals were rewarded for observing rules rather than for showing initiative. If rules said that a parcel couldn't be delivered, then it wouldn't be delivered. If the rules said that users had a right for a parcel to be accepted for delivery, the service had to accept it at a flat standard charge, regardless of the remoteness of the destination and the loss the postal service would incur on the transaction. The U.S. Mail had "users" rather than "customers," and its workers saw themselves as providing a necessary public service rather than seeking to maximize users' benefits.

While the U.S. Mail was tied down by bureaucracy, liberalization of the market saw the expansion of private-sector letter and parcel carriers, most notably United Parcel Service and Federal Express, which had invested in highly efficient operations that offered guaranteed levels of service to users, including next-day delivery. Furthermore, these private carriers were not held back by the public service obligations of the government service: they could pick and choose which customers to serve and were free to charge whatever they thought particular customers would be willing to pay.

Amid the general deregulation of services markets during the 1980s, there were repeated calls for a reorganization of the mail service to make it operate more like its private sector competitors. Yet, even many of the critics of the U.S. Mail did not go as far as to suggest an outright abandonment to the private sector.

The outcome was a reorganization to form the U.S. Postal Service, which was intended to give the restructured organization more autonomy in making decisions that were sensitive to its users' needs while at the same time respecting the fact that the wider public interest was at stake. Very slowly, accountability for results rather than enforcement of the rules began driving managers' decisions about the services they delivered. Users were seen not as captives with no choice but as customers whose business had to be earned. Marketing research was undertaken to get closer to users and better understand their needs and expectations. Innovation in new services began to flow from this research. For example, many post offices have been resited and redesigned as bright and inviting places, just like the environments that customers have come to expect from retailers in general. Express Mail and Priority Mail were developed and positioned to compete with the letter delivery services of Federal Express, offering similar levels of reliability in return for premium prices. The Postal Service began to tap into a variety of new revenue sources—for example, by selling licenses to manufacturers to reproduce the controversial "Elvis" postage stamp issued in 1993. Pricing and distribution saw increasing use of many of the practices of the private sector, for example, in the discounts offered for bulk purchase of postage stamps, which the Postal Service would deliver to customers' homes or offices.

In its newly found entrepreneurial zeal, the Postal Service made many proposals to the U.S. Postal Rate Commission for reform, for example, in the manner in which discounted postal charges are given to not-for-profit organizations. However, it still found itself facing government critics who were out to protect their own interest groups, frequently thwarting any reforms that were strictly business led. The constraints imposed by the rules of the Postal Rates Commission were seen at their most annoying in the handling of the federal government's overnight mail. The government had sought the lowest price supplier to move all its overnight mail, and several private companies put in their bids, based on an assessment of the likely viability of the contract. Federal Express won the contract—it negotiated a contract price of $3.75 per item. The U.S. Postal Service was unable to match this price, being hampered by its obligation to charge a flat rate to all users, even though it could probably have profitably carried the mail at a rate comparable to that charged by Federal Express. The fact that it has very little control over the price element of its marketing mix or the manner in which it makes its services available to groups of customers poses major barriers to the emergence of a true marketing orientation.

CASE STUDY REVIEW QUESTIONS

1. What changes would the U.S. Postal Service have to make if it were to become truly market oriented? Do you think that it would be possible for the Postal Service to implement these changes? Why or why not?

2. Compare the marketing strategies of the U.S. Postal Service with those of private mail carriers such as Federal Express. How have both organizations responded to changing technology (e.g., the spread of fax machines)?

3. Over the longer term, what do you think would be the implications for the organization's marketing managers of complete deregulation of all postal services in the United States?

1.7 *TOWARD SOCIETAL MARKETING?*

The idea that the overriding purpose of marketing is to satisfy individuals' needs profitably is increasingly being challenged. Many have argued that when a consumer buys a good, he or she is today inclined to think not just of the benefit it will bring to him or her directly but also of the benefit it will bring to society. Societal considerations can be manifested in two important ways: in the evaluation of an individual product's acceptability to society at large, and in terms of the overall societal credentials of the supplier. Initial interest in societal marketing concepts has focused on the manufactured goods sector, with environmentalism emerging as a major factor affecting consumer purchases during the 1980s. Much of the promotion of environmentally friendly aerosols, diapers, and packaging has been dismissed by many as not so much showing a concern for the environment as demonstrating a unique positioning strategy that will increase product awareness. However, a significant segment of the market for many products has expressed a need to buy products that benefit people other than themselves. Similarly, many consumers have been selective in whom they purchase from, making their purchases not from the organization best able to satisfy their own narrowly defined personal needs but from one that does more for society in general—for example, by supporting environmental or child welfare charities or by refusing to purchase supplies from countries with oppressive governments. In several well-documented cases, goods manufacturers have sold socially harmful goods and faced boycotts from consumer groups; for example, the Nestle Company's exploitation of the market for dried milk products in underdeveloped countries saw many Western consumers boycotting the company's products on principle.

As with the development of a general marketing orientation, societal marketing ideas first achieved prominence in the goods sector but have since found application within the services sector. Because of the intangible nature of services, social costs and benefits of services can be less easy to identify than for goods. Nevertheless, there is evidence that some segments of the population are widening their evaluatory criteria to include the benefits they bring to society (or the social cost they avoid). Within the financial services sector, there is now a wide range of fund management services available to investors who are concerned about the ethics of their investments (Figure 1.7). Within the travel and tourism sector, it is now recognized that intensive tourism development can create significant environmental problems, for example, the threat to the breeding habits of the loggerhead turtle on the Greek island of Zakinthos that has resulted from the intensive development of beaches for recreational purposes. Some purchasers of vacations—admittedly a small niche group at the moment—choose their vacation destination on the basis of tourism's environmental impact at a resort, and choose their service provider—the tour operator—on the basis of its policies toward environmentally benign development of resorts.

It is argued in later chapters that the promotion of service organizations' corporate brands is generally more important than the promotion of specific product brands. For this reason, many service organizations are keen to link themselves to good social causes. For example, the retailer Wal-Mart has linked its name to the support of American industry and more recently to environmentalism. The opposite—linking a corporate brand to a bad cause—can have long-term harmful effects on an organization, for example, the association of Barclays Bank with an oppressive government in South Africa during the 1970s.

Some marketers have argued that marketing itself cannot claim to be a discipline if it is unwilling to systematically investigate issues of social welfare and the impacts of market-based distribution systems.[18] Others point out that there is not necessarily any incompatibility between traditional marketing objectives and societal objectives, as the societal marketing concept does not involve a company in forgoing its long-term profitability and survival objectives,[19] although critics of the societal marketing concept argue that most external benefits provided under the guise of societal marketing are in fact rapidly internalized by their providers.[20] Thus, litter bins sponsored by a fast-food restaurant, the provision of recycling points by supermarkets, and donations to animal charities are simply new ways of gaining awareness with the public by using currently fashionable values.

Figure 1.7   Appealing to a socially responsible segment of investors. Source: The Clean Yield Group.

1.8 FURTHER REFINEMENTS IN MARKETING THOUGHT

This chapter opened with some standard definitions of marketing and has examined some of the points that have been used to define the domain of marketing. It is useful to record here some developments of the marketing approach that are of particular interest in the marketing of services. These concern the way in which an organization markets itself to its staff, the way in which sections within an organization interact with each other, and the process of turning a series of discrete exchanges with customers into a long-term relationship.

1.8.1 Internal Marketing

Marketing has traditionally focused on the external customers of an organization. However, it is increasingly being recognized—especially within the services sector—that many of the marketing processes applied to external relationships are of equal value to internal relationships. Within services organizations, much effort is often placed on selling the values of the organization to its employees. The aim is to ensure that employees share an understanding of the purpose of the organization and the service position that it seeks to adopt with regard to its external customers. Communication techniques that are commonly applied to external customers are turned inward, for example, through internal staff newsletters, educational programs, and the design of the work environment. Internal and external marketing programs frequently overlap, as when a television advertising campaign has a secondary aim of reaffirming confidence in an organization held by its employees. The subject of internal marketing is explored more fully in Chapter 6.

1.8.2 Network Marketing

Increasing attention is being paid to the idea of treating an organization as a series of producers and consumers of services who market their output to each other within the organizational structure. Many organizations have structured themselves into matrix-type structures, in which one group finds itself acting as a buyer of services produced by other groups within the organization. There is widespread evidence[21,22] that the creation of autonomous trading units within large corporations causes many internal transactions to become market-mediated rather than planned. In this way, an in-house printing service within a large organization may find itself subjected to marketing disciplines when it has to compete with outside printers—either on a job-by-job basis or as part of a periodic review—for the printing work required by other departments.

Many public services that are distributed to consumers by centrally planned methods may nevertheless be market-mediated at the point of production. Services such as trash collection and grounds maintenance are generally supplied to local authorities following competitive bidding, but the benefits are passed on to users either without charge or at a centrally administered charge.

1.8.3 Relationship Marketing

Customer relationships are emerging as an important requirement for effective services marketing. While some services can be adequately delivered by means of a series of discrete transactions, others are more effectively delivered by means of a relationship marketing strategy at the opposite end of what Gronroos[23] describes as a marketing strategy continuum. Some have gone on to argue that developing relationships has become the key focal point for marketing attention, replacing earlier preoccupation with service and before that with product development.

It has been pointed out by many[24,25] that the cost of establishing contact with a potential customer and making the first sale is often so great that the return on the initial sale is minimal, if not negative. For many services, it is only when a relationship becomes established that the customer becomes profitable to the seller. Exchanges should not be seen in isolation as a series of discrete events but should take place in order to establish and extend a relationship. It has been argued that if attention is limited to the study of single, isolated exchanges, the heart of marketing is ignored,[26] and that marketing should essentially revolve around systems where people or groups are interrelated and reach a shared goal through "patterned relationships with one another."[27]

In establishing and maintaining customer relations, sellers give what Gronroos[28] describes as a set of promises. These are connected with, among other things, the nature of a service, financial solutions, or the transfer of information. On the other hand, the buyer gives another set of promises concerning his or her commitment to the relationship. In many situations, many parties are involved in a relationship. The buyer and seller may act in a network consisting of suppliers, distributors, and other customers. Gronroos argues that for services marketing, the promise concept is as important as the exchange concept.

Various strategies are used by service providers to develop relationships with their customers. At a relatively simple level, incentives for frequent users can help to develop short-term to medium-term loyalty. In this way, many airlines reward frequent users with free or reduced-price tickets. At its more extensive, a relationship can develop to the point where the customer assigns considerable responsibility to the service provider for identifying the customer's needs and providing solutions. In this way, many manufacturing companies leave to specialist trucking companies the task of arranging delivery schedules that are most convenient for its customers, relying on the knowledge it has gained during previous dealings.

In some services, the relationship between customer and supplier involves a fundamental degree of trust. Ethics enshrined in codes of conduct may constrain the marketing decisions of many professional services providers. As an example, lawyers and accountants may be able and willing to supply services that their customers request and are able to pay for, but they are constrained from entering into a transaction because their professional code of conduct prohibits such transactions. Sometimes the relationship involves a fundamental degree of trust that overrides marketing considerations. A doctor, for example, enters into a relationship with a patient who may have little knowledge about the nature of his or her problem and may not have the ability to query any diagnosis the doctor makes. When the precise nature of a complaint is unknown, an operation may be undertaken without prior specification of the work to be carried out. If the patient is anesthetized, he or she is unable to exercise any degree of control over the relationship. In circumstances such as these, marketing promises must coexist with ethical codes of conduct.

Intermediaries are an important element in a service organization's relationship marketing strategy. Again, the focus of attention moves away from seeing each transaction between service principal and intermediary as a discrete activity. Instead, the two seek to work toward common goals through shared problem solving. Modern database technology offers many examples of how service principals have sought to add value to the total service received by the customer. The installation of an airline's software in a travel agency, for example, can help the latter to deliver faster and more reliable service to the airline's customers than might have been the case if the agency had been left to solve processing problems by itself.

While service companies seek to develop closer relationships with their clients, this has to be seen in the context of many consumers' growing confidence to venture outside a relationship. For example, there is a growing tendency for private customers to change their bank accounts whenever it seems financially attractive to do so, rather than seeing a bank as an institution that can be relied upon to satisfy a wide range of needs over a long time.

The methods used to manage relationships between producer and consumer are examined in more detail in Chapter 5.

CHAPTER REVIEW QUESTIONS

1. Discuss how a car wash business might operate if management embraced a production orientation, a sales orientation, a marketing orientation, or a societal marketing orientation.
2. Critically evaluate the marketing mix of a service organization. What elements of the marketing mix are operating smoothly? What elements have problems?
3. Of what value is the concept of an expanded marketing mix to service organizations, as opposed to the traditional "4 Ps"?
4. Why is it important for services organizations to segment their markets? Should providers of public services (e.g., city police forces) segment their markets?
5. Analyze the nature of the needs that may be satisfied by a household mortgage.
6. Using examples, consider the ways in which the marketing of a not-for-profit organization might differ from that of private companies operating in the same industry sector.

REFERENCES

1. Evans, J. and Berman, B. *Marketing,* 6th ed. (New York: Macmillan, 1994).
2. "AMA Approves New Definition," *Marketing News* (March 1, 1985): 1.
3. Crown, J. "A Hankering for Food Courts," *Advertising Age* (December 13, 1993): 23.
4. Drucker, P. F.: *Management: Tasks, Responsibilities and Practices* (New York: Harper & Row, 1973).

5. Narver, J. C. and Slater, S. F. "The Effect of a Market Orientation on Business Profitability," *Journal of Marketing* (October 1990): 20–35.

6. Maslow, A. "A Theory of Human Motivation," *Psychological Review* 50 (July 1943).

7. Bagozzi, R. P. "Marketing as Exchange," *Journal of Marketing* 39, no. 4 (1975): 32–39.

8. Alderson, W. *Marketing Behaviour and Executive Action* (Homewood, Ill.: Irwin, 1982).

9. Borden, N. H. "The Concept of the Marketing Mix," in *Science in Marketing,* ed. G. Schwartz (New York: John Wiley, 1965): 386–97.

10. McCarthy J. E. *Basic Marketing: A Management Approach* (Homewood, Ill.: Irwin, 1960).

11. Kent, R. A. "Faith in the Four Ps: An Alternative," *Journal of Marketing Management* 2, no. 2 (1986): 145–154.

12. Brookes, R. *The New Marketing* (Aldershot, UT: Gower Press, 1988).

13. Wind, Y. J. *Product Policy: Concepts, Methods and Strategy* (Reading, Mass.: Addison-Wesley, 1982).

14. Booms, B. H. and Bitner, M. J. "Marketing Strategies and Organisation Structures for Service Firms," *Marketing of Services,* ed. J. Donnelly and W. R. George (Chicago: American Marketing Association, 1981), 51–67.

15. Christopher, M, Payne, A. and Ballantyne, M. *Relationship Marketing* (London: Heinemann, 1991).

16. Gummesson, E. "Marketing-Orientation Revisited: The Crucial Role of the Part-time Marketer," *European Journal of Marketing* 25, no. 2 (1991): 60–75.

17. Kotler, P. *Marketing Management: Analysis, Planning, Implementation and Control* (Englewood Cliffs, N.J.: Prentice Hall, 1991).

18. Anderson P. "Marketing, Strategic Planning and Theory," *Journal of Marketing* (Spring 1982): 15–26.

19. Arbratt, R. and Sacks, D. "Perceptions of the Societal Marketing Concept," *European Journal of Marketing* 22 (1988): 25–33.

20. Arndt, J. "A Critique of Marketing Concepts," in *Macromarketing,* ed. P. D. White and Slater, C (University of Colorado, 1977).

21. Chandler, A. *Strategy and Structure* (Cambridge, Mass.: MIT Press, 1962).

22. Rumelt, R. P. *Strategy, Structure and Economic Performance* (Boston: Division of Research, Graduate School of Business Administration, Harvard University, 1974).

23. Gronroos, C. "The Marketing Strategy Continuum: Towards a Marketing Concept for the 1990s," *Management Decision* 29, no. 1 (1991): 7–13.

24. Berry, L. L. "Relationship Marketing," in *Emerging Perspectives of Services Marketing,* ed. L. L. Berry, et al. (Chicago: American Marketing Association, 1983).

25. Reichheld, F. "Loyalty Based Management," *Harvard Business Review* 71, no. 2 (1993): 64–73.

26. Houston, F. S. and Gassenheimer, J. B. Marketing and Exchange," *Journal of Marketing* 51 (October 1987): 3–18.

27. Levy, S. and Zaltman, G. *Marketing, Society and Conflict* (Englewood Cliffs, N. J.: Prentice Hall, 1975): 27.

28. Gronroos, C. "Defining Marketing: A Market-Oriented Approach," *European Journal of Marketing* 23, no. 1 (1989): 52–60.

SUGGESTED FURTHER READING

ANDREASAN, A. A. 1982. "Nonprofits: Check Your Attention to Customers," *Harvard Business Review* May–June, 105–10.

ASSAEL, H. 1990. *Marketing: Principles and Strategy,* 2nd ed. Fort Worth, Tex.: Dryden Press.

COLLIER, D. A. 1991. "New Marketing Mix Stresses Service." *Journal of Business Strategy* March/April, 42–45.

GRONROOS, C. 1989. "Defining Marketing: A Market-Oriented Approach," *European Journal of Marketing* 23, no. 1, 52–60

GRONROOS, C. 1991. "The Marketing Strategy Continuum: Towards a Marketing Concept for the 1990s," *Management Decision* 29, no. 1, 7–13

GUMMESSON, E. 1991. "Marketing-Orientation Revisited: The Crucial Role of the Part-Time Marketer," *European Journal of Marketing* 25, no. 2, 60–75.

HOUSTON, F. S. 1986. "The Marketing Concept: What It Is and What It Is Not," *Journal of Marketing* 50, April, 81–87.

KENT, R. A. 1986. "Faith in the Four Ps: An Alternative," *Journal of Marketing Management* 2, no. 2, 145–54.

KOHLI, A. K. and JAWORSKI, B. J. 1990. "Market Orientation: The Construct, Research Propositions and Management Implications," *Journal of Marketing* 54, April, 1–18.

KOTLER, P. and ARMSTRONG, G. 1991. *Principles of Marketing,* 5th ed. Englewood Cliffs, N. J.: Prentice Hall.

KOTLER, P. 1979. "Strategies for Introducing Marketing into Non-Profit Organizations," *Journal of Marketing* 43, 37–44.

LOVELOCK, C. H. and WEINBERG, C. B. 1984. *Marketing for Public and Nonprofit Managers.* New York: John Wiley.

NARVER, J. C. and SLATER, S. F. 1990. "The Effect of a Market Orientation on Business Profitability," *Journal of Marketing* October, 20–35.

PRIDE, W. M. and FERRELL, O. C. 1991. *Marketing: Basic Concepts and Decisions.* Boston: Houghton-Mifflin.

VANDERMERWE, S. and GILBERT, S. 1989. "Making Internal Services Market Driven," *Business Horizons* November/December, 83–89.

2

What Are Services?

CHAPTER OBJECTIVES

After reading this chapter, you should be able to understand

- the essential characteristics of services and their implications for marketing
- bases for classifying the diverse range of services according to marketing needs
- the importance of the service sector in national economies and the reasons for its emergence

2.1 INTRODUCTION

The idea that the service sector should be worthy of study in its own right is relatively recent. Early economists paid little attention to services, considering them to be totally unproductive and to add nothing of value to an economy. Adam Smith, writing in the mid-18th century, distinguished between production that had a tangible output—such as agriculture and manufacture—and production for which there was no tangible output. The latter, which included the efforts of intermediaries, doctors, lawyers, and the armed forces, he described as "unproductive of any value."[1] This remained the dominant attitude toward services until the latter part of the 19th century when Alfred Marshall[2] argued that a person providing a service was just as capable of giving utility to the recipient as a person producing a tangible product. Indeed, Marshall recognized that tangible products may not exist at all were it not for a series of services performed in order to produce them and to make them available to consumers. To Marshall, an agent distributing agricultural produce performed as valuable a task as the farmer himself—without the provision of transport and intermediary services, agricultural products produced in areas of surplus would be of no value. Today, despite some lingering beliefs that the service sector is an insubstantial and relatively inferior sector of the economy, considerable attention is paid to its direct and indirect economic consequences.

Modern definitions of services focus on the fact that a service in itself produces no tangible output, although it may be instrumental in producing some tangible output. A contemporary definition is provided by Kotler and Armstrong:

> A service is an activity or benefit that one party can offer to another that is essentially intangible and does not result in the ownership of anything. Its production may or may not be tied to a physical product.[3]

There has been, however, no consistent definition of what constitutes a service. Some definitions exclude transportation and communication on the basis that they form an integral part of goods,[4] whereas others have excluded activities such as delivery services and credit facilities when they are essentially attached to a tangible good offered for sale.[5]

In practice, it can be very difficult to distinguish services from goods, for when a good is purchased, an element of service is usually included. Similarly, a service is frequently augmented by a tangible product attached to the service. In this way, cars are commonly considered to be goods rather than services; yet they are usually sold with the benefit of considerable intangible service elements, such as a warranty or a financing facility. On the other hand, a seemingly intangible service such as an overseas vacation includes tangible elements in the purchase—use of an airplane, the hotel room, and a transfer bus, for example. In between is a wide range of products that are a combination of tangible goods and intangible services. A meal in a restaurant is a combination of tangible goods (the food and physical surroundings) and intangible services (the preparation and delivery of the food, reservation service, etc.). Figure 2.1 shows schematically that considerable diversity exists within the service sector. In fact, rather than talking about the service sector as a homogeneous group of activities, it would be more appropriate to talk about degrees of service orientation. All productive activities can be placed on a scale somewhere between being a pure service (no tangible output) and a pure good (no intangible service added to the tangible good). In practice, most products fall between the two extremes by being a combination of goods and services.

To what extent should services be considered a distinctive area of study in marketing? On the one hand, some have argued that a service contains many important elements common to goods, which makes services marketing as a separate discipline obsolete. Thus, Levitt observed:

> . . . there is no such thing as service industries. There are only industries where service components are greater or less than those of other industries.[6]

On the other hand, many have pointed to the limitations of traditional marketing principles when applied to the marketing of services, arguing that the differences

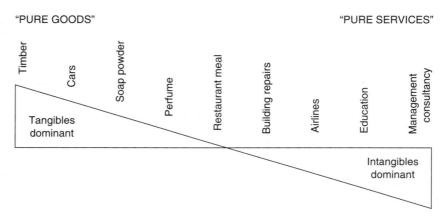

Figure 2.1 The goods and services continuum

between goods and services mean that the marketing tools used for goods marketing cannot easily be translated to services marketing.[7,8,9,10,11]

The purpose of this book is to develop frameworks within which services marketing decisions can be analyzed. In some areas—such as the analysis of the service encounter or the conceptualization of service quality—new fields of marketing thought need to be opened up. In other areas, such as setting prices and developing a promotional campaign, the basic principles of marketing have to be adapted to meet the distinctive needs of services.

The following definition of a service is used to define the scope of this book:

> The production of an essentially intangible benefit, either in its own right or as a significant element of a tangible product, which through some form of exchange satisfies an identified consumer need.

This definition recognizes that in addition to the gray area between a pure good and a pure service, some marketing activities do not easily fit on this scale at all. The first, which has attracted growing interest, is the marketing of ideas, whether of a political party, a religious sect, or a specific subject such as road safety. The second and related area is the marketing of a cause, such as famine relief in Africa or a campaign to prevent the construction of a new highway. Both of these types of activity are distinguished from normal goods and services marketing, as there is no exchange of value between the producer and the individuals or organizations to whom the marketing effort is aimed. For example, the consumer of transportation services enters into an exchange and pays for transportation services either directly and willingly, as in the case of a subway fare, or indirectly—and possibly unwillingly—through general taxation, as is the case for the use of roads. By contrast, when a pressure group mounts a campaign to bring about the building of a new road, the concept of exchange of value becomes extremely tenuous, only really occurring when, for example, a member of the public subsequently contributes to a cause—either financially or by his or her actions. Generally, though, the concept of services does not offer an appropriate framework for analyzing the marketing of ideas and causes.

This book will focus on the distinct services aspects of marketing activities rather than on the generality of marketing decisions for tangible products of which service is just one element. In this way, distribution is part of the marketing mix for building materials. As an activity, it can be seen either as an integral element of the tangible product that is essential for securing its sale, or as a discrete activity that delivers an intangible benefit—movement—the payment for which the purchaser has nothing tangible to show in return. The latter perspective will be adopted throughout this book in tackling the marketing of products that are a combination of goods and services.

2.2   DISTINGUISHING FEATURES OF A SERVICE

"Pure" services have several distinctive characteristics that differentiate them from goods and have implications for the manner in which they are marketed. These characteristics can be described as intangibility, inseparability, variability, perishability, and the inability to own a service. These characteristics will be a recurrent theme throughout this book, and they are introduced here.

2.2.1   Intangibility

A pure service cannot be assessed using any of the physical senses; it is an abstraction, which cannot be directly examined before it is purchased. A prospective purchaser of most goods is able to examine the goods for physical integrity, aesthetic appearance, taste, smell, and so on. Many advertising claims relating to these tangible properties can be verified by inspection prior to purchase. On the other hand, pure services have no tangible properties that can be used by consumers to verify advertising claims before the purchase is made. The intangible process characteristics that define services, such as reliability, personal care, and attentiveness and friendliness of staff, can be verified only when a service has been purchased and consumed.

Intangibility has several important marketing implications, which will be examined in more detail in subsequent chapters. The lack of physical evidence that intangibility implies increases the level of uncertainty consumers face when choosing between competing services. An important part of a services marketing program will therefore involve reducing consumer uncertainty by such means as adding physical evidence and the development of strong brands. Pure goods and pure services tend to move in opposite directions in their general approach to the issue of tangibility. While service marketers seek to add tangible evidence to their product, pure goods marketers often seek to augment their products by adding intangible elements such as after-sales service and improved distribution (Figure 2.2).

2.2.2   Inseparability

The production and consumption of a tangible good are two quite distinct activities. Companies usually produce goods in one central location and then transport them to the place where customers most want to buy them. In this way, manufacturing com-

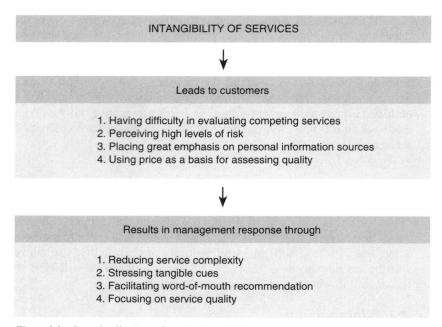

Figure 2.2   Some implications of service intangibility

panies can achieve economies of scale through centralized production and can have centralized quality control checks. The manufacturer is also able to make goods at a time convenient to itself, then make them available to customers at times convenient to customers. Production and consumption are said to be separable. On the other hand, the consumption of a service is said to be inseparable from its means of production. Producer and consumer must interact in order for the benefits of the service to be realized: both must normally meet at a mutually convenient time and place in order that the producer can directly pass on service benefits. In the extreme case of personal care services, the customer must be present during the entire production process. For example, a doctor cannot normally provide a service without the involvement of a patient. For services, marketing becomes a means of facilitating complex producer–consumer interaction, rather than being merely an exchange medium (Figure 2.3).

Inseparability occurs whether the producer is human, as with health care services, or a machine, as with a bank ATM. The service of an ATM can be realized only if the producer and consumer interact (Figure 2.4). In some cases, however, it has been possible to separate service production and consumption, especially where the level of personal contact is low. For example, a house cleaning service may clean during the day while the family is away, but the clean house is "consumed" in the evening when the family returns.

Inseparability has several important marketing implications for services. First, whereas goods are generally first produced, then offered for sale, and finally sold and consumed, service inseparability causes this process to be modified. Services are

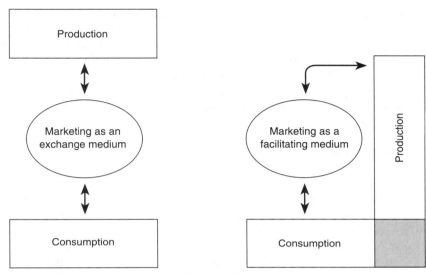

Figure 2.3   Services marketing as a facilitating medium

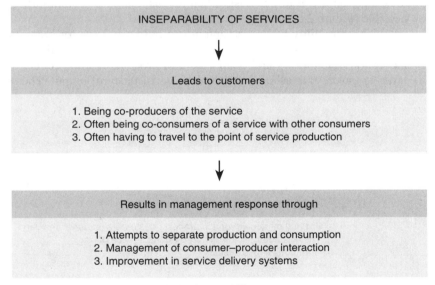

Figure 2.4   Some implications of service inseparability

generally sold first, then produced and consumed simultaneously. Second, while the method of goods production is usually (though by no means always) of little importance to consumers, production processes are critical to their enjoyment of services. With goods, consumers are not part of the production process, and in general, as long as the products that they take delivery of meet their expectations, they are satisfied (although there are exceptions, for example, where the ethics of production methods cause concern, or where quality can be assessed only with a knowledge of production stages that are hidden from the consumers' view). With services, the active participation of customers in the production process makes the process as important as outcomes in determining customers' benefits. In some cases, an apparently slight change in service production methods may totally destroy the value of the service being provided. A person buying a ticket for a concert by Tina Turner may derive no benefit at all from the concert if it is subsequently produced by Madonna instead.

2.2.3 Variability

For services, variability impacts on customers not just in terms of outcomes but also in terms of processes of production. The latter point causes variability to pose a much greater problem for services than for goods. Because customers are usually involved in the production process for a service at the same time they consume it, it can be difficult to carry out monitoring and control to ensure consistent standards. The opportunity for predelivery inspection and rejection that is open to the goods manufacturer is not normally possible with services. Variability can be particularly difficult to control when personnel are involved in providing services—such as hairdressing—on a one-to-one basis when no easy method of monitoring and control is possible (Figure 2.5).

The variability of service output can pose problems for brand building in services compared with tangible goods. For the latter it is usually relatively easy to incorporate monitoring and quality control procedures into production processes in order to ensure that a brand stands for a consistency of output. The service sector's

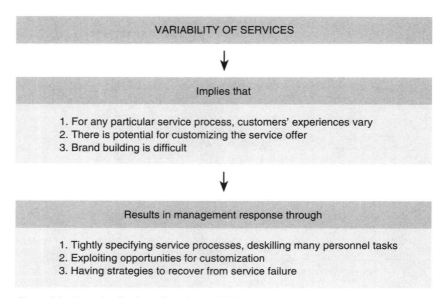

Figure 2.5   Some implications of service variability

attempts to reduce variability concentrate on methods used to select, train, motivate, and control personnel—issues that are examined in chapter 6. Refer back to the ad in Chapter 1 for "classic residence, senior living," by Hyatt. Here the Hyatt is using a brand extension strategy to assure potential customers that the quality in their senior housing will be the same as the quality in their hotel chain. In other cases, service offers have been simplified, jobs have been "deskilled," and personnel have been replaced with machines in order to reduce human variability.

2.2.4 Perishability

Services differ from goods in that they cannot be stored. A producer of cars that is unable to sell all its output in the current period can carry forward stocks to sell in a subsequent period. The only significant costs are storage costs, financing costs, and the possibility of loss through obsolescence. By contrast, the producer of a service that cannot sell all its output produced in the current period gets no chance to carry it forward for sale in a subsequent period. An airline that offers seats on a 3:00 P.M. flight from New York to Boston cannot sell any empty seats once the aircraft has left. The service offer disappears, and spare seats cannot be stored to meet a surge in demand that may occur at 5:00 P.M.

The perishability of services results in greater attention having to be paid to the management of demand by evening out peaks and troughs in demand and in scheduling service production to follow this pattern as far as possible (Figure 2.6). Pricing and promotion, two of the tools commonly adopted to tackle this problem, are discussed in Chapter 4.

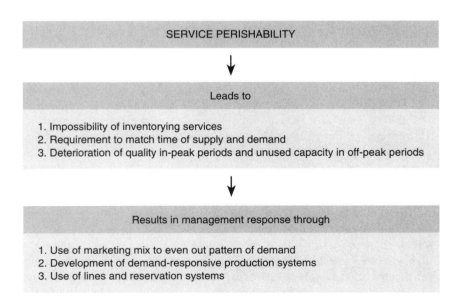

Figure 2.6   Some implications of service perishability

2.2.5 Ownership

The inability to own services is related to their intangibility and perishability. In purchasing goods, buyers generally acquire title to the goods in question and can subsequently do as they want with them. On the other hand, when a service is performed, no ownership is transferred from the seller to the buyer. The buyer is merely buying the right to a service process, such as the use of a parking lot or an attorney's time. A distinction should be drawn between the inability to own the service act and the rights that a buyer may acquire to have a service carried out at some time in the future—a theatre gift voucher, for example.

The inability to own a service has implications for the design of distribution channels. A wholesaler or retailer cannot take title, as is the case with goods. Instead, direct distribution methods are more common, and where intermediaries are used, they generally act as co-producers of the service.

2.3 ANALYSIS OF THE SERVICE OFFER

The extent to which these five features can be used to distinguish between goods and services marketing has been questioned by many. For example, on the subject of variability, some goods industries, such as fruit growing and processing, have difficulty in achieving high levels of consistent quality, whereas some service industries, such as parking lots, can achieve a consistent standard of quality in terms of speed of service, cleanliness, and so on. Similarly, many tangible goods share the problem of intangible services in being incapable of full examination before consumption. It is not normally possible, for instance, to judge the taste of a bottle of wine in a supermarket before it has been purchased and (at least partially) consumed. More recently, the development of "just in time" (JIT) techniques within the manufacturing sector has brought issues of perishability to the fore in the relationships between many industrial buyers and sellers.

This list of distinguishing features is most useful when one understands the nature of the service offer, in particular the extent to which it includes tangible goods elements. Shostack[12] has attempted to analyze the elements of a service in terms of a molecular model of interrelated services and goods components. According to this approach, an airline can be seen as offering an essentially intangible service: transportation. Yet, the total service offering includes tangible elements, such as the airplane, as well as intangible elements, such as the frequency of flights, their reliability, and the quality of inflight services. When many of these intangibles are broken down into their component parts, they too include tangible elements; for instance, inflight service includes tangible food and drink. A hypothetical application of the molecular model approach to the analysis of the complex output of a theatre is shown in Figure 2.7. This analysis highlights the tangible and intangible elements of a theatre offering. Given the large number of intangible elements, it is easy to understand, for example, why consumers would respond favorably to a service that bundles transportation, hotel, and theatre tickets into one tour package.

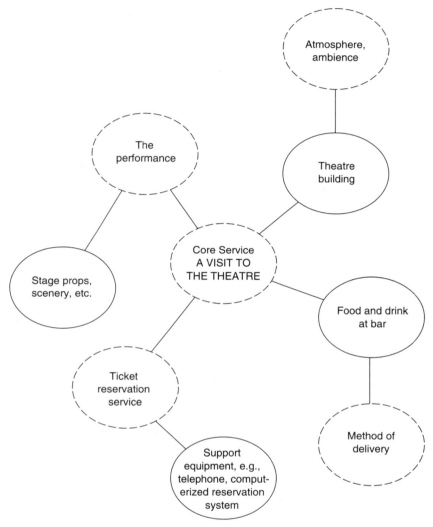

Figure 2.7   An application of Shostack's molecular model of service components to the output of a theatre

2.3.1 Goods as "Self Services"

Services that are delivered directly by organizations to consumers are distinct from services that are delivered by means of the goods the consumers have purchased. Conceptually, many goods purchases effectively result in the purchase of a stream of internally produced services. Gershuny[13] has used the term "intermediate services" to describe complex manufactured equipment that private and industrial buyers purchase in order to provide services that may otherwise have been provided as a direct service activity. In this way, an automatic washing machine provides indirect service benefits that may otherwise have been provided directly by a laundromat, and a car provides benefits otherwise provided by taxis and public transportation.

2.4 CLASSIFICATION OF SERVICES

It is too simplistic to divide the economy into goods and services sectors, for the service sector itself covers a diverse range of activities. The contrast between a simple local window cleaning service and a complex international banking operation illustrates this point. Because of this diversity, it is important that services be classified according to their particular marketing requirements. However, the most common basis for classifying services has been the type of activity performed. Statistics record service activities under such headings as banking, passenger transportation, and hotels, based largely on similarity of production methods. Banking is therefore used to classify all organizations whose main activity is the circulation of money, and passenger transportation is used to categorize all organizations that are primarily engaged in moving people, even though a local taxi operator is quite different from an airline.

Such simple classification systems are not particularly helpful to marketers. First, a single production sector can cover a very diverse range of activities with quite different marketing needs. Small bed-and-breakfast establishments and international hotels may fall within the same sector, but their marketing needs are likely to be quite different. Second, most services are in fact a combination of services. Retail stores, for example, often go beyond their traditional sectoral boundaries by offering banking facilities. Third, the marketing needs of a particular production-based subsector may have more in common with another unrelated subsector than with other areas in its own sector.

Marketers should be more interested in identifying subsectors in terms of similarity of marketing requirements. In this way, the provision of hotel services may have quite a lot in common with some airline operations in terms of the processes by which customers make purchase decisions, the methods of pricing, and promotional strategies, for example.

Defining categories of services is arguably more complex than for manufactured goods, where terms such as fast-moving consumer goods, shopping goods, and specialty goods are widely used and convey a lot of information about the marketing requirements of products within a category. The great diversity of services has hampered attempts to reduce services to a small number of categories. Instead, many analysts have attempted to classify services along a number of continua, reflecting the fact that products cannot be classified into dichotomous goods and services categories to begin with.

Many bases for classifying services have been suggested over the years. Some of the more frequently quoted ones are discussed here.

2.4.1 Marketable vs. Unmarketable Services

This first classification distinguishes between services that are freely traded and those considered by the social and economic environment of the time to be more appropriately distributed by non–market-based mechanisms. Among the latter group, many government services are provided for the public benefit, but no attempt is made to charge users of the service. This can arise when it is impossible to exclude individuals or groups of individuals from benefiting from a service. For example, it is not possible in practice for a local authority to charge individuals for the use of local sidewalks; the benefits are essentially external, in that it is not possible to restrict the distribution of the benefit to those who have entered into some form of exchange relationship. Furthermore, many public services are said to result in no rivalry in consumption, in that one person's enjoyment of a service does not keep another person from enjoying the same service. One person using a sidewalk does not generally prevent another person from using it.

A second major group of services that many cultures do not consider to be marketable include those commonly provided within household units, such as the bringing up of children, cooking, and cleaning. While many of these services are now commonly marketed within Western societies (e.g., child care services), many societies—and segments within societies—would regard the internal provision of such services as central to the functioning of family units. Attempts by Western companies to launch family-based services in cultures with strong family traditions may fail because no market exists.

As with all service classifications, a whole range of services lies between these two extremes, and the classification of any service is dynamic, reflecting changes in the political, economic, social, and technological environments. Attempts are often made to internalize many of the external benefits of public services and turn them into marketable services. As an example, users of roads throughout the world are increasingly being charged tolls, based on marketing principles of selling relatively uncongested road space to motorists. Similarly, attitudes towards which household-produced services should be considered marketable have changed over time, for example, the buying of care services for elderly relatives.

2.4.2 Producer vs. Consumer Services

Consumer services are provided for individuals who use up the service for their own enjoyment or benefit. No further economic benefit results from the consumption of the service. For this reason, the services of a hairdresser can be defined as consumer services. On the other hand, producer services are those provided to a business in order that the business can produce something else of economic benefit. In this way, a trucking company sells services to its industrial customers in order that they can add value to the goods they produce, by allowing their goods to be made available at the point of demand.

Many services are provided simultaneously to both consumer and producer markets. Here, the challenge is to adapt the marketing program to meet the differing needs of each group of users. In this way, airlines provide a basically similar service to both consumer and producer markets, but the marketing program may emphasize low price for the former and quality and greater short-notice availability for the latter.

While this is a very common basis for classifying service sectors, it could be argued that a private household may itself act as a production unit in which services are bought not for their own intrinsic value but in order to allow some other benefit to be produced. Therefore, a mortgage is not so much consumed as used to produce the benefit of homemaking. There is also evidence that industrial buyers of services do not judge a service simply on its ability to profitably add value to their own production process; rather, the personal, nonorganizational goals of individuals within an organization may cause some decisions to be based on personal consumption criteria. A car telephone service may be judged for its personal status value as well as its productive value.

2.4.3 Status of the Service in the Product Offering

It was stated earlier that most products are a combination of a goods and a service element. Services can be classified according to the role of the service in that total offering. Three principal roles can be identified:

1. A pure service exists when there is little if any evidence of tangible goods, for example, an insurance policy or a management consultancy service. With this group, the primary function of any tangible component is to support an intangible service, in the way that a tangible aircraft supports the essentially intangible service of transportation.
2. A second group of services exist in order to add value to a tangible product. This can occur when a goods manufacturer augments its core tangible product with additional service benefits, such as after-sales warranties. In other cases, the service is sold as a discrete product that customers purchase to add value to their own goods. In this way, extended warranties are purchased to enhance the value of a new car.
3. A third group of services may add value to a product more fundamentally by making it available in the first place. Such services can facilitate delivery of a tangible good from the point of production to the place where it is required by the consumer, or they can provide the means through credit arrangements that allow tangible goods to be bought. In this way, mortgages facilitate house purchase, and trucking services facilitate delivery.

2.4.4 Tangible vs. Intangible Services

Intangibility has been seen by many as a defining characteristic of services. However, it was noted earlier that a gray area exists between pure services at one extreme and pure goods at the other. The level of tangibility present in a service offer derives from four principal sources:

- tangible goods that are included in the service offer and consumed by the customer
- the physical environment in which the service production/consumption process takes place
- equipment used in the service production process
- tangible evidence of service performance

Where goods form an important component of a service offer, many of the practices associated with conventional goods marketing can be applied to this part of the service offer. Restaurants represent a mix of tangibles and intangibles; with respect to the tangible food element, few of the particular characteristics of services marketing are encountered. Production of the food can be separated from its consumption, and the perishability of food is less significant than the perishability of an empty table. Furthermore, the presence of a tangible component gives customers a visible basis on which to judge quality.

The tangible elements of the service offer comprise not just the goods exchanged but also the physical environment in which a service encounter takes place. Within this environment, the design of buildings, their cleanliness, and the appearance of staff present important tangible evidence, which may be the only basis on which a customer is able to differentiate one service provider from another. While some services are rich in such tangible cues (e.g., restaurants and shops), other services provide relatively little tangible evidence (e.g., telephone sales operations).

Tangibility is further provided by evidence of service production methods. Some services provide many opportunities for customers to see the process of production. Indeed, the whole purpose of the service may be to see the production process (e.g., a pop concert). Often this tangible evidence can be seen before a decision to purchase a service is made, either directly by observing a service being performed on somebody else (e.g., watching the work of a builder) or indirectly through a description of the service production process (a role played by brochures that specify and illustrate the service production process). On the other hand, some services provide very few tangible clues about the nature of the service production process. Not only are portfolio management services produced largely out of sight of the consumer, it is also difficult to specify in advance in a brochure what the service outcomes will be.

2.4.5 Extent of Customer Involvement

Some services can be provided only with the complete involvement of customers, whereas others require them to do little more than initiate the service process. In the first category, personal care services, almost by definition, require the complete involvement of customers during the service production and delivery process. This involvement is often interactive, as when a client of a hairdresser answers a continuous series of questions about the emerging length and style of his or her hair. For such a customer, the quality of the service production process, as well as the outcomes, assumes importance. For other services, it is not necessary for the customer to be so fully involved in the production process. Customers listening to music on a radio do not need to be involved for the service to be delivered—they can quite passively receive the service.

Customer involvement is generally lower where the service is carried out not on the mind or body directly but on customers' possessions. The shipping of goods, the cleaning of a home or office, and the operation of a bank account do not involve a service being carried out directly on the customer, whose main task is to initiate the service and to monitor performance of it. Monitoring can take the form of examining tangible evidence of service performance, such as examining whether a carpet has been cleaned to the required standard, or examining intangible evidence of performance such as a statement about an investment made on the client's behalf.

Because it is relatively difficult to maintain consistent production standards for services, many services marketing organizations have attempted to reduce the level of customer involvement in the production process. Simplification of the service production process and distant communication by mail or telephone have been used to achieve this.

With some services, the consumer may actually hope not to consume the service. In normal circumstances, consumers have little involvement with the benefits produced by an insurance policy—the current benefit can be seen as an assurance against the need to consume.

2.4.6 Degree of Variability

Two dimensions of variability can be used to classify services:

- the extent to which production standards vary from a norm, in terms both of outcomes and of production processes
- the extent to which a service can be deliberately varied to meet the specific needs of individual customers

Variability in production standards is of greatest concern to services organizations whose customers are highly involved in the production process, especially when production methods make it impractical to monitor service production. This is true of many labor-intensive personal services provided in a one-to-one situation, such as hairdressing. Some services allow greater scope for quality control checks to be undertaken during the production process, allowing an organization to provide a consistently high level of service. This is especially true of machine-based services; for example, telecommunication services can typically operate with very low failure rates.

The tendency today is for equipment-based services to be regarded as less variable than services that involve a high degree of personal intervention in the production process. Many services organizations have sought to reduce variability—and hence to build strong brands—by adopting equipment-based production methods. The replacement of human telephone operators with computerized voice systems and the automation of many banking services are typical of this trend. For example, the Sprint telephone company has developed its Voice Activated Foncard, which reduces the need for intervention by human telephone operators (Figure 2.8). Sometimes reduced personnel variability has been achieved by passing on part of the production process to the customer, in the way that self-service gasoline stations are no longer dependent on the variability of the gas station attendants.

The second dimension of variability is the extent to which a service can be deliberately customized to meet the specific needs of individual consumers. Because services are created as they are consumed, and because consumers are often a part of the production process, the potential for customization of services is generally greater than for manufactured goods. The extent to which a service can be customized is dependent on the production methods. Services that are produced for large numbers of customers simultaneously may offer little scope for individual cus-

Figure 2.8 Using equipment-based systems to put customers in control of service delivery. Source: J. Walter Thompson Company on behalf of Sprint Communications, and Vincent & Farrell Associates.

tomization—the production methods of a railroad operator do not allow individual customers' needs to be met in the way that the simpler production methods of a taxi operator may be able to. The extent to which services can be customized is partly a function of management decisions on the level of authority to be delegated to front-line service personnel. While some service operators seek to give more authority to front-line staff, the tendency is for service firms to "industrialize" their encounter with customers. This implies following clearly specified standardized procedures in each encounter. While industrialization normally reduces the flexibility of producers to meet customers' needs, it also has the effect of reducing variability of processes and outcomes.

The two dimensions of variability are clearly interrelated. In services with low variability in both dimensions, brand building by services organizations has assumed greatest importance. The two scales of variability are illustrated in Figure 2.9.

2.4.7 Pattern of Service Delivery

Two aspects of service delivery are distinguished here:

- whether a service is supplied on a continuous basis or as a series of discrete transactions
- whether it is supplied casually or within an ongoing relationship between buyer and seller

With respect to the continuity of supply, a first group of services can be identified that are purchased only when they are needed as a series of discrete transactions.

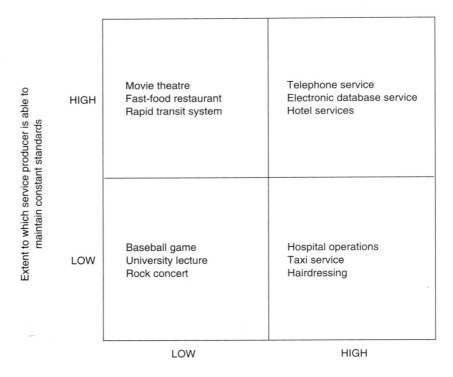

Figure 2.9   Classification of services by variability in production and adaptability to individual consumers' needs

This is typical of low-value, undifferentiated services that may be bought on impulse or with little conscious search activity (e.g., taxis and cafes). It can also be true of specialized, high-value services that are purchased only as required (e.g., funeral services are usually bought only when needed).

By contrast, other services can be identified that are impractical to supply casually. This can occur when production methods make it difficult to supply a service only when it is needed (e.g., it is impractical to provide a telephone line to a house only when it is needed; the line itself is therefore supplied continuously) or when the benefits of a service are required continuously (e.g., insurance policies).

Continuous service supply is commonly—though not always—associated with a relationship existing between buyer and seller. A long-term relationship with a supplier can be important to customers in several situations: when the production/consumption process takes place over a long time (a program of medical treatment), when the benefits will be received only after a long period of time (many financial services) and in cases where purchasers face high levels of perceived risk. Supply through an ongoing relationship, rather than by discrete transactions, can also reduce the transaction costs of having to search and order a service afresh on each occasion (for example, an annual maintenance contract on domestic equipment avoids the need to find an engineer on each occasion that a failure occurs).

Sometimes, it is sensible to supply the central element of a service through an ongoing relationship but to supply additional service benefits casually as and when required. In this way, a telephone line is supplied within an ongoing relationship, whereas individual calls are supplied casually as and when needed.

Services are classified according to the nature of their supply in Figure 2.10.

Service marketers generally try to move customers into the category where service is provided continuously rather than discretely and within an ongoing relationship rather than casually. The former can be achieved by offering incentives for the purchase of a continuous stream of service benefit (offering attractively priced annual travel insurance policies rather than selling individual short-term policies as and when required). The latter can be achieved by various strategies which are discussed more fully in Chapter 5. At the simplest level, communication programs that regularly inform existing customers of new service developments might develop producer-consumer relationships. For example, when launching the personal 1-800 number, AT&T sent direct mail pieces to all current AT&T customers. In addition, service providers might keep customers to themselves through long-term supply contracts. In this way, fitness centers seek regular business from individuals by offering annual membership schemes that effectively restrict the consumer's choice to one particular service provider.

2.4.8 Pattern of Demand

Services can be classified according to the temporal pattern of demand they face. Very few services face a constant pattern of demand through time. Many show considerable variation, which could be daily (downtown delicatessens at lunchtime), weekly (the Friday evening peak in demand for air travel), seasonal (beach hotels in summer, stores at Christmas time), cyclical (mortgages), or an unpredictable pattern

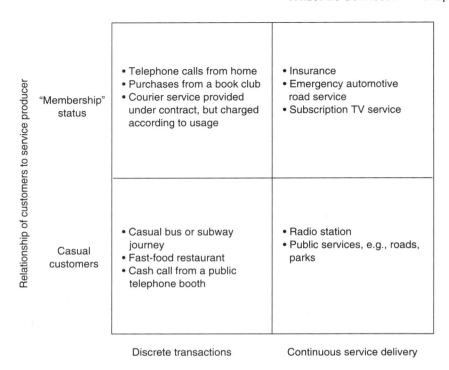

Figure 2.10   The nature of the relationship between producer and consumer

of demand (emergency building repair services, which may peak in demand after a storm). The perishability of the service offer can pose serious problems for services suppliers facing a very uneven pattern of demand. Many quite diverse service industries, such as electricity supply, hotels, and railroads, have nevertheless recognized common problems and in many cases responded with quite similar solutions. Some of these are examined in Chapter 4.

2.4.9 People-Based vs. Equipment-Based Services

Some services involve very labor-intensive production methods. A fortune teller employs a production method that is almost wholly based on human actions. At the other extreme, many services can be delivered with very little human involvement. A pay-and-display parking lot involves minimal human input in the form of checking tickets and keeping the parking lot clean.

      The management of people-based services can be very different from that of equipment-based services. While equipment can generally be programmed to perform consistently, personnel need to be carefully recruited, trained, and monitored. People-based services can usually allow greater customization of services to meet individual customers' needs. These issues are considered in Chapter 6.

2.4.10 Significance of the Service to the Purchaser

Some services are purchased frequently, are of low value, are consumed very rapidly by the recipient, and are likely to be purchased on impulse with very little prepurchase activity. Such services may represent a very small proportion of the purchaser's total expenditure and correspond to the goods marketer's definition of fast-moving consumer goods (FMCGs). A casual game on a slot machine would fit into this category. At the other end of the scale, long-lasting services may be purchased infrequently; when they are, the decision making process takes longer and involves more people. Vacations fit into this category.

Several bases for classifying services have now been presented. In practice, services need to be classified by many criteria simultaneously in order that groups of similar service types can be identified. Researchers have attempted to use a multidimensional approach to identify clusters of similar services. In one study,[14] consumers' perceptions of sixteen different personal and household services were researched, and a cluster analysis revealed two statistically significant bases for grouping services. The first—called the service locus—was defined along a scale from personal (doctors' services) to environmental (services performed on a person's possessions rather than the body). The second—service instigation—referred to the underlying reason for purchase of a service. At one extreme, a service could be purchased for basic maintenance purposes (regular visits to a dentist) while at the other, it is purchased for enhancement (health and fitness clubs).

If the clustering of service types has been carried out appropriately, it could be deduced that all services within that cluster will benefit from a broadly similar approach to marketing strategy. In Figure 2.11, a simple and hypothetical clustering has placed services along three classificatory scales: the extent of customer involvement, the extent to which the pattern of demand is peaked, and the degree of variability in production from the norm. Within the sector defined by high customer involvement, a constant pattern of demand (low peaks and troughs) and middling variability in production, three service offers can be identified: language instruction in a language laboratory, eye testing services, and graphic design services. On the basis of this analysis, each of these services could be expected to benefit from broadly similar marketing programs. These may include emphasizing the benefit to potential customers of the service's equipment base for reducing variability, developing a strong brand, and encouraging word-of-mouth recommendation. In fact, the marketing programs of three large operators in each field—Linguaphone, Pearle Vision, and Alpha Graphics—appears to converge on these points.

2.5 FURTHER DIFFERENCES BETWEEN GOODS AND SERVICES MARKETING

In addition to the distinguishing features of the services just described, environmental differences should be noted that differentiate the marketing of goods from the marketing of services. These comprise differences in the structure of services business units and differences in their operating environment.

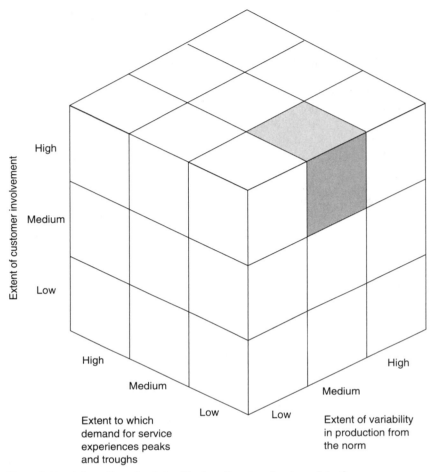

Figure 2.11   A three-dimensional classification of services showing points of convergence

2.5.1 Differences Relating to Services Producers

Although it is impossible to talk about a "typical" services organization, two key differences become apparent when they are compared with goods manufacturers. First, a wide range of services is provided on a very small scale where economies of scale are either minimal or nonexistent. Hairdressing, plumbing, legal services, painting, and decorating are usually provided by small units employing no more than a handful of people. Even a service activity such as retailing—in which the public perception is often of large supermarkets—is dominated by a very large number of small operators. In the United States in 1990, about 80 percent of the retail businesses were single outlet retailers.[15] The degree of marketing orientation of small service providers can be questioned. Evidence suggests that among other things, they may be less likely to undertake marketing research or to have formalized marketing planning processes.

A second feature of services providers is the presence of many not-for-profit providers. While there is usually little rationale for governments to supply manufactured goods, market mechanisms often fail to distribute services effectively. With some essential functions such as roads and urban transportation systems it is either impractical or undesirable for the private sector to take responsibility for provision, and government organizations assume responsibility for these functions. With many public utilities, the nature of service supply often creates potential monopoly problems, which are resolved either by direct government supply or by supply through highly regulated private sector organizations.

2.5.2 Differences Relating to the Marketing Environment

It can be argued that the marketing environment of service leads to their being subject to much more regulation and voluntary codes of ethics than the goods sector. The fact that a service is intangible makes it more difficult for a potential customer to fully examine a service before purchase. Service supply therefore involves a greater degree of trust than does the supply of goods; consequently, regulations are often designed to ensure that service delivery meets specifications. In the United States, as in most Western countries, highly intangible services such as banking, insurance, and travel services are regulated by a combination of voluntary and statutory measures. In some sectors, customers attempt to reduce their perceived risk by selecting only organizations that agree to have their relationship governed by a trade association's code of conduct.

2.6 THE EMERGENCE OF THE SERVICE ECONOMY

There is little doubt that the service sector has become an extremely important element of most Western economies. To understand the context in which services are marketed, this section looks at the role of services within national economies.

2.6.1 The Problem of Measuring Services Activity

Although it is generally acknowledged that the service sector in the United States has been growing, actually measuring the size of the sector can present as many problems as attempts to define it, for several reasons.

First, the level of accuracy with which service sector statistics have been recorded is generally less than for the manufacturing and primary sectors. The system of Standard Industrial Classifications (SICs) for a long while did not disaggregate the service sector in the same level of detail as it did the other sectors. Many service sectors do not fall neatly into one of the classifications, making it difficult to get an overall picture of that sector (for example, tourism is recorded under such diverse headings as 7011, hotels and motels; 7032, sporting and recreational camps; 7514, passenger car rental; and 8412, museums and art galleries).

Second, the intangible nature of services can make them relatively difficult to measure, especially in the case of overseas trade. Whereas flows of tangible goods through ports can usually be measured quite easily, trade flows associated with services are much more difficult to identify and measure. Furthermore, cutbacks in government statistical collection have increased the inaccuracy of many series. For example, the trade figures relating to tourism and financial services frequently have to be revised after initial publication.

Third, part of the apparent growth in the service sector may reflect the method by which statistics are collected rather than an increase in overall service level activity. Output and employment is recorded according to the dominant business of an organization. Yet, within manufacturing sector organizations, many people are employed in producing service-type activities, such as cleaning, catering, and transportation, and such employees' production is attributed to the manufacturing sector. A common occurrence during the 1980s has been for manufacturing industry to contract out many of these service activities to external suppliers. Where such contracts are performed by contract catering, office cleaning, or transportation companies, the output becomes attributable to the service sector, making the service sector look larger even though no additional services have been produced. The services have merely been switched from internal production and allocation without the use of external markets to external production and allocation by market mechanisms.

CASE STUDY

SORTING OTHER PEOPLES' MAIL DELIVERS RAPID GROWTH FOR AMERISCRIBE

The most visible evidence of the growth in the U.S. service sector is provided by the range of services we buy as private individuals—everything from home-delivered pizzas to overseas vacations and pet care. However, the most dramatic growth in the services sector has occurred within the business-to-business sector. It isn't so much that new services are being undertaken that weren't being carried out before as that firms have often found it makes more sense to buy their services from outside orginazations rather than produce the services themselves. This contracting out of some services has created new business opportunities for services suppliers, thereby increasing the total value of traded services.

A survey of one thousand of the largest corporations in the United States undertaken in January 1991 by the consulting firm Wyatt and Co. found that 86 percent of respondent firms had cut back their operations during the previous five years but that 35 percent of them had partly made up for this by making greater use of outside contractors. As a result of this trend, thousands of businesses have emerged to supply the services needs of corporate America, representing a major growth sector. Organizations that have contracted out their services can be found in all sectors of the economy—private sector profit organizations as well as not-for-profit organizations. Some companies that produce services have in turn contracted out part of their service production processes to other service suppliers.

An example of an industrial company that has turned to outside services suppliers is the Pittsburgh-based National Steel Corporation. It operates in a tough market, where it is squeezed on one side by low-cost overseas steel producers and on the other by firms that were spending more on research and development to produce new specialized steels.

Like most manufacturing industries, steel making requires the inputs of a wide range of specialized service type activities—everything ranging from cleaning offices to banking and legal services. National Steel found itself managing a huge range of activities at which it was not particularly expert. They took up valuable management time and capital that could have been better invested in the company's core business activity—making and selling steel. So National Steel analyzed just what was so central to its purpose that only the company could undertake itself, as distinct from activities that could readily be contracted out to the most efficient subcontractor. Research and development into new steels and the marketing of steel emerged at the top of the list for retention in house. For everything else, the company did not necessarily have to get involved itself—even making steel could be contracted out to producers in lower-cost countries. National Steel got to work most rapidly in contracting out its services inputs. At first it stuck to the traditional areas for contracting out by getting outside firms to run its in-house canteens and part of its transportation functions. But over time, the critical eye was cast over all its service activities, and its decision in 1990 to contract out mailroom services illustrates just how specialized business-to-business services have become.

National Steel has given the job of handling all its headquarters mail to the New York–based Ameriscribe Corporation. In return for a payment based partly on volume of mail handled, Ameriscribe sorts and distributes mail throughout the organization. It also handles a large part of National's copying work. For National Steel, Ameriscribe saves money and a lot of headaches. National has estimated that it saves more than $2 thousand a month by using an outside contractor rather than sorting its own mail. Part of this saving can be attributed to Ameriscribe's greater efficiency and experience, gained from its contracts with many large organizations. In short, it knows the mailroom business inside out in a way that National Steel could never hope to achieve internally. Cost savings also arise because Ameriscribe has much greater flexibility in the methods by which it pays its employees, in contrast to the more unionized National Steel, where pay differentials are jealously guarded.

Ameriscribe has grown fast by taking on other companies' administrative tasks, achieving a turnover of $88 million in 1990 and tripling its volume during the previous three years. Its effectiveness in handling National Steel's paperwork has been just one factor that has allowed the latter to concentrate all its energy on what it does best—selling steel—and allowed it to win back some lost markets.

CASE STUDY REVIEW QUESTIONS

1. Consider a large organization with which you are familiar. Develop a checklist that would help management decide between handling the organization's mail in-house or using an outside agency such as Ameriscribe.
2. Using the same organization as in question 1, discuss the extent to which service inputs have been contracted out. What is the potential for further subcontracting out? In other words, are there limits on firms seeking to "outsource" services?
3. What are the implications for the structure of the national economy of the increasing use of services subcontractors?

2.6.2 Key Trends in the U.S. Economy

The importance of services to the economy of the United States—and indeed to that of most developed economies—has been increasing rapidly during the past two decades. Three factors can be used to assess the changing relative importance of the service sector to the economy: (1) the share of gross domestic product (GDP) that it accounts for, (2) the proportion of the labor force employed in the sector, and (3) the contribution of services to the balance of payments. Most analyses of these indicators divide economic activity into three sectors: the primary sector (agriculture, mining, etc.), the secondary sector (manufacturing, construction, raw material processing, etc.), and the tertiary sector (services).

In respect of its share of GDP, the tertiary sector saw almost continuous growth during the period 1970–1990, increasing the proportion of the U.S. GDP that it accounts for from 57.5 percent to 66.1 percent, with banking, finance, insurance, business services, leasing, and communications being particularly prominent in this growth. By contrast, the secondary sector fell from 25.2 percent of GDP in 1970 to 19.2 percent in 1990, and the primary sector fell from 4.6 percent to 3.9 percent. Given that the secondary sector is a major consumer of the output of the tertiary sector, it seems likely that levels of growth in the service industries during the period would have been higher had the manufacturing and primary sectors not suffered decline.

These structural changes in the national economy are further illustrated by changes in the levels of employment in the three sectors over the same period. The tertiary sector's share of U.S. employment grew from 25.9 percent to 33.1 percent, mirroring changing employment patterns in many other advanced industrial economies. By contrast, employment in the primary sector fell from 4.4 percent of total employment in 1970 to 2.7 percent in 1990, and secondary sector employment declined from 32.5 percent in 1970 to 24.5 percent by 1990, with manufacturing suffering the largest number of job losses.

An interesting observation can be made by comparing the share of GDP accounted for by the tertiary sector with its corresponding share of employment. In the United States, the sector has consistently accounted for a greater share of employment than the proportion of GDP it contributes. This may give some justification to claims that the services sector as a whole is associated with relatively low earnings.

When the contribution of services to the United States balance of payments is considered, the growing relative importance of the sector can again be seen. During the past two decades, it has been usual for the United States to have a deficit in traded goods. This deficit has been made up by a surplus in invisibles, which include services, dividends, interest, and profits remitted from abroad. During the 1980s, while the visible trade balance continued to deteriorate, the net surplus in trade in services has been maintained. In 1993, while the United States visible balance was in deficit by $132.5 billion, there was an invisible surplus of $55.7 billion.[16]

2.6.3 International Comparisons

Although the OECD has found that the services sector accounted for most of the worldwide growth in employment since the oil crisis of 1973, there are still significant differences between countries in their impact.[17] There appears to be a high level of correlation between the level of economic development in an economy (as expressed by its GDP per capita) and the strength of its service sector, although whether a strong service sector leads to economic growth, or results from it, is not always clear.

The International Labor Office's Year Book of Labor Statistics illustrates the magnitude of these differences in 1990 (or the most recent year for which figures were available at that date).[18] The more highly developed economies were associated with high percentages of workers employed in the service sector, for example, the United States (75.6 percent), Canada (75.2 percent), Australia (74.2 percent), the United Kingdom (70.6 percent), and Switzerland (69.0 percent). Western countries that are considered to be less developed have proportionately fewer workers employed in the service sector, for example, Spain (59.7 percent), Portugal (53.2 percent), Ireland (53.0 percent), and Greece (49.9 percent). The lowest levels of services employment are found in the less developed countries, such as Mexico (29.9 percent), Bangladesh (28.3 percent), and Ethiopia (9.7 percent).

CASE STUDY

THE PHILIPPINES GETS A SHARE OF EMERGING WORLD TRADE IN DATA

Improvements in technology, the changing structure of industry, and its growing need for information illustrate how whole new categories of service industries can appear very quickly. Furthermore, when problems of inseparability can be overcome, new services can have a significant impact on national economies, allowing new competitive cost advantages to be exploited.

Data processing was just such a service industry. It emerged almost from nowhere during the 1980s as organizations of all kinds found increasing need to enter data into computerized databases—records of customer sales, facts about services performed, and details of rolling stock movements to name but a few. Many organizations were just beginning to appreciate the huge amount of data they were letting slip by instead of analyzing it to build up customer databases or analyze performance levels. In the early days, most firms regarded this as a back-room function that they could perform most cost-effectively by using their own staff on their own premises. With time, an increase in the volume of data to be processed, and the growing sophistication of data analysis systems, many service companies emerged to take the burden of data processing off client companies.

At first, most data processing companies operated close to their clients. Closeness was demanded by the limitations of data communication channels. However, by the late 1980s, the rapid pace of development in the telecommunications industry—especially the development of satellites and fiber optic links—allowed large volumes of data to be transmitted over long distances much more cheaply and reliably than ever before. This opened the door to an international trade in data processing, and operators around the world soon stepped in to exploit their comparative cost advantages. In particular, the development of telecommunications allowed companies to operate in overseas countries where labor costs were low, working regulations relaxed, and trade unions virtually nonexistent.

Data processing has established a firm foothold as an exportable service in areas such as the Caribbean, the Philippines, and the Irish Republic. Each of these countries is characterized by relatively low wage rates with skills at least as good as those of workers in more developed countries.

The development of the Kansas-based Saztec company illustrates the way in which new service sectors emerge and can create new international trade patterns. Saztec has won contracts from major organizations throughout the world, including several Federal government agencies, to process their data. Yet, these services are generally produced far away from either the company's or the client's base. The company employs more than eight hundred people in the Philippines, who earn an average of $50 per month—much less than the salary paid to its staff at Kansas. Staff turnover in the Philippines, at less than 1 percent, is much lower than the 30 percent annual rate at Kansas. Furthermore, the company is able to obtain a higher quality of output by the military-style organization and control of its staff—something that would not be accepted in the United States.

The Philippines has become an important exporter of data processing services by exploiting its comparative cost advantage in labor inputs, something that is useful in capturing high-volume, basic data input, in which accuracy and cost are paramount. Another country that has developed this service sector extensively is Jamaica, which in addition to exploiting its low labor costs offers the advantages of a sophisticated infrastructure—such as satellite links—and generous tax incentives. Ireland, by contrast, has exploited the fact that it has a relatively highly educated, English-speaking workforce, whose members earn about half what their counterparts would earn in the United States or the United Kingdom. Several firms, such as Wright Investor Services, have been set up in Ireland to do more sophisticated financial analysis on behalf of the big London-based banks and insurance companies.

CASE STUDY REVIEW QUESTIONS

1. Why has data processing emerged as a major new service industry?
2. What other service sectors have emerged during the past two decades? What factors explain their emergence?
3. What are the advantages to the economy of the Philippines of developing its data processing industry? Are there any disadvantages?

2.6.4 The Service Sector as a Vehicle for Economic Growth

Consider another example. According to a recent article in *Business Week,* a U.S. company, Telegroup, is waging war against Japan's phone company, KDD. Telegroup can save Japanese callers as much as 50 percent on overseas calls by routing them via the United States. The head of the company claims that it is fighting the trade deficit from Fairfield, Iowa, where the company is based.[19] How does the growth of Saztec, described in the case study, and the emergence of phone companies such as Telegroup result in economic growth to the United States?

In fact, growth in the service sector can result in economic growth to a nation in three main ways:

- by offering an exportable activity that results in a net inflow of wealth
- by reducing the need to buy services from overseas that consume domestically produced wealth

- by combining with other primary and secondary activities that allow new production possibilities for manufactured goods, increasing exports and reducing imports

While each of these categories can also be true of primary and secondary activities, the third is particularly important in the case of services which are often crucial in facilitating productivity gains in other sectors of the economy. As an example, transportation services have often had the effect of stimulating economic development at local and national levels—for instance, following the improvement of rail or road services. The absence of these basic services can have a crippling effect on the development of the primary and manufacturing sectors. One reason that Russian agriculture has not been fully exploited is the ineffective distribution system available to food producers.

Services can have a multiplier effect on local and national economies in that initial spending with a service producer triggers further expenditure. The first producer spends money buying supplies from outside (including labor), and these outside suppliers in turn purchase more inputs. The multiplier effect of this initial expenditure results in a total increase in household incomes that is much greater than the original expenditure. A good example of the multiplier effect at work in the United States is seen in the wide-ranging economic spinoffs that flowed from the Olympic Games held in Los Angeles in 1984. While the games initially created direct employment within the event itself, demand rippled out to other service sectors such as hotels and transportation. The level of activity generated additional demand for local manufacturing industry; for example, visitors require food, which may be produced locally, the producers of which may in turn require additional building materials to increase production facilities. The multiplier effects of additional service activity are limited by the propensity of suppliers to increase their own expenditure (rather than merely using up existing capacity) and the proportion of the subsequent spending that is retained within the local area (by using distant suppliers or employing casual migrant workers, much of the local economic benefit can be lost).

One approach to understanding the contribution of services to other aspects of economic activity is to analyze input-output tables of production and data on labor and capital inputs. In one study of the Canadian economy,[20] some apparently high productivity sectors were shown to be held back by the low productivity of some of their inputs, including service inputs. On the other hand, efficiency improvements in some services such as transportation were shown to have had widespread beneficial effects on the productivity contribution of other sectors.

The service sector should, in principle, be a valuable tool of regional development. Many services involve a considerable labor-based production element, and where production can be separated from consumption, production can be located close to sources of labor, free from locational constraints imposed by access to raw materials. Processing work involved in the financial services sector is a good example, where the problem of inseparability of production and consumption has been overcome by use of modern means of communication.

During the recession of the early 1980s, the service sector was seen by many as the salvation of the economy. Many politicians were eager to promote the service sector as a source of new employment to make up for the diminishing level of employment within the primary and secondary sectors. A common argument during this period was that the United States no longer held a competitive advantage in the production of many types of goods, and therefore these sectors of the economy should be allowed to decline and greater attention paid to services that showed greater competitive advantage. The logic of this argument can be pushed too far, in particular:

- A large part of the growth in the service sector during the mid-1980s reflected the buoyancy of the primary and secondary sectors during that period. As manufacturing industry increases its level of activity the demand for producer services such as accountancy, legal services, and business travel increases. The sudden decline of many financial services sectors during the late 1980s reflected the downturn in manufacturing activity, resulting in lower demand for such services as business loans and export credits.

- The assumption that the United States has a competitive advantage in the production of services needs to be examined closely. In much the same way that many sectors of American manufacturing industry lost their competitive advantage to developing nations during the 1960s and 1970s, there is evidence that the once unquestioned supremacy in certain service sectors is being challenged. American financial services organizations typify sectors that are being increasingly challenged by overseas competition. The high levels of training achieved in some of the United States' competitor nations have allowed those countries to first develop their own indigenous services and then develop them for export. Banking services, which were once a net import of Japan, are now exported by Japan throughout the world.

- Overreliance on the service sector could pose strategic problems for the United States. A diverse economic base allows a national economy to be more resilient to changes in world trading conditions.

CHAPTER REVIEW QUESTIONS

1. In Section 2.2 of this chapter, we identify the distinctive characteristics that differentiate "pure" services from goods. Discuss the extent to which you think that the principles of marketing that have been traditionally applied to the goods sector are appropriate for the services sector. Give examples.

2. Outline the reasons why it is useful, from a marketing perspective, to classify services. Select an organization that you are familiar with, and classify it along the dimensions identified in Section 2.4. Discuss the marketing implications of your classifications.

3. What is meant by inseparability? Suggest why its existence may pose problems to service organizations and methods by which its impact may be reduced.

4. Are there other methods of categorizing services?

5. Explain the reasons why governments are often eager to encourage service sectors within their countries.

6. Identify some of the problems associated with attempts to measure the size of a nation's service sector.

REFERENCES

1. Smith, A. *The Wealth of Nations* (Harmondsworth, U.K.: Penguin, 1977): 430.
2. Marshall, A. *Principles of Economics* (London: Macmillan, 1890).
3. Kotler, P. and Armstrong, G. *Principles of Marketing,* 5th ed. (Englewood Cliffs, N.J.: Prentice Hall, 1991).
4. Fuchs, V. *The Service Economy* (New York: National Bureau of Economic Research, Columbia University Press, 1968).
5. Stanton, W. J. *Fundamentals of Marketing* (New York: McGraw-Hill, 1981).
6. Levitt, T. "Production Line Approach to Service," *Harvard Business Review* (September-October 1972): 41–52.
7. Gronroos, C. "A Service Oriented Approach to the Marketing of Services," *European Journal of Marketing* 12, no. 8 (1978): 588–601.
8. Lovelock, C. "Why Marketing Needs to Be Different for Services," in *Marketing of Services,* ed. J. H. Donnelly and W. R. George (Chicago: American Marketing Association, 1981).
9. Shostack, G. L. "Breaking Free From Product Marketing," *Journal of Marketing* 41 (April 1977): 73–80.
10. Berry, L. L. "Relationship Marketing," in *Emerging Perspectives of Services Marketing,* ed. L. L. Berry et al. (Chicago: American Marketing Association, 1983).
11. Rathmell, J. M. *Marketing in the Service Sector* (Cambridge, Mass.: Winthrop, 1974).
12. Shostack, G. L. "Breaking Free From Product Marketing," *Journal of Marketing* 41 (April 1977): 73–80.
13. Gershuny, J. *After Industrial Society? The Emerging Self-Service Economy* (London: Macmillan, 1978).
14. Solomon, M. R. and Gould, S. J. "Benefitting from Structural Similarities Among Personal Services," *Journal of Services Marketing* 5, no. 2 (Spring 1991): 23–32.
15. Evans, J. and Berman, B. *Marketing* (New York: Macmillan, 1994).
16. Freadhoff, C. "Revamped Trade Report Corrects for Old Bias by Adding Services," *Investor's Business Daily* (March 23, 1994): 2.
17. OECD, "The Contribution of Services to Employment," *Employment Outlook* (September 1984): 39–54.
18. International Labour Office, *Year Book of Labour Statistics* (Geneva: International Labour Office, 1991).
19. Marbach W. and Tilsner, J. "The Great International Phone-Call Grab," *Business Week* (March 14, 1994): 6.
20. Wood, P. A. "Producer Services and Economic Change, Some Canadian Evidence," in *Technological Change and Economic Policy,* ed. K. Chapman and G. Humphreys (London: Blackwell, 1987).

SUGGESTED FURTHER READING

BATESON, J. 1977, "Do We Need Service Marketing?" *Marketing Consumer Services: New Insights.* Marketing Science Institute, Boston: Report 77-115.

BATESON, J. 1979, "Why We Need Service Marketing," in *Conceptual and Theoretical Developments in Marketing*, edited by O. C. Ferrell, S. W. Brown, and C. W. Lamb.

Chicago: American Marketing Association, 1979.

BOWEN, J. 1990 "Development of a Taxonomy of Services to Gain Strategic Marketing Insights." *Journal of the Academy of Marketing Science* (Winter): 43–50.

EIGLIER, P. and LANGEARD, E. 1977. "A New Approach To Service Marketing." *Marketing Consumer Services: New Insights*. Boston: Marketing Science Institute, Report 77–115.

JACKSON, R. W. and COOPER, P. D. 1988. "Unique Aspects of Marketing Industrial Services." *Industrial Marketing Management* (May): 111–18.

LEVITT, T. 1981. "Marketing Intangible Products and Product Tangibles." *Harvard Business Review* 59 (May-June): 95–102.

LOVELOCK, C. 1981. "Why Marketing Needs to Be Different for Services." In *Marketing of Services,* edited by J. H. Donnelly and W. R. George. Chicago: American Marketing Association.

LOVELOCK, C. H. 1983. "Classifying Services to Gain Strategic Marketing Insight." *Journal of Marketing* 47 (Summer): 9–20.

RUSHTON, A. M. and CARSON, D. J. 1985. "The Marketing of Services: Managing the Intangibles." *European Journal of Marketing* 19, no. 3: 19–41.

SHOSTACK, G. L. 1977. "Breaking Free From Product Marketing," *Journal of Marketing,* 41 (April).

SOLOMON, M. R. and Gould S. J. 1991. "Benefitting from Structural Similarities Among Personal Services." *Journal of Services Marketing* 5, no. 2 (Spring): 23–32.

ZEITHAML, V. A., PARASURAMAN, A. and BERRY, L. L. 1985. "Problems and Strategies in Services Marketing." *Journal of Marketing* 49 (Spring): 33–46.

3

The Service Product

CHAPTER OBJECTIVES

After reading this chapter, you should be able to understand

- the elements that constitute the service offer
- methods by which customers evaluate service offers
- strategic issues raised in developing the range of services offered by an organization
- procedures for developing new services and deleting old ones

3.1 INTRODUCTION

Products form the focal point for an organization's effort to satisfy its customers' needs. The features, design, styling, and ranges of the product, among other things, help the organization gain competitive advantage by meeting its customers' needs more effectively than do its competitors. Product decisions form just one set of decisions that an organization makes in order to satisfy customers' needs. They must be related to decisions about the other elements of the marketing mix in order to give a coherent market position for a service.

It was noted in Chapter 1 that the marketing mix formulation traditionally applied to goods may not be appropriate for the marketing of services. However, most reformulations of the marketing mix continue to emphasize product decisions, although the concept of a product and the nature of product decisions for services can be quite different than with goods. The purpose of this chapter is to look more specifically at the service product offering and to consider conceptual frameworks for understanding the management of products in a service context and recognizing the differences between goods and services.

3.2 THE SERVICE OFFER

The term *product* is used to describe both tangible goods offers and relatively intangible service offers. A starting point for understanding the nature of products is to take a general definition of a product:

> "A product is any good, service, or idea that satisfies a need or want and can be offered in exchange."[1]

While this definition is intended to be universal in its coverage, it must be recognized that significant differences exist between different product offers. This has led to several attempts to classify types of products. For example, Kotler[2] has proposed four categories:

- pure tangibles (e.g., salt)
- tangibles with accompanying services (e.g., automobiles)
- major services with accompanying minor goods components (e.g., air transport)
- pure services (e.g., life insurance)

It should be quite clear by now that most products are a combination of goods and services. The goods component can itself be divided into support goods and facilitating goods.[3] The former are tangible aspects of a service that aid the service provision (a textbook in education, for example), while facilitating goods must exist for the service to be provided in the first place (for example, a car is a prerequisite for the provision of a car rental service).

In reality, customers do not buy products as such but buy the benefits that products provide. The most important element of any organization's marketing mix, therefore, can be considered to be its "offer," and this chapter considers the organization's "service offer." An understanding of just what constitutes the service offer from both the buyer's and the seller's points of view is imperative. One approach[4] is to see purchase bundles, or the "service concept," as comprising three elements:

- Physical items, which are the tangible and material elements of facilitating or support goods, for example, the food or drink served in a restaurant.
- Sensual benefits, which can be defined by one or more of the five senses, such as the taste and aroma of a restaurant meal or the ambience of a restaurant.
- The psychological benefits of a service purchase bundle, which cannot be clearly defined and are determined by the customer subjectively. The existence of this type of benefit makes the management of the service offer very difficult. For example, to the student eating at a restaurant, the received psychological benefit may be increased free time to prepare for an upcoming exam.

Service offers can be distinguished from goods offers by their inseparability. The fact that a service cannot usually be separated from the person who provides it, nor from the place where it is provided, results in services being "consumed" as soon as they are produced. This therefore implies a high degree of buyer/supplier interaction. The concept of value added in the product also takes on new meaning. In both production and marketing, the concept of value added is the difference between input and output at various levels on the supply side. Since services are not resold, there can arguably only be one level of value added, with the concept of input being redefined to mean only the supplies consumed and the depreciation of capital goods used up in the production of a service. Finally, the effects of the organization/client interface and user participation have been seen as being critical elements influencing the consumer's perception of a service product.[5]

3.2.1 Analysis of the Service Offer

Several elements within the service offer can be identified. Some are fundamental to the nature of the product, whereas others refine or differentiate it. For products in general, an analysis by Kotler and Andreasen[6] distinguishes between three different levels of an individual product.

- The first level is known as the *core* product, defined in terms of the underlying need that a product satisfies. For example, a hotel offers a quiet and clean place to sleep.
- The second level is known as the *tangible* product. The core product is made available to consumers in some tangible form, expressed in terms of the product's features, styling, packaging, brand name, and quality level. For example, the Chateau Leon in Watkins Glenn, New York offers heated cabins with private baths.
- The third level is known as the *augmented* product. This is the tangible product plus additional services and benefits, included to satisfy additional needs of consumers and/or to further differentiate a product from its competitors. Many of these additional features tend to be services, such as warranties and before-sales and after-sales service. Chateau Leon also offers free breakfast and a vegetarian store.

An application of this multilevel approach to the analysis of the product offer of a car is shown in Figure 3.1.

While this analysis is held to be true of products in general, doubts have been expressed about whether it can be applied to the service offer. Is it possible to identify a core service representing the essence of a consumer's perceived need that requires satisfying? If such a core service exists, can it be made available in a form that is consumer friendly, and if so, what elements are included in this form? Finally, is there a level of service corresponding to the augmented product that allows a service provider to differentiate its service offer from its competitors in the same way a car manufacturer differentiates its augmented product from those of its competitors?

Other writers have attempted to revise this basic framework to identify different levels of the service offer. One revision talks about the substantive and peripheral

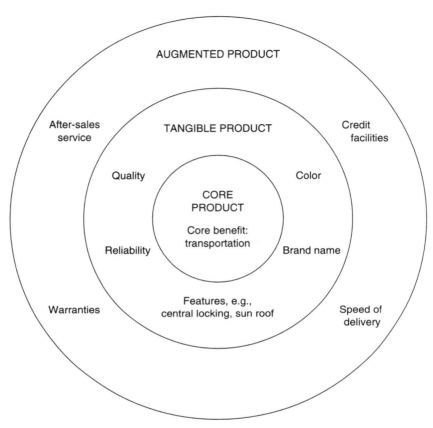

Figure 3.1   Analysis of the product offering of a car
(Adapted from P. Kotler and A. Andreasen, *Strategic Marketing for Non-Profit Organizations.*
Englewood Cliffs, N.J.: Prentice Hall, 1991)

elements of a service while another distinguishes between the service concept and
the "interactive marketing function."[7,8]

Most analyses of the service offer recognize that the problems of inseparability
and intangibility make application of the three general levels of product offer less
meaningful to the service offer. Instead, the service offer is analyzed here in terms of
two components:

- the core service that represents the core benefit
- the secondary service that represents both the tangible and the augmented product
  levels

3.3 THE CORE SERVICE LEVEL

This can be described as the *substantive* service, or the essential function that it per-
forms. Gronroos uses the term *service concept* to denote the core of a service offer-

ing, stating that it can be general, such as offering car rental as a solution to transportation problems, or it can be more specific, such as offering Chinese cuisine in a restaurant.

There seems to be little difference between services and manufactured goods when this fundamental level of a firm's offer is considered. All customer needs and wants are intangible: they cannot be seen or touched. The offer should be developed, produced, and managed with the consumers' benefit in mind in such a way that they perceive it as being successful in satisfying their needs. The offering can be a tangible good, a service, or a combination of both.

It follows that an understanding of customers' needs is vital if a service provider wishes to be successful, requiring a "common view" or "perceptual congruence" between itself and service users. This in turn requires "soft" data of a behavioral nature, which allows an understanding of what benefits the customer derives from a service. This highlights the importance of appropriate marketing research, in particular qualitative research and its attempts to measure consumers' perceptions, beliefs and attitudes. In formulating service design, market research for services should place emphasis on customer perceptions of the service itself.

3.4 *THE SECONDARY SERVICE LEVEL*

It was noted earlier that the secondary level of a service offering can be seen as representing both the tangible level of a product and the augmented level. At the augmented level, service suppliers offer additional benefits to consumers that go beyond merely delivering the core service. This is done either to meet additional consumer needs and/or to further differentiate the product from those of competitors.

As there is no "tangible" level of a service in the manner that the term is understood in a goods context, it could be argued that it is not possible to define an augmented service. However, many of the elements normally considered to be part of the augmented product relate to *how* the product is distributed or delivered, for example, installation, delivery, credit availability, and after-sales service. Service intangibility implies that when consumers are deciding on a service purchase they may not be able to experience (feel, see, hear, taste, or smell) the service before it is purchased. In many cases, services may also be mentally intangible in that they are difficult concepts to grasp.

An exploration of just what is meant by service intangibility has been made by Shostack, who sees services as being more than just intangible products:

> . . . it is wrong to imply that services are just like products except for intangibility. By such logic apples are just like oranges, except for their "appleness." Intangibility is not a modifier, it is a state."[9]

Shostack's molecular model (described in Chapter 2) is merely her way of making the point that there is a product continuum. A service dominant entity concerned primarily with intangible elements is at one extreme, and a product dominant entity consisting predominantly of tangible elements is at the other. For Shostack, the greater the weight of intangible elements in an entity, the greater the divergence from the approach of goods marketing. Services knowledge and goods knowledge are not gained in the same way. Customers of physical products can "know" their product through physical examination and/or quantitative measurement. Service reality must be defined experientially by the user, and there are many versions of this reality.

For services, therefore, the secondary level of a service offer involves combining both tangible and intangible elements in order for the customer to realize the core benefit. However, specific difficulties are involved in determining the particular combination of these tangibles and intangibles. One major difficulty is the actual articulation of the elements, for it is far easier to articulate the tangible aspects than it is to produce and display the intangibles. In addition, the intangible elements are relatively difficult to control, and therefore service managers tend to emphasize the controllable (i.e., tangible) elements rather than the more difficult intangibles. The more intangible the service, the greater the need for tangible evidence.

Another major conceptual problem in defining the service offer is that because of the inseparability of production and consumption, some elements of the secondary service level are not actually provided by the service provider but by customers themselves, for example, the student who "reads about" a subject before attending a seminar.

Notwithstanding these difficulties, the secondary level of the service offer can be analyzed in terms of several elements, some of which bear comparison with the elements used in analyzing the offer of a tangible good. The principle elements are discussed here and some of them are illustrated in Figure 3.2, where an insurance product is used as an example.

3.4.1 Features

In the tangible product, features represent specific components of the product that could be added or subtracted without changing its essential characteristics. They can be added or subtracted so that an organization produces a range of products that appeal to a variety of different market segments, each with the same core needs but each requiring marginally different products to satisfy slightly differing secondary needs.

In much the same way, most service offerings can be analyzed in terms of differentiating features (Figure 3.3). For example, banks usually offer different types of checking accounts to appeal to segments of the population with slightly differing needs. In this way, particular bundles of tangible and intangible elements that constitute the service product represent different service forms.

3.4.2 Styling

Styling means giving the product a distinctive feel or look. Is this possible with a service?

At first glance it seems easier to do this in relation to the tangible elements of the service offer than to the intangible elements. However, if a broader definition of style is used, which includes the manner, mode, or approach of service delivery rather than merely a physical quality, there is little difficulty in applying this concept to the service offer. In this instance, the customer gains the "sensual benefits" described earlier.

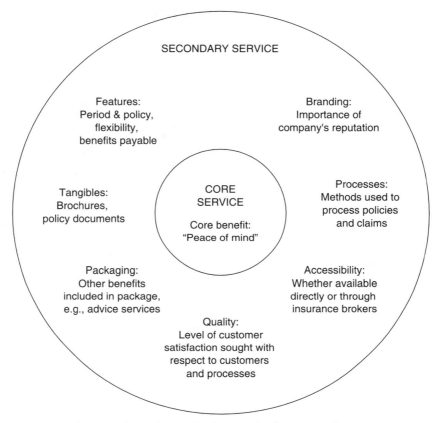

Figure 3.2   The core and secondary service elements of an insurance product

The inseparability of the service offer makes the relationship between customer and service provider of paramount importance. It is through this relationship that a service manager can develop a distinctive style. For example, McDonald's and Wendy's restaurants differ in their styles, although they are both in the business of selling relatively low-value, high-speed food and drink. The style of a service is a result of a combination of features, including tangible decor and the intangible manner in which front-line staff interact with customers. The overall service style can be established either before or after the target market is identified.

3.4.3 Packaging

The intangible nature of services prevents them from being packaged in the traditional sense of providing physical wrapping that can both protect the product and help develop a distinctive identity. However, the tangible elements of a service can be packaged, performing much the same function as the packaging of goods. Good packaging can make service consumption easier. For example, the design of takeout containers can ease the handling of fast food and also convey messages that distinguish the provider of the service from its competitors.

The Arts of the Windsor Court Hotel

The Windsor Court Hotel demonstrates that art and the art of hospitality both find fullest expression in each other's presence. Our treasured artwork which is displayed throughout the hotel creates a rich context for the ambience and caliber of service inspired by memories of great estates.

We have embraced the artistic pleasures of the discriminating traveler and bring these enjoyable experiences to you, such as the art of music expressed through our chamber players, the art of fine entertaining, and of course, the exquisite works of art which comprise the house collection.

The Arts of the Windsor Court Hotel allow us to express an elegant, warm and genuinely gracious style, rare in any time and place.

WINDSOR COURT HOTEL
300 Gravier Street
New Orleans, Louisiana 70130
(504) 523-6000 • toll free (800) 262-2662
or call your travel specialist

Figure 3.3 The Windsor Court Hotel ad emphasizes a secondary element of a hotel's service (i.e., "an elegant, warm and genuinely gracious style"), rather than the core benefit (i.e., a good night's sleep). Source: Windsor Court Hotel, New Orleans, Louisiana.

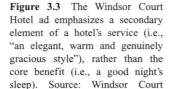

In a wider sense, service packaging can refer to the way in which tangible and intangible elements are bundled together to provide a comprehensive service offer. For example, a bank checking account may be packaged to include a credit card and discounts on a variety of consumer products.

3.4.4 Branding

The purpose of branding is to identify products as belonging to a particular organization and to enable differentiation of its products from those of its competitors. While most tangible product offers are branded in some form, the service offer itself is less likely to be branded. Instead of the individual service offer being branded, it is more likely that branding will focus on the service provider's corporate image. In this way, fast-food restaurants and accountants are usually differentiated on the basis of their corporate name and reputation rather than the specific services they offer.

In some instances, however, the service itself is branded, or there is a hierarchy of brands and sub-brands representing both corporate identity and service-specific identity. Often, service-specific branding has a tangible basis (e.g., a "Big Mac" offered by McDonald's), although at other times the product brand is based largely on intangibles (e.g., specific brand names applied to different bank accounts).

3.4.5 Physical Evidence

While manufacturers of goods tend to introduce additional services into their augmented product, service marketers are more likely to differentiate their services from the competition by adding tangible features, for example, distinctive designs of brochures, staff uniforms, and service outlets.

3.4.6 Service Delivery

Just as delivery can be an important differentiator for goods, it can also be equally important for a service. According to Gronroos, service marketers should use the concept of accessibility rather than seeing service provision in terms of distribution/delivery, as with goods. Several resources affect this accessibility: human resources (especially contact personnel), machines, buildings and other physical infrastructure, and supplementary services. These resources can be managed by a service organization to enhance the accessibility of its service to consumers. The service itself may be intangible, but these resources make the delivery of the service a reality.

3.4.7 Process

Most services are concerned with production processes as much as with any final outcomes. Service design should therefore pay attention to process and to the manner in which service personnel interact with customers during this process. One approach to designing the process is to use Shostack's "blueprinting" approach (discussed in Chapter 4).

3.4.8 People

It was noted earlier that the people involved in the process of delivering a service can be crucial in defining that service and customers' perceptions of it. Personnel therefore become an important element of the service offer, and management must define the role expectations of employees and support them with training when necessary. In addition to managing the interaction between customers and service producers' own personnel, other consumers who use or buy the service may influence the perception of the service when it is consumed in public. Many service industries therefore employ methods to control the behavior of their customers when they are likely to influence other customers' enjoyment or image of a service. Elegant restaurants, for example, may require that male diners wear a coat and tie during dinner hours.

3.4.9 Quality

The level of quality to which a service is designed is a crucial element in the total service offer. Quality is an important factor used by customers to evaluate the services of one organization in comparison with the offers of others. In fact, customers may judge not so much the quality of an individual service offer but the quality of the service provider.

In goods marketing, quality can be understood as the level of performance of a product. In services marketing, quality is the perceived level of performance of a service, but measuring it can be difficult. Not only can it be difficult to measure quality parameters, it can also be difficult to identify which quality factors customers attach importance to. A service that may be seen by the producer as having high technical quality may in fact be perceived very differently by the consumer who has a different set of quality evaluation criteria.

The intangible nature of service quality standards is reflected in the difficulty that services companies have in designing quality standards that will be readily accepted by potential customers. Customer expectations form an important element of quality—a service that fails to meet the expectations of one customer may be considered to be of poor quality, while another customer receiving an identical service but not holding such high expectations may consider the service to be of a high quality standard. In this way, an occasional traveler who has won a flight on the Concorde may consider all aspects of the service experience to exceed his or her limited expectations. On the other hand, a regular business traveler with relatively exacting expectations may rate the service as being of low quality on account of minor problems such as the speed of check-in facilities and the attentiveness of the cabin crew.

There is increasing interest in the concept of service quality among both academics and practitioners who see superior quality levels as an important means of gaining competitive advantage. For this reason, considerable research has been undertaken to understand the processes by which customers evaluate quality. A sound understanding of these processes can allow service companies to be clearer in their specification of quality levels in their offer and also to allow a more focused communication to potential customers of the service level offered.

In general, tangible goods can be designed and produced to a predetermined standard. Because such standards can generally be quantified, it is relatively easy to monitor and maintain them. With intangible services, the difficulties associated with quantification of standards makes it much more difficult for an organization to monitor and maintain a consistently high standard of service. Furthermore, the intangibility and inseparability of most services results in a series of unique buyer/seller exchanges, with no two services being provided in exactly the same way. In an attempt to reduce the problems of uniqueness, many service providers have attempted to "industrialize" their output by offering a limited range of machine-assisted services with lower variability in output.

Because of the importance of quality in the total service offering, the subject of defining, measuring, planning, implementing, and monitoring quality standards is considered in more detail in Chapter 5.

3.5 *CUSTOMER PERCEPTION OF SERVICE ATTRIBUTES*

It is important for services organizations to understand the processes by which customers evaluate the total service offer. Although customers initially assess the core service for its ability to satisfy their substantive need for a service, such as a basic need for transport, many other secondary needs, such as the need for a sense of control, trust, self-fulfillment, and status, are expressed in sought service attributes. These desired attributes have been labeled by Sasser[7] as *security* (safety of customer and/or his or her property), *consistency* (reliability), *attitude, completeness* (degree of service range), *condition* (environment), *availability,* and *timing* (length of time required for, and pace of performance of, the service). Service providers compete by producing service offerings containing a permutation of these attributes to meet customers' secondary needs better than their competitors.

An indication of the relationship between core and secondary service levels and their relationship to customer product evaluation processes is shown in Figure 3.4.

Faced with an array of service attributes, some understanding of the processes by which customers evaluate each bundle of attributes is desirable. Three possible ways can be identified by which these judgments can be made:

- First, a consumer may make a judgment based on an overpowering attribute which for that particular individual is of great importance in a given situation. For example, a person who belongs to the MileagePlus Club may fly United Air Lines all the time. This traveler would be using one attribute (i.e., whether or not he or she belongs to the frequent flyer club) as a single overpowering attribute.
- Second, judgment may be made on the basis of minimum levels of certain attributes, but final judgment may be based on the existence of a single specific attribute. Thus, a person may tell the travel agent to book a ticket only on an airline that flies between Austin and Dallas, Texas, before 9:00 A.M. on Wednesday morning and returns on Friday after 5:00 P.M. If more than two carriers meet these criteria, the traveler may then decide to take the carrier that has the frequent flyer club.

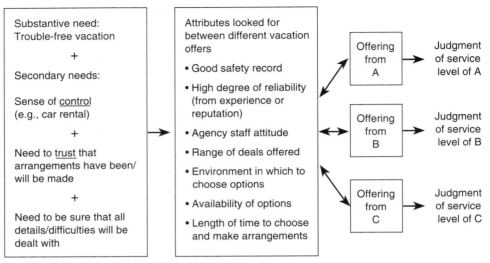

Figure 3.4 Customer judgment of the total service offer

- Third, the consumer may decide upon alternatives, using a weighted average of attributes. Such a traveler, for example, may consider not only frequent flyer clubs and times of arrival and departure but also price.

A major difficulty with this model, however, is that customers are often not consciously aware of their needs. In some respects, the service product is an *idea,* and, the need for a service is often unrecognized by the buyer until he or she becomes aware of its availability (e.g., a customer may not be aware of a need for life insurance until he or she is made aware of the benefits of life policies). Even if consumers are aware of their needs, they often have difficulty in expressing their desires to service providers. In addition, customers' needs are unlikely to remain constant as individual customers and their marketing environments change.

Although understanding customer service requirements can be difficult, it is essential that service firms do not fall into the trap of being production oriented. Customer orientation has been defined as the "consumer benefit concept"[10] in that a service offering cannot be defined in isolation from the benefit it will bring to the consumer (Figure 3.5).

3.6 SERVICE PRODUCT STRATEGIES

Few services organizations can survive by offering just one specialized service. Instead, a mix of services is usually offered. This section considers the issues involved in managing a product mix.

The service range offered by an organization can be disaggregated for analysis. The most basic unit of output is often referred to as an item: a specific version of a product. Such an item is normally part of a product line that is a group of related

There are a lot of good reasons for choosing the Quiet Company.

Some are more
important than others.

Northwestern Mutual Life
has always received the highest
possible ratings from Moody's,
Standard & Poor's, A.M. Best and
Duff & Phelps. It has been voted "the most
financially sound life insurance company" every
year in a survey sponsored by FORTUNE® magazine.
When you have a new reason for wanting the most secure
life insurance, talk to the Quiet Company. Northwestern Mutual Life.

**Northwestern
Mutual Life**®
The Quiet Company®

Figure 3.5 By using endorsements, this advertisement communicates the quality of the service provider. Source: J. Walter Thompson Company; photograph by Victor Skrebneski.

product items. The product mix is the combination of products that an organization offers to customers. A distinction can also be made between the depth of a product mix and its width. *Product depth* refers to the number of different products in a product line. *Product width* refers to the number of product lines offered by an organization.

In a services context, an example of an individual service item offered by a bank is a savings account for high school students. This in turn will form part of a line of savings accounts, the depth of which may be indicated by the presence of a wide range of savings accounts to meet the needs of customers who require ease of access, high interest, flexibility, and so on. Savings accounts represent just one line of service offering for most banks. Other lines typically include personal loans, mortgages, and credit cards.

Decisions about an organization's product mix are of strategic importance. In order to remain competitive in the face of declining demand for its principal service line, a service company may need to widen its product mix. For example, the increasing diversity in food tastes has forced many specialized fast-food outlets to widen their range. Those that have traditionally emphasized burgers have often introduced new lines such as pizzas or home delivery services. On the other hand, decisions may need to be made to delete services from the mix when consumer tastes have changed or competitive pressures have made the continuing provision of a service uneconomic. Product mix extension and deletion decisions are continually made in order that organizations can provide services more effectively (providing the right services in response to consumers' changing needs) and more efficiently (providing services for which the organization is able to make most efficient use of its resources).

The service offer of any service organization will be constrained by the capabilities, facilities, and resources at its disposal. It is therefore important for service firms to constantly examine their capabilities and their objectives to ensure that the range of services they provide meets the needs of the consumer as well as the organization. The process of ensuring that the right services are being provided in order to meet strategic objectives is often referred to as a service product audit. Key questions for an audit are these:

- What benefits do customers seek from the service?
- What is the current and continuing availability of the resources required to provide the service?
- What skills and technical know-how are required?
- What benefits are offered over and above the competition?
- Are competitors' advantages causing the organization to lose revenue?
- Does each service provided still earn sufficient financial return?
- Do services meet the targets that justify continued funding?

The answers to these and other related questions form the basis of product mix development strategy.

3.6.1 Developing the Product Mix

The growth options open to an organization can be analyzed with the help of Ansoff's Product Market Expansion Matrix.[11] The matrix sees development decisions being based on the newness of markets and the newness of products. The four main service product strategies available to a service firm are summarized here:

Market penetration.   An organization continues to supply its existing services to its existing customer segments but tries to increase sales from them. This may be achieved by increasing their total consumption of that type of service or by taking consumers from competitors. Attempting to sell more of its existing range of services to existing customers means that greater use of existing resources and facilities is required. For example, airlines recently realized that they could increase sales in the college student market by making it easier for the students to fly more often. College students travel for a variety of reasons: to visit college campuses, to go home for a long weekend, or to take a vacation. Some airlines, such as Continental and US Air, have not only introduced special youth fares for those under 25 but also dropped some restrictions, such as Saturday night stayovers and two weeks advance notice. The hope is, of course, that if these young flyers find it easy to fly on Continental or USAir, they will fly the carrier again the next time they have to travel.[12]

Market extension.   New types of consumers are found for existing services. For example, a restaurant chain established in the United States may extend its operations to a new overseas market, or universities may promote their courses to new groups of mature students. Attempting to sell existing services to new customers requires the use of existing production resources and facilities. There are, however, no market-based resources available, as the firm is entering a new market.

Service development.   New or modified services are developed to sell to the current market. For example, a bank may offer a new type of charge card to its current customer base. Attempting to sell new services to existing customers means that a firm can use market resources, but there is likely to be a lack of existing capability or resources to produce the new service.

Diversification.   New services are offered to new markets. For example, a traditional leisure vacation operator may offer a conference organizing service. Attempting to sell new services in new markets makes it less likely that there are any existing resources available.

Each of these strategies involves differing levels of risk. A market penetration strategy normally presents the lowest risk to a firm, as it is likely to be dealing with both services and consumers with which it is familiar. Both service development and market development strategies involve greater degrees of risk because the organization is dealing with something new in each situation. However, the degree of risk depends on the organization's particular strengths relative to its competitors and on the potential opportunities available. Diversification normally involves the greatest risk of all, involving an organization with both new services and new markets.

Because services go through some form of life cycle, it is essential that an organization has a strategy to maintain a balance in its portfolio of service offers. Designing the best product portfolio involves answering some important questions:

- What services should be included in the mix?
- What is the optimum range of services to offer?
- What is the most profitable mix?
- How should the mix be positioned in relation to the competition?

In order to be able to successfully manage a portfolio of services, a firm must constantly monitor the performance of its services through the use of a marketing information system.

3.6.2 Product/Service Life Cycle Concept

The product/service life cycle graphically indicates the sales of a product or service over its lifetime. The concept is based on the premise that the total sales and profitability of a product fluctuate according to some pattern during the product's life. A product life cycle shows sales and profitability on the vertical axis against time on the horizontal axis. Such a concept has been used for individual product items, product classes, and, in fact, whole industries.[13] A typical product life cycle is shown in Figure 3.6.

Figure 3.6 shows that a product's life can typically be divided into five phases:

Phase 1: Introduction.   New products are generally costly to produce and launch, and they may have teething problems. People may be wary of trying something new, especially a new service whose intangibility prevents prior evaluation. Sales therefore tend to be slow and are restricted to those who like trying out new products or who believe they can gain status or benefit by having them.

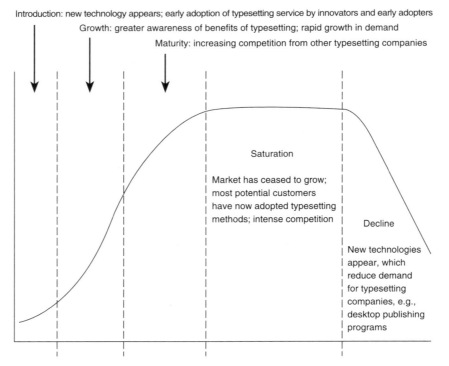

Figure 3.6   A hypothetical product life cycle for typesetting businesses

Phase 2: Growth.   By this time, the product has been tested and any problems have been resolved. The product is now more reliable and more readily available. People now start to see the benefits that can be gained by using the product. Sales start to increase greatly, and this is a signal for competitors to start entering the market.

Phase 3: Maturity.   Almost everyone who wants to buy the product has now done so, although some people may now be updating the product, having purchased it earlier in the life cycle. The number of competitors in the market has risen.

Phase 4: Saturation.   There are too many competitors and no further growth in the market. Competitors tend to compete with each other on the basis of price.

Phase 5: Decline.   With falling demand and new substitute products appearing, organizations drop out of the market.

The usefulness of the life cycle concept lies in the recognition that marketing activity for a service is closely related to the stage in the life cycle that a service has reached. In this way, promotional planning is closely related to the life cycle, with emphasis placed in the launch phase on raising awareness through public relations activity, building on this through the growth phase with advertising, resorting to sales promotion incentives as the market matures and becomes more competitive, and finally, possibly allowing promotional activity to fall as the service is allowed to go into decline. In a similar way, distribution and pricing decisions can often be related to the stage a service has reached in its life cycle.

Of course, the product life cycle presented here is a conceptual abstraction. Different products move through the life cycle at different paces. Some products have been in the maturity/saturation stage for many years (e.g., basic bank checking accounts) whereas others disappear very soon after introduction (e.g. some trendy clothes retailers). Empirical evidence also seems to imply a variety of life cycle modifications and mutations. Five of the more likely mutations are shown in Figure 3.7.

In the first example, the product has achieved a reasonably high sales level early on, but sales have failed to increase any further, although there is no sign of maturity or decline.

In the second example, the product constantly increases its sales volume in each period of time. New customers are gained, and present customers increase their purchase of the product.

The third example, however, displays the complete opposite. The product started from a strong position but now experiences falling sales, probably because of better competition entering the market.

The fourth example displays how in certain instances a product entering decline can be saved from the depths of decline. This could have occurred through product reformulation or through some form of sales promotion. Alternatively, it could have been brought about by some external factor, such as a change in customers' tastes. Whatever the cause, the product now displays a new lease on life. A

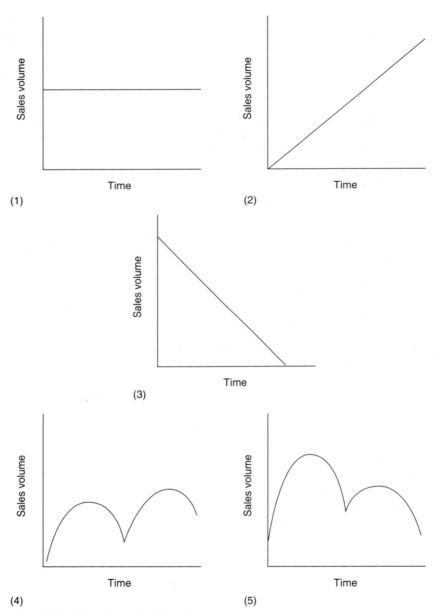

Figure 3.7 Alternative product life cycles

second cycle has developed, but, decline is on the way again, although at a higher level of sales than existed previously.

The final example displays once again the saving of a product at the decline stage. Unlike the fourth situation, however, the new cycle is at a lower level of sales than originally.

While these comments are probably true of tangible goods, to what extent is it possible to talk about a specific services life cycle?

There is evidence that many services have passed through a life cycle, for example, transatlantic air transportation. In the introductory stage (from the end of the World War II until the late 1950s), air transportation incurred large development costs, was expensive and unreliable to operate, and appealed to small market segments. The growth stage came when jet planes entered service, improving the quality of air travel, lowering its price, and making it much more competitive and accessible to additional segments. The maturity stage started in the 1970s and has continued since. This phase has been marked by a slowing of the growth rate and price competition among the increased number of operators. Services such as telecommunications, health maintenance delivery systems, leasing, and forms of outdoor communications are all in the growth stage of the life cycle. Watch repairing, bus services, and single-sex educational institutions could be considered to be moving through maturity to decline.

Instead of talking about the life cycle of a product, the inseparability of services may make it more appropriate to talk about the life cycle of service providers.[4] Five stages in the life cycle of services organizations can be identified:

Stage 1: Entrepreneurial.   An individual identifies a market need and offers a service to a small number of people, usually operating from one location. While most entrepreneurs stay at this stage, some begin to think about growth, often entailing a move to larger and/or additional sites. For example, in June 1958, two college-age brothers from Wichita, Kansas, opened the first Pizza Hut restaurant.

Stage 2: Multisite rationalization.   The successful entrepreneur starts to add to the limited number of facilities. During this stage the skills required for being a multisite operator begin to be developed. By the end of this stage, the organization gains a certain degree of stability at a level of critical mass. At this stage, franchising starts to be considered. Pleased by their success, the Carney brothers opened two more Pizza Hut restaurants within a year. They also began to develop plans for the first franchised outlet.

Stage 3: Growth.   The concept has become accepted as a profitable business idea. The company is now actively expanding through the purchase of competitors, franchising/licensing the concept, developing new company-operated facilities, or a combination of the three. Growth is influenced not only by the founder's desire to succeed but also by the pressures placed upon the company by the financial community. As you might guess, the Pizza Hut concept grew quickly. In 1963 there were 43 restaurants, and by 1968 there were 296.

Stage 4: Maturity. The number of new outlets declines, and revenues of individual facilities stabilize and in some cases decline. This tends to be caused by a combination of four factors: changing demographics within the firm's market, changing needs and tastes of consumers, increased competition, and "cannibalization" of older services by service firms' newer products. In the 1980s, as Pizza Hut moved into maturity it began to face increased competition from the delivery segment of the pizza restaurant market. Specifically, Domino's Pizza posed a major threat to Pizza Hut's leadership position. After recognizing changing consumer needs for convenience, Pizza Hut introduced delivery in its franchise stores.

Stage 5: Decline/Regeneration. Firms can become complacent, and unless a new concept is developed or new markets found, decline and deterioration soon follows.

When a company's position in the life cycle is identified, the major objectives, decisions, problems, and organizational transitions needed for the future can be anticipated. Firms can therefore plan for necessary changes rather than react to a set of conditions that could have been predicted earlier.

CASE STUDY

FAST FOOD FINDS NEW OUTLETS

By the beginning of the 1990s, the sparkle had gone out of fast-food restaurants in the United States. Growth rates had slipped to just 5 percent annually, down from the double-digit figures at the height of growth during the mid-1980s. It seemed as though fast-food restaurants had gone through the classic product life cycle; launched to an initially cautious market, they went through a rapid growth phase and now appeared to be approaching saturation. It was time for the major operators to rethink their strategies and revamp the product offering to make it more acceptable to the changed needs of consumers and to exploit new market opportunities.

The giant PepsiCo, with more than 20 thousand restaurants worldwide trading under familiar names such as Pizza Hut, Kentucky Fried Chicken, and Taco Bell, took the impending saturation of the fast-food restaurant market seriously. On the basis that it was becoming increasingly difficult to coax customers into its restaurants, it decided that it must take its food services to its customers. It had already invested heavily in takeout and home delivery services for its main brands, but during the early 1990s, attention focused on new service formats in "unconventional" sites. Unconventional sites—defined as non-freestanding sites located away from traditional eating areas—were hardly new. PepsiCo's rivals had already been trading for several years with unconventional service formats. For example, McDonald's operated outlets within hospitals and at highway rest stops, while the Little Caesar's pizza chain had more than 400 kiosks in Kmart stores throughout the country. It is the scale of PepsiCo's attack on unconventional sites that was noteworthy and resulted in its having 650 such sites by the end of 1992, compared with about 200 for McDonald's and 100 for Burger King.

Locating outlets within retail stores has been seen as one route for taking food services to customers. The Taco Bell chain has experimented with takeout kiosks located within twenty Kroger supermarkets—everybody has to shop for groceries, and research showed that people often eat immediately after they return home from shopping, so selling hot, ready-prepared food alongside the groceries appeared to be an attractive strategy. Furthermore, the so-called baby boomers, who fueled the growth of restaurants during the 1980s, are now more constrained by families and therefore tend to eat at home more. They are now poor in time but financially well off, and this provides an ideal opportunity for the home delivery of food and the sale of prepared food in supermarkets. However, one problem in developing these in-store sites is the potential for conflict with the supermarket's own deli counter. The stores themselves are philosophical about this. By positioning itself as a specialist pizza or Mexican food outlet, the PepsiCo outlet avoids some of the direct competition. Supermarkets themselves gain from PepsiCo's customers, both directly from the cut that the supermarket receives and indirectly from the increased traffic that a Taco Bell or Pizza Hut might generate in the store.

The Taco Bell chain has taken the grocery store outlets one stage further by selling its foods on supermarket shelves. At a thousand stores throughout the South and Midwest, it has experimented with a line of taco shells, salsa, and refried beans.

Wherever it sees an opportunity to exploit a new market for fast food, PepsiCo has attempted to develop an appropriate service format. While it has often started from scratch and developed its own new service format, on other occasions it has brought in formats developed by others. This was the case when it recognized that it didn't have a chain of restaurants pitched somewhere between fast food and fine dining—something likely to appeal to maturing baby boomers. In 1992, middle-market chains grew twice as quickly as the fast-food sector generally. Rather than miss out on this growth, PepsiCo paid $96 million for a two-thirds equity share in the thirty-two–restaurant California Pizza Kitchen chain and $95 million for the California-based Chevys chain. In another move, it felt unrepresented in the high-speed drive-through market, so it acquired the Michigan-based Hot'n Now chain. It operated double drive-through outlets and now is experimenting to see whether the same design format can be applied to its other chains. A more interesting move was PepsiCo's acquisition of Carts of Colorado, Inc., a company specializing in the design and supply of food vending trolleys. The Taco Bell and Pizza Hut subsidiaries have used these trolleys to take fast food to football stadiums and other outdoor events.

The development of new service formats has not been without problems for PepsiCo. The biggest obstacle has been the vociferous reaction of its existing franchisees, for whom novel outlets present a threat to their existing territory. They see inevitable cannibalization when an in-store Taco Bell opens opposite their own franchised Taco Bell. At one stage, the Association of Kentucky Fried Chicken Franchisees voted to proceed with a lawsuit against the company. To try and pacify its franchisees, KFC agreed to pay a 2 percent "pass-through" royalty to franchisees who found themselves competing against other outlets. The growth into unconventional service formats has also brought with it the problem of monitoring and maintaining quality standards.

CASE STUDY REVIEW QUESTIONS

1. Apply the Ansoff Product Market Expansion Matrix to PepsiCo. Why is it necessary for PepsiCo to develop new service formats for its fast-food businesses?

2. In what ways can PepsiCo minimize the risks associated with new service development?

3. Of what relevance is product life cycle theory to the fast-food sector?

3.6.3 Difficulties in Applying the Life Cycle Concept

Although the idea of product life cycles is appealing and seems to be validated by research, it is important to be aware of the possible failings with this conceptual approach in terms of both goods and services.

It can be argued that the product/service life cycle concept is more useful for strategic planning and control purposes than for developing short-term forecasts and costed marketing programs. In reality, life cycle patterns are far too variable in both shape and duration for any realistic predictions to be made. A second difficulty in applying the life cycle concept lies in the inability of marketers to accurately ascertain where in the life cycle a product or service actually is at any time. For example, a stabilization of sales may be a movement into maturity or simply a temporary plateau due to external causes. In fact, it is possible that the shape of the life cycle is a result of an organization's marketing activity rather than an indication of environmental factors that the organization should respond to—in other words, it could lead to a self-fulfilling prophecy.

Another criticism of the concept is that the duration of the stages will depend upon whether a product class, form, or brand is being considered. For example, the life cycle for bank checking services is probably quite flat, whereas life cycles for particular brands and types of accounts are more cyclical.

Although the applicability of the life cycle concept to services has been supported at a conceptual level,[3,4,14] a major difficulty in its application is the lack of truly valid research reinforcing the existence of such a concept for services. When these points are taken into consideration, the life cycle concept may still be helpful in aiding a firm in its product mix decisions. Although life cycles may be unpredictable for services in terms of the length of time a service may remain at a particular stage, the understanding that services are likely to change in their sales and profit performance over time implies a need for proactive product mix management by the service organization.

3.7 NEW SERVICE DEVELOPMENT

As a result of analysis and evaluation of its product mix, an organization may consider that it needs augmenting with new services. The following are typical circumstances in which new services may be necessary:

- If a major service has reached the maturity stage of its cycle and may be moving toward decline, new services may be developed to preserve sales levels.
- New services may be developed as a means of utilizing spare capacity; for example, unoccupied rooms during off-peak periods may lead a hotel operator to develop new theme weekends (e.g., murder mystery parties) to fill the empty rooms.
- New services can help to balance an organization's existing sales portfolio and thereby reduce risks of dependency on only a few services offered within a range.
- In order to retain and develop relationships with its customers, an organization may be forced to introduce new products so that it can offer them a comprehensive range of services.

- An opportunity may arise for an organization to satisfy unmet needs with a new service as a result of a competitor's leaving the market.

3.7.1 What Is Meant by a "New Service"?

The intangible nature of services means that it is often quite easy to produce slight variants of an existing service, so the term *new service* can mean anything from a minor style change to a major innovation. Lovelock[15] identifies five types of "new" services:

- Style changes include changes in decor or changes in logo or uniforms—the revised uniforms introduced by United Airlines in 1993, for example.
- Service improvements involve an actual change to a feature of a service already offered to an established market—computerization of travel agency information and booking procedures, for example.
- Service line extensions are additions to the existing service product range—new programs of study for an MBA course at a university, for example.
- New services are services that are offered by an organization to its existing customers for the first time, although they may be currently available from its competitors—telephone banking facilities, offered to bank customers, for example.
- Major innovations are entirely new services for new markets—the provision of multiuser voice mail recording services, for example.

The distinctive features of services compared with tangible goods leads to some special issues that need to be considered in new service development:

- The very intangibility of services often results in a proliferation of slightly different service products. Because of this intangibility, new services can be relatively easy to develop, and the variety of different services can cause confusion. As an example, banks frequently introduce "new" checking accounts that are only slightly differentiated from existing offers.
- The characteristic of inseparability between service production and consumption means that front-line operational staff have greater opportunity to identify new service ideas that are likely to be successful.
- As services are more likely than goods to be customized to the needs of individual customers, there could be greater opportunities for marginally different new services, each having its own unique selling proposition.

3.7.2 New Service Development Processes

Several studies have suggested that a systematic process of development helps reduce the risk of failure when new products are launched. Although a variety of different procedures have been proposed and implemented, they all tend to have the common themes of beginning with as many new ideas as possible and having the end

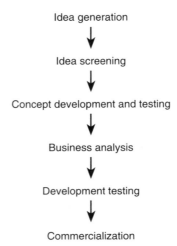

Idea generation

↓

Idea screening

↓

Concept development and testing

↓

Business analysis

↓

Development testing

↓

Commercialization

Figure 3.8 The new product development process

objective of producing a tested service idea ready for launch. One common sequence is shown in Figure 3.8, although in practice, many of the sequential stages shown are compressed or overlap with previous and subsequent stages.

Whether patterns of new product development associated with manufactured goods are equally applicable to services has been questioned by Easingwood,[16] who investigated how new service developments in services organizations reflected the intangibility, inseparability, variability, and perishability of services. Differences can occur at each of the stages. He found several differences between the processes involved for new goods and for new services.

Idea Generation. Although the generation of ideas is relatively easy for service organizations, the degree of novelty of ideas tends to be slight. Many ideas tend to be conservative, focusing on minor modifications, geographical extensions, or "me too" concepts. Ideas can be generated from within an organization and also from outside, either formally or informally. Easingwood's study found that generating new ideas is not a problem for most service firms. Inseparability means that front-line staff have a closer understanding of both service operations and customer needs, and therefore it seems logical for many new ideas to come from the operating staff. Perhaps surprisingly, this study found that the most common internal source of new service ideas was the marketing function rather than the operational function. The marketing function had constant contact with both customers and competitors and therefore had market information on tap. A much smaller proportion of new ideas originated with the operations function because new services were perceived by them as a further burden that would complicate their operations.

Customers can be an important source of ideas for new services, highlighting the importance of capturing and acting on ideas received through customers' correspondence, customer suggestion schemes, etc. A development of this is to use a network analysis approach to study the interaction between service provider and the variety of potential influences on new service idea generation.

Idea screening.   This stage involves evaluation of the ideas generated and rejection of those that do not justify the organization's resources. Criteria are usually established so that comparisons between ideas can be made, but because each firm exists in its own particular environment, there is no standard set of evaluative criteria that fits all. In Easingwood's study of service firms, a variety of screening practices were found, all with differing degrees of formality. Screening processes for financial services tend to be particularly rigorous, and it is common for each new idea to be evaluated by customer discussion groups, feedback on proposed features, and detailed scrutiny of advertising and financial projections. This rigor is partly due to the difficulties in withdrawing a financial service once it is provided.

For services in general, enhancement or support of an organization's image tends to be an important criterion used by firms in the screening process.

Concept development and testing.   An idea that survives the screening stage needs to be translated into a service concept that the organization wishes consumers to subjectively perceive. This then is tested by obtaining reactions from groups of target customers. At this stage, service positioning assumes importance and may involve the development of a visual presentation of the image of an organization's service in relation either to competitive services or to other services in its own mix.

Business analysis.   The proposed idea is now translated into a business proposal. The likelihood of success or failure is analyzed, including such resource requirements as manpower and extra physical resources. At this stage, many of the factors that will determine the financial success of the proposed new service remain speculative. In particular, the activities of competitors' new product development processes could have a crucial effect on a firm's eventual market share, as well as the price it is able to sustain for its service.

Development testing.   The idea is translated into an actual service that is capable of delivery to customers. The tangible elements as well as the service delivery systems that make up the whole service offer all have to be designed and tested. Unfortunately, testing may not always be possible, and evidence from Easingwood implies that test marketing by service firms is generally limited. One possible alternative is to introduce the new service with limited promotion just to test whether the new service operates effectively.

Commercialization.   The organization now makes decisions on when to introduce the new service, where, to whom, and how.

A successful new service development program requires an organizational culture that is conducive to changing market conditions and that can respond quickly to such changes. Within the new service development process, three roles have been identified as being crucial to success.[17] A "product champion" role is played by individuals who have the commitment and responsibility to develop and protect new ideas to the final launch. "Integrators" are people who can step across multifunctional boundaries and encourage a coordinated effort through persuasion. "Referees" are the counterbalance to the entrepreneurial process; individuals who play this role develop, and gain acceptance for, the rules by which performance will be judged.

CASE STUDY

NEW TECHNOLOGY HELPS BANKS SELL AN ENHANCED PRODUCT MIX

In times when money was scarce and financial services markets were highly regulated, banks were treated by many customers with a respect more typical of that accorded to the church. Banks enjoyed a degree of protection from competitors in many of their markets. For example, legislation restricted interstate banking and prevented near competitors from providing many core banking services. The emphasis was on customers coming to the bank rather than the bank having to go after customers.

The deregulation of the 1980s and developments in technology led banks to reassess their service mix in a bid to get a larger share of their customers' wallets. The mission statements of banks became broadened to include provision of comprehensive solutions to customers' financial needs. Needs were no longer defined narrowly in terms of the need to transfer, save, and borrow money; banks now attempted to address customers' underlying needs for financial security.

Automation has been important to banks not only in cutting operating costs but also in allowing the development of new services for customers. A major development of the 1970s was the appearance of the first ATMs, which not only cut the cost of employing tellers but also allowed new opportunities for customers to withdraw cash 24 hours a day. The development of ATMs did, however, have one unfortunate side effect for banks. Customers no longer needed to go into their branch banks for routine transactions, and this reduces the opportunities for banks to cross-sell other financial services. Offering these wider financial services was increasingly becoming crucial to a bank's success as its traditional checking business faced competition from deregulated competitors.

Recognizing the limitations of traditional ATMs in promoting uptake of its growing portfolio of financial services, Pittsburgh National Bank was among the first banks to experiment with an "intelligent" ATM. During 1992 it established an experimental remote computerized financial services outlet at Pittsburgh National Airport, allowing customers to do much more than merely withdraw and deposit cash. The facility allowed customers (and potential customers) to sit at the machine and summon up experts who could promote the bank's entire range of services, ranging from simple investment accounts to corporate loans.

To apply for a loan or credit card, or open a brokerage account, a customer sits in a booth with a phone and TV monitor that flashes a still photo and the name of the banker. After the customer indicates the desired service, a dialogue with a banker at a regional office is begun. Where appropriate, the banker uses the TV monitor to display any relevant forms or calculations that the customer may need to see. If the customer wants to take some specific information home, the banker can have it printed for the customer from a laser printer built into the remote terminal. Better still, the customer is often able to sign on the dotted line for services on the spot, needing only to hand in the completed form to the attendant on duty.

The remote terminal at Pittsburgh opens up a whole range of services to busy customers, using staff who may be located many miles away. For example, stockbroking services have proved popular and allow customers' instructions to be processed in about 15 minutes. A range of stock information, such as current prices and recent news stories about leading companies, is available to subscribers through the terminal. A customer who needs further guidance is connected via a telephone link to one of the bank's brokers working out of Philadelphia.

The Pittsburgh experimental site was undoubtedly well located in terms of accessibility to its target market of busy, higher-income, financially literate customers who are comfortable using computerized systems. Many customers still remain intimidated by this kind of remote technology, especially elderly people, whose increasingly sophisticated financial services needs are of great interest to banks. Many still prefer the personal interaction that takes place when they visit a bank branch, even for routine transactions such as cash withdrawal. Servicing elderly people in this way is becoming increasingly expensive for banks, as the costs of maintaining a branch network escalate. Attempts to replace branches with automated facilities can erode banks' valuable loyalty among elderly customers, to whom branches can make a bank appear more personal and accessible than competing mutual fund companies and security brokers who rely on toll-free numbers to sell their products. In an attempt to retain the loyalty of its elderly customers, many banks have installed minibranches in retirement communities. These are often staffed by little more than a receptionist, who acts as an intermediary to put customers in touch with regional office staff. When necessary, an appointment can be made for the two to meet, either at the minibranch or at the customers' home. With increasing familiarity with automated systems, it may only be time before a new generation of high-tech remote minibranches are established in locations—such as retirement communities—that target key groups who represent good prospects for banks' broadened product mixes.

CASE STUDY REVIEW QUESTIONS

1. Summarize the growth options open to a bank such as the Pittsburgh National Bank.
2. What problems might a bank encounter as it attempts to broaden its product range?
3. Of what use is portfolio analysis in analyzing the product range of a bank with which you are familiar?

3.8   SERVICE DELETION

Good product management depends on reliable marketing information to show when a product is failing to achieve its objectives. As well as maintaining successful services and investing in new ones, services organizations must also have the courage to eliminate services that are no longer likely to benefit the organization as a whole. This implies a need for the following:

1. establishment of targets for each service
2. periodic reviews of the performance of each service
3. modification of existing services when necessary
4. elimination of services when necessary
5. development of new services

New service development has been dealt with in the previous section. This section, therefore, deals with service deletion strategies.

In reality, an organization's portfolio of products/services is often the result of several factors:

- ad hoc responses to competitive challenges
- the history and culture of the organization
- requests from customers
- responses to technological opportunities
- takeovers and mergers

In general, there is a tendency to add on rather than subtract, and therefore many services do not die but merely fade away, consuming resources that an organization could better use elsewhere. Old products may not even cover overheads. In addition, the hidden costs of supporting dying products need to be taken into consideration:

- A disproportionate amount of management time is spent on them.
- Short and relatively uneconomic "production" runs may be required when a service has not been deleted and there is irregular demand for it.
- They often require frequent price adjustments (and stock adjustments when tangible goods are involved).
- The search for new products and services is delayed, as so much time is spent on existing products/services that the desired allocation of time to consider new ones is inadequate.

Firms should therefore have a logical planning system that incorporates product/service deletion. It would be naive, however, to assume that deletion is a simple process. For several reasons, logical deletion procedures may not be readily followed:

- Often firms do not have the information that they need to identify whether a service needs to be considered for elimination. Even if an organization is aware of a potential deletion candidate, the reasons for its failure may not be known, and therefore management may just leave things as they are and hope that the problem will go away by itself.
- Managers often become sentimental about services, hoping that sales will pick up when the market improves. Sometimes, particular elements of marketing strategy will be blamed for lack of success, with the belief that a change in advertising or pricing, for example, will improve the situation.
- Within organizations, there may be political difficulties with deleting a service. Some individuals will have vested interests in a service and may fight elimination efforts. In fact, some individuals may hide the true facts of a service's performance to ensure that deletion is not considered at all.
- Finally, there is sometimes the fear that the sales of other services are tied into the

service being deleted. For example, a car dealer who closes down the new car sales department may subsequently lose business in the service and repairs department. Furthermore, some candidates for elimination may sell their services to a small number of important customers, leading to fears that deletion would cause all of their business to go elsewhere.

In fact, many companies tackle service elimination in a piecemeal fashion, considering the matter only when a service is seen to be losing money or when some crisis leads to a cutback. A systematic approach is necessary. At regular intervals, every product/service should be reviewed in terms of its sales, profitability, average cost, market share, competitor share, and competitor prices. Today, information technology allows firms to calculate important percentages and ratios that can indicate how a product/service is performing in its marketplace.

Having acquired the relevant information, an organization can identify weak elements in its product mix, using a variety of warning signals that relate to such specifics as poor sales performance or poor profit performance and others that relate to such general factors such as new competitor introductions or increasing amounts of executive time being spent on one service. These warning signals merely indicate a need for further consideration and the possibilities of either service modification or total elimination. Identification of a weak service doesn't automatically mean that deletion is required.

One possibility for deciding which products to eliminate is the use of a product/service retention index. This can include a number of factors, each being individually weighted according to the importance attached to them by a particular firm. Each service is then ranked according to each factor, and the product retention index is thus equal to the sum of the products of the weighted index. An illustration of a product retention index is shown in Figure 3.9.

Two of the product retention factors relate to potential modification approaches, either of the service itself or of the whole marketing strategy. When poorly performing products can be saved, several possible nondeletion strategies can be identified:

1. modifying the product or service so that it meets any changed needs of customers
2. increasing the price, which may be a sensible strategy if there is fairly inelastic demand for the service
3. decreasing the price, which may generate additional sales if demand for the service is elastic
4. increasing promotional expenditure, assuming that sales of the service are sufficiently responsive to this increased promotion
5. decreasing promotional expenditure, if sales are now concentrated in a small primary market
6. revising the promotional mix, following reevaluation of the original program
7. increasing the efforts made by the sales force, giving it greater presence in competitive markets
8. decreasing sales force expenditure if sales are concentrated in a primary market
9. changing the intermediaries used in giving customers access to the service

Factor Weighting (FWi)	Factor	Product/Service Ranking (SRi)
—	Future market potential for product/service?	—
—	How much could be gained from modification?	—
—	How much could be gained from marketing strategy modification?	—
—	How much useful executive time could be released by abandoning the service?	—
—	How good are the firm's alternative opportunities?	—
—	How much is the service contributing beyond its direct costs?	—
—	How much is the service contributing to the sale of other services?	—

Figure 3.9   Product Retention Index

10. changing the physical distribution system, when there is a significant tangible element to the service offer

11. new markets or additional uses for the product or service, as indicated by additional marketing research

12. licensing/franchising agreements to another firm

If any of the nondeletion alternatives are chosen, the firm must decide how such options are to be implemented in terms of timing and size of any changes to the marketing mix.

If, on the other hand, deletion is the chosen alternative, how to implement it must be decided. This is not always a simple task, and several options are open to a company:

1. Ruthlessly eliminate "overnight." The potential problem here is that there are still likely to be customers of the service. How will they respond? Will they take their business to other competitors? Will they take their business for other services in the mix with them?

2. Increase the price and let demand fade away. This could allow the firm to make good profits on the service while demand lasts.

3. Reduce promotion or even stop it altogether. Again, this could increase profitability while demand lasts.

Whichever decision is made, an organization must consider the timing of its decision and must pay attention to some important issues:

1. Inventory level: For manufactured goods, the level of inventories influences the timing of deletion decisions. Although this is not a concern of pure services, most services include some tangible element, and the levels of such brochures and packaging materials should influence the timing of deletion.

2. Notification of consumers: Firms have everything to gain and little to lose by informing consumers that service deletion is imminent. Such a policy at least allows people time to make alternative arrangements and may also help in promoting the firm's caring image.

3. Resources: Management should move freed-up resources, particularly labor, to other appropriate services as soon as possible. This not only eliminates the possibility of idle resources and layoffs of manpower but also is an important part of internal marketing in motivating the workforce.

4. Legal implications: Service elimination may bring with it legal liabilities. In the case of suppliers, an organization may be committed to take supplies regardless of a deletion strategy. For example, a tour operator may be contractually committed to buying aircraft seats for the remainder of a season. In the case of customers, it may not be possible to delete services provided under a long-term contract until that contract comes to an end. This can be particularly important in the financial services sector, where mortgages and pension plans may allow no facility for a unilateral withdrawal of supply by the service producer, even though a policy may still have more than 30 years to run.

In addition to these considerations, firms that have decided on deletion need to be aware of possible resistance to the decision, not only from consumers but also from intermediaries and internally from its own employees. Such resistance needs to be overcome to prevent any long-term harm to the organization's image in the eyes of each of these groups. Concessions may, for example, be granted to customers who suffer hardship.

This discussion implies that firms have a choice in deciding whether a service needs to be deleted from the mix. In fact, deletion decisions are very often forced on management by circumstances beyond its control, so that by the time managers are contemplating deletion, the circumstances may well be outside management control. That is not to say that circumstances are unavoidable. In fact, by reading market conditions, monitoring the quality of their products, and assessing the fit between their current offering, the market, and future possibilities, managers are afforded greater time to consider, plan, and execute the deletion of services.

CHAPTER REVIEW QUESTIONS

1. Using as an example a car dealership in your community, describe how it sells cars and how it sells its automotive service. What are the key differences between these operations in the dealership? Evaluate how well the dealership is marketing these operations.

2. Consider the various elements of a university degree course. Having identified the core service and the secondary service elements, could these be modified to be more customer oriented?

3. Identify services that are in the following stages of the life cycle: introduction, growth, maturity, and decline. In the latter group, what do you think could have been done to forestall decline?

4. Of what relevance is product life cycle theory to services marketing management?

5. By what methods could a telecommunications company obtain ideas for new service developments? Identify the factors that might be placed on a new service screening instrument. How would you weight each factor?

6. Identify the factors that might influence an airline's decision whether or not to delete a loss-making route.

REFERENCES

1. Skinner, S. *Marketing* (Boston: Houghton Mifflin, 1994).

2. Kotler, P. *Marketing Management: Analysis, Planning, Implementation & Control* (Englewood Cliffs, N.J.: Prentice Hall, 1994).

3. Rathmell, J. M. *Marketing in the Service Sector* (Cambridge, Mass.: Winthrop, 1974).

4. Sasser, W. E., Olsen, R. P. and Wyckoff, D. D. *Management of Service Operations: Texts, Cases, Readings* (Boston: Allyn and Bacon, 1978).

5. Eiglier, P. and Langeard, E. "A New Approach To Service Marketing," *Marketing Consumer Services: New Insights* (Boston: Marketing Science Institute, Report 77–115, 1977).

6. Kotler, P. and Andreasen, A. *Strategic Marketing for Non-Profit Organizations* (Englewood Cliffs, N.J.: Prentice Hall, 1991).

7. Sasser, W. E., Olsen, R. P., and Wyckoff, D. D. *Management of Service Operations: Texts, Cases, Readings* (Boston: Allyn and Bacon, 1991).

8. Gronroos, C. "A Service Quality Model and its Marketing Implications," *European Journal of Marketing* 18, no. 4 (1984): 36–43.

9. Shostack, G. L. "Breaking Free From Product Marketing," *Journal of Marketing* 41 (April 1977): 73–80.

10. Bateson, J. "Do We Need Service Marketing?" *Marketing Consumer Services: New Insights* (Boston: Marketing Science Institute, Report 77–115, 1977).

11. Ansoff, I. H. "Strategies for Diversification," *Harvard Business Review* (September-October 1957): 113–124.

12. McCarthy, M. "Tracking Travel," *Wall Street Journal* (March 22, 1994): B1.

13. Porter, M. E. *Competitive Strategy: Techniques for Analyzing Industries and Competitors* (New York: Free Press, 1980).

14. Hise, R. T. *Product/Service Strategy* (New York: Petrocelli/Charter, 1977).

15. Lovelock, C. H. *Services Marketing, Text, Cases and Readings* (Englewood Cliffs, N.J.: Prentice Hall, 1984).

16. Easingwood, C. J. "New Product Development For Service Companies," *Journal of Product Innovation Management* no. 4 (1986): 207–219.

17. Cowell, D. *The Marketing of Services* (London: Heinemann, 1984).

SUGGESTED FURTHER READING

BOWERS, M. R. 1987. "The New Service Development Process: Suggestions for Improvements" in *The Service Challenge: Integration for Competitive Advantage*, edited by J. A. Czepiel, C. A. Congram, and J. Shanahan. Chicago: American Marketing Association.

EASINGWOOD, C. J. "New Product Development For Service Companies," *Journal of Product Innovation Management* no. 4 (1986): 207–219.

GEORGE, W. R. and MARSHALL, C. E. eds. 1984. *Developing New Services*. Chicago: American Marketing Association.

LANGEARD, E., REFFAIT, P. and EIGLIER, P. 1986. "Developing New Services" in *Creativity in Services Marketing: What's New, What Works, What's Developing* edited by M. Venkatesan, D. M. Schmalansee, and C. Marshall. Chicago: American Marketing Association.

LANGEARD, E. and EIGLIER, P. 1983. "Strategic Management of Service Development" in *Emerging Perspectives on Services Marketing,* edited by L. Berry, L. Shostack, and G. Upah. Chicago: American Marketing Association.

LOVELOCK, C. H. 1984. "Developing and Implementing New Services" in *Developing New Services*, edited by W. George and C. Marshall. Chicago: American Marketing Association: 44–64.

SCHNEIDER, B. and BOWEN, D. E. 1984. "New Service Design, Development and Implementation and the Employee" in *Developing New Services,* edited by W. R. George and C. E. Marshall. Chicago: American Marketing Association.

SCHEUING, E. and JOHNSON, E. 1989. "A Proposed Model for New Service Development." *Journal of Services Marketing* 3, no. 2: 25–34.

SHOSTACK, G. L. 1984. "Designing Services That Deliver." *Harvard Business Review* January/February: 133–9.

4

Managing the Service
Encounter

CHAPTER OBJECTIVES

After reading this chapter, you should be able to understand

- reasons for, and the consequences of, the central role played by customer encounters in service transactions

- factors that contribute toward critical incidents within the service encounter, and strategies for recovering from service failure

- the problems of matching supply and demand caused by the perishability of service offers, and strategies employed to overcome such problems

4.1 INTRODUCTION

Inseparability was introduced in Chapter 2 as one of the defining characteristics of services. Because the production of services cannot normally be separated from their consumption, the producer–consumer interaction assumes great importance within the service offer. The service process is itself important in defining the benefit received by customers—the way in which customers are handled in a restaurant forms a very large part of the benefit that customers receive from a meal out. By contrast, a company producing manufactured goods generally comes into contact with its customers only very briefly at the point where goods are exchanged for payment. In many cases, the manufacturer doesn't even make direct contact with its customers, acting instead through intermediaries. Furthermore, the processes by which goods are manufactured are usually of little concern to the consumer.

The perishability of the service offer also distinguishes the nature of contact between service producers and consumers. While goods manufacturers can normally hold stocks in order to meet fluctuating customer demand, services cannot be stored. This requires service organizations to carefully manage the contact they have with their customers, in order to avoid bottlenecks and delays in the service production process, which the customer actually takes part in.

This chapter begins by considering the basic nature of the interaction that occurs between producer and consumer, and some of the implications of this relationship that are reflected in marketing strategy. Finally, the particular problems posed by the need to spatially and temporally manage demand are examined, and appropriate marketing strategies are discussed.

4.2 THE SERVICE ENCOUNTER

Service encounters occur where it is necessary for consumer and producer to meet in order for the former to receive the benefits that the latter has the resources to provide. The concept of the service encounter has been defined broadly by Shostack as "a period of time during which a consumer directly interacts with a service."[1] This definition includes all aspects of the service firm with which a consumer may interact, including its personnel, physical assets, and other tangible evidence. In some cases, the entire service is produced and consumed during the course of this encounter. Such services can be described as "high-contact" services, and the encounter can become the only means by which consumers assess service quality. At other times, the encounter is just one element of the total production and consumption process. For such "low-contact" services, part of the production process can be performed without the direct involvement of the consumer.

From the consumer's perspective, interaction can take various forms, depending upon two principal factors.

- First, the importance of the encounter is influenced by whether the customers themselves, or their possessions, are the recipients of the service.
- Second, the nature of the encounter is influenced by the extent to which tangible elements are present within the service offer.

These two dimensions of the service encounter are shown diagrammatically in matrix form in Figure 4.1. Some of the implications flowing from this categorization are discussed here.

The most significant types of service encounters occur in the upper left quadrant of Figure 4.1, where the consumer is the direct recipient of a service and the service offering provides a high level of tangibility. These can be described as high-contact services. Examples are provided by most types of health care, where the physical presence of a customer's body is a prerequisite for a series of quite tangible operations being carried out. Public transportation offers further examples: the fundamental benefits of a rapid transit service are to physically move customers. Without their presence, the benefit cannot be received. Services in this quadrant rep-

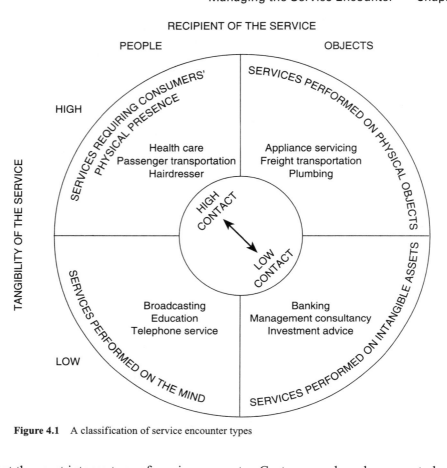

Figure 4.1   A classification of service encounter types

resent the most intense type of service encounter. Customer and producer must physically meet in order for the service to be performed, and this has several implications for the service delivery process:

- Quality control becomes a major issue, for the consumer is concerned with the processes of service production as much as with the end result. Furthermore, because many services in this category are produced in a one-on-one situation in which judgement by the service provider is called for, it can be difficult to implement quality control checks before the service is consumed.

- Because the consumer must attend during the production process, the location of the service encounter assumes importance. For example, an inconveniently located physician might fail to achieve any interaction at all.

- The problem of managing demand is most critical with this group of services. Delays in service production have an adverse consequence not only for the service outcome but for consumers' judgement of the service process. For example, although most of us could not afford an "Around the World" tour by Concorde for about $48,000 per person, we can imagine that most of the customers for this service have high expectations about service production. They would not tolerate delayed departures or misplaced hotel reservations.

The nature of the service encounter changes somewhat in the second category of services (lower left quadrant), which are essentially performed on consumers' minds. Here, consumers are the direct recipient of a service but do not need to be physically present in order to receive an intangible benefit. The intangibility of the benefit means that the service production process can in many cases be separated spatially from its consumption. In this way, young "Sesame Street" television show viewers do not need to interact with staff from the television company in order to receive the benefits. Similarly, recipients of educational services often do not need to be physically present during an encounter with the education provider; distance learning methods can include little direct contact.

A third pattern of service encounters can be observed in the upper right quadrant of Figure 4.1. Here, services are performed on customers' objects rather than on their person. An example is the repair of appliances or the transportation of goods. A large part of the production process can go unseen without any involvement by the customer, who is largely reduced to initiating the service process (e.g., delivering a car to a repairer) and collecting the results (picking up the car once a repair has been completed). The process by which a car is repaired—the substantive service—may be of little concern to the customer as long as the end result is satisfactory. However, the manner in which the customer is handled during the pre-service and after-service stages assumes great importance. It follows that while technical skills may be essential for staff engaged in the substantive service production process, skills in dealing with customers are important for those involved in customer encounters. Because the consumer is not physically present during the substantive service production process, the timing and location of this part of the process allows the service organization much greater flexibility. In this way, the car mechanic can collect a car at a customer's home (which is most convenient to the customer) and process it at its central workshops (which is most convenient to the service producer). As long as a service job is completed on time, delays during the substantive production process are of less importance to the customer than if the customer were personally involved in the production process.

The final category of service encounters is made up of services performed on a customer's intangible assets. For these services, there is little tangible evidence in the production process. It follows that the customer does not normally need to be physically present during the production process, as can be the case with most services provided by fund managers and attorneys. A large part of the substantive service production process (such as the preparation of house sale documents) can be undertaken with very little direct contact between customer and organization. The service encounter becomes less critical to the customer and can take place at a distance without any need for a physical meeting. Customers judge transactions not just on the quality of their encounter but also on outcomes (e.g., the performance of a financial portfolio).

4.2.1 Critical Incidents

Incidents occur each time producers and consumers come together in an encounter. While many incidents will be quite trivial in terms of their consequences to the consumer, some of them will be so important that they become critical to a successful encounter. Critical incidents can be defined as specific interactions between customers and a service firm's employees that are especially satisfying or especially dissatisfying.[2] While this definition focuses on the role of personnel in creating critical incidents, such incidents can also arise as a result of interaction with the service provider's equipment.

At each critical incident, customers have an opportunity to evaluate the service provider and form an opinion of service quality. The processes involved in producing services can be quite complex, resulting in a large number of critical incidents, many of which involve non–front-line staff. An estimated 50 million critical incidents occurred each year between Scandinavian Airlines and its customers.[3] On each occasion, the airline had to prove that it could meet customers' expectations.

The complexity of service encounters—and the resulting quality control problems—can be judged by examining how many critical incidents are present. A simple analysis of the interaction between an airline and its customers may reveal the following pattern of critical incidents:

Pre-sales	Initial telephone inquiry
	Making reservation
	Issue of ticket
Post-sales,	Check-in of baggage
Pre-consumption	Inspection of ticket
	Issue of boarding pass
	Advisement of departure gate
	Quality of airport announcements
	Quality of waiting conditions
Consumption	Welcome on boarding aircraft
	Assistance in finding seat
	Assistance in stowing baggage
	Reliability of departure time
	Attentiveness of inflight service
	Quality of food service
	Quality of inflight entertainment
	Quality of announcements
	Safe and comfortable operation of aircraft
	Fast transfer from aircraft to terminal
Post-consumption	Baggage reclaim
	Information available at arrival airport
	Queries regarding lost baggage, etc.

This list of critical stages of interaction is by no means exhaustive. Indeed, the extent to which any point is critical should be determined by customers' judgements rather than a technical definition by the producer. At each critical point in the service process, customers judge the quality of their service encounter.

Successful accomplishment of many of the critical incidents identified here can be dependent on satisfactory performance by support staff who do not directly interact with customers. For example, the actions of unseen baggage handlers can be critical in ensuring that baggage is reclaimed in the right place, at the right time, and intact. This emphasizes the need to treat everybody within a service organization as a "part-time marketer."[4]

4.2.2 Blueprinting

Where service production processes are complex, it is important for an organization to gain a holistic view of how the elements of the service relate to each other. "Blueprinting"[5] is a graphic approach designed to overcome problems that occur when a new service is launched without adequate identification of the necessary support functions. A customer blueprint has three main elements:

- All of the principal functions required to make and distribute a service are identified, along with the responsible company unit or personnel.
- Timing and sequencing relationships among the functions are depicted graphically.
- For each function, acceptable tolerances are identified in terms of the variation from the standard that can be tolerated without an adverse affect on customers' perception of quality.

The principles of a service blueprint are illustrated in Figure 4.2 with a suggested application of the framework to the purchase of a cup of tea in a restaurant.

A customer blueprint must clearly identify all steps in a service process—that is, all contacts or interactions with customers. These are shown in time sequential order from left to right. The blueprint is further divided into two "zones": a zone of

Stage in Production Process	Obtain seat	Take order	Make tea	Deliver tea	Pay for tea
			Repeat if tea is unsatisfactory		
Target time (mins)	1	1	3		1
Critical time	5	5	8		3
Is incident critical?	Y	N	N	Y	N
Participants	Customer	Customer Server	Cook	Customer Server	Customer Cashier
Visible evidence	Furnishings	Appearance of Staff	Tea, china, manner of service delivery		Cash collection procedure
"Line of visibility"	– – – – –	– – – – –	– – – – –	– – – – –	– – – – –
Invisible processes	Cleaning of tea room		Preparation of tea Ordering of supplies		Accounting procedures

Figure 4.2   Customer service blueprint—A simplified application to the purchase of a cup of tea in a restaurant

visibility (processes that are visible to the customer and in which the customer is likely to participate) and a zone of invisibility (processes and interactions that, although necessary to the proper servicing of a customer, are hidden from their view).

The blueprint also identifies points of potential failure in the service production process—the critical incidents on which customers base their perception of quality. Identifying specific interaction points as potential failure points can help marketers focus their management and quality control attentions on the steps most likely to cause poor judgements of service quality.

Finally, the blueprint indicates the level of tolerance for each event in the service process and indicates action to be taken in the event of failure, such as repeating the event until a satisfactory outcome is obtained.

4.2.3 Role Playing

The concept of role playing has been used to explain the interaction between service producer and service consumer[6] (Figure 4.3). It sees people as actors who act out roles that can be distinguished from their own personalities. Roles are assumed as a result of conditioning by the society and culture of which a person is a member. Individuals typically play multiple roles in life, such as family members, workers, or members of basketball teams. Each role comes with a set of socially conditioned role expectations—a person playing the role of worker is typically conditioned to act with reliability, loyalty, and trustworthiness. An analysis of the expectations associated with each role becomes a central part of role analysis. The many roles an individual plays may result in conflicting role expectations, as when the family role of a father leads to a series of role expectations that are incompatible with his role expectations as a business manager, and each role might be associated with competing expectations about the allocation of leisure time.

The service encounter can be seen as a theatrical drama. The stage is the location where the encounter takes place and can itself affect the role behavior of both buyer and seller. A scruffy service outlet may result in lowered expectations by the customer and in turn a lower level of service delivery by service personnel.[7] Both parties work to a script, which is determined by their respective role expectations—airline flight attendants are acting out a script in the manner in which they attend to passengers' needs. The script might include precise details about what actions should be performed, when, and by whom, including the words to be used in verbal communication. In reality, there may be occasions when attendants would like to do anything but wish their awkward customers a nice day. The theatrical analogy extends to the costumes that service personnel wear. When a doctor wears a white coat or a bank manager a suit, they are emphasizing to customers the role they are playing. Like the actor who uses costumes to convince his audience that he is in fact Henry VIII, the bank manager uses the suit to convince customers that he is capable of making the types of decisions that a competent bank manager makes.

In a service encounter, both customers and service personnel are playing roles that can be separated from their underlying personalities. Organizations normally employ personnel not to act in accordance with these personalities, but to act out

"The changes in the QE2 can be summed up in four words: new face, old soul.
I serve as Captain of the QE2. And my father was the original Captain. So I think I know something about this ship. It's the classic ocean liner, with big, roomy interior spaces. Miles of decks. Dining rooms galore. But today is not yesterday, and the new QE2 is not the old QE2. The ship has been handsomely refurbished. With contemporary public areas and staterooms that are even more comfortable. There's a new Yacht Club, where you can drink champagne while you watch the sun set. There's a new first class lounge. And an English Pub. But one thing that hasn't changed is the standard of service, which is, as it's always been, unsurpassed. After all, Cunard virtually invented luxury cruising. Now, you might say we've reinvented it."

You won't find people like Captain Ronald Warwick on any other cruise line. Which is why no other cruise line can give you the experience of Cunard.

Cunard. We make all the difference.

1-800-221-8200

CUNARD

Queen Elizabeth 2

Figure 4.3   In this ad for a high contact, highly tangible service, Cunard reassures customers about the experience of the captain, an important service provider on the QE2. Source: Cunard.

specified roles. Employees of a bank are socialized to play the role of cautious and prudent advisers and to represent the values of the bank in their dealings with customers. Similarly, customers play roles when dealing with service providers. A customer of a bank may try to act the role of prudent borrower when approaching a bank manager for a mortgage, even though this might be in contrast to his or her fun-loving role as a family member.

Both buyers and sellers bring role expectations into their interaction. An individual customer may have clear expectations of the role a service provider should play. Most people would expect a bank manager to be dressed appropriately to play his or her role effectively, or a store assistant to be courteous and attentive. Of interest to marketers are the specific role expectations held by particular segments of society. As an example, many young people might be happy to read by themselves an airline schedule given to them by a travel agent. On the other hand, the role expectations of many older people might be that the agent should go through the schedule and read it aloud for them. Similarly, differences in role expectations can be identified between different countries. While customers of supermarkets in most parts of the United States expect the checkout operator to pack their bags for them, this is not normally part of the role expectation held by shoppers in many European countries.

It is not just customers who bring role expectations to the interaction process. Service producers also have their ideas of the role that customers should perform within the co-production process. Hairdressers may have an expectation of customers' roles that includes giving clear instructions at the outset, arriving for the appointment on time, and giving an adequate tip. Failure of customers to perform their role expectations can have a demotivating effect on front-line personnel. Retail sales staff who have been well trained to act in their role may be able to withstand abusive customers who are acting out of role; others may resort to shouting back at their customers.

The service encounter can be seen as a process of simultaneous role playing in which a dynamic relationship is developed. In this process, either party can adapt to the role expectations held by the other. The quality of the service encounter is a reflection of the extent to which each party's role expectations are met. An airline that casts its flight attendants as the most caring attendants in the business may raise customers' expectations of their role in a manner that the attendants cannot deliver. The result would be that customers perceive a poor quality of service. By contrast, the same standard of service may be perceived as high-quality by a customer traveling on another airline which had made no attempt to try and project such a caring role on their attendants. The quality of the service encounter can be seen as the difference between service expectations and perceived delivery. When the service delivery surpasses these expectations, a high quality of service is perceived (although exceeding role expectations can sometimes be perceived poorly, as when a waiter in a restaurant offers incessant gratuitous advice to clients who simply want to be left alone).

Over time, role expectations change on the part of both service staff and their customers. Sometimes customer expectations of service staff have been raised, as in the case of standards expected from many public services. In other instances, expectations have been progressively lowered, as where customers of gasoline stations no longer expect staff to attend to their cars but are prepared to fill their tanks and clean their windshields themselves in return for lower prices. Change in customers' expectations usually begins with an innovative early adopter group and subsequently trickles through to other groups. It was mainly young people who were prepared to accept the simple, inflexible, and impersonal role played by the staff of fast-food restaurants, which many older people have subsequently accepted as a role model for restaurant staff.

WALT DISNEY MAKES EVERYONE A STAR

The Walt Disney Company is a diversified international entertainment organization whose operations include filmed entertainment, consumer products, and theme parks and resorts.

It is in the area of theme parks and resorts that the company has acquired a reputation for providing a consistently high level of consumer satisfaction. A major reason for this success lies in the careful analysis of just what visitors to its theme parks expect from their visit and detailed specification of the service standards to be provided. In delivering high-quality services, particular attention is paid to the roles played by the employees of the organization who are responsible for front-line service encounters.

The company's business mission involves making guests happy, and this mission has embedded itself in the cultural values shared by all employees. Once employed, all new employees learn about the history of the Disney Company and gain an understanding of the original philosophy of Walt Disney himself and the whole corporate culture. One approach used by Walt Disney to achieve its mission is to treat its theme parks as giant entertainment stages in which a series of satisfying service encounters take place. People paying to come into the park are considered not as customers but as guests. Similarly, employees are considered as cast members in this encounter and wear costumes appropriate to their tasks, rather than uniforms.

After being introduced to the basic cultural values of the organization, each cast member is given clear written instructions about his or her role expectations, where to report, what to wear, and how to handle typical encounters with guests. Role playing prepares cast members for a wide range of guest requests, for example, meeting their requests for directions or guidance on the best places to eat.

New employees are assigned particular roles, whose titles indicate the strength of the entertainment culture:

Role	Function
Custodial hosts	Street cleaners
Food and beverage hosts	Restaurant workers
Transportation hosts	Drivers
Security hosts	Police

Walt Disney's role scripting is based on careful analysis of what guests particularly value in the actions of cast members, and the interactions between cast members and guests are manipulated in such a positive way that the guests' expectations are exceeded. In order for roles to be performed effectively, Disney provides extensive training, including several days of training for each employee before he or she comes into contact with guests. Regular training sessions and newsletters are used to keep employees informed of new developments. Should training have failed to prepare an employee to cope with a guest's problem on the spot, the emplyee can contact backup support by telephone in order to satisfy the guest's request promptly.

In order to ensure that management is aware of the experiences of front-line staff, each member of the management team spends a week each year as a front-line member of the workforce. In addition, each member of management is also expected to bring his or her family for one day to experience the resort as a guest and thereby perceive the experience from the guest's perspective.

Finally, employees themselves are used to monitor the quality of service encounters. Peer review by current cast members is used in the selection of new recruits, the primary criterion for selection being service. All employees are expected to complete a questionnaire on their own perceptions of working for the organization. The results are then analyzed, and from the results, employee satisfaction is measured. The Disney philosophy is that if employees are satisfied with their encounters, then so ultimately will be the customer.

CASE STUDY REVIEW QUESTIONS

1. Within the context of Disney World, what is meant by "scripting"?
2. What is meant by a critical incident? How can Walt Disney identify what constitutes a critical incident and measure whether it has achieved customer satisfaction?
3. Choose any encounter that is likely to occur within Disney's theme parks and apply a "blueprinting" framework to an analysis of the encounter.

4.2.4 The Customer–Producer Boundary

Services are, in general, very labor intensive and have not witnessed the major productivity increases seen in many manufacturing industries. Sometimes, mechanization can be used to improve productivity, as will be discussed, but for many personal services, this remains a difficult possibility. An alternative way to increase the service provider's productivity is to involve customers more fully in the production process.

The inseparability of services means that customers will inevitably be an important part of the production process, especially in the case of "high-contact" services. As real labor costs have increased and service markets become more competitive, many service organizations have attempted to pass on a greater part of the production process to their customers in order to try and retain price competitiveness. At first, customers' expectations may hinder this process, but productivity savings often result when one segment takes on additional responsibilities in return for lower prices. This then becomes the norm for other follower segments. Examples where the boundary has been redefined to include greater production by the customer include the following:

- gasoline stations, which have replaced attendant service with self-service
- the U.S. Postal Service, which gives discounts to bulk mail users who do some presorting of mail themselves
- railroad operators, which have replaced porters with self-service luggage carts
- television repair companies, which require equipment for repair to be taken to them, rather than collecting it themselves
- restaurants, which replace waiter service with a self-service buffet

While service production boundaries have generally been pushed out to involve the customer more fully in the production process, some services organizations have identified customers who are prepared to pay higher prices in order to relieve themselves of parts of their co-production responsibilities. Examples include the following:

- tour operators who arrange transportation from customers' homes, and relieve customers of the need to get themselves to the airport
- auto mechanics who collect and deliver cars to the owner's home
- fast-food services that avoid the need for customers to come to their outlets by offering a delivery service

4.2.5 *The Role of Third Party Producers in the Service Encounter*

Service personnel who are not employed by a service organization may nevertheless be responsible for many of the critical incidents that affect the quality of service encounters perceived by its customers. Three categories of such personnel can be identified:

- A service company's intermediaries can become involved in critical incidents before, during, or after consumption of a service. The first contact many people have with an organization is through its sales outlets. In the case of an airline, the manner in which a customer is handled by a travel agent is a highly critical incident, the outcome of which can affect the enjoyment of the rest of the service, for example, when the ticket agent gives incorrect information about departure times, or a ticket is ordered wrongly. The incidents in which intermediaries are involved can continue through the consumption and post-consumption phases. Where services are delivered through intermediaries, as is the case with franchisees, they can become the dominant source of critical incidents. In such cases, quality control becomes an issue of controlling intermediaries.
- Service providers themselves buy services from other subcontracting organizations. Services organizations buying subcontracted services must ensure that quality control procedures apply to many of its subcontractors' processes as well as to their outcomes. Airlines buy many services from subcontractors. In some cases the purchase generates very little potential for critical incidents with the airline's passengers. Where inflight meals are bought from an outside caterer, the subcontractor has few if any encounters with the airline's customers, and quality can be assessed by the tangible evidence being delivered on time. On the other hand, some services involve a wide range of critical incidents. Airlines often subcontract their passenger checking-in procedures to a specialist handling company, for whom quality cannot simply be assessed by quantifiable factors such as length of waiting lines or numbers of lost bags. The manner in which the subcontractor's personnel handle customers and resolve such problems as overbooked aircraft, lost tickets, and general inquiries assumes critical importance.

- Sometimes staff who are not employed by the service organization or its direct sub-contractors can contribute to critical incidents in the service encounter. This occurs, for example, at airports, where airport employees, air traffic controllers, and staff working in shops within the airport contribute to airline passengers' perception of the total service. In many cases, the airline might have little—if any—effective control over the actions of these personnel. Sometimes it may be possible to relocate the environment of its service encounters—such as by changing departure airports—but it may still be difficult to gain control over some critical publicly provided services, such as immigration and passport control. The best that a service organization can do in these circumstances is to show empathy with its customers. An airline may gain some sympathy for delays caused by air traffic controllers if it explains the reason for delays to customers and does everything within its power to overcome resulting problems.

4.2.6 Service Recovery

Almost inevitably, service companies will fail at some critical incidents. At this point, organizations need a strategy by which they can try to recover from failure (Figure 4.4). There is a growing body of literature on the methods used by services organizations to recover from an adverse critical incident and to build up a strong relationship once again. The most important step in service recovery is to find out as soon as possible when a service has failed to meet customers' expectations. A customer who is dissatisfied and does not report this dissatisfaction to the service provider may never come back and, worse still, may tell friends about the bad experience. Services companies are therefore going to increasing lengths to facilitate feedback of customers' comments in the hope of being given an opportunity to make amends. Service recovery after the event might include financial compensation that is considered by the recipient to be fair, or the offer of additional services without charge, giving the company the opportunity to show itself in a better light. If service recovery is to be achieved after the event, it is important that appropriate offers of compensation are made speedily and fairly. If a long dispute ensues, aggrieved customers could increasingly rationalize their reasons for never using that service organization again and tell others not only of the bad service encounter but also of the bad post-service behavior encountered.

Rather than wait until long after a critical incident has failed, service companies should think more about service recovery during the production process. If customers' expectations of a service encounter have not been met at an early stage in the service process, it is often possible to recover them by significantly exceeding expectations at a later stage. For example, a tour operator that has announced to its customers that they will be subject to a long delay at the departure airport may subsequently exceed their expectations by taking them for a well-planned meal or entertainment as a pleasant alternative to waiting at the airport.

It can be possible for service organizations to turn a failed critical incident into a positive advantage with its customers. In adverse circumstances, a service organization's ability to empathize with its customers can create stronger bonds than if no service failure had occurred. As an example, a tour operator could arrive at a hotel

Responding to Service Failure: How Well Did They Do?

Listed below are 5 scenarios. Read each one; then evaluate how well the service provider responded to service failure. Would you patronize the provider again? Have you had similar experiences? What makes a good versus bad response to service failure?

1. **Mailing List:** A small publisher in Wisconsin purchased a mailing list from a mailing list house. To announce a new book, the publisher mailed out advertisements to each name on the list. However, the list was very old and a large number of undeliverable advertisements were returned to the publisher. The publisher had to pay for the return postage on these undeliverable items. In this case, the mailing list house responded to the service failure by offering to let the publisher use the mailing list again for free, but only if the publisher forwarded the advertisements that the post office had marked with the correct address.

2. **Rock Group:** A rock'n'roll group scheduled to perform at a theatre in Boston canceled their appearance after the warmup group had started to play. The theatre offered the audience 50 percent of their money back.

3. **Airline:** A couple took a flight that made stops in New York City, Washington DC, and State College, Pennsylvania. Due to bad weather, the flight into Washington DC was delayed one hour. The airline rebooked the couple on a later flight out of Washington DC to State College and gave them each a $25.00 coupon good for a discount on their next flight with the carrier.

4. **Dental Work:** A patient had a new crown on a back tooth. The crown came loose, and the underlying tooth cracked. The dentist gave the patient a new crown for free.

5. **Car Rental:** Arriving in San Francisco, a traveler discovered that the car rental agency did not have any subcompacts available, even though one had been reserved. The traveler received a luxury car for the price of the subcompact.

Figure 4.4   Companies know that things may sometimes go wrong; how can they reassure that they can put things right?

with a party of customers only to find that the hotel has overbooked, potentially resulting in great inconvenience to its customers. The failure to swiftly check its guests into their designated hotel could represent failure of a critical incident, which results in long-term harm for the relationship between the tour operator and its customers. However, the situation may be recovered by a tour leader who shows determination to sort things out to their best advantage. This could involve the tour leaders demonstrating to their customers that they are determined to get their way with the hotel manager and get their room allocation restored. They could also negotiate with the hotel management to secure alternative hotel accommodation of a higher standard, which customers would appreciate, at no additional charge. If the process of rearranging accommodation appears to take too long, the tour leaders could avoid the need for customers to be kept waiting in a transfer bus by arranging an alternative enjoyable activity in the interim, such as a visit to a local tourist attraction.

The extent to which service recovery is possible depends on two principal factors. First, front-line service personnel must have the ability to empathize with customers. Empathy can be demonstrated initially in the ability to spot service failure as it is perceived by customers, rather than as a technical, production-oriented definition of failure. Empathy can also be shown in the manner of front-line staffs' ability to take action that best meets the needs of customers. Second, service organizations should empower front-line staff to take remedial action at the time and place that is most critical. This may entail authorizing—and expecting—staff to deviate from the scheduled service program and, where necessary, empowering staff to use resources at their discretion in order to achieve service recovery. In the case of the tour leader facing an overbooked hotel, taking customers away for a complimentary drink may make the difference between service failure and service recovery. If the tour leader is not authorized to spend money in this way, or if approval is so difficult that it comes too late to be useful, the chance of service recovery may be lost forever.

4.2.7 The Role of Other Customers in the Service Encounter

Many service offers can sensibly be produced only in large batches, while the consumers who use the service buy only individual units of the service. It follows, therefore, that a significant proportion of the service is consumed in public. Railroad journeys, meals in a restaurant, and visits to the theatre are consumed in the presence of other customers. In such circumstances, there is said to be an element of joint consumption of service benefits—a play cannot be produced just for one patron, and a subway train cannot run for just one passenger. Several customers jointly consume one unit of service output. An environment is created in which the behavior pattern of any one customer during the service process can directly affect other customers' enjoyment of their service. In the theatre, the visitor who talks during the performance spoils the enjoyment of the performance for others.

The actions of fellow consumers, therefore, are often an important element of the service encounter, and service companies attempt to manage customer–customer interaction. By various methods, organizations try to remove adverse elements of these encounters and strengthen those elements that add to all customers' enjoyment. Some commonly used methods of managing encounters between customers include the following:

- Selecting customers on the basis of their ability to interact positively with other customers. Where the enjoyment of a service is significantly influenced by the nature of other customers, formal or informal selection criteria can be used to try and ensure that only those customers who are likely to contribute positively to service encounters are accepted. Examples of formal selection criteria include tour companies that set age limits for certain vacations, so that retired people booking a vacation can be assured that they will not be on vacation with children or teenagers whose attitudes toward loud music may have prevented enjoyment of their own lifestyle. Formal selection criteria can include inspecting the physical appearance of potential customers. Many night clubs and restaurants set dress standards in order to preserve a high-quality environment for service encounters. Informal selection criteria are aimed at encouraging some groups who add to customers' satisfaction with the service environment while discouraging those who detract from it. Color schemes, service ranges, advertising, and pricing can be used to discourage certain types of customers. Bars that charge high prices for drinks and offer a comfortable environment informally exclude the segment of the population whose aim is to get drunk as cheaply as possible.

- Determining rules of behavior expected from customers. Examples of the way in which the actions of one customer can affect another's enjoyment of a service include smoking in a restaurant, talking during a movie, and playing loud music on public transportation. The simplest strategy for influencing behavior is to make known the standards of expected behavior and to rely on customers' goodwill to act in accordance with these expectations. With increasing recognition by most people in society that smoking can be unpleasant for others, social pressures alone may induce most smokers to observe no-smoking signs. Where rules are not obeyed, the intervention of service personnel may be called for. Failure to intervene can result in a negative service encounter continuing for the affected party. Moreover, the service organization may be perceived as not caring by its failure to enforce rules. Against this, intervention that is too heavy handed may alienate the offender, especially if the rule is perceived as one with little popular support. The most positive service encounter results from intervention that is perceived as a gentle reminder by the offender and as valuable corrective action by other customers.

- Facilitating positive customer–customer interaction. For many services, an important part of the overall benefit is derived from positive interaction with other customers. Vacationers, people attending a conference, and students of a college can all derive significant benefit from the interaction with their peer groups. A vacation group in which nobody talks to the others may restrict the opportunities for shared enjoyment. The service providers can attempt to develop bonds between customers by, for example, introducing customers to one another or arranging venues where they can meet socially.

4.2.8 Industrializing the Service Encounter

Service organizations face a dilemma, for while most try to maximize the choice and flexibility of services available to customers, they need to reduce the variability of service outcomes in order that consistent brand values can be established. They also need to pursue methods for increasing productivity, in particular by reducing the amount and cost of skilled labor involved in production processes.

Complex and diverse service offers can require personnel to use their judgement and to be knowledgeable about a wide range of services. In many services sectors, giving too much judgment to staff results in a level of variability which is incompatible with consistent brand development. Multiple choices in the service offer can make training staff to become familiar with all the options very expensive, often matched by the minimal level of income that some service options generate. For these reasons, service organizations often seek to simplify their service offer and to "deskill" many of the tasks performed by front-line service staff. By offering a limited range of services at a high standard of consistency, the process follows the pattern of the early development of factory production of goods. The process, sometimes described as the industrialization of services, can take various forms:

- Simplifying the range of services available. Organizations may find themselves offering services that are purchased by relatively few customers. The effort put into providing these services may not be justified by the financial return. Worse still, the lack of familiarity of many staff with little-used services could make them less than proficient at handling service requests, resulting in a poor service encounter that reflects badly on the organization as a whole. Where peripheral services do not produce significant net revenue but offer wide scope for the organization to make mistakes, a case can often be made for dropping them. As an example, retailers have sometimes offered a delivery service at an additional charge, only to experience minimal demand from a small segment of customers. Moreover, the lack of training often given to sales staff (e.g., on details of delivery areas) and the general complexity of delivery operations (such as ensuring that there is somebody at home to receive the goods) could justify a company dropping the service. Simplification of the service range to just offering basic retail services may allow a wide range of negative service encounters to be avoided while driving relatively few customers to competitors. It also allows service personnel to concentrate their activities on doing what they are best at—in this case, shop floor encounters.
- Providing "scripts" for role performance. It was noted earlier that service personnel act out their role expectations in an informally scripted manner. More formal scripting allows service staff to follow the expectations of their role more precisely. Formal scripting can include a precise specification of the actions to be taken by service staff in particular situations, often with the help of machine-based systems. In this way, a telephone sales person can be prompted what to say next by messages on a computer screen. Training in itself can help staff understand how they should handle a service encounter—for example, the manner in which flight attendants greet passengers boarding an aircraft.
- Tightly specifying operating procedures. In some instances, it may be difficult to set out operating procedures that specify in detail how service personnel should handle each encounter. Personal services such as hairdressing rely heavily on the creativity of individual staff, and operating procedures can go no further than describing general conduct. However, many service operations can be specified with much greater detail. At a managerial level, many jobs have been deskilled by instituting formalized procedures, which replace much of the judgement previously made by managers. In this way, bank managers use much less judgement in deciding whether to give credit to a client—the task is decided by a computer-based credit scoring system. Similarly, local managers in sectors such as retailing and hotels are often given little discretion over such matters as the appearance of their outlets and the type of facilities provided. These are specified in detail from the head office, and the branch manager is expected to follow closely. In this way, organizations can ensure that many aspects of the service encounter will be identical, regardless of the time or place.
- Replacing human inputs with machine-based inputs. Machines are generally more

predictable in delivering services than humans. They also increasingly offer cost savings, which may give a company a competitive price advantage. Although machines may break down, when they are functioning they tend to be much less variable than humans, who may suffer from tiredness, momentary inattentiveness, or periodic boredom. In addition to reducing the variability of service outcomes, machine-based encounters offer other advantages over human-based encounters:

- The service provider may be able to offer a much wider range of encounter possibilities. For example, bank ATMs allow many bank transactions to be undertaken at a time and place convenient to the customer.
- It is often possible to program machinery to provide a range of services reliably in a manner that would not have been possible in the encounter based on a human service producer. Many telephone companies now offer a wide range of automated telephone services (e.g., call interception services), which can be delivered with high levels of reliability.
- Studies have suggested that automated encounters give many customers a feeling of greater control over an encounter. A bank customer phoning the local branch to ask for an account balance may feel that he or she is having to work hard to get the information out of a bank employee and may feel too intimidated to ask additional questions. By contrast, a caller to an automated banking information system can feel in complete control over dealings with the computer.

4.3 THE MANAGEMENT OF CUSTOMER DEMAND

The task of managing markets and ensuring a good fit between supply and demand is usually much more complex for services than for goods. Because goods manufacturers are able to separate production from consumption, they have the ability to hold stocks of goods, which can be moved to even out regional imbalances in supply and demand. Stocks can also be built up to cater to any peaks in demand. For example, lawn mower manufacturers can work during the winter months, making mowers to store to meet the sudden surge in demand that occurs each spring. Mowers that are not sold in the spring can be sold later in the year at a lower clearance price or put back into stock for the following year.

Many of the strategies for managing supply and demand that are open to goods manufacturers are not available to services producers. The perishability and inseparability of the service offer means that it is not sufficient to broadly match supply and demand over the longer term within a broadly defined geographical market. Instead, supply and demand must be matched temporally and spatially. An excess of production capacity in one time period cannot be transferred to another period when there is a shortage, nor can excess demand in one area normally be met easily by excess supply that is located in another area.

The concept of demand can in itself be ambiguous, with economists and marketers adopting somewhat varying definitions of demand. It is therefore useful to begin by identifying possible demand conditions that a service organization may face. Eight types of demand situations have been identified by Kotler:[8]

- Negative demand occurs where most or all segments in a market possess negative feelings toward a service, to the extent that they may even be prepared to pay a price to avoid receiving the service. Many medical services are perceived as unpleasant and are purchased only in distress, even though there may be benefit to individuals from receiving regular preventive treatments. Here the task of marketing management is to identify the cause of negative feelings and to counter these feelings with a positive marketing program. Dentists have introduced relaxing interior design of dental offices, background music, friendly personnel, and a promotion campaign to stress both the pleasantness of modern dental offices and the valuable long-term health benefits. These measures may overcome the problems of negative demand.

- No demand occurs when a product is perceived by certain segments as being of no value. In the financial services sector, young people often see savings and pension policies as being of no value to themselves. The task of marketing management attempting to create demand in such segments is to reformulate the product offering and promotional methods so that the product's benefits are more readily comprehended by the target segments.

- Latent demand occurs when an underlying need for a service exists but no product exists that can satisfy this need at an affordable price to consumers. The task of marketing management becomes one of identifying methods by which new services can be either developed or made available at a price that allows latent demand to be turned into actual demand. Within the U.S. travel market, a latent demand for leisure travel to the Far East exists, but it is prevented from becoming actual demand by the high cost of air fares. The development of more fuel-efficient wide-bodied aircraft and the gradual liberalizing of air licensing regulations have allowed for some lowering of fares, thereby turning some of this latent demand into actual demand.

- Faltering demand is characterized by a steady fall in sales that is more than a temporary downturn. The task of management is to identify the causes of this downturn and to develop a strategy for reviving demand. Small "Mom and Pop" stores in the United States have often found themselves facing a faltering demand, which has sometimes been successfully transformed by the introduction of longer opening hours and by refocusing the range of goods sold.

- Irregular demand is characterized by a very uneven distribution of demand through time. The inability to store services from one period of low demand to another of high demand means that this pattern of demand poses major problems for many service industries. It can be overcome by a combination of demand management designed to reduce the irregularity of demand, and supply management aimed at meeting demand as closely as is practical. These issues are considered in more detail further on.

- Full demand exists when demand is currently at a desirable level and allows the organization to meet its objectives. A hotel in a historic city with no scope for further physical expansion may have an occupancy rate that is difficult or impractical to improve. The management task moves away from increasing the volume of demand to improving its quality—by concentrating on high-value activities aimed at high-spending segments, for example.

- Overfull demand occurs when there is excess demand for a service on a permanent basis. A rock group may find that tickets for all its concerts are sold out very quickly and could be sold many times over again. The marketing management task is to stifle demand in a manner that does not cause long-term harm (stifling demand by high prices alone may build up an exploitative image, which may be harmful in the future should demand need to be stimulated once more). It also involves increasing supply, when this is possible and does not detract from the exclusive image of the product (e.g., more concerts or substitutes for concerts, such as video recordings).

- Unwholesome demand occurs when an organization receives demand for a service it would prefer not to have. It may be forced to meet the demand because of legal requirements (e.g., the U.S. Postal Service cannot normally refuse to deliver letters for customers who are very expensive to service) or because of a long-standing commitment to supply service to a customer (a medical insurance company that agrees to automatically renew premiums each year regardless of changes in the customer's state of health will consider renewal requests from sick customers to be a form of unwholesome demand). Marketing management's task here is to try to eliminate new demand through reduced promotional activity and higher prices, among other things.

4.3.1 Managing Irregular Demand

The fact that services cannot be stored does not generally cause a problem when demand levels are stable and predictable. However, the demand for most services shows significant temporal variation. Peaks in demand can take several forms:

- daily variation (commuter railroad services in the morning and evening peaks, leisure centers during evenings)
- weekly variation (nightclubs on Saturday nights, airlines on Friday evenings)
- seasonal variation (ski resorts in winter, department stores in the Christmas shopping season)
- cyclical variation (mortgages, architectural services)
- unpredictable variation (building repairs following storm damage)

In practice, many services experience demand patterns that follow more than one of these peaks. A restaurant, for example, may have a daily peak (at midday), a weekly peak (Fridays), and a seasonal peak (December).

Financial success for organizations in competitive markets facing uneven demand comes from being able to match supply with demand at a lower cost than its competitors, or a higher standard of service, or both. In free markets, service organizations must take a strategic view of the level of demand they should cater to. In particular, they must decide whether to even attempt to meet peak demands, rather than turn business away. The precise cutoff point is influenced by several factors:

- Infrequently occurring peaks in demand may be very expensive to provide for when they require the organization to provide a high level of equipment or personnel that cannot be laid off or used alternatively during slack periods. Commuter railroad operators often do not stimulate peak period demand—or even try to choke it off—because they would be required to purchase and maintain additional rolling stock whose entire overhead cost would be carried by those few journeys during the peak when they operate. Similarly, enlarged platforms at terminals may be required in order to cater to just a few additional peak trains each day.

- Peaks in demand may bring in a high level of poor-quality demand. Restaurants in tourist areas may regard the once-only demand brought by Memorial Day visitors to be of less long-term value than catering for the relatively stable all-year trade from local residents.

- Quality of service may suffer when a service organization expands its output beyond optimal levels. Restaurants that squeeze in more tables at peak periods and employ additional casual wait staff may find a fall in quality as their efforts become too stretched.

- On the other hand, some organizations may lose valuable core business if they do not cater to peaks. A bank that frequently suffers long lunchtime waiting lines for cash checking facilities may risk losing an entire relationship with customers if the latter transfer not only their checking facility to a competing bank but also their mortgage and insurance business.

An indication of the financial implications for organizations of uneven patterns of demand is shown in Figure 4.5, where two levels of capacity are indicated. The optimum capacity is notionally defined as that for which a facility was designed. Any additional demand is likely to result in long lines or discomfort. The maximum available capacity is the upper technical limit of a service to handle customers (e.g., a seventy-seat railroad car can in practice carry as many as two hundred people during rush hour). At the peak, business is lost; when demand is satisfied above the opti-

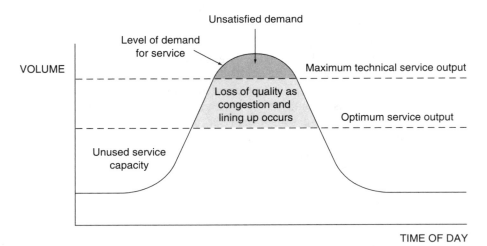

Figure 4.5   Implications of uneven service demand relative to capacity

mum capacity level, customer service suffers; in the slack period, resources are wasted.

Once a strategic decision has been made about the level of demand that it is desirable to meet, tactics must be developed to bring about a match between supply and demand for each time period. The task of marketing management can conceptually be broken down into two components:

- managing the supply of service to match the pattern of customer demand
- managing the state of demand to even out peaks and troughs

4.3.2 Managing Service Capacity

The output of services organizations is determined by the productive capacity of their equipment and personnel. The extent to which an organization is able to adjust its output to meet changes in demand is a reflection of the elasticity of these factor inputs. Capacity is said to be inelastic over the short term when it is impossible to produce additional capacity. It is not possible, for example, to enlarge a historic house to cater to a demand peak on summer Sunday afternoons. Capacity is said to be elastic when supply can be adjusted in response to demand. Highly elastic supply allows an organization to meet very short-term variations in demand by introducing additional capacity at short notice. Sometimes, capacity can be elastic up to a certain point but inelastic beyond it. A railroad operator can provide additional trains to meet morning commuter peaks until it runs out of spare rolling stock and terminal facilities, when supply becomes very inelastic. Any discussion of the concept of elasticity of supply requires a time frame to be defined. Supply may be inelastic to very sudden changes in demand, but it may be possible to supply additional capacity with sufficient advance planning.

In the area of supply management, marketing management cannot be seen in isolation from operations management and human resource management. Typical strategies used within services industries for making supply more responsive to demand include the following:

- Equipment and personnel can be scheduled to switch between alternative uses to reflect differing patterns of demand for different services. A hotel complex can switch a large hall from meeting a peak demand for banquets and parties in the evenings to meeting a peak demand for conferences during the working day. Similarly, personnel can be trained to allow different jobs to be performed at different peak periods. Tour operators often train staff to be resort representatives in beach resorts during the summer peak and skiing representatives during the winter skiing peak.
- Efforts are often made to switch resources between alternative uses at very short notice. For example, a store assistant engaged in restocking shelves can be summoned at short notice to perform much more perishable and inseparable service functions, such as giving advice on products or reducing check-out lines.
- Capacity can be bought in on a part-time basis specifically at periods of peak demand. This can involve both personnel resources (e.g., bar staff hired in the

evenings only, tour guides hired for the summer only) and equipment (aircraft leased for the summer season only, shops rented on short leases for the Christmas shopping season).

- Operations can be organized so that as much backup work as possible is carried out during slack periods of demand. This particularly affects the tangible component of the service offering. In this way, equipment can be serviced during the quiet periods (e.g., winter overhaul programs carried out on an airline's fleet of aircraft), and personnel can do as much preparation as possible as a peak approaches (a theatre restaurant can take orders for drinks and meals before a performance and prepare them ready to serve after the performance).

Although it is desirable for the supply of service components to be made as elastic as possible, these components must not be looked at in isolation. The benefits of elasticity in one component can be negated if they are not matched by elasticity in other complimentary components of a service. For example, a strategy that allows a tour operator to increase the carrying capacity of its aircraft at short notice will be of only limited value if it cannot also increase the availability of additional hotel accommodations. Capacity management must therefore identify critical bottlenecks that prevent customers' demands from being satisfied.

4.3.3 *Managing the Pattern of Customer Demand*

When demand is highly peaked, an organization could simply do nothing and allow waiting lines to develop for its service. This is bad strategy, both in harming the long-term development of relationships and in denying the short-term opportunities that peaks and troughs can present. A simple waiting line strategy is most typical of services operating in noncompetitive environments, for example, some aspects of publicly provided services. In competitive markets, a more proactive market-oriented strategy is needed to manage the pattern of demand. The methods most commonly used are described below:

- Demand is frequently stimulated during the off-peak periods by using all of the elements of the marketing mix. Prices are often reduced during slack periods in various tactical forms (e.g., "off-peak" railroad tickets, the "happy hour" in bars, and money-off vouchers valid only during slack periods). The product offering can itself be reformulated during the off-peak period by bundling with other services or goods (family weekends in business hotels to fill spare room capacity). Distribution of a service could be made more favorable to customers during slack periods. For example, during quiet times of the day or season, a takeout restaurant may offer a free home delivery service. Promotion for many service companies is concentrated on stimulating demand during slack periods.

- For some services whose consumption takes place in public, stimulating demand in quiet periods may be important as a means of improving the quality of the service itself. In theatres, more customers not only increase income, but create a greater ambience for all customers who come for the atmosphere created by the interaction of a live performer and audience.

- Similarly, demand is suppressed during peak periods by using a reformulation of the marketing mix. Prices are often increased tactically, either directly (surcharges for railroad travel during the morning rush hour, higher vacation prices in August), or indirectly (removing discounting during peak periods). Promotion of services associated with peak demand is often reduced (many urban transportation operators concentrate most of their advertising on leisure travel rather than on the highly peaked journey to work). Distribution and the product offering are often simplified at peak periods (restaurants and cafes frequently turn away low-value business during peak periods).

4.3.4 Waiting and Reservation Systems

When demand exceeds the supply capacity of a service, and demand and supply management measures have failed to match the two, some form of waiting line management or reservation system is often desirable. A formal reservation system is preferable to a random free-for-all, for many reasons.

First, from an operational viewpoint, advance reservation systems allow an organization to identify when peaks in demand will occur. When there is reasonable mid- to short-term supply elasticity, supply can be adjusted to meet demand, either by bringing in additional capacity to meet an unexpected surge in demand or by laying off capacity when demand looks as though it will fall below the expected level. In this way, advance reservations for an airline can help it to schedule its fleet to accommodate as many potential passengers as possible. A low level of advance reservations could lead to some unpromising-looking flights being canceled or "consolidated."

Second, reservation systems allow organizations to develop a relationship with their customers from an early stage. This relationship can be formed at the simplest level by use of a telephone inquiry to gain some degree of commitment from a potential customer and to offer a service at a time when both customer and supplier can be assured of achieving their objectives. Alternatively, the relationship can be developed from the time when a potential customer walks into a service outlet and joins a waiting line. The way customers are handled in the line forms part of their assessment of the total service quality. Techniques commonly used to manage this waiting time include the following:

- Organizations should be careful about the promises they make with regard to waiting time. When expectations of a short wait are held out, any lengthening of the waiting time will be perceived as a service failure. This could have serious implications for customers' perception of subsequent stages in the service they are about to receive. It may be better to warn customers to expect a long delay; then, if the actual delay is subsequently shorter, customers will perceive this as exceeding their expectations. They will then enter the next stage of the service process with a more positive mind.
- Waiting time will appear to pass by more quickly when the customer can perceive that progress is being made, for example, by seeing that a line is moving steadily. Uncertainty about the length of waiting time left causes anxiety and makes the per-

ceived time longer. Customers should also be able to perceive that the line is being processed fairly.

- Attempts are made during the waiting process to take customers' minds off of their wait, for example, by providing a comfortable television lounge for customers waiting for their cars to be serviced.

- When a delay is of uncertain duration, regular communication to customers makes time appear to pass by more quickly. The hardship caused by delay in waiting for a plane can be lessened with appropriate communication to customers explaining the cause of the delay.

- A waiting line represents an opportunity for an organization to make its customers more familiar with other services they may be interested in at some other time. Diners waiting for a meal may have the time and interest to read about a program of special events offered by associated hotels within the chain.

- Sometimes, the organization may be able to use a line for one service to try and cross-sell a higher-value service. In this way, a potential customer for an economy-class air ticket may be persuaded to buy a first-class air ticket rather than wait for the next available second-class seat.

CASE STUDY

LOVING OUR NATIONAL PARKS TO DEATH?

Seventy-five years ago, President Woodrow Wilson signed the Organic Act, thus creating the National Park system. The National Park Service has the task of conserving and preserving scenery, wildlife, and our historic heritage for the enjoyment of future generations. Today, though, our national parks face a multitude of problems, one of which should be of particular interest to service marketers: how to manage the demand for the parks. *National Parks* magazine suggests that we are loving our parks to death because visitations levels are so high.[9] National parks preserve unique ecosystems, but must withstand thousands of visitors a day. As usage increases, so does the damage to the fragile protected environment.

The Park Service and the Forest Service are beginning to experiment with new management models. For example, at Channel Islands National Park and National Marine Sanctuary in California, the Park Service has limited visitor access to the islands by setting daily limits on the number of visitors who can go to the sanctuary. On the mainland, the Park Service also established a visitor center, where park staff educate visitors about the island ecosystems. In other words, the Park Service is trying to provide a broad educational experience while preserving resources.

Similarly, in the national parks of Alaska, demand management issues have arisen.[10] A typical problem appears at Denali National Park and Preserve in the summer. One ninty-mile road, which goes into the center of Denali, gives visitors the chance to see some spectacular mountains and unusual wildlife such as moose, caribou, and grizzlies. Buses operated by the Park Service and by a concession transport the bulk of the visitors; people driving cars and recreational vehicles are allowed only part way up the road unless they have campground reservations. On a day in January, there was only one visitor, a reporter from *Wilderness* magazine, but during the hundred-day summer season, six hundred thousand tourists come to the park so that about fifty-five buses a day travel along the road. One ranger says, "We can't meet the demand. . . . We could put on more buses, but what suffers is the visitor experience. Right now we sometimes have five or six buses stopped to look at one bear."

Demand is expected to keep increasing at Denali by about 7 percent a year. Several things explain the steadily increasing traffic. The Anchorage–Fairbanks Highway was completed in 1972, giving thousands of tourists and their cars access to the park. In the mid-1980s, ship and train tours began delivering hundreds of travelers a day to the park hotel and to a nearby tourist village with hotels and amenities such as minigolf.

CASE STUDY REVIEW QUESTIONS

1. Identify the different segments of consumers that visit national parks like Denali. Describe the demographic and psychographic characteristics of these segments. In each segment, discuss the factors that affect why customers from this segment choose to use a national park like Denali when they do.
2. Discuss the pros and cons of instituting a reservation system at Denali. Do you think a reservation system could help shape demand patterns in all segments?
3. Suggest how you would use other marketing mix elements to shape demand patterns in each segment.

CHAPTER REVIEW QUESTIONS

1. What distinguishes high-contact services from low-contact services? How do marketing issues differ between the two types of services?
2. Choose one high-contact service sector with which you are familiar and identify the critical incidents that occur during the service production/consumption process.
3. Design a questionnaire that would help a fast-food restaurant identify service failure. Suggest strategies the restaurant could employ to recover from service failure most effectively.
4. During heat waves in the south, utility companies must "demarket" their electricity. Suggest strategies to accomplish this.
5. Using a service that you know well, plot out demand on a chart over an appropriate time frame. Define and discuss the levels of maximum and optimal capacity. Finally, indicate how you might use marketing mix variables to control the pattern of demand so that it is more favorable.
6. Choose a capacity constrained service industry and identify the options that are available to increase its elasticity of supply.

REFERENCES

1. Shostack, G. L. "Planning the Service Encounter," in *The Service Encounter,* ed. J. A. Czepiel, M. R. Solomon, and C. F. Suprenant. Lexington, Mass.: Lexington Books, 243–54.
2. Bitner, M. J., Booms, B. H., and Tetreault, M. S. "The Service Encounter: Diagnosing Favorable and Unfavorable Incidents," *Journal of Marketing* 54 (January 1990): 71–84.
3. Carlzon, J. *Moments of Truth* (Cambridge, Mass.: Ballinger Books, 1987): 3.

4. Gummesson, E. "Marketing-orientation Revisited: The Crucial Role of the Part-time Marketer," *European Journal of Marketing* 25, no. 2 (1991): 60–75.

5. Shostack, G. L. "Designing Services That Deliver," *Harvard Business Review* (January/February 1984): 133–9.

6. Solomon, M. R., Suprenant, C., Czepiel, J. A. and Gutman, E. G. "A Role Theory Perspective on Dyadic Interactions: The Service Encounter," *Journal of Marketing* 49 (Winter 1985): 99–111.

7. Bitner, M. "Evaluating Service Encounters: The Effects of Physical Surroundings and Employee Responses," *Journal of Marketing* vol 51 (April 1990): 69–82.

8. Kotler, P. *Marketing Management: Analysis, Planning, Implementation and Control* (Englewood Cliffs, N.J.: Prentice Hall, 1994)

9. Craig, B. "Diamonds and Rust," *National Parks* (May/June 1991): 41–4.

10. Daniel, J. "A Chance to Do it Right," *Wilderness* 56, no. 201 (1993): 11–33.

SUGGESTED FURTHER READING

BERRY, L. L. 1983. "Relationship Marketing," in *Emerging Perspectives of Services Marketing,* edited by L. L. Berry et al. Chicago: American Marketing Association.

BITNER, M. 1990. "Evaluating Service Encounters: The Effects of Physical Surroundings and Employee Responses." *Journal of Marketing* 51 (April): 69–82.

BITNER, M. J., BOOMS, B. H., and TETREAULT, M. S. 1990. "The Service Encounter: Diagnosing Favorable and Unfavorable Incidents." *Journal of Marketing* 54 (January): 71–84.

CARLZON, J. 1987. *Moments of Truth.* Cambridge, Mass.: Ballinger Books.

CHASE, R. B. 1978. "Where Does the Customer Fit in a Service Operation?" *Harvard Business Review* (November/December): 137–42.

LEVITT, T. 1976. "The Industrialization of Service." *Harvard Business Review* (September/October): 63–67.

LOVELOCK, C. H. YOUNG, R. F. 1979. "Look to Consumers to Increase Productivity." *Harvard Business Review* (May/June): 168–78.

SASSER, W. E. 1976. "Match Supply and Demand in Service Industries." *Harvard Business Review* (November-December): 61–65.

SHOSTACK, G. L. 1985. "Planning the Service Encounter" in *The Service Encounter,* edited by J. A. Czepiel, M. R. Solomon, and Carol. F. Suprenant. Lexington, Mass.: Lexington Books, 243–54.

SHOSTACK, G. L. 1984. "Designing Services That Deliver." *Harvard Business Review* (January/February): 133–9.

SOLOMON, M. R., SUPRENANT, C., CZEPIEL, J. A., and GUTMAN, E. G. 1985. "A Role Theory Perspective on Dyadic Interactions: The Service Encounter," *Journal of Marketing* 49 (Winter): 99–111.

SUPRENANT, C. F., and SOLOMON, M. R. 1987. "Predictability and Personalization in the Service Encounter." *Journal of Marketing* 51 (April): 86–96.

5

Buyer Behavior and Relationships with Customers

CHAPTER OBJECTIVES

After reading this chapter, you should be able to understand

- the importance of studying service purchase decision processes
- the role of intangibility in contributing to the perceived risk of services purchases
- the reasons why services organizations seek to turn casual transactions with customers into ongoing relationships
- the methods by which relationship marketing strategies are developed and implemented

5.1 INTRODUCTION

Services can be highly complex products for consumers to evaluate. Unlike goods, services cannot be evaluated before a purchase decision is made. A student going to a rock concert cannot judge the quality of the service on any particular night until after the service has been consumed. Sometimes the service is not only intangible but mentally intangible as well. Very many people, for instance, find it difficult to grasp what exactly financial services offer. Moreover, if we make a mistake in choosing a service, the consequences are often felt more personally than if we make a mistake in choosing goods. A failed surgical operation, a bad experience at an airport or a poor concert are events we have to endure. We are involved in the service production process and cannot easily brush the consequences aside, as we can if we buy an unpleasant type of candy, then decide to throw it away.

It follows that evaluating a service can be much more risky than evaluating a tangible good. We cannot rely on our senses to judge quality before purchase, so we look for evidence of service performance, especially tangible cues. As a means of managing our exposure to risk, we are more likely to canvass the opinion of friends and to rely on word-of-mouth recommendation.

The traditional idea that consumers enter into a series of discrete transactions with service providers is increasingly being challenged. Instead of evaluating competing services on each occasion that we need that type of service, it is increasingly likely that we enter into a relationship with a supplier. Rather than calling a repair service each time a heating system fails, a house owner may instead take out a maintenance contract, which will automatically bring service when it is needed. For customers of services, the move toward relationships can reduce perceived levels of risk and transaction costs. To the provider of a service, relationships help to develop loyalty from customers who recognize the added value in a relationship and restrict their search activity for competing services.

The first part of this chapter reviews some basic issues on how consumers go about choosing one service against another. This is followed up in the second part with a discussion of the methods used by service providers to try and turn casual one-time purchases into a more continuous supply of services within the context of a relationship.

5.2 RESEARCHING BUYER BEHAVIOR

It is very important for service marketers to gain an insight into the processes and critical factors involved in customers' purchase decisions. In particular, an organization should be able to understand

- who is involved in making a purchase decision
- how long the decision making process takes
- what the set of competing services is from which consumers make their choice
- the relative importance attached by decision makers to each of the elements of the service offer
- the sources of information that are used in evaluating competing service offers

The basic processes involved in purchase decisions are illustrated in Figure 5.1. Simple models of buyer behavior usually see an underlying need triggering a search for solutions to satisfy the need. When possible solutions have been identified, they are evaluated according to some criteria. The final purchase decision is seen as a product of the interaction between the final decision maker and a range of influencers. Finally, after purchase and consumption, the consumer develops feelings about the purchase, which influence future decisions. In reality, service purchase decision processes, can be complex iterative processes, involving large numbers of

Figure 5.1   Simplified stages in the buyer decision process

influencers and diverse decision criteria. Needs can themselves be difficult to understand and should be distinguished from expectations. The intangible nature of services and the general inability of people to check the quality or nature of a service until after it has been consumed adds to the importance of understanding the sources of information used in the evaluation process.

5.2.1 Researching the Decision Making Unit (DMU)

Few services purchase decisions are made by an individual in total isolation. Usually other people are involved in some role and have a bearing on the final purchase decision. It is important to recognize who the key players in this process are, in order to configure the service format to meet these peoples' needs. Also, promotional messages can be adapted and directed to the key individuals involved in the purchase decision. Various roles can be identified among people involved in the decision process:

- *Influencers* are people or groups of people whom the decision maker refers to in the process of making a decision. Reference groups can be primary, in the form of friends, acquaintances, and work colleagues, or secondary, in the form of remote personalities with whom there is no two-way interaction. Where research indicates that the primary reference group exerts major influence on purchase decisions, this could indicate the need to take measures that will facilitate word-of-mouth communication, e.g., giving established customers rewards in return for the introduction of new customers. An analysis of secondary reference groups used by consumers in the decision process can be used in several ways. It will indicate possible personalities to be approached who may be used to endorse a product in the company's advertising. It will also indicate which opinion leaders an organization should target as part of its communication program in order to achieve the maximum "trickle-down" effect. The media can be included within this secondary reference group— what a newspaper writes in its columns can have an important influence on purchase decisions.

- *Gatekeepers* are most commonly found among commercial buyers. Their main effect is to act as a filter on the range of services that enter the decision choice set. Gatekeepers can take various forms. A junior manager may screen out what he or she considers to be unsuitable products so that they do not get considered by a senior manager who is responsible for making the final decision. In many organizations, it can be difficult to establish just who is acting as a gatekeeper. Identifying a marketing strategy that gains acceptance by the gatekeeper or bypasses the gatekeeper completely is therefore made difficult. Larger organizations—the public sector in particular—may have a list of suppliers who are invited to submit bids for work. Without being on this list, a provider of services is unable to enter the decision set.

  Although gatekeepers are most commonly associated with the purchase of business services, they can also affect consumer purchases. In the case of many household services, an early part of the decision process may be collecting brochures or telephoning to invite quotations for a service. While the final decision may be the subject of joint discussion and action, the initial stage of defining the decision set is more likely to be left to one person. In this way, one member of a family delegated to pick up vacation brochures acts as a gatekeeper, restricting the family's subsequent choice to the vacations of those companies whose brochures appealed to him or her.

- *Orderers* are the people who place an order for service. In some cases, ordering a service may be reduced to a routine task and delegated to an individual. Commercial organizations may leave low-budget items that are not novel to the discretion of a buyer. In this way, casual window cleaning may be contracted by a buying clerk within the organization without immediate reference to anybody else. In the case of modified rebuys, or novel purchases, the decision making unit is likely to be larger.

- *Users* of a service may not be the people responsible for making the actual purchase decision to use a particular service. This is particularly true of many industrial service purchases. Nevertheless, research should be undertaken to reveal the extent to which users are important elements in the decision process. It is important for a business air travel manager to understand the pressure the actual traveler can exert on the choice of airline, as opposed to the influence of a company buyer (who might have arranged a long-term contract with one particular airline), a gatekeeper (who may discard promotional material relating to new airlines), or other influencers within the organization (e.g., cost center managers, who might be more concerned with the cost of using a service in contrast to the user's overriding concern with its quality).

- The *decision maker* is the person (or group of individuals) who makes the final decision to purchase, either executing the purchase or instructing others to do so. With many family-based consumer services, it can be difficult to identify just who within the family carries most weight in making the final decision. Research into family service purchases that are purchased jointly has suggested that wives dominate in making the final decision about vacations, whereas husbands dominate the final descision about mortgages. Within any particular service sector, an analysis of how a decision is made can realistically be achieved only by means of qualitative in-depth research. For decisions made by commercial buyers, the task of identifying the individuals responsible for making a final decision—and their level within the organizational hierarchy—becomes even more difficult.

5.2.2 Researching the Choice Set

Most buyers of services do not act with total rationality. To do so would imply identifying all possible sources of supply and applying a logical evaluatory criteria to each. Although it is often suggested that organizational buyers act with more rationality than private buyers, they are still likely to show great scope for irrationality in decision making. A company buyer may prefer the simple and relatively risk-free approach of sticking to the services with which he or she is familiar, rather than seeking to review all possible choices periodically. In fact, choice is made from a select set of possibilities, and these consumer choice sets can be classified according to their selectivity:

- The total set comprises all services that are capable of satisfying a given need.
- The awareness set comprises all the services that the consumer is aware of (the unaware set is the opposite of the awareness set).
- The consideration set includes those items within the awareness set that the consumer considers buying.
- The choice set is the group of services from which a final decision is ultimately made.
- Along the way to defining the choice set, some services would have been rejected as they are perceived to be unavailable, unaffordable, unsuitable, etc. These comprise the infeasible set.

Research should seek to establish the choice set against which a company's service is being compared. On this basis the marketing program can be adapted to achieve competitive advantage against other members of the set. In the case of a proposed new service, research may be undertaken to establish the criteria consumers use to include a particular service within their choice set.

5.2.3 Models of Buyer Behavior

The very basic model of buyer behavior described in Figure 5.1 provides a useful starting point and conceptual framework for analyzing buying processes. If a model is to have value to marketing managers, it should be capable of use as a predictive tool, given a set of conditions on which the model is based. For this reason, a number of researchers have attempted to develop models that explain how buying decisions are made in specified situations, and from this to predict the likely consequences of changes to marketing strategy. Modeling buyer decision processes poses many problems. At one extreme, simple models such as that presented in Figure 5.1 may help in very general terms in developing marketing strategies, but they are too general to be of use in any specific situation. At the other extreme, models of buyer behavior based on narrowly defined sectors may lose much of their explanatory and predictive power if applied to another sector where assumptions on which the original model were calibrated no longer apply. In any event, most models of buyer behavior provide normative rather than strictly quantitative explanations of buyer behavior and there can be no guarantee that the assumptions on which the model was originally based continue to be valid.

The earliest models of buyer behavior focused attention on explaining the decision processes involved in goods purchases. They see consumers as a "black box," processing inputs (product information, method of promotion, etc.) to arrive at purchase decisions (Figure 5.2). The processing determinants are seen as being influenced by a range of psychological and sociological factors. One widely used framework that has been applied to consumer service purchase decisions is that developed by Howard and Sheth,[1] which identified the following elements in the decision process:

- Inputs: information about the range of competing services that may satisfy a consumer's need. Information may be obtained from personal or published sources.
- Behavioral determinants: an individual's predisposition to act in a particular way. This predisposition, which the individual brings to the purchase decision, is influenced by the culture he or she lives in, family, and personality factors, among others.
- Perceptual reaction: different interpretation of inputs by different individuals, based on their unique personality makeup and the conditioning that results from previous

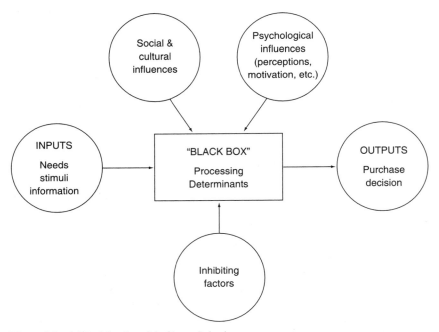

Figure 5.2 A "black box" model of buyer behavior processes

purchase experiences. While one person might readily accept the advertising messages of a bank, another might have been disappointed by that particular bank in the past or by banks' advertising in general, and is therefore less likely to perceive such inputs as credible.

- Processing determinants: the way in which a decision is made. Important determinants include the motivation of the individual to satisfy a particular need, the individual's past experience of a particular service or organization, and the weight attached to each of the factors that are used in the evaluation. Some consumers for some services may have critical product requirements that must be present if a product is to be included in the decision set. At other times, consumers attach weights to each of a product's attributes and select the one with the highest weighted "score."

- Inhibitors: factors that might prevent an individual from moving toward making a decision to purchase a particular service, such as the ease of access to the service, the price of the service, and the terms and conditions of service delivery.

- Outputs: the outcome of the decision process, which may be either to go ahead and purchase, or not to buy, or to defer a decision to a later date.

The Howard-Sheth model was developed as a general framework to explain both goods and services decision processes. More recently it has been recognized that this type of model does not fully address the issue of producer–seller interaction that occurs during the evaluation process. The intangibility of services and the inability of consumers to evaluate a service before consumption can also result in a much more complex process of information collection and evaluation than is the case with goods.

One example of a model based specifically on the service sector has been developed by Fisk[2] and is shown diagrammatically in Figure 5.3. The model sees the purchase process as being divided into three stages: pre-consumption, consumption, and post-consumption. The pre-consumption stage comprises the range of activities that commonly take place before a purchase decision is made, beginning with initial problem recognition, collection of information, and identification of the choice set. At this stage, consumers identify what they expect to be the best solution. In the following consumption stage, consumers actually decide through experience what they consider to be the best choice. During this phase, expectations raised during the pre-consumption phase are compared with actual service delivery. A gap between the two results in attempts to reduce dissonance; for example, dissatisfaction resulting from failure to meet expectations may be resolved by complaining. In the post-consumption phase, the whole service encounter is evaluated, and this determines whether consumers will be motivated to continue to consume the service. Like most models, this model simplifies the buying process—for example, by showing evaluation as three distinct elements—whereas in reality a service is progressively evaluated.

More specific models of buyer behavior have been developed as a result of research into specific services sectors. Many of them have attempted to rank in order of importance the factors that contribute to the purchase decision and to identify critical factors, the absence of which will exclude a possibility from a decision set. As

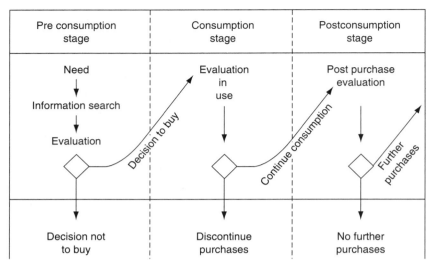

Figure 5.3   The Consumption/Evaluation Process for Services
(Based on R. P. Fisk, "Toward a Consumption/Evaluation Process Model for Services," in
Marketing of Services, ed. J. H. Donnelly and W. R. George (Chicago: American Marketing
Association, 1981): 191–195.

an example, one study into restaurant choice decisions[3] identified five key factors
used in the evaluation of a restaurant: food quality, menu variety, price, atmosphere,
and convenience. However, the research also found that the importance attached to
each of these factors differed according to the implicit purpose of the visit to the
restaurant. The factors influencing a choice of restaurant for a celebration were quite
different from those used for a general social occasion. For most categories of use,
image and atmosphere appeared to be the critical factors that distinguished between
restaurants within the choice set. When consumers had no independent transportation, location close to the town center was found to be a necessary factor for further
consideration.

5.2.4 Consumer and Organizational Buyer
Behavior Compared

The processes by which private consumers purchase services normally differ from
the way in which organizations buy services, for several reasons:

- Two sets of needs are being met when an organization buys services: the formal
  needs of the organization and the needs of the individuals who make up the organization. While the former might be thought of as being the more rational, the needs
  that individuals attempt to satisfy are influenced by their own perceptual and behavioral environment, very much the same as would be true of private consumer purchases (Figure 5.4).
- More people are typically involved in organizational purchases. High-value services

Figure 5.4 This ad appeals to both emotional and rational sides of an organizational buyer. Source: BRX/Global, Inc., Rochester, NY.

purchases may require evaluation and approval at several levels of an organization's management hierarchy. Research might indicate for particular organizations or types of organizations the level at which a final decision is made. Analysis of the decision making unit might also reveal a wider range of influencers present in the decision making process.

- Organizational purchases are more likely to be made according to formalized routines. At its simplest, such a routine may involve delegating to a junior buyer the task of making repeat orders for services that have previously been evaluated. At the other extreme, many high-value service purchases may be made only after a formal process of bidding and evaluation has been undertaken.

- The greater number of people involved in organizational buying also often results in lengthening the whole process. A desire to minimize risk is inherent in many formal organizational motives and is informally present in many individuals' motives, often resulting in lengthy feasibility studies. In some new markets, especially overseas markets, trust in service suppliers may be an important factor used by purchasers when evaluating competing suppliers, and it may take time to build up a trusting relationship before any purchase commitment is secured.

- The elements of the service offering that are considered critical in the evaluation process are likely to differ. For many services, the emphasis placed on price by many private buyers is replaced by reliability and performance characteristics by the organizational buyer. In many cases, poor performance of a service can have direct financial consequences for an organization. A poor parcel delivery service might merely cause annoyance to a private buyer but might lead to lost production output or lost sales for an organizational buyer.

- The need for organizational buyers' risks to be reduced and their desire to seek the active cooperation of suppliers in tackling shared problems has resulted in greater attention being paid to the development of organizational buyer-seller relationships over time rather than to individual purchases in isolation. Furthermore, as the complexity of services increases, the organizational buying unit perceives a greater need for confidence and trust in its services suppliers.

CASE STUDY

SUPERMARKETS GET READY FOR A NEW GENERATION OF YABS

The range of grocery stores available to shoppers in most Western countries today is greater than ever. Large Kroger and Safeway supermarkets operate alongside the chains of much smaller high-price/high-convenience stores such as Circle K and Seven-Eleven. The supermarkets themselves are adopting specific positions to appeal to different segments of the grocery-buying population, and much effort has gone into understanding the needs that different segments of the population try to fulfill on a visit to a supermarket.

A study undertaken by the Henley Center for Forecasting illustrates how research on the future of the market can form a basis for strategic change. In this instance, the research was concerned with predicting patterns of shopping behavior in the mid-1990s and particularly with establishing a set of market segments based on behavior patterns.

The outcome of the Henley Center's investigation was the identification of several different types of shopper, based on a multivariable approach, which took account of demographic factors such as age, sex, and income as well as lifestyle, personality, and attitude toward the shopping experience. As with so many of these studies, the resultant new breeds of shopper have been labeled with catchy titles.

The Harried Hurrier, the most important type of new shopper, is typically burdened with squabbling children and crippled by a severe lack of time. Hurriers are averse to anything, such as having too much choice, that eats into their precious minutes and makes them impatient. Another large group, but spending less money will be the middle-aged Young-at-Heart, who in contrast to the first group have time on their hands and like to try new products. An important and growing species of grocery shopper is the Young, Affluent, and Busy (or "YABs"), who are not much constrained by money in their quest for convenience and more interesting products but who do have a low boredom threshold. Two other types who are expected to grow in importance are the Fastidious, who are attracted by in-store hygiene and tidiness, and the mainly male Begrudgers, who shop only out of obligation to others. At the same time, the Perfect Wife and Mother, who is concerned with balanced diet, appears to be on her way out. She is likely to be more than compensated for by the Obsessive Fad-Followers, whose choice of food tends to be dominated by brand image and current trends.

The new breeds are expected to act as a catalyst for a shopping revolution. Although the already established need for convenience will still predominate, retail analysts anticipate some significant changes such as in-store traffic routing systems, one-way layouts, and food centers themed by nationality. Much appears to be gained from transforming the sometimes stressful encounter with the supermarket into a pleasurable leisure activity.

However, balancing the needs of all these groups may prove to be a difficult task, which may lead to greater specialization within the sector. For example, it is not impossible to imagine chains of specialty food retailers that act as menu stores offering the YABs the alternative of buying different dinner party food on different days, switching the emphasis from French to Italian to Indian recipes.

CASE STUDY REVIEW QUESTIONS

1. To what extent are segment descriptions such as those used for YABs and Harried Hurriers useful to supermarkets in marketing planning?
2. What research methods would be appropriate to a supermarket chain trying to find out more about its customers' expectations?
3. Can grocery retailers learn anything from studying organizations in other service sectors?

5.3 DEVELOPING RELATIONSHIPS WITH CUSTOMERS

Traditional marketing theory has focused attention on encounters as being a series of discrete events, too often viewed in isolation from preceding exchanges, and without analysis of both parties' expectations for future exchanges. Some services can be supplied quite adequately on the basis of a series of discrete, casual encounters. Most people taking taxis in New York, or seeking a bar in a tourist center, would have little need for a relationship with a supplier. However, a relationship-based series of encounters can be useful for both customers and producers in many circumstances:

- Some services involve a multistage production process, and it would not be sensible for a customer to switch service producers during production and thereby require the new supplier to have to establish what was already been carried out during previous stages. A doctor who keeps records is able to perform an operation with the benefit of the knowledge gained during previous inspections and operations. A newly introduced doctor would probably have to begin with fresh diagnostic checks.
- The service provider may be required to monitor the results of a service after it has been delivered, and therefore needs to engage in some form of relationship. An engineer who has installed a new heating unit may need to check the operation of the unit after it has been used for a while.
- Legislation may require some form of relationship to exist between buyer and seller before a service can be provided. Sometimes, a license allows a company to only

supply bona fide members of a club (e.g., conditions frequently attached in some states to licenses for night clubs or casinos).

- Where services are complex, or allow significant adaptations to meet customers' differing needs, there is evidence that customers are more likely to seek a relationship with suppliers. Risk tends to increase with complexity, and a relationship is one strategy by which customers can seek to reduce the level of perceived risk.

- In some markets, customers may seek the reassurance that a relationship can bring in terms of the ability to obtain preferential treatment or semiautomatic responses to requests for service. For example, a customer signing up for a regular maintenance contract on domestic appliances avoids the need to formally initiate service requests each time service is needed. By entering into such a relationship, buyers can also avoid the significant transaction costs associated with multiple service ordering.

- It has also been suggested that both suppliers and customers seek the security of relationships when the market environment is turbulent.

- To the supplier of services, the development of strong relationships helps to facilitate loyalty from customers whose loyalty is challenged by competing brands. By developing a relationship with customers, suppliers add to the differentiation of their products and give their customers a reason to remain loyal.[4] In highly competitive markets, suppliers may be able to attract new users to their services only at a high cost in terms of promotional activity and price incentives. Research has indicated that for many services, the cost of recruiting new customers exceeds the revenue earned from the first transaction. It is only by pursuing a long-term relationship that an organization is able to make profits. In other words, it has to develop an ongoing relationship.[5]

- A more formalized relationship with customers facilitates suppliers' task of collecting feedback from their customers.

Increasingly, organizations attempt to move their interaction with customers along what Gronroos has described as a marketing strategy continuum.[6] The aim is to move away from delivering goods and services, by a series of discrete transactions, toward continuous delivery through an ongoing relationship. Sheth has defined relationship marketing as "the understanding, explanation and management of the ongoing collaborative business relationship between suppliers and customers."[7]

5.3.1 Strategies Used by Services Organizations to Develop Relationships with Customers

There is nothing new about the way in which firms have tried to develop ongoing relationships with their customers (Figure 5.5). In simple economies where production of goods and services took place on a small scale, business owners could know each customer personally and come to understand their particular characteristics. They could therefore adapt service delivery to the needs of individuals on the basis of knowledge gained during previous transactions, and they could suggest appropriate new product offers. They were also able to form an opinion about customers' creditworthiness. With the growth in size of organizations, the personal contact

Build Your College Savings With Fidelity

With college costs spiraling upward, you know you should probably be saving for your child's education. And now, the Fidelity College Savings Plan can help make it easy to take the first step.

It's Easy To Start

The Fidelity College Savings Plan offers you four specially selected mutual funds. And to help you take that important first step, there are no sales charges plus a special low minimum* of $1,000 or $100 per month with our Starter Account – just for college savers.

Save Regularly Over Time

With Fidelity's Plan, you can also choose to make automatic monthly or quarterly investments right from your bank account into your child's College Savings Plan account. It's easy with Fidelity Automatic Account Builder.**

Our Free Planning Guide Can Help

We've created a common sense college planning guide to help you put it all together. From special offers for UGMA/UTMA custodial accounts to easy-to-follow planning worksheets, the Fidelity College Savings Plan gives you everything you need to start saving now.

Call 24 Hours For A Free Fact Kit
1-800-544-8888

Fidelity Investments®

2r *Share prices (except for money market funds), yields and returns will vary. The load waiver on Fidelity Blue Chip Growth Fund and Fidelity Growth & Income Portfolio and the $1,000 minimum investment on these funds and on Fidelity Cash Reserves and Fidelity Asset Manager™ apply to custodial (UGMA/UTMA) accounts only. Starter Account Option available only in Cash Reserves. An investment in Cash Reserves is not insured or guaranteed by the U.S. government, and there is no assurance that a $1 share price can be maintained. For more complete information including management fees and expenses, call for a free prospectus. Read it carefully before you invest or send money. **Periodic investment plans do not protect against loss in declining markets nor do they assure a profit. Fidelity Distributors Corporation.

Figure 5.5   Fidelity Investments is cultivating long-term relationships with its clients. The parents targeted by this ad are not the parents of college-age kids but the parents of young toddlers (hence the pictures of building blocks). Fidelity is trying to build an 18-year relationship with its target market, during which time it will doubtless attempt to extend its relationship, for example, by developing opportunities arising from parents' growing anxieties over their pensions. Source: Reprined with Permission by Fidelity Investments © 1994.

between an organization and its customers has been diluted. Instead of being able to reassure customers on the basis of close relationships, organizations often attempt to provide this reassurance through the development of strong brands. The recent resurgence of interest in relationship marketing has occurred for two important reasons:

- In increasingly competitive markets, good service alone is insufficient to differentiate an organization from its competitors. Customers increasingly judge service providers on the basis of superior relationship quality.
- The development of powerful user-friendly databases has allowed organizations to recreate in a computer what the individual business owner knew in his or her head.

Attempts have been made to analyze the development of relationships, often using the principles of life cycle theories. A theoretical model of relationship proposed by Dwyer, Schurr, and Oh[8] identifies five stages of relationship development: awareness, exploration, expansion, commitment, and dissolution. Their model proposed that a relationship begins to develop significance in the exploration stage when it is characterized by attempts of the seller to attract the attention of the other party. The exploration stage includes attempts by each party to bargain and to understand the nature of the power, norms, and expectations held by the other. If this stage is satisfactorily concluded, an expansion phase follows. Exchange outcomes in the exploratory stage provide evidence about the suitability of long-term exchange relationships. The commitment phase of a relationship implies some degree of exclusivity between the parties and results in reduction or elimination of the information search for alternatives. The dissolution stage marks the point where buyer and seller recognize that they would be better able to achieve their respective aims outside the relationship. Several studies have validated the existence of a relationship life cycle.[9]

Service organizations use various strategies to move their customers through the stages of relationship development:

- The possibility that relationships will develop can occur only when the parties are aware of each other and of their mutual desire to enter into exchange transactions. At this stage, the parties may have diverging views about the possibility of forming a long-term relationship. The supplier must be able to offer potential customers reasons why they should show disloyalty to their existing suppliers. In some cases, low introductory prices are offered by services organizations and provide a sufficient incentive for disloyal customers of other companies to switch suppliers. Non–price-related means of gaining attention include advertising and direct mail aimed at the market segments with whom relationships are sought. Over time, the supplier tries to build value into the relationship so that customers have little incentive for seeking lower-price solutions elsewhere. Inevitably, sellers face risks in adopting this strategy. It may be difficult to identify and exclude from a relationship invitation those segments of the population who are likely to show most disloyalty by withdrawing from the relationship at the point where it is just beginning to become profitable to the supplier.
- On entering into a relationship, buyers and sellers make a series of promises to each

other.[10] In the early stages of a relationship, suppliers' promises result in expectations being held by buyers about the standard of service that will actually be delivered. Many studies into service quality have highlighted the way in which the gap between expected performance and actual service performance determines customers' perception of quality (see Chapter 6). Quality in perceived service delivery is a prerequisite for the development of a quality relationship.[11]

- At the first encounter, many service organizations record information about customers that will be useful in assessing their future needs. In an initial encounter, a financial adviser can record the type of services that a customer prefers. Gradually, the adviser can refine this profile as subsequent transactions occur. In this way a financial service can build up a database that the company can use to alert customers to new service developments of specific interest to them.

- Financial incentives are often given to customers as a reward for maintaining their relationship. These can range from a simple money-off voucher, valid for a reduction in the price of a future service, to a club-type of scheme, which allows a standard level of discount for club members. Incentives that are purely financially based can defeat the service supplier's central objective of getting greater value out of a relationship. It is often expensive to initiate a relationship, and organizations therefore attempt to achieve profits at later stages by raising price levels to reflect the value that customers attach to the relationship. However, in some cases, greater bonding between customer and supplier can be achieved by selling membership plans to customers that allow subsequent discount, as is the case with store discount cards. Having invested in a membership plan, customers are likely to rationalize their reasons for taking advantage of it rather than taking their business elsewhere.

- Rather than offer price discounts, companies can add to the value of a relationship by offering other nonfinancial incentives. For example, many retailers offer special preview evenings for customers who have joined their membership clubs. Incentives for frequent users can help to develop short- to medium-term loyalty. Many airlines, for example, reward frequent business passengers with free or reduced-price vacation tickets.

- A strategy used by some companies is to create relationships by trying to turn discrete service delivery into continuous delivery. In this way, companies offering travel insurance often encourage customers to buy year-round coverage rather than purchasing a policy each time they travel abroad.

- By retaining information about preferences a firm can tailor future service offers to the specific needs of the individual customers. A travel agent booking accommodation for a corporate client can select hotels on the basis of preferences expressed during previous transactions. By offering a more personalized service, the travel agent is adding value to the relationship, increasing the transaction costs to the customer of transferring to another travel agent.

- A more intensive relationship can develop when customers assign considerable responsibility to a service provider for identifying their needs. An auto mechanic may attempt to move away from offering a series of discrete services initiated by customers to taking total responsibility for maintaining a customer's car, including diagnosing problems and initiating routine service appointments.

In some low-contact service industries, the development of relationships focuses on interaction with a very limited number of people, typically the organization's sales force. This is characteristic of the financial services sector, where despite a long-term relationship between a company and client, the client may seldom need to consult anybody other than the sales person, and the bulk of the substantive service is processed in the client's absence. Many studies have attempted to analyze the characteristics of sales personnel that are most closely associated with successful customer interaction and the ways in which these characteristics can result in the development of long-term relationships.[12] Two important elements used to explain relationship quality are trust in the salesperson and satisfaction with the salesperson's performance so far. The quality of a relationship has also been identified with the salesperson's ability to reduce the perceived riskiness of a highly intangible service purchase.[13]

The emerging relationship between buyer and seller has frequently been identified with the concept of trust, often building upon models used in social psychology. Trust can be defined in a marketing context as "...a belief that a party is reliable and will fulfill their obligations in an exchange relationship."[14] While relationships may endure as a result of one or both parties having no choice but to remain with the other party (e.g., a monopoly supplier), trust has been seen as a crucial function in a relationship, which allows tensions to be worked out.[15]

Although there has been much recent interest in relationship marketing—for goods as well as for services—this has tended to emphasize the producer's perspective on a relationship. It can be argued that with increasing knowledge and confidence, consumers are increasingly happy to venture outside a long-term relationship with a service provider. This is reflected in the observation that in 1990 43 percent of a sample of bank customers in the United States had changed banks within the last five years,[16] running counter to earlier anecdotal observations that the relationship of individuals with their banks is more enduring than the relationship with their spouses. With increased knowledge of financial services, consumers are more willing today to venture to another bank that offers the best personal loan or the most attractive credit card. Also, a long-term relationship often begins with attractive introductory discounts, and a significant segment of many service markets is prepared to move its business regularly to the service provider that offers the most attractive discount. The motorist who reviews his or her car insurance each year, for example, may not allow an insurance company to develop a long-term profitable relationship. Many business-to-business service contracts may be reviewed regularly as a matter of course, as in the competitive bidding that is required for many government purchases of services. In such circumstances, it is often not possible to add value and higher prices to a long-term relationship.

CASE STUDY

RELATIONSHIPS SOUGHT TO BOOST THE SAGGING PRESTIGE OF AMERICAN EXPRESS

During the 1980s, the market for charge cards in the United States approached saturation as a proliferation of new cards appeared. Visa and Mastercard had dominated the market for some time, bolstered by the growing number of affinity cards launched in collaboration with industrial companies, such as the AT&T Universal Visa card. The Sears group had weighed in with the launch of its Discover card. Among the plethora of cards, American Express (Amex) had tried to position its card as an exclusive status symbol—a card that could not be compared with the likes of Visa and Mastercard.

By the early 1990s, American Express was facing a tough time in the card market. Since 1989, its archrival, Visa, had been targeting Amex instead of its traditional rival, Mastercard. Banks began adding privileges to their cards, such as free travel accident insurance, once considered a privilege of the Amex card. It seemed that the Amex card was becoming a commodity item undifferentiated from its competitors' offers. By the 1990s, the card had lost much of its prestigious image, a loss not helped by consumers' increasing consciousness of card charges and willingness to shop around for the best card. The outcome of all these factors was to reduce Amex's worldwide market share from 20.3 percent in 1987 to 14.5 percent in 1991. By contrast, Visa's market share had increased from 44.7 percent to 51.0 percent.

Not only was Amex loosing favor with cardholders, it was becoming increasingly derided by merchants, from whom Amex obtained about two-thirds of its card income. In 1991, Amex continued charging its merchants fees of 3 percent to 4 percent of charge value, while Visa had whittled its fee down to an average of just 1.82 percent. Merchants knew that about 90 percent of all Amex cardholders also carried a Visa card, and many tried to "suppress" the use of Amex by encouraging customers to use Visa instead. Some merchants stopped accepting Amex completely, a potentially dangerous strategy for any business relying on business expense customers traveling with corporate cards. There were numerous local rebellions against Amex's charges, the most notable being the so-called "Boston fee party" in which Boston restauranteurs led many other businesses throughout the country in refusing to accept Amex cards following the refusal of the company to lower its merchant fees.

Amex initially underestimated its competition but eventually attempted to regain profitable business through the development of loyal relationships between the company and both its cardholders and its merchants. Amex recognized the limitations of its 1980s strategy of simply acquiring new cardholders and then taking their business for granted. Instead, it realized that it would make more financial sense to sacrifice numbers if the result would be a quality base of loyal customers. Similarly, the company recognized that it wasn't good enough to simply sign up more merchants—it would be better to have a core of merchants who were committed to working with the company to increase use of its cards.

Amex decided to focus its attention on the 20 percent of its cardholder base who accounted for 80 percent of charge volume. For this core group of customers, the company made an effort to tailor its service to meet the specific needs of each individual, for example, in the way that it allowed cardholders to receive their monthly statement on any chosen day. It also refined its customer database so that it could send mailings for goods and services that most accurately reflected its customers' interests and lifestyles. To try to get itself seen as a partner in problem solving, Amex offered many more services; for example, it offered to reserve tickets at concerts for its gold and platinum card holders. In a bid to encourage a greater proportion of its cardholders' spending to be charged to Amex cards rather than to competitors' cards, Amex developed its Membership Miles scheme, a form of frequent flyer program, which awarded miles on selected airlines in return for charge volume.

More importantly, Amex developed closer relationships with its merchants. To discourage defectors, the company promised to be more attentive to merchant concerns such as discount rates, speedy payment, and marketing support. The company reassigned the duties of its merchant service representatives by requiring them to make more frequent visits to existing merchants, rather than spending most of their time looking for new ones. Where a problem had been identified, representatives were also empowered to make deals on the spot in an attempt to resolve it.

In a further attempt to develop loyalty with its merchant members, Amex agreed to be sensitive in its own direct marketing efforts, which in the past had upset many merchants by directly competing with their own goods and services. Finally, Amex demonstrated its enthusiasm for working with its merchants through a series of television advertisements that focused on a specific business—usually a small, rapidly growing business with a high level of awareness among cardholders—and promoted the business as much as the Amex card.

Amex had determined that in the increasingly fierce charge card market, features and benefits were no longer adequate to give its card a competitive edge. Its strategy was designed to sell much wider, high-quality relationships through which cardholders and merchants could receive a total service that met their specific needs. Only time will tell whether merchants and cardholders are prepared to pay a premium price to reflect the value of such relationships, or indeed whether similar emphasis on relationships becomes the norm for all charge cards, again causing Amex to lose its competitive advantage.

CASE STUDY REVIEW QUESTIONS

1. Demographers have recently begun to call attention to a growing demographic group—teenagers. *Business Week,* April 11, 1994, said: "They are the leading edge of a demographic wave that will wash over the U.S. during the next two decades, transforming our culture and economy." Advise Amex: how can that company use relationship marketing to gain a competitive edge among these young people?

2. Suggest further strategies that might be appropriate to American Express in its bid to develop relationships with its cardholders and merchants.

3. Review the positioning strategies open to American Express for its card services.

CHAPTER REVIEW QUESTIONS

1. Explain why a thorough understanding of buyer behavior processes may be important for a cinema chain seeking to enhance its service offer.

2. Using Fisk's model, identify the activities that occur when a person is selecting a dentist for himself or herself. How does your list change when the person is selecting a dentist for a child's first visit to the dentist?

3. Consider a high school senior's decision making process in selecting a college. The decision typically starts in the fall of the senior year, when the student must write away for college applications. It ends in May, when the student must send in a deposit to the chosen college. Who are typically the influencers, gatekeepers, users, and decision makers? Now, advise a small liberal arts college about ways to reach the people playing each role.

4. What are the potential benefits to an airline of developing relationships with its customers?

5. Identify and critically assess the effectiveness of methods used by banks to develop relationships with their customers.

6. Using a service that you are familiar with, trace the development of your relationship with that organization. In other words, what happened during each of the five stages identified earlier: awareness, exploration, expansion, commitment, and dissolution? What stage are you in currently? How good a marketing job has the service organization done as you moved through the stages?

REFERENCES

1. Howard, J. A. and Sheth, J. N. *The Theory of Buyer Behavior* (New York: John Wiley, 1969).

2. Fisk, R. P. "Toward a Consumption/Evaluation Process Model for Services," in *Marketing of Services,* ed. J. H. Donnelly and W. R. George (Chicago: American Marketing Association, 1981).

3. Lewis, R. "Restaurant Advertising: Appeals and Consumers' Intentions," *Journal of Advertising Research* 21, no. 5 (1981): 69–74.

4. Day, G. S. and Wensley, R. "Marketing Theory with a Strategic Orientation," *Journal of Marketing* 47 (Fall 1983): 79–89.

5. Reichheld, F. "Loyalty Based Management," *Harvard Business Review* 68, no. 5 (1993): 105–11; L. L. Berry, "Relationship Marketing," in *Emerging Perspectives of Services Marketing,* ed. L. L. Berry, et al. (Chicago: American Marketing Association, 1983); and Jackson, B. B. "Build Customer Relationships That Last," *Harvard Business Review* (November/December 1985): 120–28 .

6. Gronroos, C. "The Marketing Strategy Continuum: Towards a Marketing Concept for the 1990s," *Management Decision* 29, no. 1 (1991): 7–13.

7. Sheth, J. N. "Relationship Marketing: An Emerging School of Marketing Thought." Paper presented June 23, 1993 at the 1993 Services Marketing Faculty Consortium, hosted by First Interstate Center for Services Marketing, Department of Marketing, Arizona State University.

8. Dwyer, F. R., Schurr, P. H., and Oh, S. "Developing Buyer and Seller Relationships," *Journal of Marketing* 51 (April 1987): 11–27.

9. Palmer, A. and Bejou, D. "Buyer-Seller Relationships—A Conceptual Model and Empirical Investigation," *Journal of Marketing Management* 10(6) (1994): 495–512.

10. Gronroos, C. "Defining Marketing: A Market-Oriented Approach," *European Journal of Marketing* 23, no. 1 (1989): 52–60.

11. Crosby, L. A. "Maintaining Quality in the Service Relationship," in *Quality in Services,* ed. S. W. Brown and E. Gummesson (Lexington, Mass.: Lexington Books, 1989).

12. Crosby, L. A., Evans, K. R., and Cowles, D. "Relationship Quality in Services Selling: An Interpersonal Influence Perspective," *Journal of Marketing* 54 (July 1990): 68–81.

13. Zeithaml, V. A. "How Consumers' Evaluation Processes Differ Between Goods and Services," in *Marketing of Services,* ed. J. H. Donnelly and W. R. George (Chicago: American Marketing Association, 1981): 186–90.

14. Schurr, P. H. and Ozanne, J. L. "Influences on Exchange Processes: Buyers' Preconceptions of a Seller's Trustworthiness and Bargaining Toughness," *Journal of Consumer Research* 11 (March 1985): 939–53.

15. Sullivan, J. and Peterson, R. "Factors Associated with Trust in Japanese-American Joint Ventures," *Management International Review* 22 (1982): 33–40.

16. Lewis, B. R. "Bank Service Quality," *Journal of Marketing Management* 7, no. 1 (1991): 47–62.

SUGGESTED FURTHER READING

Fisk, R. P. 1981. "Toward a Consumption/Evaluation Process Model for Services" in *Marketing of Services,* edited by J. H. Donnelly and W. R. George. Chicago: American Marketing Association.

JOHNSTON, W. L. and BONOMA, T. V. 1981. "The Buying Center: Structure and Interaction Patterns." *Journal of Marketing* (Summer): 143–56.

STOCK, J. R. and ZINSZER, P. H. 1987. "The Industrial Purchase Decision for Professional Services." *Journal of Business Research* (February): 1–16.

ZEITHAML, V. A. 1981. "How Consumers' Evaluation Processes Differ Between Goods and Services" in *Marketing of Services,* edited by J. H. Donnelly and W. R. George. Chicago: American Marketing Association, 186–90.

BERRY, L. L. 1983. "Relationship Marketing" in *Emerging Perspectives of Services Marketing,* edited by L. L. Berry et al. Chicago: American Marketing Association.

CROSBY, L. A., EVANS, K. R., and COWLES, D. 1990. "Relationship Quality in Services Selling: An Interpersonal Influence Perspective." *Journal of Marketing* 54 (July): 68–81.

DWYER, F. R., SCHURR, P. H. and OH, S. 1987. "Developing Buyer and Seller Relationships." *Journal of Marketing* 51 (April): 11–27.

GRONROOS, C. 1990. "Relationship Approach to Marketing in Service Contexts: The Marketing and Organizational Interface." *Journal of Business Research* 20: 3–11.

JACKSON, B. B. 1985. "Build Customer Relationships that Last," *Harvard Business Review* (November/December); 120–128.

REICHHELD, F. F. 1993. "Loyalty Based Management." *Harvard Business Review* 71, no. 2: 64–73.

SHOSTACK, G. L. 1985. "Planning the Service Encounter" in *The Service Encounter,* edited by J. A. Czepiel, M. R. Solomon, and C. F. Suprenant. Lexington, Mass.: Lexington Books, 243–54.

SHOSTACK, G. L. 1984. "Designing Services that Deliver." *Harvard Business Review* (January/February): 133–39.

6

Service Quality

CHAPTER OBJECTIVES

After reading this chapter, you should be able to understand

- frameworks for understanding the concept of service quality

- methods of measuring service quality

- approaches used to set quality standards

- strategies used to deliver and monitor quality services

6.1 INTRODUCTION

Quality is seen as an increasingly important element that differentiates between competing services. It is correspondingly an important element in marketing mix planning, as is evidenced by the Profit Impact of Marketing Strategies (PIMS) study of the Strategic Planning Institute, which concluded that the single most important factor affecting a business unit's performance is the quality of its goods and services relative to that of its competitors.[1]

The quality of tangible goods can usually be assessed by examining them. However, the quality of services is less easily testable; normally it can be assessed only when the service has been consumed. For this reason, the purchase decision process for a service usually involves more risk than with goods. Understanding just what dimensions of quality are important to customers in this evaluation process can be difficult. It is not sufficient for companies to make assumptions and deliver quality standards in accordance with their own assumptions of customers' expectations.

A further problem in defining service quality lies in the importance customers often attach to the quality of the service provider as well as the quality of its services. The two cannot be separated as easily as is usually possible with goods.

This chapter first considers the conceptual problems encountered by academics in trying to define just what is meant by service quality. Within these conceptual frameworks, methods of measuring service quality and managing its delivery are then reviewed.

6.2 DEFINING SERVICE QUALITY

Quality is extremely difficult to define in a few words. At its most basic, quality has been defined as "conforming to requirements."[2] This implies that organizations must establish requirements and specifications; once these specifications are established, the quality goal of the various functions of an organization is to comply strictly with them. However, the questions remain: whose requirements and whose specifications? Thus, a second series of definitions states that quality is all about fitness for use. Such definitions are based primarily on satisfying customers' needs.[3] These two definitions can be united in the concept of customer perceived quality: quality can be defined only by customers and occurs when an organization supplies goods or services to a specification that satisfies their needs.

Many analyses of service quality have attempted to distinguish between objective measures of quality and measures based on the more subjective perceptions of customers. One definition used by Swan and Comb[4] identified two important dimensions of service quality: *instrumental* quality, the physical aspects of a service, and the *expressive* dimension, its intangible or psychological aspects. More recent work by Gronroos[5] identifies *technical* and *functional* quality as being the two principle components. Technical quality refers to the relatively quantifiable aspects of service delivery. Because it can easily be measured by both customer and supplier, it forms an important basis for judging service quality. Examples of technical quality include the waiting time at a supermarket check-out and the reliability of airline services. This, however, is not the only element that makes up perceived service quality. Because services involve direct consumer–producer interaction, consumers are also influenced by *how* the technical quality is delivered to them—functional quality, which cannot be measured as objectively as technical quality. In a supermarket checkout line, functional quality is influenced by such factors as the environment in which waiting takes place and consumers' perceptions of the manner in which waiting lines are handled by the supermarket's employees. Gronroos also sees an important role for a service firm's corporate image in defining customers' perceptions of quality, corporate image being based on both technical and functional quality. Figure 6.1 illustrates diagrammatically Gronroos's conceptualization of service quality as applied to an optician's practice.

If quality is defined as the extent to which a service meets customers' requirements, the problem remains of identifying just what those requirements are. The general absence of easily understood criteria for assessing quality makes articulation of customers' requirements and communication of the quality level offered much more

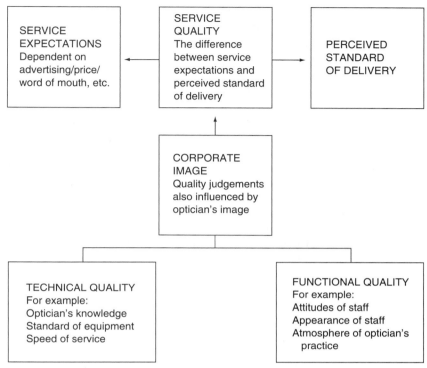

Figure 6.1   Consumer perception of technical and functional quality applied to an optician's practice (Based on C. Gronroos, *Strategic Management and Marketing in the Service Sector*, Bromley, U.K.: Chartwell-Bratt Ltd., 1984.)

difficult than with goods. Service quality is a highly abstract construct, in contrast to goods, where technical aspects of quality often predominate. Many conceptualizations of service quality therefore begin by addressing consumers' abstract expectations of quality.

Consumers subsequently judge service quality as the extent to which perceived service delivery matches up to these initial expectations. In this way, a service that is perceived as being average may be considered of high quality when compared against low expectations, but of low quality when assessed against high expectations. Much research remains to be done to understand the processes by which expectations of service quality are formed. Zeithaml, Berry, and Parasuraman[6] have suggested that three levels of expectations can be defined against which quality is assessed: the desired level of service, reflecting what the customer wants; the adequate service level, defined as the standard customers are willing to accept; and the predicted service level, that which they believe is most likely to actually occur.

While the desirability of measuring service quality is now widely recognized, there is relatively little understanding of the mechanisms by which service quality leads to customer satisfaction and in turn leads to purchase intentions. An attempt to understand these linkages has been made by Cronin and Taylor,[7] who showed how

service quality is an antecedent of consumer satisfaction, which in turn has a significant effect on purchase intentions. Their empirical investigation suggested that consumer satisfaction has greater effect on purchase intentions than quality as it is more
narrowly defined.

Analysis of service quality is further complicated by the fact that production
and consumption of a service generally occur simultaneously, with two interfaces
existing between producer and consumer. The first interface comprises the traditional
marketing mix elements; the additional interface comes through the process of
buyer–seller interaction. A buyer of manufactured goods encounters only the traditional marketing mix variables of a manufacturer, i.e., the product, its price, its distribution, and how these are communicated to him or her. Usually, production
processes are unseen by consumers and therefore cannot be used as a basis for quality assessment. By contrast, service inseparability results in the production process
being an important basis for assessing quality. A further problem in understanding
and managing service quality flows from the intangibility, variability and inseparability of most services and the resulting series of unique buyer–seller exchanges in
which no two services are provided in exactly the same way.

CASE STUDY

BANK PUTS ITS MONEY WHERE ITS MOUTH IS

Until the 1970s, marketing-led approaches to quality management were not high on the
agenda of most banks. They operated in an environment in which professional ethics and standards of conduct were the main constraint on their activities. Furthermore, promoting quality
standards was often seen as undesirable, possibly undermining the implicit trust that people
were assumed to have in their bank. This approach may have suited banks well until the
1970s, but since that time, the banking environment in many countries has became increasingly competitive. In the context of deregulated financial markets, customers of banks were
increasingly able and willing to shop around for financial services that best met their expectations. Moreover, consumers' expectations in general had been heightened in other consumer
service markets, and they saw no reason why banks should not operate to the same standards
as an airline or a car rental company.

Against this background, many banks in the United States began setting quality standards for their dealings with customers. While many banks had for some time given guarantees to their customers on such matters as the accuracy of statements, one bank decided to
back up its quality guarantees with financial compensation schemes. The Colorado National
Bank developed a quality program appropriately called "PIMWIMI" (Put Your Money Where
Your Mouth Is"). The bank made specific promises to its customers:

- Customers would not wait more than three minutes to be served by a teller, or five
  minutes for a personal banking, personal loan, or customer assistance inquiry.
- Staff would offer a friendly greeting to each customer by name.
- All inquiries and applications for personal loans would be turned around within no
  more than one working day.
- Statements would be accurate.

These items were selected for inclusion in the customer guarantee as a result of previous research, which had shown them to be of importance to customers. Before offering the guarantee, the bank determined that it had the resources to deliver service to these standards.

If it failed to deliver in accordance with its guarantee, the bank promised that it would send a personal letter from the bank's president to the customer apologizing for the failure to meet the quality standard, along with a $5 bill.

In the first year of the PIMWIMI program's operation, the bank was not called upon to make any payment in respect to its guarantee of courteous service. With respect to the other elements of its guarantee, it paid out just $885 in the first three months, representing a very low rate of failure among its 256,000 transactions during the period and less than had been expected.

The principle benefit of the PIMWIMI program was to focus the attention of the bank's employees on meeting clearly defined quality targets. The program was linked to the bank's reward system, which linked individuals' pay to the quality of service reported by customers.

CASE STUDY REVIEW QUESTIONS

1. What possible risks does a bank face when it offers such guarantees? What can it do to reduce this risk?
2. Do you think it is a good idea to link this bank's guarantee scheme to its employees' salaries? What problems and opportunities does this present?
3. How does a service quality guarantee relate to other elements of a bank's marketing mix planning?

6.3   RESEARCHING SERVICE QUALITY

One of the prime causes of poor quality performance by service firms is not knowing what their customers expect. Many organizations are eager to provide good quality of service, but fall short simply because they do not accurately understand what customers expect from the company. The absence of well-defined tangible cues makes this understanding much more difficult than it would be if the organization were marketing manufactured goods. Marketing research is a means of eliciting information about customers' expectations and perceptions of services. Services organizations should ask the following key questions;

- What do customers consider the important features of the service to be?
- What level of these features do customers expect?
- How is service delivery perceived by customers?

Several methods for researching customers' expectations and perceptions are available and will be examined here. However, as a set of general principles for the effective measurement of service quality, a research program should be adopted which is:

1. Varied: Every research method has its limitations, and in order to overcome them and to achieve a comprehensive insight into a problem, a combination of qualitative and quantitative research techniques should be used.

2. Ongoing: The expectations and perceptions of customers are constantly changing, as is the nature of the service offer provided by companies. It is therefore important that a service research process is administered on a continuous basis so that any changes can be picked up quickly and acted upon if necessary.

3. Undertaken with employees: The closeness of staff to customers within the services sector makes it important that they are asked about problems and possible improvements as well as their personal motivations and requirements.

4. Shared with employees: Employees' performance in delivering service quality may be improved if they are made aware of the results of studies of customer expectations and complaint analysis.

6.3.1 Regular Customer Surveys

The incidence of customer satisfaction surveys is increasing throughout the services sector. Today, members of the public are in constant receipt of literature from a wide range of service providers—both private and public—asking for comments on the quality of service received. It is probably true that most large service providers have jumped on this quality bandwagon, although it is often questionable whether the most appropriate methods are employed to gather the information. Typical applications include filling in a questionnaire after a meal in a restaurant, or being asked by a hospital to complete a survey on attitudes toward the hospital. Such surveys usually ask recipients to relate any complaints that they may have about the services provided and any comments or suggestions for improving them. Most people assume that data from such surveys will be used to direct corrective action when expectations are not reached. It must, however, be stated that many of these surveys are of dubious quality and therefore of limited value. Many of them represent a superficial approach to marketing, research, and the issue of quality service. More rigorous and comprehensive expectation and perception studies would often be of much more value. These are discussed here.

6.3.2 Customer Panels

Customer panels can provide a continuous source of information on customer expectations. Groups of customers, generally frequent users, are brought together regularly by a company to study their opinions about the quality of service provided. On other occasions they may be employed to monitor the introduction of a new or revised service. For example a panel could be brought together by a bank following the experimental introduction of a new branch design format.

The use of continuous panels can offer organizations a means of anticipating problems and may act as an early warning system for emerging issues of importance. Retailers have been involved in the operation of continuous panels to monitor their level of service provision and also let panels contribute to new service development research.

However, the validity of this research method is quite dependent on how well the panel represents consumers as a whole. Careful selection should therefore be undertaken to ensure that the panel possesses the same characteristics as the population of customers being analyzed, such as social, economic, demographic, and frequency of use.

6.3.3 Transaction Analysis

Transaction analysis, an increasingly popular method of evaluative research, involves tracking the satisfaction of individuals with particular transactions that they have recently been involved in. This type of research enables management to judge current performance, particularly customers' satisfaction with the contact personnel with whom they have interacted, as well as their overall satisfaction with the service.

The research effort normally involves a mail or telephone survey of individual customers immediately after a transaction has been completed. A wide range of services organizations in the United States is now using this approach. For example, banks often track customers following the completion of a loan transaction. An additional benefit of this research is its capability to associate service quality performance with individual contact personnel and link it to reward systems.

6.3.4 Perception Surveys

Perception surveys use a combination of qualitative and quantitative research methods. Many professional services organizations have employed such studies in order to develop future marketing strategies. Their aim is to achieve a better understanding of how customers view an organization in order to help the firm see itself as clients see it. The initial qualitative stages of a study involve researchers in identifying the attitudes of clients (past, present, and future) to the firm as well as how the firm is perceived by the community at large. This may involve eliciting information from journalists, intermediaries, and even competitors. Group discussions and/or in-depth interviews are used for assessing the perceptions of people at this stage. In the quantitative phase of a survey, clients are asked to judge the company's performance by use of a battery of attitude statements. Perception studies often include an analysis of the perceptions of a firm's employees.

6.3.5 Mystery Shoppers

Mystery shopping is a method of auditing the standard of service provision, particularly the staff involvement. A major difficulty in ensuring service quality is overcoming the nonconformance of staff with performance guidelines. This so-called service-performance gap is the result of the inability and/or unwillingness of employees to perform the service at the desired level. An important function of mystery shopper surveys is therefore to monitor the extent to which specified quality standards are actually being met by employees.

This method of researching actual service provision involves the use of trained assessors who visit service organizations and report back their observations. Audits tend to be tailored to the specific needs of a company and to focus on an issue that the company wishes to evaluate. The format of the inquiry is therefore determined by the client and the research organization in collaboration.

The constructive nature of this research technique has to be emphasized, as the mystery shopper can quite easily be mistaken by staff as an undercover agent spying on them on behalf of the management. If the techniques are applied correctly, they can allow management to know what is really happening on the front line of their business. To be effective, mystery shopping surveys need to be undertaken independently, should be objective, and must be consistent. The training of assessors is critical to the effective use of this research method and should include, for example, training in observation techniques that allow them to distinguish between a greeting and an acknowledgement. Is the welcome given by a dentist's receptionist slow and cold, possibly indicating the tone of the substantive service delivery process, or is it warm and inviting?

6.3.6 Analysis of Complaints

Dissatisfaction of customers is most clearly voiced through the complaints they make about service provision. For many companies, analyzing these complaints may be the sole method of keeping in touch with customers. Complaints can be made directly to the provider or indirectly through an intermediary or a regulatory agency. Complaints by customers, referring to instances of what they consider poor quality service, may provide a rich source of data on which to base policies for improving service quality, if they are treated constructively.

However, customer complaints are at best an inadequate source of information. Most customers don't bother to complain, remain dissatisfied, and tell others about their dissatisfaction. Other customers simply change to another supplier and do not offer potentially valuable information to the first provider about the factors that caused them to leave (although this could, of course, be researched by the service provider).

In truly market-oriented organizations, complaints analysis can form a useful pointer to where the process of service delivery is breaking down. As part of an overall program for keeping in touch with customers, the analysis of complaints can have an important role to play. The continuous tracking of complaints is a relatively inexpensive source of data that enable a company to review the major concerns of customers on an ongoing basis and perhaps rectify any evident problems. In addition, the receipt of complaints by the firm enables staff to enter into direct contact with customers and provides an opportunity to interact with them about their concerns. As well as giving their opinions on these issues in particular, complainants can also contribute views about customer service in general. Customer feedback about service provision problems can only be encouraged. A notable example in this respect is the use by some airlines (e.g., British Airways) of video recording booths at airports that allow customers to alleviate their pent-up feelings, thus giving the airline useful information on which to act.

6.3.7 Employee Research

Research undertaken among employees can enable their views about the way that services are provided and their perceptions of how they are received by customers to be taken into account. Data gathered from staff training seminars and development exercises, feedback from quality circles, job appraisal and performance evaluation reports, and so on can all provide valuable information for planning quality service provision. One way in which formal feedback from staff can be built into a systematic research program is a staff suggestion scheme. The proposals that staff make about how services could be provided more efficiently and/or effectively have an important role in improving service quality.

Research into employees' needs can also help identify policies that improve their motivation to deliver a high quality of service. Many of the techniques employed to elicit the views of employees as internal customers are in principle the same as those used in studies of external customers. Interviews and focus groups of employees may be used in the collection of qualitative data on employee needs, wants, motivations, and attitudes toward working conditions, benefits, and policies. This can be followed up with appropriate quantitative analysis, such as the SERVQUAL methodology to be described, which can be equally applied to internal employee studies.

In Chapter 7 the issue of obtaining involvement and participation of the workforce is considered in some detail. Involving employees in the research process and its findings, for example, by using them to gather data, showing them videotapes of group discussions and interviews with customers, and circulating the findings of research reports among them, can do a lot to improve their understanding of service quality issues throughout their organization.

6.3.8 Similar Industry Studies

Customers' quality expectations in other similar service industries can be a useful source of information for managers. It is often apparent that customer needs may be similar between different industries, even though the service product is outwardly quite different. Many common dimensions cut across the boundaries of industries and apply to services in general—for example, courteous and competent staff, a pleasant environment, and helpfulness, to name but a few. It can therefore be beneficial to investigate the nature of service provision in closely related service areas and to draw on the findings of any available research. In particular, it is worthwhile to investigate what is known in those services sectors that have a good track record of analyzing and responding to customers' needs and identify whether it is applicable to an industry that has only recently adopted a customer-led approach.

6.3.9 Intermediary Research

As has already been noted, services intermediaries often fulfill a valuable function in the process of service delivery, performing their role in quite a different manner from that of goods intermediaries. Research into intermediaries focuses on two principal concerns:

- First, where intermediaries form an important part of a service delivery processes, the quality perceived by customers is largely determined by the performance of intermediaries. In this way, the perceived quality of an airline may be tarnished if a travel agent that it works through is perceived as being slow or unhelpful to customers. Research through such techniques as mystery shopper surveys can be used to monitor the standard of quality delivered by intermediaries. In addition, qualitative research is often undertaken through focus groups of intermediaries to learn more about their motivations and attitudes toward the service principal.

- Second, intermediaries as co-producers of a service are further down the channel of distribution and closer to customers. They are therefore in a position to provide valuable feedback to the service principal about consumers' expectations and perceptions. As well as conducting structured research investigations of intermediaries, many services principals find it possible to learn more about the needs and expectations of their final customers during the process of providing intermediary support services, such as training.

6.4 COMPREHENSIVE EXPECTATION AND PERCEPTION STUDIES

Quality is clearly an important but complex concept. Recently, service organizations have recognized that although quality is a means of gaining competitive advantage, it cannot be satisfactorily measured by a series of isolated ad hoc studies. Instead, organizations need comprehensive programs to research customers' expectations and perceptions of service quality. Preeminent among these comprehensive studies is the work of Berry, Parasuraman, and Zeithaml, who have been strong advocates of the need for services organizations to learn more about their customers through a rigorous marketing-research–oriented approach that focuses on the expectations and perceptions of customers. Their research program, which began in 1983, is still in progress; yet, its findings so far offer several insights into the marketing of services that should benefit practitioners throughout the sector. Their research concentrates on the belief that service quality is measurable, although because of intangibility it may be more difficult to measure than goods quality. Their research tackles two basic dimensions of service provision—outcomes and processes—and also considers additional dimensions of service quality that transcend these two basic dimensions. Furthermore, Berry, et al., make the point that the only relevant factors in determining service quality are those that customers perceive as being important. Only customers judge quality—all other judgments are considered to be essentially irrelevant. They therefore set out to determine what customers expect from services and just what the characteristics are that define those services (effectively, what is the service in the mind of the customer?). Subsequently, they endeavored to develop an instrument for measuring customers' perceptions of service quality compared with their expectations. Their findings have evolved from a set of qualitative marketing research procedures to culminate in the quantitative technique for measuring service quality known as SERVQUAL.

The SERVQUAL technique can be used by companies to better understand the expectations and perceptions of their customers. It is applicable across a broad range of service industries and can be easily modified to take account of the specific requirements of a company. In effect, it provides a skeleton for an investigatory instrument that can be adapted or added to as needed.

SERVQUAL is based upon a generic twenty-two-item questionnaire designed to cover five broad dimensions of service quality that Berry, et al., consolidated from their original qualitative investigations. The five dimensions covered, with some description of each and the respective numbers of statements associated with them, is as follows:

Dimension	Number of Statements
tangibles (appearance of physical elements)	4
reliability (dependability, accurate performance)	5
responsiveness (promptness, helpfulness)	4
assurance (competence, courtesy, credibility, security)	4
empathy (easy access, good communications, customer understanding).	5

Customers are asked to respond to twenty-two company specific statements relating to their expectations and perceptions about service delivery. They are asked to score in each instance on a Likert scale, from 1 (strongly agree) to 7 (strongly disagree), whether or not they agree with each statement. In addition, the survey asks for respondents' evaluation of the relative importance they attach to each of the dimensions of quality, any comments they would care to make about their experiences of the service, and their overall impression of it. They are also asked for supplementary demographic data.

To measure the level of customer satisfaction for a service provided by a particular company, the results for perceptions and expectations need to be calculated for each customer. From this, measures of service quality can be derived quite simply by subtracting expectation scores from perception scores, either unweighted or weighted to take into consideration the relative importance of each dimension of quality or the relative importance of different customer groups. The outcome of a one-time study is a measure that tells the company whether its customers' expectations are exceeded or not.

Beyond this simple analysis, SERVQUAL results can be used to identify which components or facets of a service the company is particularly good or bad at. It can be used to monitor service quality over time, to compare performance with that of competitors, or to measure customer satisfaction with a particular service industry generally.

An organization or industry group can use the information collected through SERVQUAL to improve its position by acting upon the results and ensuring that it continuously surpasses customers' expectations. Additionally, the expectations-perceptions results, along with the demographic data, may facilitate effective customer segmentation.

It is important that service providers decide upon a target level of service quality and then communicate the level of service offered to both consumers and employees. This allows employees to know what is expected of them, and customers will have an idea of the level of service they can expect.

The SERVQUAL model highlights the difficulties in ensuring a high quality of service for all customers in all situations. More specifically, it identifies five gaps where there may be a shortfall between expectation of service level and perception of actual service delivery.

Gap 1: Gap between Consumer Expectations and Management Perception.   Management may think that they know what consumers want and proceed to deliver it when in fact consumers may expect something quite different.

Gap 2: Gap between Management Perception and Service Quality Specification.   Management may not set quality specifications or may not set them clearly. Alternatively, management may set clear quality specifications, but they may not be achievable.

Gap 3: Gap between Service Quality Specifications and Service Delivery.   Unforeseen problems or poor management can lead to failure of a service provider to meet service quality specifications. This may be due to human error but also to mechanical breakdown of facilitating or support goods.

Gap 4: Gap between Service Delivery and External Communications. There may be dissatisfaction with a service because of the excessively heightened expectations developed through the service provider's communications efforts. Dissatisfaction occurs when actual delivery does not meet up to the expectations held out in a company's communications.

Gap 5: Gap between Perceived Service and Expected Service.   This gap occurs as a result of one or more of the previous gaps. The way in which customers perceive actual service delivery does not match up with their initial expectations.

The five gaps are illustrated in Figure 6.2, where a hypothetical application to a restaurant is shown.

6.4.1 Criticisms of SERVQUAL

While the SERVQUAL technique has attracted a lot of positive attention for its conceptualization of quality measurement issues, it has also attracted criticism. Some researchers have debated whether the dimensions of SERVQUAL are consistent across industries; others have suggested better wording for some of the scale items.[8,9]

In addition, researchers have asked whether the calculated difference scores (the difference between expectations and perceptions) are appropriate from a measurement and theoretical perspective.[10,11] From a measurement perspective, there are three psychometric problems associated with the use of difference scores: reliability, discriminant validity, and variance restriction problems. A study by Brown,

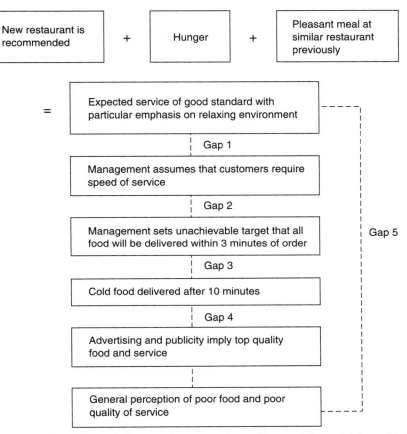

Figure 6.2   Sources of divergence between service quality expectation and delivery (Modified from A. Parasuraman, V. A. Zeithaml, and L. L. Berry, "A Conceptual Model of Service Quality and Its Implications for Future Research." *Journal of Marketing* (Fall 1985): 41–50.)

Churchill, and Peter[10] found evidence that these psychometric problems indeed arise with the use of SERVQUAL; they recommend, instead, the use of nondifference score measures, which display better discriminant and nomological validity. However, Parasuraman, Zeithaml, and Berry[11] respond by arguing that the alleged psychometric deficiencies of the difference-score formulation are less severe than have been suggested by critics. Despite their argument that the difference scores offer researchers better diagnostics than separate measurement of perceptions and expectations, from a theoretical perspective there is little evidence to support the relevance of the expectations-performance gap as the basis for measuring service quality.[12] Instead, considerable research supports a more straightforward approach of assessing quality on the basis of simple performance-based measures.[13,14] It has also been suggested that merely meeting customer expectations is no longer adequate. With large numbers of suppliers able to offer a broadly similar level of satisfaction, a company can stand out only by "delighting" its customers with service delivery that is far in excess of expectations. When quality levels between suppliers is similar, the quality of buyer–seller relationships may supersede a more narrow definition of product quality in consumers' quality evaluations.

6.5 SETTING QUALITY STANDARDS

The specification of service levels serves a valuable function in communicating the standard of quality that consumers can expect to receive. It also serves to communicate the standards expected of employees. While the general manner in which an organization promotes itself may give a general impression of the level of quality it attempts to deliver, more specific standards can be stated in other ways, which are considered here:

- At its most basic, an organization can rely on its terms of business as a basis for determining the level of service to be delivered to customers. These generally act to protect customers against excessively poor service rather than being used to proactively promote high standards of excellence. The terms of business of tour operators, for example, make very few promises about service quality, other than offers of compensation if delays exceed a specified standard or if accommodation arrangements are changed at short notice.
- Generally worded customer charters go beyond the minimum levels of business terms by stating in a general manner the standards of performance the organization aims to achieve in its dealings with customers. In this way, banks often publish charters that specify in general terms the manner in which accounts will be conducted and complaints handled.
- Specific guarantees of service performance are sometimes offered, especially in respect of service outcomes. As an example, parcel delivery companies often guarantee to deliver a parcel within a specified time and agree to pay compensation if they fall below this standard (Figure 6.3). Guarantees sometimes concentrate on the manner in which a service is produced rather than specifically on final outcomes. In this way, banks and retailers sometimes give guarantees about the length of time customers will have to wait in line for service. While there can be great benefits from publicizing specific guaranteed performance standards to customers, failure to perform could result in heavy compensation claims, or claims about misleading advertising. Many highly specific targets are therefore restricted to internal use, where their function is to motivate and control staff rather than to provide guarantees to potential customers. While most banks give their branch managers targets for such quality standards as waiting time for teller staff and availability of working ATMs, they do not guarantee a specified level of service to their customers.
- Many service companies belong to a trade or professional association and incorporate the association's code of conduct into their own service offerings. Codes of conduct adopted by members of professional associations as diverse as auto mechanics, funeral directors, and attorneys specify minimum standards below

Figure 6.3 UPS makes a commitment to provide a high level of service on one important dimension: arrival. Source: United Parcel Service.

which service provision should not fall. The code of conduct provides both a reassurance to potential customers and a statement to employees about the minimum standards that are expected of them.

• Of more general applicability is the adoption of a general quality standard, for example, the International Standard Organization's quality standard ISO 9002. An increasing number of service industries are now receiving Baldrige quality awards, administered by the Commerce Department's National Institute of Standards and Technology (see case study). Contrary to popular belief, a company working to either of these standards does not guarantee a high level of quality for its service. Instead, the awards are granted to organizations that can show that they have in place management systems for ensuring a *consistent* standard of quality. Whether the standard itself is high or low is largely a subjective judgment.

6.6 MANAGING THE MARKETING MIX FOR QUALITY

Service quality management is the process of attempting to ensure that the gap between consumer expectations and perceived service delivery is as small as possible. This task has several important dimensions.

First, the marketing mix formulation and its communication to potential customers must be as realistic as possible. Exaggerated claims merely lead to high expectations, which an organization may not be able to deliver. Therefore unrealistic expectations can lead to the perception that the service delivers poor quality.

Second, non–marketer-dominated factors, such as word-of-mouth information and traditions, also need to be considered, as their presence too may have the effect of increasing expectations.

Finally, service companies must recognize that the relationship between customer perceptions and expectations is dynamic. Merely maintaining customers' level of perceived quality is insufficient if their expectations have been raised over time. Marketing mix management is therefore concerned with closing the quality gap over time, either by improving the service offer or by restraining customers' expectations (Figure 6.4).

Quality affects all aspects of the marketing mix. Decisions about service specification cannot be made in isolation from decisions concerning other elements of the

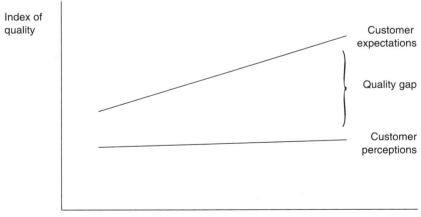

Figure 6.4   The changing quality gap

mix. All can affect the level of customer expectations and the perceived standard of service delivery.

- *Promotion* decisions have the effect of developing consumers' expectations of service quality. When marketer-dominated sources of promotion are the main basis for evaluating and selecting competing services, the message as well as the medium of communication can contribute in a significant way to customers' quality expectations. Invariably, promotion sets expectations, which organizations struggle to meet.

  On some occasions, however, the image created by promotion may actually add to the perceived quality of the service. This is quite common with goods, where the intangible image added to products such as beer can actually lead to the belief by consumers that the beer is of higher quality than another beer of identical technical quality that has been promoted in a different way. The possibility for achieving this with services is generally less, because of the greater involvement of customers in the production/consumption process and the many opportunities that occur for judging quality. It is, however, possible in some publicly consumed services, that high-profile advertising may in fact add to the perceived quality of the service. In this way, promotion of a gold charge card may add to a customer's sense of having bought an exclusive and prestigious facility. Without the advertising, the prestigious value of the card would not be recognized by others.

- *Price* decisions affect both customers' expectations and their perceptions of service quality, as well as the service organization's ability to produce quality services. When all other factors are equal, price can be used by potential customers as a basis for judging service quality. If two outwardly similar restaurants charge different prices for a similar meal, the presumption may be made that the higher-priced restaurant must offer a higher standard of service, which the customer will subsequently expect to be delivered. Against this benchmark the service delivery will be assessed.

  The price charged can influence the level of quality that a service organization can build into its offering. While any price position along a line from high price/high quality to low price/low quality may be feasible, high price/low quality and low price/high quality positions are not generally sustainable over the long term. As an example, airlines that have attempted to offer high levels of service as well as low prices have often gone bankrupt if they maintained the position for any significant time.

- *Accessibility* decisions can affect customer expectations of quality as well as actual performance. A poor-quality service sold through a high-quality intermediary may give heightened expectations of quality. Poor delivery may subsequently harm the image of the intermediary itself, which partly explains why many travel agents are reluctant to continue to act as intermediaries for tour operators or airlines with poor service quality records. The manner in which an intermediary initiates, processes, and follows up the service delivery process can often affect the perceived quality received by the customer. An agent who incorrectly fills out the departure time for a bus ticket harms the quality of the service that the customer receives. For these reasons, an important element of quality management involves the recruitment and monitoring of a network of intermediaries who are able to share the service principal's commitment to quality standards.

- *Personnel* (more particularly, the "contact personnel") are important elements of consumers' perceptions of functional quality. Therefore, the buyer–seller interaction becomes crucial in the management of service quality. Recruitment, training, motivation, and control of personnel therefore become important elements of the marketing mix, which impacts on quality standards. Those employees who directly perform a service have the best possible vantage point for observing it and are the most able to identify any impediments to its quality. Whether these contact personnel have the ability to articulate these failings is another matter.

CASE STUDY

AT&T GETS A BALDRIGE ON ITS CARDS

In the world of business they have become something like an Oscar or a Pulitzer prize. A Baldrige Award has been trumpeted loudly by organizations that have won one and can help the careers of people who have been associated with the award. The Baldrige Award—known officially as the Malcolm Baldrige National Quality Award—was seen by the Reagan administration as an important incentive in getting American firms up to the quality standards set by overseas competitors. The award is given each year to firms in three categories: large manufacturers, large service organizations, and businesses employing fewer than five hundred people. Since they were launched in 1987, Baldrige Awards have been given to a select number of services organizations, including Federal Express, AT&T's Universal Card division, and Atlanta's Ritz-Carlton Hotel.

What is the value of the Baldrige Award? Winners have been quick to exploit the award in their advertising. In the public mind, the award has come to be associated with high quality. This last point is a misunderstanding of what the Baldrige Award is all about. In fact, the judges concentrate on the processes of a business rather than its outcomes, something that explains why the maker of Cadillac cars received an award in 1990 even though Cadillac came in at a poor seventeenth place in an independent survey of defects per new car. Applicants for the award must carefully follow procedures set out by the Commerce Department's National Institute of Standards and Technology. After reading a 42-page set of instructions, applicants must submit a mass of data about quality controls and processes, leadership, training, and personnel practices—in all, a total of 75 pages of questions and answers. Volunteer examiners then grade all applications, and those scoring 750 or more points out of a possible 1,000 are visited by a team of examiners, who make recommendations to nine judges.

Although recipients of a Baldrige Award have capitalized on it in their advertising, the true value of the award lies in the discipline it inspires within an organization. By forcing its employees to examine their processes and how these processes relate to fulfilling customers' needs, opportunities for bringing about improvements can be identified. In fact, many organizations have adopted the Baldrige procedure as an internal measure for reviewing and improving quality. As an example, AT&T, whose Universal Card unit won an award in 1992, encourages all of its business units to compete for its own internal quality award, which is based on Baldrige. During 1993, 85 percent of its business units applied, and although some of them would have no hope of winning a national award, the process was considered extremely valuable for concentrating managements' attention on quality issues.

The Baldrige Award is not without its critics. Many have pointed to the valuable management time and effort that can be eaten up in the application process, deflecting attention from other important strategic issues. It has been estimated by Corning—whose telecommunications division unsuccessfully applied for an award in 1989—that the process soaked up more than seven thousand man-hours. Winning a Baldrige Award alone does not guarantee financial success. In fact, several previous recipients, such as IBM, have subsequently found themselves in financial difficulty.

As fault-free services become the norm, it has been argued that the kinds of things that Baldrige looks for will become increasingly irrelevant in bringing about market success for an organization. The bureaucratic procedure of the Baldrige process pays little attention to what has been called the "glow and tingle" factor, which causes a customer to choose one service supplier rather than another. Furthermore, in a market where all service suppliers achieve similar levels of consistent quality, competitive advantage will be gained by the firms best able to develop quality relationships with customers that inspire confidence and long-term loyalty.

CASE STUDY REVIEW QUESTIONS

1. In the case of AT&T's Universal Card unit, what do you consider to be the important factors defining service quality?
2. In the context of services, how important is it to measure service processes as distinct from service outcomes?
3. What are likely to be the most important effects on employees of applying for—and winning—a Baldrige award?

6.7 ORGANIZING AND IMPLEMENTING SERVICE QUALITY

Service quality doesn't come about by chance. Organizations need to develop strategies for ensuring that they deliver consistent, high-quality services. Many people have attempted to identify the organizational factors most commonly associated with successful quality management. Research undertaken by Kotler[15] into successful service firms in the United States brought about the following list of key requirements:

1. A strategic concept that is customer focused.
2. A history of commitment by top management to quality—that is, seeing quality indicators as being just as important as financial indicators.
3. Setting high standards and communicating these expected standards to employees.
4. Systems for monitoring performance. Top service firms regularly evaluate their own and their competitors' performances.
5. Systems for satisfying complaining customers. It is important to respond quickly and appropriately to customer complaints.
6. Satisfying employees as well as customers. Successful organizations understand the importance of contact personnel and see an important role for internal marketing—that is, applying the philosophies and practices of marketing to people who serve the external customers so that (1) the best possible people can be employed and retained and (2) they will do the best possible work."[12]

Service personnel have emerged as a key element in the process of quality management. Maintaining a consistent standard of quality in labor-based services becomes very difficult because of the inherent variability of personnel compared with machines. Furthermore, as has already been noted, the inseparability of most services does not generally allow an organization to undertake quality control checks between the points of production and consumption. In this section, strategies to reduce the variability of the human input are examined.

6.7.1 Total Quality Management

Total quality management (TQM) is an approach to improving the effectiveness and flexibility of an organization as a whole. It is a multidisciplinary approach, in that marketing inputs to TQM processes cannot be seen in isolation from issues of operations management and human resource management. Total Quality Management is essentially a means of organizing and involving everybody employed in an organization, in all activities, in all functions, and at all levels. The approach recognizes that the activities of every staff member (including non-contact personnel) have an impact on the quality received by customers. Therefore, an important aim of TQM is to generate a widespread awareness of customer needs among employees, in particular, the standards of quality that are expected by customers.

In addition to focusing on meeting customer requirements effectively, TQM is concerned with the efficiency with which these requirements are met. An important element of TQM, therefore, comprises strategies to reduce waste—defined as anything that neither adds value nor contributes to meeting customer requirements. One target for cost reductions is transaction costs, which are distinguished from production costs and represent the costs of governing production systems, that is, the costs of monitoring and negotiating work contracts and their level of performance.[17] In this way, many services organizations have budgeting procedures that can be slow and cumbersome in responding to changed customer expectations, resulting in greater cost or loss to the organization. For example, a publicly owned leisure center may consider it necessary to upgrade the standards of its facilities in the face of competition from a newly opened privately operated leisure center. Permission to spend the necessary money to improve standards might require prolonged negotiation with senior managers and possibly a committee of the authority. By the time that approval is given for the quality improvement, the competition may have taken away a significant share of its market, representing a transaction cost of not having in place an effective system for TQM.

Total quality management may be introduced as part of a package of other quality initiatives, such as just in time (JIT) production methods to control stock levels, which are now widely employed by the retail sector. Within the services sector, the concept of JIT can be extended to the deployment of staff, whereby extra staff are brought in at short notice to meet peak demands.

Total quality management has many points of congruence with marketing in its internal and external manifestations. It rests upon the generation of an organizational mission or philosophy that encourages all employees and functional areas to regard themselves as providers and customers of other departments. Human resource management policies play a key role in facilitating TQM, for example in the way that total quality training and quality appraisals are incorporated by line areas in their efforts to contribute to overall corporate goals. In this respect, the dissemination and fitting processes of the Harvard and Matching schools (described in Chapter 7) are important.

6.7.2 Quality Circles

Quality circles (QCs) often work within a TQM framework. They consist of small groups of employees who meet together with a supervisor or group leader to discuss their work in terms of production and delivery standards. If quality circles are to be used in the delivery of services, the marketing aims of the service organization must be incorporated into the TQM package and the agenda of the QCs. Quality circles are especially suited to high-contact services in which there is considerable interaction between employees and consumers. Front-line service staff who are in a position to identify quality shortcomings as they impact on customers are brought together with operational staff who may not interact directly with customers but can significantly affect service quality. By sitting down and talking together, employees have an opportunity to jointly recognize and suggest solutions to problems. In this way, a QC run by a car repair business would bring together reception staff, who interact with the public, and mechanics, who produce the substantive service. By analyzing a quality problem identified by the receptionists (e.g., delays in collecting completed jobs), the mechanics might be able to suggest solutions (e.g., rescheduling some work procedures).

To be successful, the QC leader has to be willing to listen to and act upon issues raised by QC members. This is essential if the QC is to be sustained. Circle members must feel that their participation is real and effective; thus, the communication process within the QC must be two-way. If the QC appears to become only a routinized listening session, circle members may consider it to be just another form of managerial control. While circle members might consent to such control, their active participation in processes to improve service quality may be absent.

Members of the QC need speedy and real feedback on ideas they come up with to solve operational problems. When a QC has successfully identified reasons why marketing objectives are not being attained, its suggestions should be commented on in a constructive manner. The effectiveness of QCs can be improved if staff reward mechanisms are linked to performance.

6.7.3 Reducing Dependency on Human Resources

Most service industries contain opportunities to replace potentially variable human inputs with relatively predictable machine-based inputs. While this may result in a loss of customization to meet the needs of individual customers, the quality of service outcomes and processes can generally be made more predictable. At one extreme, human contact personnel can be dispensed with completely (e.g., telephone banking). At the other extreme, equipment is used to moderate the behavior of contact personnel (e.g., scripted computer-generated messages used by airline reservation staff). Personnel replacement policies are considered in more detail in Chapter 7.

CHAPTER REVIEW QUESTIONS

1. Discuss the reasons why quality has become an increasingly important issue in services marketing.
2. In what ways can an airline attempt to measure the quality of its services?
3. Using a not-for-profit organization of your choice, give examples of the methods by which the organization can manage quality.
4. Giving examples, distinguish between the concepts of functional quality and technical quality.
5. Critically assess the usefulness of the SERVQUAL technique for measuring quality in an industry of your choice.
6. In what ways can the personnel input to services be managed in order to achieve more consistent quality standards?

REFERENCES

1. Buzzell, R. D. and Gale, B. T. *The PIMS Principles: Linking Strategy to Performance* (New York: Free Press, 1987).
2. Crosby, P. B. *Quality Without Tears* (New York: New American Library, 1984).
3. Juran, J. M. *Upper Management and Quality* (New York: Juran Institute, 1982).
4. Swan, J. E. and Comb, L. J. "Product Performance and Consumer Satisfaction: A New Concept," *Journal of Marketing* (April 1976): 17–30.
5. Gronroos, C. "A Service Quality Model and Its Marketing Implications," *European Journal of Marketing* 18, no. 4 (1984): 36–43.
6. Zeithaml, V. A., Berry, L. L., and Parasuraman, A. "The Nature and Determinants of Customer Expectations of Service," *Journal of the Academy of Marketing Science* 21, no. 1 (1993): 1–12.
7. Cronin, J. J. and Taylor, S. A. "Measuring Service Quality: A Reexamination and Extension," *Journal of Marketing* 56 (July 1992): 55–68.
8. Babakus, E. and Boller, G. "An Empirical Assessment of the SERVQUAL Scale," *Journal of Business Research* 24 (May 1992): 253–68.
9. Bolton, R., and Drew, J. H. "A Multistage Model of Customers' Assessments of Service Quality and Value," *Journal of Consumer Research* 17, no. 4 (1991): 375–84.
10. Brown, T., Churchill, G., and Peter, J. P. "Research Note: Improving the Measurement of Service Quality," *Journal of Retailing* 69 (spring 1993): 127–39.
11. Parasuraman, A. Zeithaml, V., and Berry, L. "Research Note: More on Improving Service Quality Measurement," *Journal of Retailing* 69 (spring 1993): 127–39.
12. Carman, J. M. "Consumer Perceptions of Service Quality: An Assessment of the SERVQUAL Dimensions," *Journal of Retailing* 66, no. 1 (1990): 33–55.
13. Bolton, R. and Drew, J. "A Multistage Model of Customers' Assessments of Service Quality and Value," *Journal of Consumer Research* 17 (March 1991): 375–84.
14. Churchill, G. and Suprenant, C. "An Investigation into the Determinants of Customer Satisfaction," *Journal of Marketing Research* 19 (November 1982): 491–504.
15. Kotler, P. *Marketing Management: Analysis, Planning, Implementation and Control* (Englewood Cliffs, N.J.: Prentice Hall, 1994).
16. Berry L. L. "Services Marketing is Different," *Business* 30, no. 3 (May/June 1980): 24–9.

17. Williamson, O. *Markets and Hierarchies: Analysis and Antitrust Implications* (New York: The Free Press, 1975).

SUGGESTED FURTHER READING

BOLTON, R. and DREW, J. 1991. "A Multistage Model of Customers' Assessments of Service Quality and Value." *Journal of Consumer Research* 17 (March): 375–84.

BROWN, S. W. and SWARTZ, T. A. 1989. "A Gap Analysis of Professional Service Quality." *Journal of Marketing* (April): 92–8.

CARMAN, J. M. 1990. "Consumer Perceptions of Service Quality: An Assessment of the SERVQUAL Dimensions." *Journal of Retailing* 66 (1): 33–55.

CHURCHILL, G. and SUPRENANT, C. 1982. "An Investigation Into the Determinants of Customer Satisfaction." *Journal of Marketing Research* 19 (November): 491–504.

CINA, C. 1989. "Creating an Effective Customer Satisfaction Program." *Journal of Consumer Marketing* (Fall): 31–40.

CRONIN, J. J. and Taylor, S. A. 1992. "Measuring Service Quality: A Reexamination and Extension." *Journal of Marketing* 56 (July): 55–68.

CROSBY, L. A. 1989. "Maintaining Quality in the Service Relationship" in *Quality in Services*, edited by S. W. Brown and E. Gummesson. Lexington, Mass.: Lexington Books.

CROSBY, P. B. 1984. *Quality Without Tears*. New York: New American Library.

GRONROOS, C. 1984. "A Service Quality Model and Its Marketing Implications." *European Journal of Marketing* 18, no. 4: 36–43.

PARASURAMAN, A., Zeithaml, V., and Berry, L. 1988. "Servqual: A Multiple-Item Scale for Measuring Consumer Perceptions of Service Quality," *Journal of Retailing* 64, no.1: 12–37.

PARASURAMAN, A., ZEITHAML, V. A., and BERRY, L. 1985. "A Conceptual Model of Service Quality and Its Implications for Future Research." *Journal of Marketing* 49 (Fall): 41–50.

ZEITHAML, V. A., PARASURAMAN, A., and BERRY, L. L. 1990. *Delivering Quality Service*. New York: Free Press.

ZEITHAML, V. A., BERRY, L. L., and PARASURAMAN, A. 1993. "The Nature and Determinants of Customer Expectations of Service." *Journal of the Academy of Marketing Science* 21, no. 1: 1–12.

7

Marketing and Human Resource Management

CHAPTER OBJECTIVES

After reading this chapter, you should be able to understand

- the role played by operational personnel in services marketing
- the relationship between personnel performance and service quality
- human resource management policies and their role in improving marketing orientation among personnel
- methods of recruiting, motivating, and controlling service personnel

7.1 INTRODUCTION

The importance of people as a component of the service offer has often been emphasized in this book. Human attributes embed themselves in the service offer in three principal ways:

- Most service production processes require the service organization's own personnel to provide significant inputs to the service production process, both at the front-line point of delivery and in the parts of the production process that are invisible to the final consumer. In many one-to-one personal services, the service provider's own personnel constitute by far the most important element of the total service offer.
- Many service processes require the active involvement of the consumers of a service, and the nature and level of their involvement contributes to the definition of the service offer.

• Other people who simultaneously consume a mass-produced service (e.g., other visitors to a theatre) can affect the nature of the service offer and therefore the benefits that any individual customer receives.

The focus of this chapter is on the first of these categories: personnel employed by the service organization. For most service providers, employees constitute a very important component of the service offering. The management of this input, in terms of recruiting the best personnel and training, motivating, rewarding, and controlling them, becomes crucial in influencing the quality of service output.

Services management has often been described as the bringing together of the principles of marketing, operations management, and human resource management. It can sometimes be difficult—and undesirable—to draw distinctions between the three orientations (Figure 7.1). In this way, methods to improve the service provided by staff of a fast-food restaurant can be seen as a marketing problem (the need to analyze and respond to customer needs for such items as speed and cleanliness), or an operations management problem (scheduling work in a manner that reduces bottlenecks and allows a flexible response to patterns of demand), or a human resource management problem (selecting and motivating staff in a way that maximizes their ability to deliver a specified standard of service that meets identified customer needs).

This chapter analyzes the key marketing-related decisions that services organi-

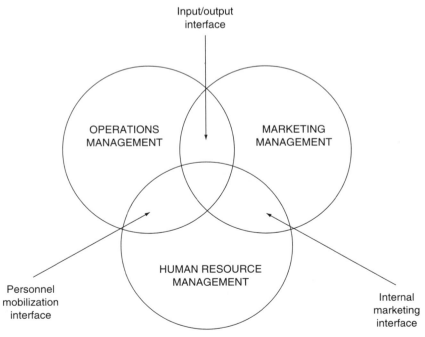

Figure 7.1 The interfaces between marketing management, operations management, and human resource management

zations must make about their employees. A general background to the management of the employment relationship is introduced, with analysis of how this relationship can be managed in order to bring about a greater marketing orientation within services organizations. In analyzing the personnel element of services processes, this chapter returns to many of the issues first discussed in Chapters 4 and 6, where the service offer was defined, especially in the all-important area of service quality.

7.2 THE IMPORTANCE OF PERSONNEL TO THE SERVICE OFFERING

It can be almost a cliché to say that for some businesses, the employees *are* the business. If they are taken away, the organization is left with very few assets to enable it to gain competitive advantage in meeting customers' needs. In some organizations, personnel can be seen as just another asset to be managed; in other organizations, human resource management is so central to the activities of the organization that it cannot be seen as a separate activity from marketing. Some indication of the importance attached to human resource management within any organization can be gained by examining two aspects of a firm's personnel:

1. the proportion of total costs that are represented by personnel costs
2. the importance within the service offer of personnel encounters with customers

In Figure 7.2 these two dimensions of personnel significance are shown in a matrix form with examples. In human resource management, the most critical group of services is found where personnel account for a high proportion of total costs and form an important part of the service offer perceived by consumers. Many personal services, such as hairdressing, fall into this category. In other cases, personnel costs may be a small proportion of total costs but the employees may significantly affect consumers' perceptions of a service. In this way, personnel costs are typically a relatively small proportion of the costs of a telephone service, yet the performance of key front-line staff, such as telephone operators or service engineers, can significantly affect judgements of quality.

The human input to services can by its nature be highly variable, resulting in variability of output. For this reason, many service organizations have replaced personnel with equipment-based inputs, which often results in fewer but more highly trained personnel being required. Equipment-based personnel replacement strategies are discussed later in this chapter.

The importance attached to human resource management is also a reflection of the competitiveness of the environment in which an organization operates. At one extreme, the highly competitive environment that faces American fast-food restaurants requires organizations to ensure that their staff meet customers' needs for speed, friendliness, and accuracy more effectively than do their competitors. On the other hand, organizations with relatively protected markets, such as many government services, can afford to be less customer led in their management of human resources.

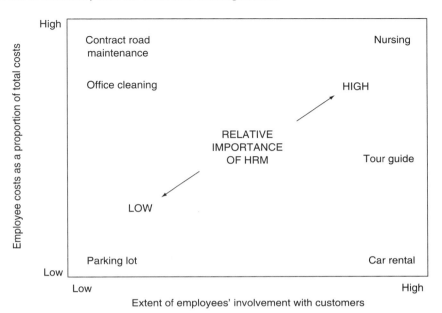

Figure 7.2   The importance of personnel within the service offer

7.3 *WHAT IS MEANT BY HUMAN RESOURCE MANAGEMENT?*

The employees of a service organization are a resource that should be effectively managed if the organization's corporate goals are to be achieved. In much the same way they develop strategic plans in relation to the markets they serve, organizations should also develop strategic plans to develop their human resources. In labor-intensive, market-oriented service organizations, the development of human resource management plans must be closely linked to marketing plans. This section considers in general terms what is meant by human resource management and how it relates to marketing management.

Human resource management (HRM) is concerned with the deployment and provision of human resources. At a strategic level, two broad approaches have been identified: the matching school and the Harvard school.[1] The former, based on the work of Formbrun,[2] focuses on the importance of establishing a close fit between HRM and business strategy, viewing HRM as something that is "done" to employees in order to achieve predefined business goals. By contrast, the Harvard model[3] focuses on the crucial importance of involving the general managers in the dissemination of an organization's central mission to all employees. The role of employees in delivering this mission is crucial; without this dissemination, HRM would be seen as merely a set of independent specialist activities without a strategic business contribution. Strategic integration and improved quality are seen as outcomes of strategic HRM. Therefore, recruitment, selection, appraisal, development, and participation are not considered narrowly as component parts of personnel activity but are seen as parts of corporate strategy that contribute to marketing effectiveness.

Human resource management can be contrasted with the more traditional personnel management, which is often seen as being isolated and separate from the business aims of firms. Personnel management has frequently been oriented toward control and administrative activities rather than the alignment of human resources toward achieving strategic organizational goals. Consequently, personnel management has often become too concerned with achieving its own set of subgoals, which are not necessarily related to the marketing needs of an organization. In this way, the maintenance of a uniform pay structure may have been seen as a desirable objective in its own right by personnel managers even though the marketing needs of an organization may require more flexibility in the manner of paying staff.

7.3.1 Soft and Hard HRM Compared

In the context of services organizations, an important distinction can be made between what has come to be known as "hard" HRM and "soft" HRM.[4] Hard HRM is primarily concerned with the economic outcomes of a business, typically measured in terms of efficiency and worker productivity. Where a worker's tangible output can be measured, piecework payment methods are a form of hard HRM.

Soft HRM, on the other hand, emphasizes the importance to organizations of seeing their employees as essential assets to be developed. Such an approach also entails encouraging employees to participate within the organization. By participating, employees begin to identify with corporate goals and to see how their functions contribute to these goals. Soft HRM also facilitates the process of change within an organization. For service industries where workers produce their service in full view of their customers, it may be inappropriate to treat workers as economic objects that simply turn inputs into outputs. Their customers are concerned with workers' commitment to doing their job with a smile, something that can be facilitated with soft HRM policies.

7.3.2 HRM and Its Relationship to Marketing

The role of marketing, above all else, is to achieve organizational goals by satisfying customers' needs. Human resources management is concerned with achieving organizational goals. It therefore follows that HRM must itself be concerned with satisfying the needs of external customers. Within services organizations, HRM has three client groups which it must deal with efficiently if it is not to remain distinct and independent from marketing:

- Employees. For example, HRM concerns itself with recruiting and motivating staff and may direct internal marketing efforts toward employees.
- Senior management. In all functional areas, senior management must be aware of the way HRM contributes to both management activities and the overall success of the organization. The HRM contribution is the central message of the Harvard model of HRM.

- External groups. The external public includes prospective employees and, more indirectly, potential customers, intermediaries, and other interested groups such as pressure groups and government regulatory bodies. An organization may be able to accomplish its objectives with respect to each of these groups only if it has succeeded in managing its human resources effectively.

Success for the HRM function requires that it demonstrate its central significance to overall corporate goals. It therefore must integrate itself with other functions. In services marketing, such integration has to revolve around the consumer and has three elements:

- Identifying with client needs. The HRM department must work backward from the position of the client or customer and support the marketing effort by such means as the recruitment and training of staff who are most able to satisfy customers' needs. The marketing function can itself feed back information to the HRM function through regular monitoring surveys of customer satisfaction. Such data can be used in staff appraisal schemes and integrated into the organization's total quality management processes.
- Follow-up and evaluation. The activities of HRM must be evaluated against performance and their contribution to corporate goals. For example, an analysis of reasons for low levels of repeat business might show that telephone sales staff have a poor level of sales skills. This may suggest a need to improve the training given to them.
- Organizational gain. The activities of all functional areas, including HRM, should contribute to overall organizational gain. If this is not the case, an activity should be terminated or amended. This may cause some ill feeling between people in different functions if they do not take a global view of their contribution to the success of an organization.

7.4 MOTIVATION, CONSENT, AND INVOLVEMENT

Motivation, consent, and participation form essential focal points for an organization's HRM strategy. In HRM the emphasis is on the individual employee and his or her importance to the organization. This importance cannot be made real unless employees feel motivated to share organizational goals.

Motivation concerns the choices that employees make between alternative forms of behavior in order to attain their own personal goals. The task of management is to equate the individual's personal goals with those of the employing organization—that is, getting employees morally involved with the service they help to produce. This in turn requires employees to consent to the management of their work activities. When this consent is obtained, employees can be motivated by some form of participation in the organization. Such participation gives the employee a small stake in the organization, be it financial or in the form of discretionary control over the performance of their work function.

Understanding what motivates an employee to perform well is particularly important where service employees are under the constant view of customers.

7.4.1 Motivation

Motivation concerns goals and rewards. Maslow[5] has argued that motivation is based on individuals' desire to satisfy various levels of need. These levels range from the need to realize potential and develop the self to basic needs such as hunger, thirst, and sex. The rewards for reaching goals can be tangible (money) or intangible (commendations or awards that add to status or self-esteem). Through an appropriate motivation package, an organization can bring about a congruence between its own goals and those of its employees. For example, a bank should not reward its tellers solely on the number and accuracy of the daily transactions if the bank wants to offer fast, accurate, friendly service. Instead, the bank will need to design a motivation package that rewards speed, accuracy, and friendliness. The components of the package might include both direct financial awards (a bonus) and recognition (a handwritten note from the president of the bank).

In many service industries employing low-wage, part-time employees, raising pay levels will probably not increase their motivation to work if their primary motive for doing the job is to get out of the house and meet people. Redesigning the service production process may achieve greater motivation by involving the employee directly. For example, employees may experience role overload (excessive contact with too many customers). Instituting frequent breaks and variation in work tasks may reduce the feelings of overload and motivate employees to work toward the corporate goals.

7.4.2 Consent

The term *consent* covers a variety of management-led initiatives and strategies that support management's authority without actively emphasizing its coercive power. For many services provided on a one-to-one basis, direct monitoring and supervision of employees by management may be impossible to achieve. Active consent is therefore of great use to the management of services organizations.

During the twentieth century, various forms of employee participation and involvement have been designed to aid management in the generation of consent. Such initiatives include scientific management, industrial management, the human relations approach, welfare, paternalism, professionalized and proceduralized personnel management, and, more recently, HRM. Each initiative has its own prescription for the generation of consent.

Scientific management approaches seek cooperation between employer and employee in terms of the division of labor, when employees work in narrowly defined work roles as directed by management. Advocates of scientific management saw mutual benefits for the employee and employer. Specializing in one work activity gives employees the opportunity to earn more, especially through piece-rate pay systems. Assigning employees to one work activity gives management greater work control and higher productivity. However, such work assignments may also generate employee hostility to what is often described as de-skilling. Within the services sector, many attempts have been made to de-skill jobs in accordance with the scientific management prescription. However, it is necessary to balance the benefits of specialization and improved efficiency against employees' sense of alienation from their jobs, which occurs when they are involved in only a very small part of a total service delivery process. Scientific management might suggest that a restaurant could be operated most efficiently by having specialist staff separately responsible for order taking, meal delivery, beverages, and payment. However, a much greater sense of involvement from employees may occur if staff are trained to be able to deliver to each customer the whole service from beginning to end.

Paternalism is associated with attempts by employers to show that they are interested in the welfare of their workforce at home as well as at work. Many employers take a paternalistic attitude toward their employees by providing such benefits as on-site child care services, temporary accommodation for their employees, and subsidized health and fitness clubs. These are designed to encourage employee identification with the company, and therefore loyalty, which legitimizes managerial authority and hence employees' consent to it.

In contrast to the economically based consent strategies of scientific management, the human relations approach looks at people as social animals. Mayo's study of General Electric argued that productivity was unrelated to work organization and economic rewards as suggested by scientific management.[6] Instead, he emphasized the importance of atmosphere, social attitudes, group feelings, and employees' sense of identification. He suggested that separation of employees, which scientific management had created, prevented them from experiencing the sense of identification and involvement that is essential for all humans. One solution was to design group structures into production processes.

Mayo's work is similar in focus to that of Herzberg, who suggested that humans have lower- and higher order needs. The former are the basic economic needs of food and shelter, whereas the latter are more psychologically based in terms of recognition and contribution to the group and organization.

All the management initiatives and strategies described in this section are in part efforts to generate employee consent to management authority without management exercising its authority by way of coercion (Figure 7.3).

7.4.3 Moral Involvement

Moral involvement refers to a mechanism that allows employees to identify with the corporate goals of their employer and relay their feelings about these goals back to management. For this to happen, employees need some institutional process through which, directly or indirectly, they can voice their concerns over decisions that affect them. Within the service sector, employees who feel morally involved with the work of their employer are more likely to put the company and its customers' interests first when there is a potential clash with their own interests.

Mechanisms to develop moral involvement are closely related to policies that generate consent. Mechanisms can operate collectively, as with collective bargaining or through consultation with employees on decisions made by management. Alternatively, moral involvement can be developed individually, through quality circles, team briefings, appraisals or the open door policies encouraged by the human relations approach.

Alfred Satterfield,
Volunteer Social Worker

"I hope that in the end they'll say, 'Al did his part.' "

Alfred Satterfield,
Department Manager, Roxboro, NC

"Customers come here, not just for the low prices, but because they know we care. I want people to leave here knowing that I did my best to help!"

© 1994 WAL·MART

Caring and Low Prices. We go the distance... **WAL★MART** *Always*

Figure 7.3 In this ad, Wal-Mart communicates to its customers that its employees go the extra distance to help. It also increases department managers' motivation through recognition of outstanding performance. Source: Wal-Mart Stores, Inc., Bentonville, AR.

CASE STUDY

HAMPTON INNS GUARANTEES SATISFACTION FOR CUSTOMERS— EMPLOYEES COME TO LIKE IT TOO

The importance of linking personnel practices to total quality management is quite clearly seen in the rapid and successful growth of the Hampton Inns hotel chain. Founded in 1987, it had grown five years later to a nationwide chain of over two hundred hotels operating in forty states. To maintain its growth, the company had to tackle two major but closely related problems:

- First, it had to maintain a standard of quality as good as that of any other hotel in the sector. With an increasingly large operation, there was a danger that Hampton Inns might become too large to be able to pay attention to the small details that discerning customers look for. The company wanted to develop loyalty from its customers based on their satisfaction with quality.
- Second, Hampton Inns faced an industry-wide problem of trying to retain staff. Individuals typically showed little loyalty to their employer and moved quickly to other hotels offering better wages or working conditions.

In 1989, Hampton Inns became the first major chain to offer an unconditional 100 percent satisfaction guarantee to all its customers. Customers who had an unresolved problem or complaint during their stay would be given one night's free accommodation. When customers invoke the guarantee, their complaints are analyzed at the company's Memphis headquarters. From this, the company learns a lot about how well it is meeting customers' expectations. Wherever it is found to be failing, practices can be changed across the entire chain.

From a management perspective, the customer guarantee could be made to work only through the efforts of its staff. Crucial to this process was the empowerment that the company gave all employees to take whatever action they considered necessary to keep customers satisfied. This empowerment extended not just to hotel managers or front-desk personnel but to all staff who might come into contact with guests. For example, a housekeeper might notice that a guest was having trouble getting the room key to fit. Rather than referring the guest to reception for the problem to be resolved, the housekeeper was expected to take responsibility for resolving the problem, for example, by getting a new key or having a new lock installed. If the guest still wasn't happy with the resolution of the problem, the housekeeper was empowered to refund the cost of the hotel room without having to explain the problem again to the manager.

Such empowerment is not what most housekeepers would expect in a job. Similarly, most employers have traditionally looked on hourly paid staff as employees hired to do a simple job—management were paid to do the thinking. The hourly paid staff at Hampton Inns did not at first see themselves as trouble-shooting problem solvers. Clearly, training was needed to bring about a change in values.

Before launching the customer service guarantee, the company conducted training seminars at each of its hotels. The seminar leaders explained how all employees should view their jobs in the wider context of providing total customer satisfaction, rather than seeing themselves merely as housekeepers or handymen. Although the company tried to explain that the traditional rule book had been thrown away and that employees were expected to use their own initiative, this met some resistance at first. Many employees felt uncomfortable not knowing what the rules were. Would the company actually stand by their decisions, whatever the consequences? Managers felt uncomfortable too. Would their authority be usurped by this freedom given to employees? How could managers hope to maintain discipline when employees had been told to break the rules? If they reported too many customer complaints to headquarters, or gave away too many free nights, wouldn't this make them look like bad managers in the eyes of the company?

Given these comments from its employees, the company revamped its training program to emphasize that the company would stand behind any decision made by employees that was made with customer satisfaction first and foremost in mind. Managers were also won over. They came to see that the payoff for this uncomfortable cultural change would be greater loyalty from customers and a competitive advantage over rivals. They were convinced that the effect of giving out for free nights need not harm their bottom line. The strategy was sold on the basis that it would ensure increases in revenue over the longer term.

One year after the introduction of the customer guarantee, marketing research identified several benefits. Two percent of its customers said that they stayed at Hampton Inns specifically because of the guarantee it offered. Set against this, the guarantee was invoked for less than 0.1 percent of total room nights. Research showed that when customers had invoked the guarantee before leaving the hotel, the overwhelming majority said they would return to a Hampton Inn, and nearly half of them actually had. The company also noticed an improvement in the retention of its employees. A survey of staff had shown that they now felt more motivated and enthusiastic about their jobs. While it wasn't clear whether empowerment had caused this lower turnover rate, it was quite evident that it had caused them to work harder at satisfying guests' needs and to pay more attention to quality on the job.

CASE STUDY REVIEW QUESTIONS

1. What other factors not mentioned in this case study do you consider to be important in achieving a commitment to quality from Hampton Inn's employees?
2. What is meant by total quality management in the context of Hampton Inns?
3. Why do you think so many hotels specify their employees' roles much more narrowly?

7.5 THE FLEXIBLE FIRM

It was noted in Chapter 4 that demand for many services can be highly variable, with peaks and troughs that can be daily, weekly, annual, seasonal, cyclical, or unpredictable in pattern. Various methods of managing demand have been suggested in previous chapters, including differential pricing to encourage off-peak consumption and reformulating the service offer to provide added benefits during off-peak periods. On the supply side, great importance is attached to the flexible management of service personnel in such a way that they can respond rapidly to meet changes in the volume of service demand.

As well as being able to achieve short-term flexibility, services organizations must also have longer-term flexibility to shift their human resources from areas in decline to those where there is a prospect of future growth. For example, in order to retain its profitability, a bank must be able to move personnel away from relatively static activities such as cash handling and basic checking toward the more profitable growth area of financial services.

Flexibility within a service organization can be achieved by segmenting the workforce into core and peripheral components. Core workers have greater job security and have defined career opportunities within an internal labor market. In return for this job security, core workers may have to accept what has been called functional flexibility,[7] in that they become responsible for a variety of job tasks. As part of a hard HRM approach, the work output of this group is intensified. In order for this to be successful, employees must be effectively trained and motivated. Finally, methods must be found to encourage employee participation in descision making.

Peripheral employees, on the other hand, have less job security and limited career opportunities. These employees are numerically flexible, while financial flexibility is brought about through the process of distancing. In this situation, a firm

may utilize the services and skills of specialist labor but acquire it through a commercial contract rather than an employment contract. This process is referred to as
subcontracting. The principal characteristics of the flexible firm are illustrated in
Figure 7.4.

As a strategic tool, the model of the flexible firm has important implications
for services organizations that experience fluctuating demand. However, critics of the
concept suggest that the strategic role attributed to the flexibility model is often illu-
sory, with many organizations introducing "flexibility" in very much an opportunis-
tic manner.[8]

7.6 MANAGING THE EMPLOYMENT RELATIONSHIP

Attention is now given to the application of several important principles of human
resource management referred to above. For example, service providers recognize
that methods of recruiting, selecting, training, and rewarding staff impact on their
marketing activities.

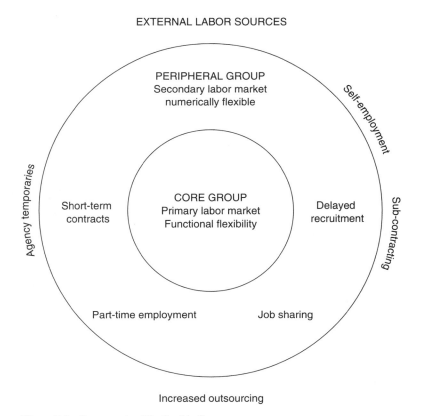

Figure 7.4   Components of the flexible firm

7.6.1 Recruitment

Recruitment is the process by which an organization secures its human resources. Traditionally the recruitment function has been performed by personnel specialists who are removed from line management. Current HRM practice favors the integration of the recruitment function into the line areas where a potential employee will be working.

The focus of recruitment activity is to attract (and preferably retain) the right employee for the right job within the organization. Clearly, the recruitment process is intimately linked to that of selection. The process of selection (to be described) concerns how potential recruits are tested in terms of the job and person specifications.

In order to recruit the right personnel, service organizations must carefully consider just what they want from particular employees. For example, tour operators recruiting representatives to work in overseas resorts recognize that academic qualifications are not in themselves important in new recruits. Instead, the ability to work under pressure, to empathize with clients, to work in groups, and to be able to survive for long periods without sleep may be identified from previous experience as characteristics that allow representatives to perform their tasks in a manner that meets customers' expectations.

Five principal recruitment tasks can be identified:

- development of recruitment policies
- establishment of routine recruitment procedures
- establishment of job descriptions
- development of a person specification
- advertising of job vacancies

Traditionally, all five areas have been considered to be the preserve of the personnel department. Within an HRM approach, recruitment policies, job descriptions, and person specifications can all become the responsibility—at least in part—of line managers, largely on the grounds that they are better able to understand the needs of the organization.

7.6.2 Selection

The recruitment process is concerned with attracting enough appropriate candidates for potential selection. The process of selection is concerned with identifying and employing the most suitable candidate. Six key tasks within the selection process can be identified:

- examining candidates' resumes
- short-listing candidates
- inviting candidates for interviews
- interviewing and testing candidates

- choosing a candidate for employment
- offering and confirming the employment

As with the process of recruitment, the preinterview selection, short-listing, interviewing, and choosing of a candidate can all be wholly or in part delegated to the line areas. Again, it is argued that line managers are closer to understanding the requirements of a job and can use previous experience in selecting new recruits.

7.6.3 Training and Development

Hard HRM emphasizes labor as a factor of production to be used as effectively as any other input. This effective use of labor can be attained in a variety of ways, for example, by forcing labor to become more flexible or to work more intensively. However, there is a danger that this process might cause labor to become alienated and poorly motivated. Soft HRM, on the other hand, emphasizes the need to train and develop labor as the organization's most valuable asset. Both soft and hard HRM are concerned with the corporate aims of efficiency and profitability. The most effective organizations are those that can use elements of soft HRM in order to ensure that they do in fact get the economic benefits of hard HRM. Therefore, the two dimensions of HRM are not mutually exclusive but highly integrated, with soft HRM operating as the front end of hard HRM. Training and development are essential elements within the process of ensuring effective economic performance by employees.

Training refers to the acquisition of the specific knowledge and skills that enable employees to perform their jobs effectively. The focus of staff training, therefore, is the job. In contrast to this, staff development concerns activities that are directed to the future needs of the employee, which may themselves be derived from the future needs of the organization. For example, workers may need to become familiar with personal computers, fax machines, and other aspects of information technology that as yet are not elements within their own specific job requirements.

Appropriate training is essential if any process of change is to be actively consented to by the workforce. Initially, an awareness training program may be used to communicate the nature of change to the workforce as a precursor to the actual changes. This may involve making employees aware of the competitive market pressures that the organization faces and how it proposes to address them. An opportunity may be taken to allow employees to make their views known and to air any concerns they might have. This can help to generate some moral involvement in the process of change and could itself be the precursor to an effective participation forum.

If marketing is to be integrated into the jobs of all employees, so that everybody becomes a "part-time marketer," marketing managers cannot merely state this need at strategic HRM meetings. It is also essential to develop programs by which such strategies can be operationalized. In many cases, it may be possible to identify tasks appropriate for different people within the organization. For example, bank tellers might be required to learn about specific financial services offered by the bank and to be able to make appropriate suggestions of service offers to customers.

Failure to develop general sales skills and disseminate knowledge of specific services available could result not only in lost sales opportunities but in a feeling of alienation by tellers who haven't been given the training to allow them to do a job that is expected of them.

A practical problem facing many services organizations that allocate large budgets to staff training is that many other organizations in their sector may spend very little, relying on staff being stolen from the company doing the training. This occurs, for example, within the banking sector, where many smaller banks have created new facilities using the skills of staff attracted from the major banks. The problem also occurs in many construction-related industries and in the car repair business.

The ease with which an organization can lose trained staff may be one reason to explain the reluctance of many U.S. companies to spend money on training and development. However, policies can be adopted to maximize the benefits of such expenditure to the organization. Above all else, training and development should be linked to broader soft HRM policies, which have the effect of generating longer-term loyalty by employees. Judged by hard HRM policies alone, training can be seen as a short-term risky activity that adds relatively little to the long-term profitability of an organization.

When soft HRM policies alone are insufficient to retain trained staff, an organization may attempt to retain an individual by seeking reimbursement of any expenditure if the employee leaves the organization within a specified time. Reimbursement is most likely to be sought when the expenditure was aimed at developing the general abilities of an individual rather than ability to perform a functional and organizational specific task. An organization might therefore try to recover the cost of supporting an individual to undertake an MBA program, but not a product-specific sales training course.

An organization that is an industry leader may have no alternative but to accept a certain level of waste in return for maintaining a constant competitive advantage over other organizations. In this way, the Marriott hotel chain provides a level of training that is highly praised within the hotel sector. A manager or receptionist who is trained by Marriott can readily find employment with a competitor. Against such potential loss, the Marriott chain enjoys a very good reputation with guests. This in turn has allowed it to position itself as a high-quality service provider, removing much of the need for price discounting, which has harmed many of its rivals.

7.6.4 Career Development

Another mechanism that can assist an organization in its goals of recruiting and retaining staff is a clearly defined career progression pathway. In Atkinson's model,[7] this mechanism is more relevant to core employees than to the large number of "peripheral" workers (catering assistants, part-time shop assistants, hotel housekeeping staff), to whom short-term reward systems are likely to be greater motivators than the possibility of career progression.

Career progression refers to a mechanism that enables an employee to visualize how his or her working life might develop within a particular organization. Clearly defined expectations of what an individual employee should be able to achieve within an organization, and clear statements of promotion criteria, can be helpful. Additionally, the creation and use of an internal labor market—for instance, through counseling and the dissemination of job vacancy details—can be vital. An organization can introduce vertical job ladders or tenure-based remuneration and promotion programs to assist in the retention of core employees.

During periods of scarcity among the skilled labor force, offers of defined career paths may become essential if the right caliber of staff are to be recruited and retained. As an example, many retailers that had previously operated relatively casual employment policies introduced career structures for the first time during the tight labor market of the mid-1980s. Conversely, during the period of recession that followed, it became very difficult for employers to maintain their promises, and the consequence was a demotivational effect on staff. In this way, the fall in profitability of branch banking in the United States in the early 1990s has brought about considerable disillusionment among core bank employees, who see their career progression prospects made considerably more difficult than they had expected, despite good work performance.

7.6.5 Rewarding Staff

The process of staff recruitment, and more crucially the retention of staff, is directly influenced by the quality of rewards offered. The central purpose of a reward system is to improve the standard of staff performance by giving employees something they consider to be of value in return for good performance. What employees consider to be a good reward is influenced by the nature of the motivators that drive each individual. Therefore, a standardized reward system is unlikely to achieve maximum motivation among a large and diverse workforce.

Rewards to employees can be divided into two categories: nonmonetary and monetary. Nonmonetary rewards cover a wide range of benefits, some of which will be a formal part of the reward system—for example, subsidized housing or sports facilities or public recognition for work achievement (as where staff are given diplomas signifying their level of achievement). At other times, nonmonetary rewards could be informal and represent something of a hidden agenda for management. In this way, a loyal, long-standing restaurant waiter may be rewarded by being given a relatively easy schedule of work that eliminates unpopular Saturday nights.

The soft HRM approach does not recognize these nonmonetary benefits as being part of a narrowly defined reward system. Instead, they are seen as going to the root of the relationship between staff and employer. Subsidized sports facilities are not merely a reward but part of a total work environment that encourages consent, moral involvement, and participation by the workforce. When informal nonmonetary rewards are part of a hidden agenda, the soft HRM approach would see them as being potentially harmful to the employment relationship by reducing the level of consent from the workforce at large.

Monetary rewards are a more direct method of improving the performance of employees, and they form an important element of hard HRM policy. In the absence of well-developed soft HRM policies, monetary rewards can form the principal motivator for employees. Several methods are commonly used in the services sector to reward employees financially:

- Basic hourly wages are used to reward large numbers of "peripheral" workers, who are generally rewarded according to their inputs rather than their outputs. In comparison with the manufactured goods sector, it is generally more difficult to measure service outcomes and to use them as a basis for payment. Nevertheless, such measurement sometimes occurs. Delivery drivers employed by a pizza restaurant may, for instance, be paid a fixed amount for each pizza delivered. Paying employees by the number of completed tasks can have potentially harmful effects on customers. The delivery driver who is paid solely on the basis of the number of pizzas delivered may concentrate on delivering them as quickly as possible but with little regard for driving safely or courtesy with people.
- A fixed salary is more commonly paid to the core workers of an organization. Sometimes the fixed salary is related to length of service. As well as being administratively simple, a fixed salary avoids the problems of trying to assess individuals' eligibility for bonuses, which can be especially difficult when employees work in teams.
- A fixed annual salary plus a variable commission is commonly paid to service personnel who are actively involved in selling. A problem for organizations that use this approach is that a sales person who aims to maximize his or her commission earnings is often not involved in the service production and delivery process and therefore is not in a position to maximize customer satisfaction and secure repeat business. When service production employees are in fact involved in selling (many restaurant waiting staff), this form of payment can be a motivator to good service delivery as well as increasing sales.
- Performance-related pay (PRP) systems are assuming increasing importance within the services sector. These systems seek to link some percentage of an employee's pay directly to his or her work performance. In some ways, PRP represents a movement toward the individualization of pay.

  A key element in any PRP system is the appraisal of individual employees' performance. The outputs of some workers can be quantified relatively easily. For example, most bank managers' performance-related pay is based partly on the level of new accounts opened. More qualitative aspects of job performance are much more difficult to appraise—for example, the quality of advice given by doctors or dentists. Qualitative assessment raises questions about which dimensions of job performance are to be considered important in the exercise and who is to undertake the appraisal. If appraisal is not handled sensitively, employees could suspect that it is a means of rewarding some individuals according to a hidden agenda. Many services industries also have the problem that service outcomes are the result of joint activity by several employees; therefore, the team may be a more appropriate unit for appraisal than the individual employee.

  Nevertheless, some form of performance-related pay is generally of great use to services organizations. It can allow greater management control and—if linked to appropriate performance measurement methods—can enable management to quickly identify good or bad performers. If handled appropriately, it can also assist in the generation of consent and moral involvement because employees will have a direct interest in their own performance.

- Profit-sharing plans can operate as a supplement to the basic wage or salary and can assist in the generation of employee loyalty through greater commitment. Employees can be made members of a trust fund set up by their employer so that a percentage of profits are held in trust on behalf of employees, subject to agreed eligibility criteria. Profit-sharing plans have the advantage of encouraging staff involvement in their organization. Such plans, however, have a major disadvantage: profits may fall because of some external factor such as an economic recession, despite employees' most committed efforts. There is also debate about whether profit-sharing really acts as a motivator to better performance in large companies or merely becomes part of basic pay expectations. In the United States, a good example of a profit-sharing plan is provided by the retailer Wal-Mart, which, despite paying relatively low wages, achieves high levels of employee loyalty. One of the reasons is its practice of paying profit-related stock into a trust fund that employees can cash in when they leave the company. Long-serving employees have been known to leave with payments of several hundred thousand dollars.

- In many services organizations, an important element of the financial reward is derived from outside the formal contract of employment. In particular, many employees expect tipping by customers in return for good service. The acknowledgment of tipping by employers puts greater pressure on front-line service staff to perform well and in principle puts the burden of appraisal directly on the consumer of a service. It also reduces the level of basic wage expected by employees. Against this, reliance on tipping poses some problems. Support personnel may be important contributors to the quality of service received by customers but may receive none of the benefits of tipping received by front-line staff. A chef may be an important element of the benefit received by a restaurant customer, but tipping tends to emphasize the quality of the final delivery system. On the other hand, attempts to institutionalize tipping by levying service charges and sharing proceeds among all service staff may reduce individual motivation. A fixed service charge also reduces the ability of consumers to tip on the basis of perceived quality. A further problem of reliance on tipping is that customers might be put off by the prospect of feeling obliged to pay a tip. For this reason many service providers prohibit their employees from receiving tips. While customers from some cultures—such as the United States—readily accept the principle of tipping, others—including the British—are more ambivalent. In the public sector, attempts at tipping are often viewed as a form of bribery.

CASE STUDY

MORE MANAGED HEALTH CARE SYSTEMS USE INCENTIVE PAY TO REWARD "BEST DOCTORS"

"I'm a doctor with professional ethics, not an entertainer to be judged by uninformed observers," commented one New Jersey doctor about attempts to measure his performance.

He was reacting to the debate in the United States over health care. By the late 1980s, this seemed to be running out of control, with few checks on costs and even less on value for money.

People with traditional health insurance policies are able to choose their own doctors and pass on the bill to their insurers. Because individuals do not pay the bill (except for any deductible), they are not too concerned with assessing value for money. Partly for this reason, health insurance policies were getting more and more expensive for employers to buy, forcing many to turn to an alternative method of delivering health care services: health maintenance organizations (HMOs).

Health maintenance organizations collect premiums from employers, in return for which they provide specified health care facilities for the firm's employees. However, employees are not free to choose any doctor they wish; instead, they must consult a doctor who has been contracted by the HMO. Payments to contracting doctors vary between HMOs, but they have traditionally been on the basis of either a fixed fee per patient per year or a fee per visit. Doctors typically expect to have five-thousand patients on their lists—a single HMO may account for half of these. U.S. Healthcare, Inc. is one of a growing number of HMOs that has introduced an incentive plan to the way it pays its doctors. Each year, it surveys its subscribing members to see how they like their doctors, and it links doctors' payments to these results. In 1992, its doctors received performance bonuses that averaged 15 percent.

Among the questions that the company uses in its questionnaire for assessing doctors' performance are these:

- How easy is it to make appointments for checkups?
- How long is the waiting time in a doctor's office?
- How much personal concern does the doctor show?
- How readily can patients follow up test results?
- Would patients recommend their doctor to others?

In addition, the company monitors the percentage of each doctor's patients who transfer to another doctor during the course of the year.

Incentive pay plans for doctors are gaining popularity, spurred by a belief that they may help upgrade the quality of medical care provided by HMOs and other managed care programs. However, some questions have been raised about the legitimacy of this approach. Skeptics don't like the idea of basing incentives on patients' sense of "quality," arguing that patients rely too much on fringe issues such as a receptionist's attitude or a doctor's punctuality. The skeptics would prefer to see assessment based on more sophisticated studies of illnesses, treatments, and patient outcomes—something much more difficult to evaluate.

Another problem often raised is that individual doctor's incentive payments can disrupt their ability to work together in a collegial way. The Harvard Community Health Plan is typical of HMOs that introduced and then withdrew incentive plans following arguments between doctors about the size of their respective bonuses. Another group of skeptics argue that where incentive payment schemes have been introduced for doctors, they have had only a short-term effect on doctors' behavior.

The methods used by HMOs to monitor the quality and costs of their doctors have received considerable attention in the debate about the spiraling costs of health care in the United States. Many advocates of incentive payment plans hope that current shortcomings can be remedied by more sophisticated measuring systems and that this will help allow HMOs to play an increasing role in health care in the United States.

CASE STUDY REVIEW QUESTIONS

1. What are the marketing benefits of attempting to measure the performance of doctors? If you were a marketing manager for an HMO, how would you like to see doctors appraised?
2. What part do you think ethics play in determining doctors' performance? Do you think performance assessment is really within the domain of marketing management?
3. Other professional groups—e.g., lawyers, professors, engineers, and architects—should perhaps institute performance appraisals. If you were a marketing manager for an organization housing one of these professional groups, how would you evaluate the organization members' professional performance? What marketing benefits would you see from instituting routine appraisals? What resistance would you expect to encounter in implementing an appraisal system?

7.6.6 *Monitoring and Controlling Staff*

When production methods are based largely on human inputs, the control of the workforce assumes primary importance as a means of controlling service quality. The problem of control is particularly great with service industries, as it is usually not possible to remove the results of poor employee performance before their effects are felt by customers. While the effects of a poorly performing car worker can be concealed from customers by checking his or her tangible output, the inseparability of the service production/consumption process makes quality control difficult to achieve for services.

Control systems are closely related to reward systems in that pay can be used to control performance. For example, bonuses can be forfeited if performance falls below a specified standard. In addition, warnings, or ultimately dismissal, form part of a control system. In an ideal service organization with a well-developed soft HRM policy, employees' involvement in their work should lead to considerable self-control or informal control from their peer group. Where such policies are less well developed, three principal types of control are used: simple, technical, and bureaucratic controls.

*   Simple controls are typified by direct personal supervision of personnel. For example, a headwaiter can maintain a constant watch over junior waiters and directly influence performance when it deviates from standard.
*   Technical controls can be built into the service production process in order to monitor individuals' performance. For example, a supermarket check-out can measure the speed of individual operators and control action (e.g., training or redeployment) taken toward those shown to fall below standard.
*   Bureaucratic controls require employees to document their performance. For example, a service engineer can complete work sheets of visits made and jobs completed. Control action can be initiated toward employees who on paper appear to be underperforming.

In addition to these internal controls, the relationship that many front-line service personnel develop with their customers allows customers to exercise a degree of informal control. A university professor teaching a class wishes to avoid, in most cases, the hostility from the class that might result from a consistently poor standard of performance. In other words, the class can exercise a type of informal control.

7.7 INDUSTRIAL RELATIONS

The service sector spans organizations from small family businesses to large multinational corporations. It covers external environments ranging from protected and regulated to highly competitive. In reflection of this diversity, there is great variety in the manner in which managements negotiate employment conditions with their workforces. In services organizations employing large numbers of staff, much of the employment relationship has traditionally been conducted collectively between the employer and groups of employees.

7.7.1 Collective Bargaining

The essential features of collective bargaining are threefold.

- First, collective bargaining recognizes organized labor groups with whom management negotiates on substantive issues such as pay and procedural issues, e.g., discipline and layoffs. Collective bargaining, therefore, formally recognizes the presence within the organization of an outside body.
- Second, collective bargaining emphasizes a divergence of interests between the employer and a large body of employees. This divergence is considered best settled by a process of compromise and negotiation.
- Third, collective bargaining recognizes that disruptive activities—for example, bans on overtime, slowing down, and withdrawal of labor—might be used to further employees' interests. This third feature of collective bargaining is exaggerated by the media, some academics, and politicians. As an element in collective bargaining, it becomes a consideration only when the first two elements have failed.

Many presume that collective bargaining is not suited to many areas of employment in the service sector. It is more accurate to argue that the mechanisms used to administer and manage the employment relationship within the services sector do not encourage the use of collective bargaining as a method of participation. Several reasons for this can be identified:

- Many service providers operate on a small scale, making collective agreements unnecessary.
- The concept of collective action has often appeared alien to the cultural values of many services workers. Bank workers, travel agents, and accountants typify workers in services where collective attitudes are relatively weak on the part of both the employer and employee.
- Flexibility in production requires many service industries to employ large numbers of part-time staff, who are less likely to be organized collectively.

- The very personal relationship that can develop between service personnel and their clients can result in personnel identifying more with their clients than with their peer group of workers.

Efforts to emphasize employees' close identification with business objectives via HRM do not sit easily with the presence of an outside body that emphasizes the significance of collective action. Services organizations that do not feel secure with organized labor groups are likely to attempt to marginalize their impact by not recognizing them and by creating organization-specific employee relations policies. Within the service sector, many organizations have moved away from the traditional view of industrial relations and now speak of employee relations.

7.7.2 Employee Relations

Employee relations focuses on the aspect of managerial activity that is concerned with fostering an identification with the employing organization and its business aims. It therefore concerns itself with direct relations between employees and management—that is, independently of any collective representation by organized labor groups. The term *employee relations* has become fashionable and appears to be less adversarial than *industrial relations.* Use of the term has grown, although organizations often use the term without changing behavior.[9]

Employee relations may in fact become one element within a wider corporate and HRM strategy. The movement toward employee relations and the changed emphasis of managerial strategy and employee participation are at the core of HRM.

7.8 STRATEGIES TO INCREASE EMPLOYEE PARTICIPATION

The methods an organization uses to encourage participation by its employees are likely to be influenced by the type of people it employs and the extent to which their jobs present opportunities to exercise autonomy (that is, the extent to which employees are able to control their own work processes) and discretion (the degree of independent thinking they can exercise in performing their work). Participation entails giving employees a direct personal stake in the overall business objectives of their organization. It forms the focus of strategic HRM. If management strategy is effective, there should be little difference between the aims of an organization's business plan and the aims of employees. Management strategy should be to make the two aims congruent by facilitating increased participation.

In general, participation by employees refers to the inclusion of nonmanagerial employees in an organization's decision making processes (Figure 7.5). This section considers various forms of participation and comments on their suitability for services organizations.

In practice, organizations are more likely to be concerned with securing greater employee involvement by making individual employee objectives more congruent with those of the whole organization rather than by increasing collective participation. This type of involvement may be available to all employees, but the extent to

THREE STEPS OF SERVICE	"We Are Ladies and Gentlemen Serving Ladies and Gentlemen"	THE RITZ-CARLTON CREDO
1 A warm and sincere greeting. Use the guest name, if and when possible. 2 Anticipation and compliance with guest needs. 3 Fond farewell. Give them a warm good-bye and use their names, if and when possible.		The Ritz-Carlton Hotel is a place where the genuine care and comfort of our guests is our highest mission. We pledge to provide the finest personal service and facilities for our guests who will always enjoy a warm, relaxed yet refined ambience. The Ritz-Carlton experience enlivens the senses, instills well-being, and fulfills even the unexpressed wishes and needs of our guests.

Figure 7.5 The hotel chain Ritz-Carlton® recognizes that its personnel significantly affect consumers' perceptions of service. Therefore, the hotel empowers its employees to take whatever action is necessary to keep customers satisfied. Source: Ritz-Carlton® materials were provided by the Ritz-Carlton Hotel Company. RITZ-CARLTON is a federally registered trademark of The Ritz-Carlton Hotel Company.

which their participation is real and effective may well depend on where they are positioned in the employment hierarchy—that is, whether they are within the core group or the peripheral group of workers. Increased participation is brought about by team briefings and a combination of consultation and communication methods.

- Open door policies encourage employees to air their grievances and make suggestions directly to their superiors. The aim of this approach is to make management accessible and employee friendly. To be effective, the human relations approach would require employees to feel that they have a real say in managerial matters. As a consequence, management must appear to be open and interested in employee relations. It is likely that this approach to managerial style and strategy will emphasize open management through some of the methods described here.

- Team briefings are a system of communication within the organization by which a group leader provides group members (up to about twenty) with management-derived information. The rationale behind briefing is to encourage commitment to and identification with the organization. Team briefings are particularly useful in times of organizational change, although they can be held regularly to cover such items as competitive progress, changes in policy, and points of future action. Ideally, they should result in a "cascade" of information down through an organization. The difference between briefing and quality circles (discussed next) is in their respective contents. Briefing sessions are likely to be more general and to relate to the whole organization, whereas quality circles relate to the specific work activity of a group of employees. Any general points of satisfaction or dissatisfaction can be aired in briefings and then taken up in specific quality circles.

- Quality circles (QCs) are small groups of employees who meet with a supervisor or group leader in an attempt to discuss their work in terms of production quality and service delivery. QCs usually work within a total quality management approach (see Chapter 6). To be successful, the QC leader has to be willing to listen to and act upon issues raised by QC members.

- Total quality management (TQM) policies (already discussed in more detail in Chapter 6) set out to create and disseminate an organizational mission that encourages all employees to identify methods by which they can carry out their tasks more efficiently (producing any given level of output for less cost) and more effectively (meeting customers' requirements more closely). Employees are encouraged to act outside of what they may see as a narrowly defined role and to appreciate the impact their actions will have on customers' service perceptions.

- The pattern of ownership of an organization can influence the level of consent and participation. Where the workforce own a significant share of a business, there should in principle be less cause for "us and them" attitudes to develop between management and the workforce. For this reason, many labor-intensive service organizations have significant proportions of worker stockholders.

7.9 *INTERNAL MARKETING*

Internal marketing describes the application of marketing techniques to audiences within the organization, as a means of securing the motivation, participation, consent, and moral involvement of employees. Definitions of internal marketing vary. Some see it as being limited to communication programs, whereas others see it as encompassing the whole relationship between an organization and its employees. One definition describes internal marketing as "the means of applying the philosophy and practices of marketing to people who serve the external customers so that (1) the best possible people can be employed and retained and (2) they will do the best possible work."[10]

In services marketing, internal marketing has two aspects:

- First, all employees operating in their functional areas interact with other functional specialist in a quasi-trading manner. In this way, the personnel department can be seen as providing recruitment expertise for an organization's accounting department, whereas the latter can be seen as providing payment systems on behalf of the personnel department. Therefore, each functional group within an organization can be seen as engaging in trade with other functional groups as though those functions were external customers.

- Second, all functional staff must work together in support of an organization's mission and business strategy. All staff must be able to share a common purpose and be able to work with rather than against other functional specialists in achieving the organization's aims. The mission of an organization must therefore be communicated to employees much as brand values are communicated to external customers.

Internal marketing has come to be associated with efforts to sell the message of an organization to its internal audience, using techniques similar to those used in the organization's relationships with external audiences. In reality, of course, true internal marketing would encompass all the HRM policies that have been described, which are designed to attract, select, train, motivate, direct, evaluate, and reward personnel. In this way, internal marketing becomes a core business philosophy, just as the traditional marketing philosophy involves more than merely using the tools of promotion.

The focal point of the narrower understanding of internal marketing lies in communicating the values of an organization to its employees in order to increase their level of consent, participation, motivation, and moral involvement. The following are commonly observed internal marketing techniques used by service organizations:

- The organization's mission statement must be clearly formulated and communicated to employees. An organization's mission statement should leave employees in no doubt about its essential purpose, which could be to become the largest or highest-quality provider within a particular sector or geographical area.

- Internal newsletters help to develop a sense of involvement of individuals within a business and can be used to inspire confidence by reporting significant new developments. Newsletters are commonly used to inform the workforce about achievements of individual employees.

- External advertising should regard the internal labor force as a secondary target market. Advertisements on television for a company's services can have the effect of inspiring the confidence of employees in their management.

- Staff uniforms and the physical working environment can be used to inspire staff members' confidence in the organization and to convey the organization's personality.

7.10 REDUCING DEPENDENCY ON HUMAN RESOURCES

Employees represent an expensive and difficult asset to manage. Furthermore, the quality of output received by final consumers can be perceived as being highly variable. Services organizations therefore often replace human operatives with machines, both to reduce variability (where machines can achieve high levels of reliability) and to reduce operating costs. Several methods used to reduce dependency on the organization's employees can be identified:

- At one extreme, the human element in a service production and delivery process can be almost completely replaced by automatic machinery. Examples include bank ATMs, vending machines, and automatic car washes. Constraints on employee replacement come from the limitations of technology (for example, completely automatic car washes can seldom achieve such high standards of cleanliness as those where an operator is present to perform some operations inaccessible to machinery), the cost of replacement machinery (only within the past few years has the cost of telecommunications equipment fallen to the point where mass-market automatic telephone banking has become a possibility), and the attitudes of consumers toward automated service delivery (many segments of the population are still reluctant to use ATMs, preferring the reassurance provided by human contact).

- Equipment can be used alongside employees to assist them in their tasks. This often has the effect of de-skilling their tasks by reducing the scope they have for exercising discretion, thus reducing the variability in quality perceived by customers. In this way, computerized accounting systems in hotels reduce the risk that staff will add up a client's bill incorrectly. Similarly, the computer systems used by many airline reservation staff include promptings that guide their interaction with clients.

- The inseparability of the service offer means that consumers of a service are often also involved as co-producers of the service. The involvement of the service provider's personnel can be reduced by shifting a greater part of the production process to the consumer. In this way, most gas stations expect customers to fill their own car with fuel rather than have this task undertaken by an employee. Similarly, a television repair company may require customers to bring TV sets to its premises for repair. In both cases, customers have greater control over the quality of service by undertaking part of it themselves.

CHAPTER REVIEW QUESTIONS

1. What are the principal ways in which the management of personnel is likely to be different in a service organization compared with a manufacturer?
2. Discuss the ways in which a fast-food restaurant can increase the level of participation by its staff.
3. Using an industry with which you are familiar, identify methods by which the effects of variability of the personnel inputs can be minimized in order to produce a consistent standard of service.
4. What is the link between personnel and service quality?
5. What are the shortcomings of traditional personnel management for the effective marketing of services?
6. Using examples, show how human resource management policies can help to overcome the problems associated with peaked patterns of demand.

REFERENCES

1. Boxall, P. "Strategic HRM: Beginnings of a New Theoretical Direction," *Human Resource Management Journal* 2, no. 3 (1992): 40–51.
2. Formbrun, C. *Strategic Human Resource Management* (New York: John Wiley, 1984).
3. Beer, M., et al. *Managing Human Assets* (New York: Free Press, 1984).
4. Guest, D. "HRM and Personnel Management: Can You Spot the Difference?" *Personnel Management* (January 1989): 40–51.
5. Maslow, A. *Motivation and Personality* (New York: Harper and Row, 1954).
6. Mayo, E. *The Social Problems of Industrial Civilization* (London: Routledge and Kegan Paul, 1949).
7. Atkinson, J. "Manpower Strategies for Flexible Organizations," *Personnel Management* (August 1984): 28–31.
8. Pollert, A. "The Flexible Firm; Fact or Fixation?" *Work, Employment and Society* 1, no. 1

(1988): 29–31; and P. Marginson, "Employment Flexibility in Large Companies: Change and Continuity," *Industrial Relations Journal* 20 (1989): 24–29.

9. Marchington, M. and Parker, P. *Changing Patterns of Employee Relations* (London: Harvester Wheatsheaf, 1990).

10. Berry L. L. "Services Marketing is Different," *Business* 30, no. 3 (May/June 1980): 24–9.

SUGGESTED FURTHER READING

BEER, M., et al. 1984. *Managing Human Assets*. New York: Free Press.

BERRY, L. L. 1981. "The Employee as Customer." *Journal of Retail Banking* (March)

COLLINS, B. and PAYNE, A. 1991. "Internal Marketing: A New Perspective for HRM," *European Management Journal* 9, no. 3, 261–70

COMPTON, F., GEORGE, W. R., GRONROOS, C., and KARVINEN, M. 1987. "Internal Marketing" in *The Service Challenge: Integration for Competitive Advantage,* edited by J. A. Czepiel, C. A. Congram, and J. Shannon. Chicago: American Marketing Association.

FIRNSTAHL, T. W. 1989. "My Employees Are My Service Guarantee," *Harvard Business Review* (July/August): 28–37.

FORMBRUN, C. 1984. *Strategic Human Resource Management*. New York: John Wiley.

GEORGE, W. R. 1990. "Internal Marketing and Organizational Behavior: A Partnership in Developing Customer-Conscious Employees at Every Level." *Journal of Business Research* 20: 63–70.

GEORGE, W. R. 1986. "Internal Communications Programs as a Mechanism for Doing Internal Marketing," in *Creativity in Services Marketing*, edited by M. Venkatesan et al. Chicago: American Marketing Association.

GLASSMAN, M. and McAfee, B. 1992. "Integrating the Personnel and Marketing Functions." *Business Horizons* 35, no. 3 (May/June): 52–9.

GRONROOS, C. 1981. "Internal Marketing—an Integral Part of Marketing Theory," in *Marketing of Services* edited by J. H. Donnelly and W. E. George. Chicago: American Marketing Association Proceedings Series, 236–8.

GRONROOS, C. 1985. "Internal Marketing—Theory and Practice," in *Services Marketing in a Changing Environment,* edited by T. M. Bloch, C. D. Upah, and V. A. Zeithaml. Chicago: American Marketing Association.

HERZBERG, F. 1966. *Work and the Nature of Man*. New York: Staples Press.

HOFFMAN, D. K. and INGRAM, T. N. 1991. "Creating Customer Orientated Employees: The Case in Home Health Care." *Journal of Health Care Marketing* 11 (June): 24–32.

KELLEY, S. W. 1992. "Developing Customer Orientation Among Service Employees," *Journal of the Academy of Marketing Science* (Winter): 27–36.

WINTER, J. P. 1985. "Getting Your House in Order With Internal Marketing: A Marketing Prerequisite." *Health Marketing Quarterly* 3, no. 1: 62–69.

8

Making Services Accessible

CHAPTER OBJECTIVES

After reading this chapter, you should be able to understand

- factors affecting the choice of service outlet sites, and the extent to which service production and consumption are spatially flexible

- methods used to reduce the effects of inseparability on service production and delivery

- the role of intermediaries in making services accessible to consumers

- the diversity of service intermediaries and the factors that influence their selection

- the principles of physical distribution management as they affect the tangible elements of service offers

8.1 INTRODUCTION

The methods by which a service is made available to customers is an important defining characteristic of the service offer—the method by which banks, restaurants, and shops make their service offers accessible to customers often *is* the service. Without a strategy to make a service accessible to customers, a service is of no value. The inseparability of services makes the task of passing on service benefits much more complex than is the case with manufactured goods. Inseparability implies that services are consumed at the point of production. In other words, a service cannot be produced by one person in one place and handled by other people to make it available to consumers in other places. A service cannot therefore be produced where costs are lowest and sold where demand is greatest. Customer accessibility must be designed into the service production system.

In this chapter, strategies to make services accessible to customers will be analyzed by focusing on four important, but related issues:

- Where and when is the service to be made available to the consumer?
- What is the role of intermediaries in the process of service delivery?
- How are intermediaries selected, motivated, and monitored?
- How are tangible goods, which form a part of many service offers, to be made available to final consumers?

8.2 SERVICE LOCATION DECISIONS

In this section, choices facing service providers about the place and time at which a service is to be provided are considered. First, it should be repeated that because consumers of services are usually involved as co-producers of the service, the time and place where they are expected to take part in this process become important criteria for evaluation. Production location decisions therefore cannot be taken in isolation from an analysis of customers' needs. While services organizations often desire to centralize production in order to achieve economies of scale, consumers usually seek local access to services, often at a time that may not be ideal for the producer to cater for. Service location decisions therefore involve a trade-off between the needs of the producer and the needs of the consumer.

For some services, production is very inflexible with respect to location, resulting in relatively production-led locational decisions. At the other extreme, production techniques may by their nature allow much greater flexibility, but location decisions are constrained by the inflexibility of consumers to travel to a service outlet, whether because of physical inability or unwillingness. Some intangible, low-contact services are able to separate production from consumption, using some of the methods described later in this chapter. Such services can be produced in the most economic location and made available wherever customers are located.

A typology of service location decisions is shown in Figure 8.1. Here inseparable services are classified in a matrix according to their degree of flexibility in production and consumption.

8.2.1 Flexibility in Production

Extreme inflexibility in production is found in services whose whole purpose is to be at one unique location. For example, tourism-related services based on a unique historic site cannot be moved by their very nature. Other services are locationally inflexible because they can be sensibly produced only in large-scale centralized production facilities. This can be the case when the necessary supporting equipment is expensive but offers opportunities for significant economies of scale. When this

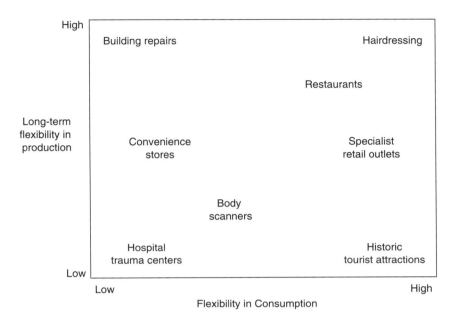

Figure 8.1   Locational flexibility in production and consumption of inseparable services

equipment is also highly immobile, customers must come to a limited number of central service points to receive service. This is true with much of the specialized and expensive equipment needed for complex medical care, such as body scanners, which tend to be provided at a small number of central locations. When the equipment offers less scope for economies of scale and is more easily transported, service production can be distributed more widely. This explains why mammogram services are frequently taken to users, whereas users must travel to body scanners.

Some service organizations operate a "hub and spoke" system whereby the benefits of large-scale, centralized production of specialized services is combined with locally accessible outlets (Figure 8.2). The specialized business and investment services of banking can often be competitive only if they are produced in units with a high enough critical mass to support the payment of an expert in that field of activity and to cover associated overhead. Many major banks have therefore developed specialized business advisory centers located in a few key locations. Their services are subsequently made available through local branches by a combination of telephone, mail, computer link, or a personal visit from the centrally based expert. Similarly, much of the processing work involved in producing a service can be transferred to an efficient regional center, leaving local outlets to make the service available to the public. In this way, many banks have transferred mortgage loan processing from small branches, leaving the latter to act as little more than sales outlets.

As well as internal economies of scale, external economies of scale sometimes feature in a firm's location decisions. The first kind of external economy occurs when a location close to other service producers reduces a firm's input costs. For this reason, many diverse financial services companies have congregated in the financial district of Manhattan, where a commodity trading company may find significant

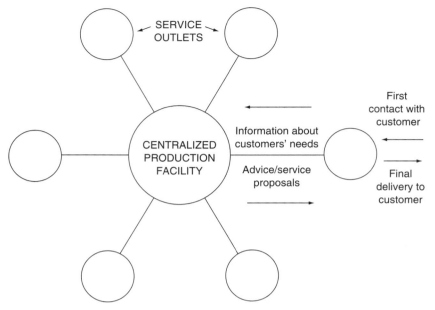

Figure 8.2 A hub and spoke system of service production and delivery

benefits from being located within walking distance of commercial banks, foreign exchange dealers, and insurance companies. Similarly, clusters of advertising agencies, graphic designers, typographers, and typesetters can be found to maximize benefits from internal trading, to the benefit of suppliers and customers alike. However, the importance to locational decisions of such external economies of scale is declining because of technological developments that allow production to be separated from consumption. In both of the examples just given, service benefits can now be delivered electronically without any need for direct interaction. A second kind of external economy of scale can result from locating in a recognized local marketplace, as occurs where jewelers or realtors congregate in one neighborhood of a town. Because the existence of the marketplace is widely recognized, any firm locating within it will need to spend less on promotion to attract potential customers to its location.

Production considerations are likely to be a less important influence on location decisions where economies of scale are insignificant. In a market environment, competitive advantage will be gained by maximizing availability though more widespread distribution outlets rather than by saving costs through centralization. To illustrate this, hairdressing offers little scope for economies of scale, and competitive advantage is gained by providing small outlets that are easily accessible to customers.

Finally, the competitiveness of the market environment can affect the locational flexibility of service producers. A service producer that is able to be flexible in its location decisions may nevertheless be unwilling to be flexible if its customers have little choice of supplier. For this reason, many government-provided services (e.g., driver licensing) are provided through centralized administrative offices, which may be inconveniently located for most users.

8.2.2 Flexibility in Consumption

Decisions on service location are also influenced by the extent to which consumers are willing or able to be flexible about where they consume a service. Inflexibility on the part of consumers can arise for various reasons:

- When a service is to be performed on a customer's possessions, those possessions may themselves be immovable, requiring the supplier to come to the customer (e.g., building repairs).
- Sometimes the customer may also be physically immobile (e.g., physically challenged users of health care services).
- For impulse purchases, or services to which there are many competitive alternatives, customers are unlikely to be willing to travel far to seek out a service.
- For specialist services, customers may show more willingness to be flexible about where they are prepared to receive the service, compared with routine purchases that they would be unwilling to travel for.

In reality, most service consumers' decisions involve a trade-off between the price of a service, the quality of delivery at a particular location, the amount of choice available, and the cost to the consumer in terms of time and money involved in gaining access to a service. The consumer picking up a few odd items of groceries is likely to consider price and choice less important than ease of access—hence the continued existence of many small convenience stores. The consumer purchasing the week's groceries is likely to consider price and selection much more important than ease of access. For more specialized services, such as the purchase of an overseas vacation, consumers may be willing to travel longer distances to a travel agent who offers competitive prices and/or a wide selection of vacations.

Access strategies should be based on the identification of market segments made up of users with similar accessibility needs. Access strategies can then be developed that meet the needs of each segment.

- Age frequently defines segments in terms of the level of access sought. Many elderly users of personal care services are sometimes unwilling or unable to leave the home, making home availability of a service a desirable attribute. Other groups, such as older teenagers, may be attracted by the very act of getting away from home to receive a service. This could explain continuing interest in going out to see a movie at a theatre even when competing alternatives are provided by local video rental shops or premium cable television services.
- Segmentation on the basis of an individual's economic status can be seen in the willingness of more affluent people to pay premium prices in order to consume a service at a point and time convenient to themselves rather than the service

provider. Evidence of this is provided by home delivery food services that target groups with relatively high disposable incomes.

- Psychographic segmentation can be seen in the way groups of people seek out services that satisfy their life style needs. As an example, people in some segments of the population are prepared to travel long distances to a restaurant whose design and ambience appeals to them.

- The cultural background of some individuals can predispose them to seek out a particular kind of accessibility. This can be seen in the reluctance of some groups to become involved in service delivery methods that remove regular personal contact with the service provider. Insurance companies that collect premiums from the homes of customers may reassure some people who have been brought up to distrust impersonal organizations, whereas a periodic visit to a bank or an annual payment by mail may satisfy the needs of others.

- Access strategies can be based on the type of benefit that users seek from a service. As an example, customers are often prepared to travel a considerable distance to a restaurant for a celebration meal but would prefer a more easily accessible restaurant for a business lunch.

- High-frequency users of a service may place a higher premium on easy accessibility than casual users.

- In business-to-business services, the level of access to a service can directly affect the customer's operating costs. A computer repair company that makes its services available at buyers' offices avoids the costs that the latter would incur if it had to perform part of the service—delivery and collection—itself.

For many services, the location of the service delivery point is the most important means of attracting new business. This can be true of low-value services whose consumers show little willingness to preplan their purchase or to go out of their way to find the service. Location is also very important to impulse purchasing. Gas stations and bars in tourist areas are typically chosen as a result of a customer encountering the service outlet with no prior planning. It is unlikely, for instance, that many motorists would follow media advertisements and seek out a gas station located on a side street. A visible location is a vital factor influencing such a choice.

Because of the perishability of service offers, their time accessibility is as important as their spatial location. Again, customers can be segmented according to their flexibility with respect to the time when they are prepared to consume a service. At one extreme, people in some segments for some services may be prepared to wait until a specified time to receive the service. Ardent fans of a rock 'n' roll group would probably buy a ticket for a concert regardless of its time and date. At the other extreme no purchase is made if a service is not instantly available. A taxi operator that makes its service available only at specified times will probably lose all business outside these times to other operators.

Service accessibility by time can be used to give an organization competitive advantage in much the same way as spatial accessibility. Banks have frequently used longer opening hours to gain a competitive advantage over other banks by attracting people who found the standard banking hours too restrictive.

8.2.3 Service Location Models

Before a network of service outlets can be designed, an organization must clearly define its accessibility objectives. In particular, it must have a clear idea of the volume of business, market share, and customer segments that it wishes to attract. Accessibility objectives derive from the positioning strategy for a service. A high level of accessibility may, for example, only be compatible with business objectives if it is also associated with a premium price position. A high level of accessibility may also reduce and change the role played by promotion within the marketing mix. By contrast, a strategy that involves a low level of accessibility may need to rely heavily on promotion to make potential customers aware of the location of service outlets.

These are some examples of accessibility objectives that an organization may set itself in designing a network of service outlets:

- to provide a hotel location in all United States towns with a population of fifty thousand or more
- to develop supermarket sites that are within ten minutes' driving time of at least fifty thousand people
- to locate retail sites where pedestrian or vehicular traffic exceeds a specified threshold

Service location decisions are used at both macro and micro levels. At the macro level, organizations seek the most profitable areas or regions in which to make their service available, given the strength of demand, the level of competition and the costs of setting up in an area. At the micro level, decisions refer to the choice of specific sites.

Macroanalysis begins with a clear statement of the profile of customers that an organization is targeting. Areas are then sought that have a profile closely matching that of the target market. At their simplest, indicators can be used to identify potentially attractive locations. As an example, a company undertaking to create a national chain of travel agencies targeted at the affluent, elderly market could get an initial feel for the best locations by studying the statistics about who travels most (from the National Travel Survey) and average income and age (from the U.S. Bureau of Census). The attractiveness of a market could be indicated by a weighted index of these factors and subjected to a more detailed analysis of competitors' activities in each area. Other, more specialized segmentation methods have been developed that allow organizations to evaluate the profile of an area, for example, the *Sourcebook of Zip Code Demographics* (published annually by CACI).

Methods used by an organization to select service outlet locations tend to become more complex as the organization grows. In the early stages of growth, simple rule-of-thumb methods may be acceptable. With further growth, simple indexes and ratios are commonly used. When more service outlets have been established, an organization can begin to gather sufficient data to analyze the performance of its existing outlets and from this analysis to develop models that can be used to predict the likely performance of proposed new locations. Regression techniques are used to identify relationships between variables and the level of significance of each variable in explaining the performance of a location. The development of regression models requires considerable initial investment in creating an information base and calibrating the model, but once calibrated, these models can help reduce the risk inherent in new service location decisions. However, models cannot be extrapolated to cover types of decisions that were not envisaged in the model as originally calibrated. For example, a model calibrated for site location decisions in the United States may be inappropriate for making location decisions in Mexico.

Additional problems in the application of regression modeling techniques can be noted. Because such techniques require large amounts of data for calibration, they are really suited only to high-volume services. It can also be difficult to identify the key variables that cause variation in sales turnover or to exclude interaction among the variables. Finally, regression is essentially an incremental planning technique, which is less appropriate for designing networks of service outlets like those that may occur when two service organizations merge and consequently need to rationalize outlets. In such a case, an alternative approach is to use a spatial location model.

Spatial location models measure the geographical dispersion of demand and attempt to allocate this demand to service outlets on the basis that the probability of a consumer's using a particular outlet will be

- positively related to the attractiveness of that outlet
- negatively related to its distance from the points where demand is located

These principles are developed in the following model, which has frequently been used as a basis for retail location models but also has applications in locating recreational facilities, health services, and so on.[1]

$$P_{ij} = \frac{\dfrac{A_j^a}{d_{ij}^b}}{\displaystyle\sum_{n=1} \dfrac{A_j^a}{d_{ij}^b}}$$

where P_{ij} = the probability of a trip from origin i to destination j
A_j = the attractiveness of destination j
d_{ij} = the distance between origin i and destination j
a and b = parameters to be empirically determined

The intuitive appeal and simplicity of such a model can hide conceptual and practical problems in its application—problems that have triggered considerable research in an attempt to specify the basic model. The concept of attractiveness can be difficult to measure, and it has been pointed out that although an individual may believe that a location is attractive, this attractiveness may not be important to that particular individual.[2] Distance itself can be difficult to determine; it can be measured objectively (mileage or average traveling times) or subjectively (users' perceptions of distance). There is evidence that subjectively perceived distances increase proportionately less than the objective measured distance.[3]

Spatial location-allocation models are powerful tools that emphasize long-term marketing strategies rather than short-term decisions about opening or closing a specific location. They can be used to evaluate all combinations of location possibilities in relation to the geographical pattern of demand. The criteria for selecting the most efficient network of outlets involve balancing the need to maximize its attractiveness to customers against the service provider's need to minimize the cost of operating the network. Sophisticated computer models allow assumptions about consumer behavior to be varied—for example, the maximum distance that people are prepared to walk to an outlet. Such models are expensive because extensive data and specialized staff are needed to develop them. When the risks associated with a bad location decision are low, it may be more cost-effective to use rule-of-thumb methods than to commission such a model. In the United States, the high cost of acquiring and refurbishing property in the mid-1980s led to spatial location models becoming very popular as risk reducers. However, the fall in property-related costs—and associated risk levels—in the early 1990s saw many companies dropping the use of these models and reverting to more cost-effective rule-of-thumb methods or regression models.

CASE STUDY

MODELS USEFUL IN LOCATION DECISIONS

Example 1: Regression Model Helps Supermarket Plan Future Store Sites

The level of risk associated with opening a new supermarket in a fiercely competitive environment can be considerable. While a small general retailer may be able to rent shop space on low-risk short-term leases, modern supermarkets often require considerable investment in specially designed facilities that meet customers' ever-increasing needs and expectations. A study by Jones and Mock[4] of a small American supermarket chain illustrates the value of regression modeling techniques. The supermarket chain being studied had previously relied on rule-of-thumb methods for store allocation, but as the size of its new stores increased, so too had the level of risk. As its business grew, it was also able to gather more data to help it understand the factors associated with the success of a particular store.

The planners started the regression modeling by grouping sites according to similarities in their environments. On the basis of socioeconomic data, five distinctive environments were identified: city center, suburbs, old established shopping streets, the urban fringe, and nonmetropolitan locations. To find out which of the many variables available were the most relevant for each retailing environment, a series of cross-tabulations between individual key variables was carried out. The relevant variables were then put into a series of stepwise regression models, one for each environment, allowing the identification of the variables that were most effective in explaining sales performance. In suburban stores, variation in store sales was best explained by three measures: the percentage of the neighborhood that had recently been developed, the accessibility of the site by car, and the number of competitors located within three blocks. Each increase of 1 percent in the share of new houses resulted in an additional weekly sales turnover of $120, whereas each nearby competitor reduced sales by $656.

Example 2: Rationalizing Service Station Outlets

Goodchild and Noronha[5] reported on a study to evaluate the most efficient network of service station outlets in a small town. The merger of two gas station chains had left the new chain with a total of thirty-one outlets in the town, but it appeared that the new chain would be most profitable if it operated only twenty outlets. The company decided that four of the newest and highest-volume locations would be retained, leaving it the task of deciding which sixteen of the remaining twenty-seven locations should be retained. Rather than evaluating on a site-by-site basis using multiple regression techniques, the company used a spatial location-allocation model on account of its interactive ability to adjust sales volumes of all outlets in the network simultaneously.

The potential demand for gasoline was measured by reference to these factors:

- the residential population in each of 600 census enumeration areas in the city
- the traffic flow (number of cars x length of link) in each of 560 road links
- Against these positive determinants of demand, a distance decay effect was intro-duced to the model, indicating that demand would decrease as customers' distance from a service outlet increased.

A model was developed of this form:

$$\text{Demand}_j = A\sum_i \frac{\text{Population}_i}{\left(1 - \text{ad}_{ij}\right)} + B\sum_k \frac{\text{Traffic}_k}{\left(1 - \text{ad}_{kj}\right)}$$

where demand at service station j was calculated as the sum total of population at all i enu-meration districts divided by a factor reflecting the distance of the outlet from each enumera-tion district (1-ad_{ij}), plus the sum total of traffic on all links, divided by a factor reflecting the distance of the outlet from each link (1-ad_{kj}). A and B are weights that could be modified to favor either local catchment area demand or traffic flow demand. The location-allocation pro-cedure was able to indicate the sales and market share at each site—including competitors—and how a site might be even more effective if it were slightly relocated. The analysis could be repeated by use of different distance decay parameters and different weights for A and B in the equation to reflect different marketing strategies. An emphasis on local catchment area demand (high value for A) favored central locations, whereas an emphasis on traffic flow gen-erated more dispersed site locations.

CASE STUDY REVIEW QUESTIONS

1. What are the advantages of the regression model and the spatial location-allocation models over simpler approaches to location decisions?
2. Identify possible weaknesses inherent in the approaches.
3. What is the value of location models to the task of service marketing management?

8.2.4 Reducing Locational Dependency

The traditional idea that service production and consumption are inseparable appears at first sight to pose problems in achieving both maximum productive efficiency and maximum accessibility to a service. One method of resolving this apparent problem is to try and make production and consumption separable—that is, to design a ser-vice that can be produced where it is most efficient and consumed where it is most needed. It can sometimes be conceptually quite difficult to identify just where a service is produced. However, several methods can be identified by which production can be removed from the point of consumption.

- Telecommunications allow the substantive element of a service to be produced at a central processing unit and made available at any point of consumers' choice. Information databases used by businesses and prerecorded telephone information lines fit into this category. Banks have recognized the distribution implications of telephone banking services, and many large banks in the United States have created systems that allow private and business customers to receive spoken telephone statements and to transfer funds from one account to another, or to pay bills to outside organizations from any telephone. Some banks have offered more sophisticated services by allowing customers to receive information and give instructions via a telephone line and the customer's own personal computer terminal. The locational implications of such delivery systems are quite significant. It will doubtless prove possible to reduce the size of banks' costly branch networks as some segments of the population and some categories of the banks' services are distributed to any point chosen by the consumer. As well as offering distribution at any place, telephone delivery systems can operate from an efficient central base capable of offering twenty-four hour service delivery every day of the year.

- Postal services can be used to make intangible services available at almost any location, much like telecommunications-based accessibility strategies. The development of database marketing has allowed direct mail to be used not only for promotion but also to increase accessibility. Insurance companies now make many services, such as personal loan checks and insurance coverage, available at the homes of consumers, while the service itself is processed at a remote office.

- A more novel means of separating production and consumption is to provide a surrogate for a service that allows the service itself to be provided at a time and place of the consumer's choice. The best example of a surrogate is provided by a credit card. Providing short-term credit is a service offered by credit card companies; yet, the card company is not required to take part in every act of service delivery—that is, every time customers use their cards in a shop or a restaurant. The credit card acts as a mediating device between a store owner and the customer by stating that the credit card company agrees at some remote point to transfer funds into the store owner's bank account and the shopper agrees to send to the credit card company payment for the goods purchased plus the agreed cost of any ancillary services such as extended credit. The service of providing credit is therefore made available at a potentially enormous range of outlets, quite independently of any involvement by the card company.

8.3 THE ROLE OF INTERMEDIARIES IN DISTRIBUTING SERVICES

In the context of manufactured goods marketing, an intermediary can be understood as a person who handles goods as they pass from the organization that manufactured them to the individuals or businesses that consume them. The intermediary may physically handle the goods, splitting them into progressively smaller volumes as they pass through channels of distribution, or may simply buy and sell the rights to goods in the role of a commodity dealer.

Any discussion of service intermediaries immediately raises some conceptual issues:

- Services cannot be owned; therefore, it is difficult to talk about rights to service ownership being transferred through channels of distribution.
- Pure services are intangible and perishable; therefore, inventories cannot exist.
- The inseparability of most services should logically require an intermediary to become a co-producer of a service.

A distinction should be made between intermediaries as co-producers and their role as mere sales agents. While the former is an active part of the production process, the latter does not actually deliver a service itself—it delivers only the right to a service. As an example, an outlet selling postage stamps is not significantly involved as a co-producer of postal services. It can be difficult to distinguish between these two situations. A theatre ticket agency, in addition to merely selling the right to a service, may provide a valuable service for consumers in procuring specific seats.

Service intermediaries perform important functions on behalf of service producers (often referred to as "service principals"). The role expectations of intermediaries vary according to the nature of the service in question. Some of the most important are described here:

- As a co-producer of a service, an intermediary assists in making a service available to consumers at a place and time convenient to consumers. A contract post office assists in the process of making services such as money orders and parcel dispatch available to consumers. In other cases, an intermediary may become the dominant partner involved in co-production. A national key-cutting or shoe-heeling service may put almost the entire service production process in the hands of intermediaries, leaving the principal to provide administrative and advertising support and to monitor standards.
- Intermediaries help to make a service locally available. A personal loan can be said to be created at the head office of a finance company where bulk funds are acquired and documentation produced, but for many customer segments, the loan must be made available through an intermediary with a local outlet where potential customers can discuss their needs. This outlet could be the finance company's own branch or an appointed intermediary.
- Intermediaries usually provide sales support at the point of sale. A two-way personal dialogue with a local intermediary may be more effective at securing a sale from some customers of personal services than advertising messages derived centrally from a service principal.
- Consumers may prefer to buy services from an intermediary who offers a wide choice, including the services offered by competing service principals. A travel

agency selling only its tours directly to the public may encounter resistance from segments of the population who prefer to have choices presented to them at one location.

- Consumers may enjoy trusting relationships with intermediaries and prefer to choose between competing alternatives on the basis of the intermediaries' advice. In the financial services sector, intermediaries develop trust with their clients in guiding them through often complex choices. To be successful with buyers in such segments, a financial services company must establish its credentials with the intermediary if its products are to enter the final consumer's choice set.

- As co-producer of a service, an intermediary often shares some of the risk of providing a service. This can come about when a service principal requires intermediaries to contribute some of their own capital to the cost of acquiring equipment, and both share any subsequent operating profit or loss.

- The use of independent intermediaries can free up capital, which a service principal can reinvest in its core service production facilities. An airline that closes its own ticket shops and directs potential customers to travel agents is able to reinvest the proceeds in updating its aircraft or reservation systems. This action may give it greater competitive advantage than having its own ticket outlets.

- Once the initial service act is completed, there may be a requirement for after-sales support to be provided. Intermediaries can make this support more accessible to the consumer and assist the service principal as co-producer of the after-sales support. Insurance is a good example: many segments of the insurance-buying public feel happier with easy access to a local agent who can give advice about making a claim. The agent, in turn, simplifies the task of the insurance company by handling much of the paperwork involved in making a claim, thereby reducing the latter's workload.

8.4 *"PUSH" AND "PULL" RELATIONSHIPS WITH INTERMEDIARIES*

"Push" and "pull" channels of distribution are familiar concepts in the marketing of manufactured goods, but they also have application within the services sector. A traditional "push" channel of distribution involves a service principal aggressively promoting its service to intermediaries by means of personal selling, trade advertising, and trade incentives. The intermediary, in turn, aggressively sells the service to final consumers, often having to strike a balance between maximizing the customer's benefit and maximizing the incentives received by the intermediary from the service principal. This approach sees the service as essentially a commodity—the consumer starts with no preference of service principal and seeks the best value available from an intermediary.

For service principals, "push" strategies can be quite risky, as any product differentiation policy can be effective only if the intermediary effectively communicates the unique benefits to potential customers rather than relying on price alone as the point of differentiation. To reduce this risk, service principals can aim messages directly at consumers, attempting to establish at an early stage in the buying process the values that their brand stands for. Having developed an attitude toward a brand, consumers are more likely to specifically ask for that brand from an intermediary or to express a preference for it when offered a choice by the intermediary. In the "pull" strategy, the intermediary's role is reduced to one of dispensing presold branded services. Many pension companies have tried to develop brands in this way, aiming to develop favorable images in the minds of potential customers before they approach their brokers. "Push" and "pull" strategies are compared in Figure 8.3.

It can sometimes be difficult to distinguish between pure "push" and pure "pull" strategies. A company may act as an intermediary for some services but as a service principal for other similar services. As well as selling a service for a principal as an intermediary, the company could buy rights to services as though the principal were a subcontractor. In this way, small local travel agents sometimes put together vacations aimed at segments of their own market. An agent that acts as intermediary for the sale of other tour operators' vacations might buy hotel, travel, and sightseeing services direct from the principals and sell the entire tour under its own brand name. The travel agent effectively becomes a principal. While there is potential benefit from being able to earn both the retail agent's and the tour operator's profit margin, this strategy poses potential risk for the intermediary, who must cover all the fixed costs of the principal rather than earning a commission on every service sold.

8.5 SERVICE CHARACTERISTICS AS AN INFLUENCE ON CHANNEL DESIGN

Services are not homogeneous, and this is reflected in the selection of intermediaries. While some services can be handled by many intermediaries, others cannot easily be handled by intermediaries at all. The characteristics of services and of customers' expectations need to be considered before an accessibility strategy is developed.

- Some services experience highly variable outcomes, making efforts at controlling quality through intermediaries very difficult to achieve. This is particularly true of

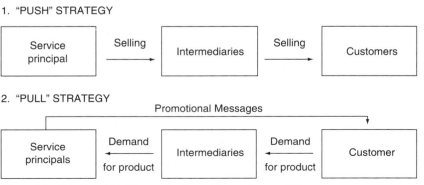

Figure 8.3 "Push" and "Pull" strategies for making services available to consumers

personal services, such as hairdressing, which are most commonly provided by small businesses directly to final consumers without the use of intermediaries.

• Some services may be highly specialized and likely to be neglected by intermediaries with inadequate training or knowledge. A principal may gain no competitive advantage if intermediaries are incapable of giving appropriate sales and co-production support. When a service is complex, the service principal must pay careful attention to the selection of intermediaries, or alternatively deal directly with consumers. In the vacation industry, skiing and activity holidays are quite specialized services, and most travel agents do not know enough about them to handle them effectively. Some operators of these holidays have therefore chosen to operate through specialized intermediaries such as specialist outdoor pursuit agencies, while many more prefer to deal directly with their target markets.

• Margins available on a service may be insufficient to support many intermediaries, if any at all. Domestic and industrial cleaning services often operate on very low margins; as a result most services are provided directly to consumers.

• Legislation or voluntary codes of conduct may limit the choice of intermediary available to a service principal or make it impossible to act through an intermediary at all. Most states have laws governing who can legally distribute intangible services, such as financial services.

8.6 DEVELOPING A STRATEGY FOR INTERMEDIARIES

The development of a strategy to make services accessible to users begins with a clear analysis of an organization's accessibility objectives for a service. Accessibility strategies could be designed around meeting the following typical objectives:

• to gain market share for an existing service in an established market
• to gain entry to a new market
• to prevent penetration of an established market by a market challenger

The following sections discuss the merits of several types of intermediaries and their ability to contribute to the service principal's accessibility objectives. One option is for the service principal to make a service available directly to consumers without the involvement of intermediaries. In some of the circumstances described in the previous sections, this could be the most appropriate strategy, for example, when the service is complex and the service principal wishes to ensure that greater accessibility through intermediaries is not achieved at the expense of quality standards. In other cases, service principals can achieve their accessibility objectives better by working with intermediaries. Here, decisions must be made about the most appropriate type of intermediary for the service in question.

8.7 DIRECT SALE

Direct sale is a particularly attractive option for service providers when the service offering is complex and variable and when legal constraints make the involvement of intermediaries difficult. The attractions of direct sale are numerous:

- The service provider is in regular direct contact with consumers of its service, making faster feedback of customer comments a possibility. This can facilitate the process of improving existing services or developing new ones.

- It can be easier for service principals to develop relationships with customers if they are in regular contact. Databases can be built up to provide a profile of individual customers, allowing for more effective targeting of new service offers. Banks—which have traditionally dealt directly with their customers—in theory may segment their customers by age, income, and stage in the family life cycle. A bank could then present a series of offers to selected market segments. This strategy may not yield short-term profits but could be used to build a long-term profitable relationship.

- Intermediaries may jealously guard their customers from the service principal in the fear that any initial direct contact between the service principal and consumer could result in a diminished role for the intermediary. Having spent time and effort attracting their customer, they do not wish to see the service principal picking up the long-term benefits of repeat business without the revenue-earning involvement of the intermediary. The service principal can therefore lose a lot of valuable feedback.

- In the public sector, political considerations or fears over confidentiality may prevent services being provided by private sector intermediaries. Definitions of what is politically acceptable change over time. In the United States, many have considered that school catering, trash collection, and educational transportation are vital public services that could only be supplied directly by public sector bodies. It is now routinely accepted that all of these can be provided through service intermediaries of one form or another, although debate continues about the desirability of delivering more contentious services, such as security services, through private sector intermediaries.

- The service principal can retain for itself the profit margin that would have been paid to an intermediary. This could be beneficial when its own service delivery costs are lower than the commission that it would have paid to an intermediary.

Quite often, service principals choose to make their services available both directly and through intermediaries. This can be an attractive option, as it allows the principal to target segments that have quite different buying behaviors. For example, one segment of the vacation-buying public may seek the reassurance provided by being able to walk in and talk to a travel agent, while another segment—more confident, price-sensitive, and short of time—may find direct booking with a tour operator by telephone more attractive. Although there are advantages with segmenting the market in this way, there can also be problems. Intermediaries can become demotivated if they see a principal for whom they are working as agent selling the same services directly to the public. To make matters worse, direct sale promotional material often emphasizes the benefits of not using an intermediary—typically, lower prices and faster service. Occasionally, agents' trade associations have threatened to boycott the products of principals who act in this way. One solution is to split an organization into two distinct operating units, each with its own brand identity, one to operate through intermediaries and the other to sell directly to the final consumer.

8.8 *SELECTION OF INTERMEDIARIES*

Service intermediaries take many forms in terms of their size, structure, legal status, and relationship to the service principal. Because of this diversity, attempts at classification can become confused by the level of overlap. In this section, attention is focused on the characteristics of four important types of intermediary: agents, retailers, wholesalers, and franchisees.

8.8.1 *Service Agents*

An agent is someone who acts on behalf of a principal and has the authority to create a legal relationship between the customer and service principal as if it were made directly between the two. Principals are vicariously liable for the actions of their agents. Agents are usually rewarded for their actions by being able to deduct a commission before payment is passed on to the principal, although in many cases agents may be paid a fixed fee for the work actually done—for example, in preparing a new market prior to the launch of a new service.

For service principals, the use of agents offers many advantages:

- Capital requirements for creating a chain of distribution outlets are minimized, allowing reinvestment in core service production.
- Consumers may expect choice at the point of service purchase, and it is usually easier for an independent agent, rather than the service principal, to set up distribution outlets that sell competing products.
- When a service principal enters a new market, it may lack the knowledge that allows it to understand buyer behavior and the nature of competition in that market. Many overseas financial institutions with a poor understanding of the United States financial services market have therefore acted through locally appointed agents who have first-hand knowledge of local market conditions.
- In overseas markets, it may be illegal for a service principal to deal directly with the public—a problem that can be remedied by acting through a local licensed agent.
- In some cases, special skills are required by a service principal that would be very costly to develop in house. This partly explains why commercial banks employ specialist stockbrokers to sell stock on the stock exchange.

8.8.2 *Retail Outlets*

The notion of a retailer in the service sector poses conceptual problems, for it has already been established that a retailer cannot carry an inventory of services—one of the important functions of a retailer of goods. The distinction between a retailer and an agent or franchisee can be a fine one. In general, a retailer operates in a manner that does not create legal relations between the service principal and the final customer. The customer's relationship is only with the retailer.

Many services that pass through retailers have a significant goods element. As an example, many film processing companies sell their services through retail stores under each store's own brand name, and the store takes a profit margin while allowing the film processing company to make its service available locally. Many services, such as key cutting and fast-food catering are often retailed in the form of a franchise agreement, which will be discussed more fully.

Sometimes service retailers undertake another of the traditional goods retailer's function by taking risk. A retailer can buy the right to a block of service transactions, and if these rights are not sold by the time the service is performed, the value of these rights disappears. This can happen when a ticket agent buys a block of tickets on a no-return basis from an event organizer.

8.8.3 Service Wholesalers

Similar conceptual problems apply to the role of the wholesaler. In services, the term is most sensibly understood when an intermediary buys the right to a large volume of service transactions and then proceeds to break them down into smaller units so that retailers or other intermediaries can handle them. Hotel booking agencies that buy large blocks of hotel accommodation earn their margin by buying in volume at low prices and adding a markup as a block booking is broken down into smaller units for sale to retailers or agents. As with retailers, it can be difficult to distinguish a wholesaler from an agent. A hotel wholesaler may have some rights to return unsold accommodation to the hotels concerned and may include in its dealings with customers a statement that the transaction is to be governed by conditions specified by the hotel.

8.9 FRANCHISED SERVICE DISTRIBUTION

The term *franchising* refers to a relationship in which one party—the franchisor—provides the development work on a service format and monitors standards of delivery while coming to an arrangement with a second party—the franchisee—who is licensed to deliver the service, taking some share of the financial risk and reward in return. Vertical franchising occurs where a manufacturer allows a franchisee an exclusive right to make the goods that it has produced available to the public. The more recent business format franchising occurs where an organization allows others to copy the format of its own operations.

The International Franchise Association defines a franchise operation as follows:

> a contractual relationship between the franchisor and franchisee in which the franchisor offers or is obliged to maintain a continuing interest in the business of the franchisee in such areas as know-how and training; wherein the franchise operates under a common trade name, format or procedure owned by or controlled by the franchisor, and in which the franchisee has made or will make a substantial capital investment in his business from his own resources.

The private services sector has recognized the value of franchising and has witnessed significant growth. The number of nonautomotive and gasoline franchises in the United States grew from 312,800 in 1987 to some 424,500 in 1992. During the same period, comparable total franchise sales rose from $80 billion a year to $250 billion. Franchising offers particular opportunities for service industries that are people intensive. It combines the motivation of self-employed franchisees with the quality control and brand values of the franchisor (Figure 8.4).

Franchise agreements cover a diverse range of services, from car rental to fast food, kitchen design services, veterinary services, and hotels. Of the top ten business franchise operations (in terms of turnover), all are involved in essentially service-based activities. Although most franchisees are self-employed individuals or small companies, they can also be very large corporations. It is quite common to find corporate franchisees who operate a large number of hotels or restaurants for a franchisor, making the franchisee a very large organization. Franchising also has applications within the not-for-profit sector.

8.9.1 The Nature of a Franchise Agreement

The franchise agreement sets out the rights and obligations of the franchisor and franchisee. A franchise agreement typically includes the following main clauses:

- The nature of the service to be supplied by the franchisee is specified. This can refer to particular categories of service: for example, a car servicing franchise would probably indicate which specific service operations (such as brake replacement or engine tuning) are covered by the franchise agreement.
- The territory in which the franchisee is given the right to offer a service is usually specified. The premium that a franchisee is prepared to pay for a franchise usually reflects the exclusivity of its territory.
- The length of a franchise agreement is specified. Most franchises run for five to ten years with options to renew at the end of the period.
- The franchisee usually agrees to buy the franchise for an initial fee and agrees to the basis on which future payments are to be made to the franchisor. The level of the initial fee reflects the strength of an established brand. A high initial fee for a strong established brand can be much less risky for a franchisee than a low price for a relatively new franchise. Payment of ongoing fees to the franchisor is usually calculated as a percentage of turnover. The agreement also usually requires the franchisee to buy certain supplies from the franchisor.
- The franchisee agrees to follow instructions from the franchisor concerning the manner of service delivery. Franchisees are typically required to charge according to an agreed scale of prices; maintain standards of reliability, availability, and performance in the delivery of the service; and ensure that any franchisee-produced advertising follows the franchisor's guidelines.
- The franchisee usually agrees not to act as an intermediary for any other service principal. Franchisors insist that their franchised outlets show the same loyalty to the organization as if they were actually owned by the organization. It follows that the operator of a Pizza Hut franchise cannot use a franchised outlet to sell the services or goods of a competing organization such as Burger King. Franchising implies that the franchisor has a degree of control over the franchisee. A retail

agent, in contrast, usually has considerable discretion over the manner in which he or she conducts business. For the franchisor, considerable harm could result if its promotion were used to draw potential customers into the franchisee's outlets, only for them to be cross-sold a service over which the franchisor has no control nor is likely to receive any financial benefit. However, in many cases, service franchises are sold on the understanding that they will form just one small part of the franchisee's operations. For example, a franchise to operate a parcel company's collection point may be compatible with the business of a gas station or convenience store franchisee.

- The franchisor agrees to provide promotional support for the franchisee. The aim of such support is to establish the values of the franchisor's brand in the minds of potential customers, thereby reducing the promotion that the franchisee is required to undertake. The franchise agreement usually requires certain promotional activities of the franchisee to be approved by the franchisor.
- The franchisor usually agrees to provide some level of administrative and technical support for the franchisee. This can include the provision of equipment (e.g., printing machines for a fast-print franchise) and administrative support, such as accounting.
- Franchise agreements usually give either party the right to terminate the franchise and for the franchisee to sell the franchise. The right to terminate can act as a control mechanism should either party fail to perform in accordance with the conditions of the franchise. A successful franchisee would want a clause in an agreement allowing him or her to sell the goodwill of a franchise that has been developed over time.

8.9.2 Franchise Development

Once franchising has taken hold within an organization, it tends to expand rather than contract. If a franchisor has built up a successful brand format, coupled with successful management, it can usually achieve greater returns on its capital by selling the right to use its name than by operating its own outlets. There is, however, a limit to which operations can be franchised, and most franchisors choose not to franchise their operations entirely. There are two important reasons for this. First, new service development is usually easier to carry out in house rather than at a distance through a franchise, and thus franchisees are not alienated if experimental new services fail. Second, some operations may be too specialized for a franchisee to have the standard of training to ensure a consistent standard of delivery, and the franchisor may choose to retain responsibility for providing these operations.

Maintaining and motivating franchisees is a constant challenge for franchisors. Franchisees can become only too aware of the payments that the franchisor takes from them on an ongoing basis, sometimes with little to show by way of the franchisor's contribution to the franchise relationship. As franchising has matured, there have been well-publicized arguments between franchisees and franchisors—the level of franchisees' complaints to the Federal Trade Commission rose from 253 in 1990 to 620 in 1992. Franchisees are often tempted not to renew their franchises at the end of their agreement and to either go into business alone or sign up with other fran-

FRANCHISE OPPORTUNITIES

Listed below are some franchising opportunities. Which ones seem like good opportunities to you?

Name/Address	Number of Franchisees	Description/Training	Equity Capital Needed
Tax Offices of America Box 4098 Waterbury, CT 06704	15	Income tax preparation for individuals & small businesses. Estate planning & business consulting services. Exclusive territories. Training program.	$19,500 & up
Car-X-Muffler & Brake 8430 W. Bryn Mawr Avenue Chicago, IL 60631	135	Retail automotive repair chain specializing in exhaust, brake, suspension, and front-end services. Six week training program.	Equity capital need $200,000; Franchise fee $18,500
Hertz System, Inc. 225 Brae Boulevard Park Ridge, NJ 07656	1,100+	Drive yourself truck/car and non-vehicle equipment rental; Zone System manager trains new franchisee before operation opens; Visits by system manager on a periodic basis; training classes, manuals, etc.	Varies according to location
Duds 'N Suds 3000 Justin Drive Des Moines, Iowa 50322	85	Full service and self-service laundry, soda fountain with pop, coffee, beer, big screen TV. On site training.	$60,000–$80,000
Pilot Air Freight Corporation PO Box 97 Media, PA 19063	70	Domestic/international freight service. Training in classroom with emphasis on operation, customer services, sales, and accounting procedures.	$10,000–$30,000, Determined by market
Coverall North American, Inc. 3111 Camino del Rio North San Diego, CA 92108	1,050	Commercial cleaning and janitorial service. Two week on-the-job training.	$3,250–$33,600

Figure 8.4   Franchising opportunities are available for a variety of services. Sources: *1994 Directory of Franchising Organizations,* Pilot Industries: Babylon, NY 11702 and *1991 Franchise Opportunities Handbook,* United States Department of Commerce, Minority Business Development Agency, U.S. Government Printing Office: Washington, D.C. 20402.

chise operations. Where brands are strong, the former route can be very risky. For example, Benetton retail franchisees who have used their premises to provide their own competing service format have lost customers when the franchisor created a new outlet in the locality. Payment of franchise fees represents good value to a franchisee as long as it receives good backup from the franchisor and a steady supply of customers who are attracted by the reputation of the franchise brand.

Buying a franchise is a popular way for many Americans to realize their dream of owning their own business. Franchisees buy a tested business format and, in return for payments to the franchisor, get the benefits of the latter's market knowledge, business expertise, and centralized promotion. A franchise is also considered a safe bet. The U.S. Small Business Administration has estimated that while 63 percent of all new businesses fail within six years, the comparable figure for new franchisees is just 5 percent. In the early days of franchising, franchisors and franchisees saw themselves as partners working together on a contract that may have been no more than a page or two long.

The easygoing attitude toward franchising changed during the 1990s. A recession, oversaturation in many markets, and huge debt loads from leveraged buyouts put new pressures on franchisors to squeeze their franchisees. Franchising appeared to be going through some form of life cycle in which problems of maturity were beginning to appear. Franchisees' complaints to the Federal Trade Commission were rising, and they were becoming increasingly willing to organize and to lobby legislators to press for a better deal in their dealings with franchisors. Indeed, many franchisees had grown to the point where they had become powerful multi-outlet corporations in their own right. More recent surveys of franchisees carried out by consultants had suggested that the franchisee failure rate was in fact as high as 10 to 12 percent a year.

CASE STUDY

BLIMPIE GETS OUT OF A PICKLE WITH ITS FRANCHISEES

The Blimpie sandwich franchise chain shows what can go wrong and also shows the steps that franchisors can take to ensure that franchisee and franchisor continue to work together as partners. Toward the end of the 1980s, the franchisor's parent—the New York based Astor Restaurant Group—found itself in bad shape, largely as a result of an overenthusiastic and expensive expansion into Mexico. The venture soaked up a lot of capital and management effort at a time when Blimpie's archrival, Subway, was making rapid progress. Morale at Blimpie's 149 franchise outlets was at an all-time low.

While some franchisors were using most of their energy fighting off calls for more regulation of franchise agreements, Blimpie's cofounder and chief executive, Anthony Conza, saw the signals from his franchisees and set about regaining their trust. Part of this trust involved opening communication channels with franchisees in a way they had never seen before. To this end, Conza launched a regular newsletter and set up an 800 hotline to give tips to franchisees and answer their inquiries. To improve feedback still further, he formed a franchisee advisory council to get their comments on key issues, including new products and pricing. He also gave franchisees more control over advertising by forming regional advertising co-ops.

A test of the new relationship between Blimpie and its franchisees came following its expansion into the highly competitive Chicago market, where Subway had already established preeminence. Three of the nine Chicago franchisees were failing, blaming inadequate advertising by Blimpie for failing to make the chain stand out from its much better-known rivals. Recognizing the problem, Blimpie decided that for the time being its franchisees would be allowed to divert their 6 percent royalty fees to support an expanded advertising program. At the top of its mind must have been the negative publicity that would have been picked up by potential franchisees in other areas where Blimpie sought to expand.

The approach adopted by Blimpie appears to be having the desired effects. Between 1987 and 1992, Blimpie's system-wide sales increased by 38 percent from $96 million to $132 million, while the number of outlets has risen from 149 to 570. Most significantly, the franchisee failure rate was down from 10 percent to just 3 percent.

CASE STUDY REVIEW QUESTIONS

1. Explain why Blimpie was able to expand so rapidly between 1987 and 1992.
2. What are the attractions to investors of investing in a Blimpie franchise rather than setting up their own sandwich bar?
3. When, if at all, should government intervene to regulate relationships between franchisor and franchisee?

8.9.3 Franchising within the Not-for-Profit Sector

Although franchising is most commonly associated with services provided by private sector organizations within competitive markets, it is also has valuable benefits within the not-for-profit services sector. Here it can take various forms:

- The right to operate a vital public service can be sold to a franchisee, who in turn has the right to charge users of the facility. The franchisee is normally required to maintain the facility at a required standard and to obtain government approval of prices to be charged. In this way, the National Parks Service sells franchises to private firms for the right to operate hotels and restaurants within the national parks.

- Government can sell the exclusive right for private organizations to operate a service that is of public importance. In the United States, the government has auctioned the rights to operate cellular telephone services to the highest bidders. The successful bidders must operate their services in accordance with regulations laid down by the government.

- In the United States, the U.S. Postal Service has for some time operated through franchised outlets. In addition to government-owned and -operated post offices, contract post offices have been licensed to provide a more limited range of postal services in local communities. Franchises have been taken up by a variety of small businesses, which often combine a post office counter service with the business of a retail shop.

8.10 ACCESSIBILITY THROUGH CO-PRODUCTION

Some services organizations choose to make their services available to consumers in combination with other goods and services with the collaboration of another producer. The outputs of the two organizations can be quite diverse. For example, a finance company could offer loan facilities in conjunction with a company selling hi-fi equipment. Other examples include a combined railroad fare and museum admission ticket and a combined hotel and travel offer.

Other services can be made available in combination with similar services provided by potential competitors. The basis for doing this is that the combined value of the enlarged service offer will generate more business and ultimately be of benefit to all the service providers involved. In this way, many regional travel tickets allow passengers to travel on the subways and buses of potentially competing operators, thereby making public transportation as a whole a relatively attractive option. Similarly, banks benefit by sharing cash dispenser networks. Those sharing them gain a competitive advantage over a bank that chooses to go it alone with its own dedicated but smaller network. In the United States, as in most Western countries, antitrust legislation restricts such co-production where it is deemed to restrict competition in a manner that is against the public interest.

8.11 DEVELOPMENTS TO INCREASE ACCESSIBILITY

The means by which an organization makes its services available to consumers need to be periodically reviewed to reflect the changing marketing environment, especially competition, technological developments, and new legislative constraints and opportunities. The needs of the service as it passes through its life cycle and the changing strengths and weaknesses of the organization might also call for a reassessment of strategy. Here, several important factors affecting future service accessibility decisions are considered.

- New technology can allow a much greater integration of intermediaries and a reduction of the slow bureaucratic procedures that can sometimes result from their use. As an example, new data processing techniques allow airlines and tour operators to provide much quicker and more comprehensive facilities through travel agents, overcoming many of the previous communications constraints imposed by mail and telephone methods of making services available. In the future, continuing developments may even allow the intermediary to be cut out completely by making services available interactively through customers' own video terminals.

- In many services industries, the effects of new technology and the desire of organizations to develop closer relationships with their customers can result in a reduction in the number of intermediaries used and the greater use of direct marketing techniques.

- Having established itself in a market through an independent intermediary, a service principal may attempt to gain more influence over its outlets by acquiring its own branch network.

8.12 MAKING THE TANGIBLE COMPONENTS OF THE SERVICE OFFER AVAILABLE TO CONSUMERS

In some services, tangible goods are a vital element of the overall offering, and a strategy is needed for making them available to consumers. Managing the availability of tangibles assumes importance for several reasons:

- Tangibles may be vital in giving presales evidence of a service offering in the form of printed brochures, order forms, and so on. Imagine the logistical problems an airline with twenty thousand ticket agents would face if it decided to distribute a brochure to potential customers. If the airline were to distribute just fifty copies of its timetable booklet to each agent, it would need to move one million booklets. The fact that airlines often also produce additional supplementary brochures—such as vacations brochures—makes the logistical task even greater.
- Tangibles often form an important component of a service offer, and failure to deliver tangibles reduces the quality of a service or makes it impossible to perform at all. This is true of fast-food restaurant chains, for whom perishable raw materials have to be moved regularly and rapidly.
- Sometimes the fundamental purpose of a service process is to make goods available. Retailers and equipment rental companies provide a service, but without a strategy to move the associated goods effectively, their service becomes of little value (Figure 8.6).
- The trucking industry exists solely to move goods.

When tangibles form an important part of a service offer, their efficient and effective distribution can give an organization a competitive advantage. An inefficient and unreliable distribution system can negate a restaurant chain's efforts at improving service quality if it is unable to deliver the meals it advertises. Here, a very brief overview of the key elements of a physical distribution system as they affect services companies is offered.

8.12.1 Physical Distribution Management

The design of a physical distribution system begins with the setting of objectives. Ideally, a system should make the right goods available in the right places at the right time. Against this must be balanced the need to minimize the cost of distribution, so objectives are stated in a form that involves a trade-off. For example, an airline might realistically aim to deliver 80 percent of brochure requests to travel agents within three working days at the minimum possible cost. Distribution objectives, in turn, are based on an assessment of distribution needs. While a fast-food restaurant chain might be happy to live with a three-day delivery objective for orders for packaging materials, twenty-four-hour delivery (or less) may be required for perishable foods. The importance of rapid and reliable delivery of fresh food would be reflected in a greater willingness to pay premium prices for a service that is capable of meeting objectives; failure to deliver could have a harmful effect on sales and reputation.

A physical distribution system can be seen as comprising six basic elements, which can be manipulated to design an optimum system. They are shown in Figure 8.5. The management decisions to be made in respect of each are considered here.

Suppliers.   A marketing-oriented services organization must balance the need to have supply sources close to customers against the economies of scale that may be obtained from having one central point of supply. Where markets are turbulent, the distribution system may favor suppliers who are closest to the customer rather than necessarily the cheapest sources of production. During a period of market turbulence, a vacation operator may source brochures at home rather than wait for them to be delivered from a possibly cheaper source overseas.

Outlets.   These can range from the individual household to the largest supermarket. If the unique offer of a service is home delivery, strategy must identify the most efficient and effective means of moving associated tangibles to customers' homes.

Inventories.   These need to be held in order to provide rapid availability of goods and to provide contingencies against disruptions in production. Inventories

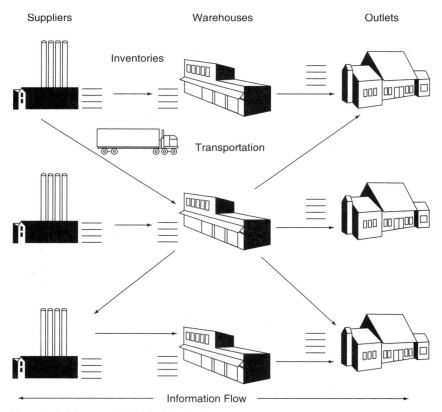

Figure 8.5   Elements of a physical distribution system

Figure 8.6   This advertisement points out a distinctive advantage of renting a car from Hertz—the 1800 European locations. Source: © 1994 Hertz System Inc. Hertz is a registered service mark and trademark of Hertz System Inc.

also occur because of the need to achieve economies of scale in production, resulting in initially large inventories that are gradually reduced until the next production run. Seasonal patterns of production and consumption may also contribute to fluctuating inventories. The need to make goods readily available has to be offset against the need to minimize the cost of holding inventories that can result from capital charges, storage charges, and the risk of obsolescence.

Warehouses.   These are incorporated into a system to provide a break of bulk point and to hold inventories. A company must decide on the number and nature of the warehouses to be incorporated into its system, in particular the balance between the need for local and accessible warehouses and the need for efficiency savings that favors large warehouses. Automation of warehouses with the development of computerized picking systems is increasingly favoring larger warehouses. A national retailer in the United States may include just a dozen strategically located warehouses in its distribution system to serve a national chain of outlets.

Transportation.   This moves inventories from manufacturers to retail outlets and sometimes—as in mail order—to final consumers. Transportation is becoming an increasingly important element of distribution systems, with goods tending to travel for longer average distances within the system, largely reflecting the trend toward large, highly efficient warehouses.

Information flow.   The need to respond to customer requirements rapidly, while at the same time keeping down stockholding levels, demands a rapid flow of information. The development of "just in time" (JIT) systems has been possible only with improvements in data processing techniques. The introduction of bar codes has achieved notable results in this respect. A supermarket can now know minute by minute the state of inventories for all of its products and can order replacement stocks, by an electronic data link, for delivery from a regional distribution center the following day. Similarly, the regional distribution centers can rapidly reorder stocks from their suppliers. The development of "just in time" systems not only has allowed a more reliable level of availability of goods to the final consumer but also has allowed retailers to reduce the warehouse space provided within shops. Because it is no longer necessary to hold large stocks locally, warehouse space can be turned over to more valuable sales floor space.

CHAPTER REVIEW QUESTIONS

1. What are the most important factors influencing the location decision for a proposed new health club facility?
2. Of what value are modeling techniques in deciding on retail store location?
3. How does a travel agent assist tour operators in making vacations available to its customers?
4. In what situations is a service principal likely to prefer dealing directly with its customers rather than through intermediaries?
5. Using examples, contrast the role of "push" and "pull" methods of making services available within the services sector.
6. Analyze the potential problems and opportunities for a dry cleaning company seeking to expand through franchising.

REFERENCES

1. Huff, D. L., "A Programmed Solution for Approximating an Optimal Retail Location," *Land Economics* 42 (1966): 293–303.
2. Fishbein, M. *Readings in Attitude Theory and Measurement* (New York: John Wiley, 1967).
3. Mayo, E. J. and Jarvis, L. P. *The Psychology of Leisure Travel* (Boston: CBI Publishing Co., 1981).

4. Jones, K. G. and Mock, D. R., "Evaluating Retail Trading Performance," in *Store Location and Store Assessment Research,* ed. R. L. Davies and D. S. Rogers (London: John Wiley, 1984).

5. Goodchild, M. F. and Noronha, V. T. "Location Allocation and Impulsive Shopping: The Case of Gasoline Retailing," in *Spatial Analysis and Location Allocation Models,* ed. A. Ghosh and G. Rushton (New York: Van Nostrand and Reinhold, 1987).

SUGGESTED FURTHER READING

CARBONE, T. C. 1989. "Formula for Success: Franchising Means Having a Business Without All the Risk." *Management World* 18 no. 2: 32–3.

COYLE, J. J. 1992. *The Management of Business Logistics,* 5th ed. St. Paul, Minn.: Est Publishing.

DONNELLY, J. H. 1976. "Marketing Intermediaries in Channels of Distribution for Services." *Journal of Marketing* (January): 55–70.

GEORGE, W. R. 1977. "The Retailing of Services—A Challenging Future." *Journal of Retailing* 53, no. 3: 85–98.

GHOSH, A. and RUSHTON, G., eds. 1987. *Spatial Analysis and Location Allocation Models.* New York: Van Nostrand and Reinhold.

GHOSH, A. and CRAIG, S. 1986. "An Approach to Determining the Optimal Location for New Services." *Journal of Marketing Research* (November): 354–62.

HERRON, D. P. 1979. "Managing Physical Distribution for Profit." *Harvard Business Review* (May/June): 121–32.

KELLY, P. J. and GEORGE, W. R. 1982. "Strategic Management Issues for the Retailing of Services." *Journal of Retailing* (Summer): 26–43.

O'NEIL, B. F. and IVESON, J. L. 1991. "Strategically Managing the Logistics Function." *The Logistics and Transportation Review* (December): 359–78.

NORTON, S. W. 1988. "An Empirical Look at Franchising as an Organizational Form." *Journal of Business* 61, no. 2: 197–218.

RAAB, S. S. 1987. *The Blueprint for Franchising a Business.* New York: John Wiley.

STERN, L. W. and EL-ANSARY, A. 1989. *Management in Marketing Channels.* Englewood Cliffs, N.J.: Prentice Hall.

9

Pricing of Services

CHAPTER OBJECTIVES

After reading this chapter, you should be able to understand

- the role of price in developing the marketing mix for services
- factors influencing an organization's price decisions, including organizational objectives, cost levels, strength of demand, level of competition, and external price regulations
- the development of price strategies for services
- methods of implementing a program of tactical pricing
- specific issues raised in the pricing of public services and internally traded services

9.1 INTRODUCTION

For services distributed through market mechanisms, price is the financial mediating device by which exchange takes place between service providers and their customers. Within the services sector, the term *price* often goes by various names, sometimes reflecting the nature of the relationship between customer and provider in which the exchange takes place. Professional services companies therefore talk about *fees,* whereas other organizations use terms such as *fares, tolls, rates, charges,* and *subscriptions.* The art of successful pricing is to establish a price level that is low enough for the exchange to represent good value to consumers, yet high enough to allow a service provider to achieve its financial objectives.

The importance of pricing to the development of marketing strategy is reflected in the diverse range of strategic uses to which it is put.

- At the beginning of the life of a new service, pricing is often used to gain entry to a new market. As an example, a firm of real estate agents seeking to extend its operations to a new region may initially offer very low commission rates in order to raise awareness and gain entry to the local market.
- Price is used as a means of maintaining the market share of a service during its life and is used tactically to defend its position against competitors.
- Ultimately, for organizations working toward financial objectives, prices must be set at a level that allows them to meet those objectives.

While most services are market mediated through the price mechanism, services are more likely than goods to be made available to consumers by methods in which price is not the focal point of the exchange. Many not-for-profit services are supplied to the end user either at no charge or at a charge that bears little relation to the value of the service to the consumer or the producer. Public services, such as museums and schools, that have adopted marketing principles often have no control over the price element of the marketing mix. For example, the reward for attracting more visitors to a museum or pupils to a school may be additional centrally derived grants rather than income received directly from the users of the service.

9.2 ORGANIZATIONAL INFLUENCES ON PRICING DECISIONS

Organizations show diversity in their objectives, and an analysis of corporate objectives is a useful starting point for understanding the factors that underlie price decisions. These are some of the more commonly found organizational objectives and their implications for price decisions:

9.2.1 Profit Maximization

It is often assumed that all private sector organizations exist primarily to maximize their profits and that this is the dominant influence on their pricing policies. In fact, the notion of profit maximization needs to be qualified with a time dimension, for marketing strategies that maximize profits over the short run may damage long-term profits. An organization charging high prices in a new market may make that market seem very attractive to new entrants, thereby increasing the level of competition in subsequent years. Over the longer term, this could actually reduce profitability. Also, the time frame over which profitability is sought can affect pricing decisions. If a new innovative service is given an objective to break even after just one year, prices may be set at a low level in order to capture as large a share of the market as quickly as possible, whereas a longer-term profit objective may have allowed the organization to tap relatively small but high-value segments of its markets in the first year and to exploit lower-value segments in subsequent years. The notion of profit maximization has an additional weakness in the service sector, where it can be difficult to establish clear relationships between costs, revenue, and profits.

9.2.2 Market Share Maximization

It is frequently argued that it is unrealistic to expect the managers of a business to put all their efforts into maximizing profits.[1] First, there can be practical difficulties in establishing relationships between marketing strategy decisions and the resulting change in profitability. Second, management often does not directly receive any reward for increasing its organization's profits—its main concern is to achieve a satisfactory level of profits rather than the maximum possible. It can be argued that managers are more likely to benefit from decisions that increase the market share of their organization. Sales growth can result in increased promotion prospects and job security for managers, even though greater overall profits could probably have been achieved by more ruthless pruning of activities that made little contribution to overhead.

An objective to maximize market share may be very important to service industries in which it is necessary to achieve a critical mass in order to achieve economies of scale and therefore competitive advantage. The price competition that has accompanied the development of some grocery retail chains in the United States has often been based on the desire of companies to obtain long-term profitability by achieving economies of scale in buying, distribution, and promotion.

9.2.3 Survival

Sometimes, the idea of maximizing profits or market share is a luxury to a service provider, whose main objective is simply to survive and to avoid going into bankruptcy. Most businesses fail when they run out of cash for debts when they become due for payment. In these circumstances, prices may be set at a very low level simply to get sufficient cash to help the organization get past its short-term problems. During the Persian Gulf War in 1991, demand for air travel fell significantly. This put severe pressure on the resources of many smaller airlines, which suffered doubly from the increase in aviation fuel prices. Many airlines were forced to lower fares dramatically to keep cash flowing into the business long enough to surmount what they thought would be the last hurdle before regaining a long-term growth path.

9.2.4 Social Objectives

Profit-related objectives still have little meaning to many not-for-profit organizations. The price of some public services represents a tax levied by government, based on wider considerations of the ability of users to pay for the service and the public benefits of that service. As an instrument of social policy, educational services aimed at disadvantaged groups are often priced at very low prices or at no charge at all.

Although social objectives are normally associated with public services, they can sometimes be found within the private sector. For example, within benefits packages, employers often provide services for their staff at prices that do not reflect the true value of the service. Examples include staff restaurants and sports clubs, which are often priced at much lower levels than their normal market value.

In practice, organizations work to a number of objectives simultaneously. For example, a market share objective over the short term may be seen as a means toward achieving a long-term profit maximizing objective.

9.3 FACTORS INFLUENCING PRICING DECISIONS

An organization's objectives specify the desired results of pricing policies. Strategies are the means by which price is used to achieve these objectives. Before pricing strategy is discussed it is useful to lay the groundwork by analyzing the underlying factors that influence price decisions. Four important bases for price determination can be identified:

- what it costs to produce a service
- the amount that consumers are prepared to pay for it
- the price that competitors are charging
- the constraints on pricing that are imposed by regulatory agencies

The cost of producing a service represents the minimum price that a commercial organization would be prepared to accept over the long term for providing the service. The maximum price achievable is what customers are prepared to pay for the service. This will itself be influenced by the level of competition. Government regulation may intervene to prevent organizations from charging the maximum price that consumers would theoretically be prepared to pay. These principles are illustrated in Figure 9.1.

9.3.1 "Cost Plus" Pricing

Many empirical studies have shown the importance of costs as a basis for determining prices within the service sector. For example, in their study of service firms in the United States, Zeithaml, Parasuraman, and Berry found that cost was the dominant basis for price determination.[2]

At its most simple, a "cost plus" pricing system works by using historical cost information to calculate a unit cost for each type of input used in a service production process. Subsequent price decisions for specific services are based on the number of units of inputs used, multiplied by the cost per unit (adjusted for inflation), plus a profit margin. This method of setting prices is widely used in service industries as diverse as catering, building, accountancy, and vehicle servicing. An example of how a truck operator might calculate its prices on this basis is shown in Figure 9.2.

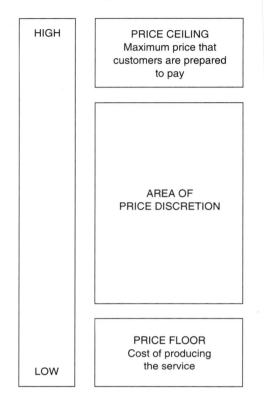

Figure 9.1   The key influences on price decisions

"Cost plus" type pricing methods are very popular within the services sector, for several reasons:

- Selling prices are easy to calculate; sales staff can easily calculate the price of services that have to be tailored to the individual needs of customers. For example, every building job, vehicle repair, or landscape gardening job is likely to be unique, and a price for each job can be calculated by junior staff using standard unit costs for the inputs required to complete the job and a predetermined profit margin.
- When an agreement is made to provide a service, but the precise nature of the actual service is unknown at the outset, a contract may stipulate that the final price will be based in some way on costs. A garage agreeing to repair a car with an unidentified engine noise cannot realistically give the customer a price quotation before undertaking the job and examining the nature of the problem. In these circumstances, the customer may agree to pay an agreed amount per hour for labor, plus the cost of any parts.
- Trade and professional associations often include codes of conduct that allow the service provider to increase prices beyond those originally estimated only on the basis of the actual costs incurred. Attorneys and accountants, for example, who

Cost information for most recent trading year:

Total drivers' wage cost $675,000
Total drivers' hours worked   45,000
Cost per driver's hour $15.00
Total vehicle running costs $100,000
Total mileage operated   250,000
Vehicle operating costs per mile $0.40

Total other overhead costs $30,000
Overhead per mile operated $0.12

Required return on sales   15%

For a price quotation based on a 200-mile journey requiring 12 hours of driver's time:

Total Price:

200 miles × $0.40 = $80.00
12 hours × $15.00 = $180.00
Overheads (based on
    mileage):
200 miles × $0.12 = $24.00

Total = $284.00
Add 15% margin = $42.60

TOTAL PRICE = $326.60

Figure 9.2   "Cost plus" method of price setting for a truck operator

need to commit more resources than originally expected to complete a job, are bound by their professional bodies to pass on only their reasonable additional costs.

Against these attractions, pricing services solely on a "cost plus" basis presents several problems:

- In itself, cost-based pricing does not consider the competition a service faces at any particular time nor the fact that some customers may value the same service more highly than others.
- Calculating the costs of a particular service can in fact be very difficult—often more difficult than in the case of goods—because of the structure of costs facing many services businesses.
- While it may be possible to determine costs for previous accounting periods, it can be difficult to predict what these costs will actually be at the time they are produced. This is a particular problem for services that are contracted to be provided at some time in the future. Unlike goods, services cannot be produced at known cost levels in the current period and stored for consumption in some future period. Historical cost information is often adjusted by an inflation factor when service delivery is to be made in the future, but it can be difficult to decide what is the most appropriate inflation factor to use for a specific input. When input costs are highly volatile (e.g., aviation fuel), one solution is for a service producer to pass on part of the risk of unpredictable inflation to customers. Charter airlines frequently do this

by requiring customers to pay for any increase in fuel costs beyond a specified amount.

9.3.2 The Problem of Cost Allocation

The costs of producing a service are both variable and fixed. Variable costs increase as service production increases, whereas fixed costs remain unchanged if an additional unit of service is produced. Fixed costs, therefore, cannot be attributed to any particular unit of output. In between these two extremes of costs are semifixed costs, which remain constant until production reaches a certain level of output that necessitates expenditure on additional units of productive capacity. The particular problem of many services industries is that fixed costs represent a very high proportion of total costs, resulting in great difficulty in calculating the cost of any particular unit of service.

The importance of fixed costs for a number of services industries is illustrated in Table 9.1, where a variable cost is defined as any cost that varies directly as a result of one extra customer consuming a service for which there is currently spare capacity. One more passenger on a domestic flight from New York to Boston results only in nominal additional variable costs of an extra inflight meal and the airport departure tax that has to be paid for each passenger. The cost of flight attendants and aircraft depreciation does not change, nor do the more remote fixed costs such as head office administration and promotion.

It can be argued that over the long term, all costs borne by a business are variable. In the case of the airline, if the unit of analysis is a particular flight rather than one individual passenger, the proportion of variable costs increases. So, if the airline withdrew just one return journey between the two points, it would save fuel costs, making fuel a variable cost. It would probably also save some staff costs, but it may still have to incur aircraft depreciation costs and the more remote head office admin-

TABLE 9.1   FIXED AND VARIABLE COSTS IN SELECTED SERVICE INDUSTRIES

Service	Fixed costs	Variable costs
Restaurant	Building maintenance Rent and rates Waiters and cooks	Food
Bank mortgage	Staff time Building maintenance Corporate advertising	Sales commission Paper and postage
Domestic air journey	Aircraft maintenance and depreciation Head office administrative costs	Airport departure tax Inflight meal
Hairdresser	Building maintenance Rent and rates	Shampoos used

istration costs. If the whole route were closed, even more costs would become variable—staff employed at the terminal could be cut, as could the flight crews. It might be possible for the airline to avoid some of its aircraft depreciation costs by reducing the size of its fleet. Even promotional costs would become variable, as part of the airline's advertising would no longer be incurred if the service were closed completely.

High levels of fixed costs are associated with high levels of interdependency between different service outputs that share common inputs. As an example, the cost of maintaining a retail bank branch network is fixed over the short to medium term, yet the network provides facilities for a wide range of different service activities—current accounts, mortgages, business loans, and foreign currency business, to name but a few. Staff may be involved in handling each of these activities in the course of a working day, and it is likely that no special space is reserved exclusively for each activity. For many of these activities, the short-term direct costs are quite negligible. For example, the direct cost of one order to change dollars into an overseas currency is little more than the cost of a receipt slip. But users of this service would be expected to contribute toward the overhead costs of staff and space. There is frequently no obvious method by which these fixed costs can be attributed to specific units of output or even to particular types of service. The fixed costs for money exchange, for instance, could be allocated on the basis of the proportion of floor space occupied, proportion of staff time used, proportion of total turnover, or some combination of these factors. Allocation bases are often the result of judgement and political infighting. They can change as a result of arguments between cost center managers, who invariably feel that their product is contributing excessively to fixed costs. Each manager may argue that their pricing base is putting them at a disadvantage against competitors who have a simpler cost structure. In the end, cost allocation is a combination of scientific analysis and bargaining.

9.3.3 Marginal Cost Pricing

A special kind of cost-based pricing occurs when firms choose to ignore their fixed costs. The price charged to any individual customer is based not on the total unit cost of production but only on the additional costs that result directly from serving that additional customer. It is used when the bulk of a company's output has been sold at a full price that recovers its fixed costs, but in order to fill remaining capacity, the company brings its prices down to a level that at least covers its variable, or avoidable, costs. Marginal cost pricing is widely used in service industries with low short-term supply elasticity and high fixed costs. It is common in the airline industry, where the perishability of a seat renders it unsalable after departure. Rather than receive no revenue for an empty seat, an airline may prefer to get some income from a passenger, as long as the transaction provides a contribution that more than covers additional costs (e.g., food and departure taxes).

Against the attraction of filling spare capacity and getting a contribution toward fixed costs where otherwise there would be none, marginal cost pricing does have its problems. The biggest danger is that it can be taken too far, allowing too high a proportion of customers to be carried at marginal cost, with too few customers charged at full price to cover the fixed costs. Many airlines and vacation tour operators have fallen into the trap of selling vacations on this basis, only to find that their fixed costs have not been fully covered. Another problem is that it may devalue customers' perception of a service. If a service promoted for its prestige value can be sold for a fraction of its original price, it may leave potential customers wondering just what the true value of the service is. It may also cause resentment from customers who had committed themselves to a service well in advance, only to find that their fellow consumers obtained a lower price by booking later (and thereby also making marketing planning much more difficult for many service operators). Companies can try to overcome problems of marginal cost pricing by differentiating the marginally costed product from the one purchased at full price. Cruise operators, for instance, reduce the price of last-minute standby cruises but offer no guarantee of the precise accommodation to be made available.

9.3.4 Demand-Based Pricing

The upper limit to the price of a service is determined by what customers are prepared to pay for it. In fact, different customers often put differing ceilings on the price they are prepared to pay. Successful demand-oriented pricing is therefore based on effective segmentation of markets to achieve the maximum price from each segment. Price segmentation can be carried out on different bases:

- segmentation between different groups of users
- segmentation between different points of use
- segmentation between different types of use

Price segmentation between different groups of users.   Effective price segmentation requires groups of consumers to be segmented in such a way that maximum value is obtained from each segment. Sometimes this can be achieved by simply offering the same service to each segment but charging a different price. In this way, a hairdresser can offer seniors a haircut identical to the one offered to all other customer groups in all respects except price. The rationale could be that this segment is more price sensitive than other segments, and therefore additional profitable business can be gained only by sacrificing some element of profit margin. By performing more haircuts, even at a lower price, a hairdresser may end up having increased total net revenue from this segment while still preserving the higher prices charged to other segments.

On other occasions, the service offering is slightly differentiated and is targeted to segments of people who are prepared to pay a price that reflects its differential advantages. This is particularly important when it is impossible or undesirable to restrict the availability of a lower price to certain predefined groups. Take the example of airlines operating between London and New York. Most operators offer a variety of fare and service combinations to suit the needs of several segments. One segment requires the ability to travel at short notice and is typically traveling on business; because the cost of not being able to travel at short notice may be high, this business traveler is prepared to pay a relatively high price in return for ready availability. A subsegment of this market may wish to arrive refreshed and ready for a day's work and is prepared to pay more for the differentiated first class accommodation. Nonbusiness travelers may be happy to accept a lower price in return for committing themselves to a particular flight at least two weeks before departure. Another segment with less income to spend on travel may be prepared to take the risk of obtaining a last-minute standby flight in return for a still lower-priced ticket.

The intangible and inseparable nature of services make the possibilities for price segmentation between different groups of users much greater than is usually the case with manufactured goods. Goods can easily be purchased by one person, stored, and sold to another person. If price segmentation allowed one group to buy bread at a discounted price, it would be possible for this group to buy bread and resell it to people in higher-priced segments, thereby reducing the effectiveness of the segmentation exercise. Because services are produced at the point of consumption, it is possible to control the availability of services to different segments. Therefore, a hairdresser who offers a discounted price for seniors is able to ensure that only such people are charged the lower price—seniors cannot go into the hairdresser's to buy a haircut and then resell it to a higher price segment.

CASE STUDY

LAWYERS FORCED TO TAKE THE PLUS OUT OF "COST PLUS" PRICING

Lawyers have charged for their services on the basis of "cost plus" methods for a long time. As their service is very labor intensive, the principal cost is the remuneration of attorneys, while the "plus" is the margin that a firm feels it can charge to cover its overhead expenses and provide an adequate profit. Law firms generally enjoyed the boom years of the mid-1980s—the "plus" element of their charges had gradually became bigger and bigger. During a period when businesses in general were prosperous, and there was a shortage of qualified attorneys, law firms could charge by the hour with few questions being asked. It was not uncommon for them to bill their clients at rates of up to $450 per hour.

By contrast, the recession of the late 1980s found many corporate clients eager to trim their overhead costs, including the amount they paid for legal services. Their quest for a more realistic charging basis was bolstered by the glut of newly trained lawyers being produced by law schools and the growth of in-house legal services departments operated by their clients. Law firms had to consider alternative charging methods that met the price expectations of their clients.

Hourly "cost plus" charging had become very popular because it was very often difficult at the outset to know just what work would be involved in a case. This is especially true in product liability and personal injury work, where it is often impossible to foresee all of the twists and turns in a case and hence predict its actual length and cost. However, "cost plus" charging had come to give entirely the wrong economic incentives to law firms. A 1991 study by the Brookings Institution showed that hourly billing led to needless and expensive work: attorneys were tempted to stretch out their time rather than aim for efficiency or results. Common abuses included loading cases with bloated teams of attorneys, sending two lawyers to take a deposition when only one was needed, and assigning high-priced attorneys to summarize depositions, answer complaints, and do other routine work that could easily be undertaken by less expensive paralegals.

In the changed environment of the 1990s, law firms have responded to the demands of corporate clients by agreeing to new methods of pricing. New upstart firms, hungry for business, have been particularly eager to experiment. An example is the Dallas-based firm of Bickel and Brewer, which charges fixed fees for over two-thirds of its work. Fixed fees work well where the amount of work required on a case can be quite easily predicted, as with real estate transactions and routine worker's compensation claims. Many law firms have combined fixed-rate billing with payments that are related to the outcome of a case. Without the incentive to roll up hours, attorneys could be more aggressive about settling a claim and more efficient in tackling it.

Where there is no realistic alternative to "cost plus" pricing methods, many law firms have agreed to the demands of their clients that the law firm's costs be monitored and audited. Big users of law services, such as the insurance company Fireman's Fund, use outside auditing agencies to check for waste. As a result of its own initiative, Fireman's Fund estimates that it has saved about $1 million a year on costs not agreed to.

The message for law firms is clear. To succeed in an increasingly competitive market place, they cannot rely on traditional methods of pricing their services. Their clients' expectations have changed, and firms that respond to these changed expectations are likely to be the most successful. While Bickel and Brewer—a firm willing to experiment with fixed-rate pricing—reported record profits in 1991, some of the more traditional practices began talking about limiting the hiring of new recruits to meet a declining level of demand.

CASE STUDY REVIEW QUESTIONS

1. Other industries such as car repair also use cost-based charging systems. Summarize the problems inherent in such systems.
2. In an industry such as legal service, what factors are likely to precipiate a move away from cost-based pricing? What factors are likely to limit changes in pricing practices?
3. What ethical considerations might be raised by moving from cost-based to results-based methods of charging for services?

Price segmentation between different points of consumption. Services organizations frequently charge different prices at different service locations. The inseparability of service production and consumption allows services firms to define their price segments on the basis of both the point of consumption and the point of production, and they often take the production outlet as a basis for price segmentation in its own right. An example is found in retail store chains, which in addition to using price to target particular groups of customers, also often charge different prices at different stores. Many use a variety of lists that are applied to branches according to the local strength of demand—this itself can reflect the level of local competition, the prevailing general level of prices, and the retailer's local strength in terms of location and brand recognition.

Some production locations may offer unique advantages to consumers. Unlike goods, the service offering cannot be transferred from where it is cheapest to produce to where it is most valued. Service providers can therefore charge higher prices at premium sites. Hotel chains charge high premiums for hotels located in vacation areas. A hotel room in the center of Manhattan offers much greater benefits to business and leisure consumers who wish to visit central New York without a long drive back to their accommodation. Hotel prices for comparable standards of hotel therefore fall as distance from the city increases.

Transportation services present an interesting example of price segmentation by location, as operators frequently charge different prices at each end of a route. The New York to London air travel market is quite different from the London to New York market. The state of the respective local economies, levels of competition, and customers' buying behavior differ between the two markets, resulting in different pricing policies in each. Because of the personal nature of an airline ticket and the fact that discounted return tickets specify the outward and return dates of travel, airlines are able to restrict tickets from being purchased in the low-priced area and used by passengers originating from the higher priced area.

Price segmentation by time of production.   Goods produced in one period can usually be stored and consumed in subsequent periods. Charging different prices in each period could result in customers buying goods for storage when prices are low and using up their stockpiles when prices are high. Because services are instantly perishable, much greater price segmentation by time is possible.

Services often face uneven demand that follows a daily, weekly, annual, seasonal, cyclical, or random pattern. At the height of each peak, pricing is usually a reflection of these factors:

- the greater willingness of customers to pay higher prices when demand is strong
- the greater cost that often results from service operators trying to cater for short peaks in demand

The main reason that strong demand at certain times of the day results in a greater willingness to pay high prices is the shortage of supply relative to demand and the fact that customers may have no realistic alternative. In the case of railroad services into the major urban centers, workers must generally arrive at work at a specified time, and congested roads may limit alternative means of getting to work. A railroad operator can therefore sustain a higher level of fares during the daily commuter peak period. Price segmentation can occur not only between different periods of the day but between different periods of the week (e.g., higher fares for many air services on a Friday evening) or between different seasons of the year (beach hotels during the summer months).

Price segmentation by time can be effective in inducing new business at what would otherwise be a quiet period. Hotels in holiday resorts frequently lower their prices in the off-peak season to tempt additional customers. Many of the public utilities lower their charges during off-peak periods. For example, telephone companies offer lower rates at night to stimulate relatively price-sensitive long-distance demand by personal customers.

In most cases of price segmentation by time, there is also some relationship to production costs. The argument of telephone operators is typical of many service industries in claiming that the marginal cost of producing additional output during off-peak periods is relatively low. As long as peak demand has covered the fixed costs of providing equipment, off-peak output can be supplied on a marginal cost basis.

9.3.5 Competitor-Based Pricing

In very few situations can an organization set its prices without taking account of its competitors' activities. Competition can be defined in terms of the similarity of the service offered or merely the similarity of the needs which it satisfies. For example, a chain of video rental shops can see its competition narrowly in terms of other rental chains, or more widely to include movie theatres and satellite television services, or more widely still to include any form of entertainment.

Having established what market it is in and who the competition is, an organization must establish what price position it will adopt relative to its competitors. This position will reflect the service's much wider marketing mix strategy, so if the company has invested in providing a relatively high-quality service whose benefits have been effectively promoted to target users, it may justifiably pitch its price level higher than its competitors do.

For services targeting similar subsegments of a market, the pricing decisions of competitors will have a direct bearing on an organization's own pricing decisions. Price is used in these circumstances as a tactical weapon to gain short-term competitive advantage over rivals. In a market where the competitors have broadly similar cost structures, price cutting can be destabilizing and can result in costly price wars with no sustainable increase in sales or profitability. An example of price being used to gain short-term competitive advantage has been seen in periodic attempts by airlines to increase their market share by cutting fares. While their market share has often increased in the short term, their efforts have often been neutralized shortly afterward by the retaliatory price cutting of competitors, leaving all the competitors temporarily worse off.

Going rate pricing. In some services markets that are characterized by a fairly homogeneous service offering, demand is so sensitive to price that a firm would risk losing most of its business if it charged just a small amount more than its competitors. On the other hand, charging any less would result in immediate retaliation from competitors, so that nobody would be any better off. For example, in some areas several restaurants cluster closely together, all offering a basically similar service at a similar price. For the price-sensitive diner, the "dish of the day" may be set at the going rate, while more specialized dishes for which there is less direct competition are priced at a premium rate.

When cost levels are difficult to establish, charging a going rate can avoid the problems of trying to calculate costs. As an example, it may be very difficult to calculate the cost of renting out a video film, as the figure will depend on assumptions made about the number of uses over which the initial purchase cost can be spread. It is much easier to make price decisions on the basis of the going rate among nearby competitors.

Sealed bid pricing. Many industrial services are provided by means of a sealed bidding process whereby interested parties are invited to submit a bid for supplying services on the basis of a predetermined specification. In many government contracts, the organization inviting bids may be legally obliged to accept the lowest bid, unless exceptional circumstances can be proved. Price therefore becomes a crucial concern for bidders, regardless of their efforts to build up long-term brand values, which in other markets might have allowed them to charge a premium price. The first task of a bidding company is to establish a minimum bid price based on its costs and required rate of return, below which it would not be prepared to bid. The more difficult task is to try to put a maximum figure on what it can bid. This is based on expectations of what its competitors will bid, following an analysis of their strengths and weaknesses.

9.4 DISTORTIONS TO MARKET-LED PRICING DECISIONS

It is sometimes presumed that organizations set prices on the basis of market forces and that markets themselves are competitive. In practice, services are more likely than goods to be supplied in noncompetitive environments, and this results in government intervention in pricing decisions. The nature and consequences of such market distortions are discussed here.

9.4.1 Pricing in Noncompetitive Markets

In most Western countries there is a presumption that competition is necessary as a means of minimizing prices charged to consumers. However, while price competition may appear to act in the short-term interests of consumers, this normally restrains the combined profits of competitors. It is common, therefore, for competing organizations to want to come to some sort of agreement among themselves about prices to be charged in order to avoid costly price competition. To counter this, most Western governments have actively attempted to eliminate practices that reduce the level of competition in a market. In the United States, price fixing is considered a conspiracy under the Sherman Act and the Federal Trade Commission Act. The law has been used in the airline industry on several occasions, for example, in a price fixing case during the early 1990s in which several major carriers were implicated.

Although marketers like the attractiveness of charging different prices for different groups of buyers, this could be considered an anticompetitive activity. The Robinson-Patman Act makes any price discrimination illegal where price differences are not based on cost differences or the need to meet competition. It is illegal for a large company to use artificially low predatory prices in an attempt to drive a smaller competitor out of business (e.g., the attempt by Northwest Airlines in 1993 to use predatory pricing to undermine competition from the much smaller Reno Air).

9.4.2 Regulation as a Factor Influencing
Pricing Decisions

In addition to some publicly provided services whose prices are set as a matter of social policy, many private sector services companies must consider regulations when setting their prices. These regulations can be classified as follows:

- direct government controls to regulate monopoly power
- government controls on price representations

Direct government controls to regulate monopoly power.   Many private sector utilities provide their services without any direct competition, and government therefore attempts to protect consumers from monopoly exploitation. The most effective long-term solution is to create a more competitive market by encouraging more suppliers in a market. In many cases, however, the development of a competitive market is either impractical or undesirable. For this reason, the government has until recently allowed just one company to provide local telephone services in an area (although in this case, the possibility that cable television companies will be able to carry telephone calls may help increase competition). In such cases, government has the powers to regulate the prices charged (as well as the power to determine service standards). Most states use legislation to control prices charged by electricity, gas, and local telephone utilities. Even in the cable television market, whose prices had been deregulated since 1986, operators were ordered by the Federal Communications Commission in 1993 to cut their charges where a single company enjoyed a monopoly. A study had shown that monopoly advantage had been used to increase average charges by 53.4 percent between 1986 and 1991—more than double the general rate of inflation.

Government controls on price representations.   In addition to controlling or influencing the actual level of prices, government regulation can affect the manner in which price information is communicated to potential customers. The most general legislation derives from the Wheeler Lea Amendment, which bans unfair or deceptive acts in commerce. More specific regulations govern price representations made in respect of financial services. For example, it is unlawful to make misleading claims about the true rate of interest charged on a personal loan.

9.5 PRICING STRATEGY

The factors that underlie pricing decisions have now been identified. This section analyzes ways in which these factors can be manipulated to give strategic direction to pricing policy in order that organizational objectives can be met. The challenge here is to make pricing work as an effective element of the marketing mix, combining with the other mix elements to give a service provider a profitable market position. An effective strategy must identify the roles price will play as a service moves through the different stages in the life cycle from the launch stage through growth to maturity.

This analysis of pricing strategy will consider, first, the development of a strategy for a new service launch, and second, price adjustments to established services. In practice, of course, it is often not easy to distinguish the two situations, as when an existing service is modified or relaunched.

9.6 NEW SERVICE PRICING STRATEGY

In developing a price strategy for a new service, two key issues need to be addressed:

- What price position is sought for the service?
- How novel is the service offering?

The choice of price position cannot be separated from other elements of the marketing mix. In many consumer services, the price element can itself interact with the product quality element of a positioning strategy. This can happen when consumers have difficulty in distinguishing between competing services before consumption, and the price charged is seen as an important indication of quality. Private consumers choosing a painter or decorator with no knowledge of his or her previous work record may be cautious about accepting the cheapest quotation because it may reflect an inexperienced worker with a poor quality record.

The novelty of a new service offering can be analyzed in terms of whether it is completely new to the market, or merely new to the company providing it but already available from other sources. In the case of completely new innovative services, the company will have some degree of monopoly power in its early years. For example, when a bank introduces the first ATM facility to a town, it will have a monopoly for a while. On the other hand, the launch of a "me too" service to compete with established services is likely to face heavy price competition from its launch stage. The distinction between innovative services and copycat services is the basis of two distinct pricing strategies: price skimming and saturation pricing.

9.6.1 Price Skimming Strategy

Most completely new product launches are aimed initially at the segment of users who can be labeled "innovators"—consumers who have the resources and inclination to be the trend-setters in purchasing new goods and services. This group includes the first people to buy innovative services such as portable telecommunication services. Following them will be a group of early adopters, followed by a larger group often described as the "early majority." The subsequent "late majority" group may take up the new service only when the product market itself has reached maturity. "Laggards" are the last group to adopt a new service and do so only when the product has become a social norm and/or its price has fallen sufficiently. A diffusion model is illustrated in Figure 10.2.

Price skimming strategies attempt to gain the highest possible price from the innovators. When sales to this segment appear to be approaching saturation level, the price level is lowered in order to appeal to the early adopter segment, which has a lower price threshold at which it is prepared to purchase the service. This process is repeated for the following adoption categories.

The art of effective pricing of innovative services is to identify who the earliest adopters are, how much they are prepared to pay, and how long this price can be sustained before competitors come on the scene with imitation services at a lower price. A price skimming strategy works by gradually lowering prices to gain access to new segments and to protect market share against new market entrants. In this way, pricing strategy is closely related to the concept of the product life cycle. A typical price skimming strategy showing price levels through time is shown in part (a) of Figure 9.3.

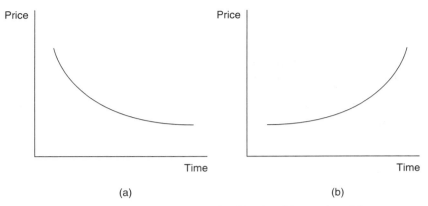

Figure 9.3   Pricing strategies compared: (a) price skimming; (b) saturation pricing

It can be argued that diffusion patterns for new industrial services are generally different from those for consumer services. There is less desire to be a trend-setter and a different type of rationality in purchase decisions. This limits the opportunities for price skimming to situations where commercial buyers can use innovative service inputs to gain an early competitive advantage.

For many innovative services, the trend of falling prices may be further enhanced by falling costs. Lower costs can be caused by economies of scale (e.g., the cost per customer of providing the technical support for a home shopping service declines as fixed costs are spread over more volume) and also by the experience effect—the process by which costs fall as experience in production is gained.[3] The experience effect is of particular strategic significance to service industries, since by pursuing a strategy to gain experience faster than its competitors, an organization lowers its cost base and has a greater scope for adopting an aggressive pricing strategy. The combined effects of these two factors can be seen in the portable telephone market, where high initial prices have been brought down by the ability of network operators to spread their capital costs over increasing numbers of users. Also, operators have learned from experience to provide a given level of service more efficiently (for example, through adjusting transmitter locations).

9.6.2 Saturation Pricing Strategy

Many "new" services are launched as copies of existing competitors' services. In the absence of unique product features, a low initial price can be used to encourage people who show little brand loyalty to switch service suppliers. Once an initial trial has been made, a service provider would attempt to develop increased loyalty from its customers, as a result of which they will be prepared to pay progressively higher prices. A saturation pricing strategy is shown diagrammatically in part (b) of Figure 9.3.

The success of a saturation pricing strategy is dependent on a sound understanding of the buying behavior of the target market (Figure 9.4) and these aspects in particular:

Figure 9.4　Midland is practicing a saturation pricing strategy. Source: The Midland Certified Reagent Company, Midland TX.

- The level of consumers' knowledge about prices. For some services, such as credit cards, consumers typically have little idea of the rate of interest they are currently paying or indeed of the "going rate" for such charges. Therefore, any attempt to attract new customers on the basis of a differential price advantage may prove unsuccessful. Other incentives (e.g., free gifts or money-off vouchers) may be more effective at inducing new business. Companies offering a diverse range of services may sometimes offer low prices on services for which price comparisons are commonly made, but charge higher prices on other related services about which consumer knowledge is lower. Customers of attorneys may shop around for a standard service such as representation during a house purchase but may be more reluctant to do so when faced with a nonroutine purchase such as civil litigation.

- The extent to which the service supplier can increase prices on the basis of perceived added value of the service offering. The purpose of a low initial price is to encourage new users of a service to try a service and return later, paying progressively higher prices. If the new competitor's service is perceived to offer no better value than that of the existing supplier, the disloyalty that caused the initial switching could result in switching back at a later date in response to tactical pricing. Worse still, a newly launched service could experience start-up problems in its early days, doing nothing to generate a perception of added value.

- The extent to which the service supplier can turn a casually gained relationship into a long-term committed relationship. Incentives are frequently offered to lessen the attractiveness of switching away from a brand. This can take the form of a subscription rate for regular purchase of a service, or offering an ever-increasing range of services that together raise the cost to the consumer of transferring business elsewhere. Banks may offer easy transfers between various savings and investment accounts and, in doing so, aim to reduce the attractiveness of moving one element of the customer's business elsewhere.

In some cases, a high initial consumer adoption of a new service may itself add value to the service offering. This can be true when co-production of benefits among consumers is important. A telecommunications operator offering data exchange facilities will be able to offer a more valuable service if large numbers of users are contracted to its system, offering more communications possibilities for potential new users. In the same way, airport landing slots become increasingly valuable to an airline operator as an airport becomes progressively busier, as each airline is able to offer a more comprehensive and valuable set of potential connections to its customers. In both cases, a low initial price may be critical to gain entry to a market, while raising prices is consistent with increasing value to the users of the service.

9.6.3 Evaluating Strategic Pricing Options

In practice, pricing strategies often contain elements of skimming and saturation strategies. The fact that most new services are in fact adaptations and are easy to copy often prevents a straightforward choice of strategy. Even when a price strategy has been adopted and implemented, it may go off target, for any of several reasons:

- Poor market research may have misjudged potential customers' willingness to pay for a new service. The service provider may have misjudged the effect of price competition from other services, which, although different in form, satisfied the same basic needs.

- Competitors may emerge sooner or later than expected. The fact that new services are often easily and quickly copied can result in a curtailment of the period during which an organization can expect to achieve relatively high prices. For example, an optician opening the first eye care center in an expanding community may expect to enjoy a few years of higher price levels before competitors drive them down, only to find that another optician has a similar idea and opens a second eye care center shortly afterwards.

- Government regulation may extend or shorten the period during which a company has a protected market for its service. In the United States, local telephone companies' monopoly of local services may be ended by government action that removes previous restrictions on cable television companies using their infrastructure to provide telephone services. Price competition may occur earlier than had otherwise been anticipated.

9.6.4 Price Leader or Follower?

Many services markets are characterized by a small number of dominant suppliers and a large number of smaller ones. Perfect competition and pure monopoly are two extremes that rarely occur in practice. In markets that show some signs of interdependency among suppliers, firms can often be described as price makers, or price followers. Price makers, as a result of their size and power within a market, are able to determine the levels and patterns of prices, which other suppliers then follow. Price takers, on the other hand, tend to have a relatively low size and market share and may lack product differentiation, resources, or management drive to adopt a proactive pricing strategy. For this reason, the smaller real estate agents in a local area may find it convenient to simply respond to pricing policies adopted by the dominant firms. To take a proactive role themselves may bring about a reaction from the dominant firms, which they would be unable to defend on account of their size and standing in the market.

CASE STUDY

PRICING BEHAVIOR BRINGS BLOODBATH TO UNITED STATES AIRLINE INDUSTRY

A bloodbath quite vividly describes the United States airline industry during the early 1990s. In the two years leading up to 1992, the airlines between them lost $6 billion—more than their entire profits during the previous twenty years. More than a decade after deregulation of the industry, the struggle for market share saw airlines continuing to use a deadly weapon in their marketing mix: pricing.

Price wars have been frequent since deregulation, ranging from local skirmishes between an established operator on a route and a new upstart to all-out nationwide price-cutting campaigns. It has been argued by many that price wars have been used by the strong carriers as a means of consolidating their hold of a market by keeping challengers at bay. The accusing finger has often been pointed at American Airlines, which with a 1991 annual revenue of $13 billion had become the largest airline in the United States. The philosophy of American's chairman, Robert Crandall, has been quite clear: the airline business is an intensely competitive business, and American will not give a price advantage to its competitors. In this brutal world, market mechanisms will remove airlines whose prices do not cover their costs.

A major skirmish occurred in 1992, initiated in April by American's launch of a new fare structure that offered just four basic fares on any one route. The structure—which was dubbed "value pricing"—replaced the myriad of convoluted special fares that had targeted small segments of fliers and had become so confusing to travelers. Corporate discounts were dropped, but American lowered its coach fares by 38 percent to roughly the level that those previously receiving corporate discounts would have paid. It was American's stated hope that simpler, cheaper, and more equitable fares would eventually stimulate demand and increase traffic generally.

However, other airlines saw this new pricing strategy as an attack. TWA saw the lower fares as an attack on the niche group of fliers who do not get discounts—precisely the group that TWA had been targeting. Another struggling carrier, Northwest, also felt threatened by the new fare structure. A few weeks after American's value pricing was launched, Northwest announced a two-for-one promotion. American saw that move as a challenge to its new pricing system and responded with a price cut that matched the promotion while preserving its new fare structure. In a drastic move, American halved its summer advance purchase fares. The savageness of these cuts earned American's chairman a reputation as the "big bad bully" of the industry. Inevitably, most other airlines were forced to match these cuts. As a result, the airline sector in the United States took its biggest losses ever during 1992.

Critics claimed that American had become so dominant that it had become a de facto regulator of the airline industry—they set the price, and any competitor who deviated would be punished. Some observers have drawn the conclusion that it has been American's strategy all along to eliminate rivals, allowing it to raise its own prices once they are gone. Inevitably, such allegations over American's pricing strategy has led rivals—including Northwest and Continental—to sue, alleging unfair trading practices.

American was in the fortunate position of not having the debts that many airlines had accumulated during the 1980s. Its balance sheet was strong enough to allow it to resist price challenges from its more highly geared competitors. However, one thorn remained in the side of American—the large number of airlines who were flying under the protection of Chapter 11 bankruptcy. At carriers such as Continental, TWA, and America West, receivers were often seen as being too eager to set low prices simply to recover money for their creditors.

Another problem facing the long-term ability of American to set price levels is the presence of highly efficient, small regional airlines whose cost levels allow them to charge low fares and still earn a profit. The most notable success in this respect has been enjoyed by Southwest Airlines, which in 1991–1992 had a turnover of $1.5 billion and managed to earn a profit of $74 million despite the price wars going on around it. This customer-centered airline had managed to keep its costs down by controlling its wage bill and by cutting out many expensive frills such as inflight meals and the free transfer of passengers' luggage to other airlines. By operating a simple route network, Southwest also avoided the expense of maintaining a network of hub airports. Such has been Southwest's success in cost-led price cuts that American now accepts that its own pricing in Southwest's California stronghold is governed by the latter.

CASE STUDY REVIEW QUESTIONS

1. In what ways could another large airline hope to achieve a sustainable price advantage over American?
2. What public policy issues are raised by the pricing behavior of American?
3. How can a small airline hope to survive against the strength of airlines such as American?

9.7 SERVICE MIX PRICING

Multi-output service providers usually set the price of a new service with reference to the prices charged for other services within their mix. Three product relationships can be identified as being important for pricing purposes:

- optional additional services
- captive services
- competing services

Optional additional services are those which a consumer chooses whether or not to add to the core service purchase, often at the time the core service is purchased. As a matter of strategy, an organization could charge a low lead-in price for its core service but recoup a higher margin from the additional optional services. Breaking a service into core and optional components may allow for the presentation of lower price indicators, which through a process of rationalization may be more acceptable to certain groups of customers. Research may show that the price of the core service is in fact the only factor that potential customers consider when choosing between alternative services. In this way, many car rental companies cut their margins on the core vehicle rental rate but make up some of their margin through charges levied for insurance and fuel.

Captive services occur when the core service has been purchased and additional services can be provided only by the original provider of the core service. When the captive services are not specified at the time of purchasing the core service, or are left up to the discretion of the service provider, the latter is in a strong position to charge a high price. However, the company must consider whether consumers will perceive such prices for captive services as exploitive and whether such pricing practices undercut customer loyalty. An example of captive service pricing is provided by car insurance companies, which, after selling the core insurance policy, can treat customers as captive in adding additional coverage.

Competing services exist within the mix when a new service targets a segment of the population that overlaps the segments served by other products within the organization's mix. By a process of "cannibalization," a service provider could find that it is competing with itself. In this way, an airline offering a low priced direct service from Miami to Toronto may find that the low-price—in addition to generating completely new business—has an important side effect in abstracting traffic from its connecting services from Miami to Washington and from Washington to Toronto.

9.7.1 Price Bundling

Price bundling is the practice of marketing two or more services in a single package for a single price. Bundling is particularly important for services because:

- First, the high ratio of fixed to variable costs that characterize many services organizations makes the allocation of costs between different services difficult and sometimes arbitrary.
- Second, there is often a high level of interdependency between different types of service output. In this way, the provision of an ATM card, which most banks do not charge for separately, becomes part of a bank checking account.

Price bundling of diverse services from an organization's service mix is frequently used as a means of building relationships with customers (Figure 9.5). In this

Figure 9.5 This ski package bundles lift tickets, meals, and lodging. Source: Historic Delaware Hotel, Leadville, CO.

way, a mortgage could be bundled with a household contents insurance policy or a legal protection policy. When the bundle of service represents ease of administration to the consumer, the service organization may be able to achieve a price for the bundle greater than the combined price of the bundle's components.

"Pure" bundling occurs when services are available only in a bundled form (e.g., when a tour operator includes insurance in all of its vacations), whereas "mixed" bundling allows customers to choose which specific elements of the service offering they wish to purchase. One study has shown that as service firms expand their range of service outputs, simple cost-based or price follower strategies become too simplistic.[4] As the number of services offered by an organization increases, the opportunities for differentiation and bundling are enhanced. Also, the high ratio of fixed to variable costs typical of many services industries makes average costing increasingly arbitrary as fixed cost allocations change with the expansion of the service range. Bundling reduces the need to allocate fixed costs to individual services.

9.8 TACTICAL PRICING

Pricing strategy determines the position that price is to play within the marketing mix over the strategic planning period. In practice, maneuverability around the central strategy will be needed to allow detailed, local application of the overall strategy. This is the role of tactical pricing. The distinction between strategic and tactical pricing can be difficult to draw. In highly competitive, undifferentiated services markets, the development of tactical plans can be all-important and can assume much greater importance than in a service where an organization has more opportunity for developing a distinctive strategic price position. Some of the tactical uses of pricing are discussed here.

Tactical pricing can provide short-term competitive advantage. Periodic price reductions can be a means of inducing potential customers to try a service, whether it is new or established. The price cut can be a general across-the-board reduction, or it can be targeted (e.g., by the use of vouchers). How much demand increases when demand is temporarily reduced depends on consumers' price sensitivity. When purchasing some services, such as expensive root canals, consumers may not compare prices. Consumers may not be able to respond to price reductions if they are tied to a relationship with another supplier. For example, a garage that reduces car servicing charges may attract no additional demand from people who have long-term maintenance contracts with other organizations. Finally, consumers may perceive a price discount as a signal of inferior service quality. The latter point is important, for economic rationality may not always be present in the way tactical price adjustments are viewed by target customers. Indeed, a price reduction may reduce the perceived value of a service, leading to a feeling that its quality has been eroded. Subsequent price increases may lead to the feeling that the service is overpriced if it could be offered previously at a lower price. There may also be significant price points at which a service is perceived as being of good value—a transatlantic air ticket priced at $499 may be perceived as offering much better value than a ticket priced at $500.

Even if economic rationality is assumed on the part of consumers, it can be difficult to predict the effects of a price change. Comparison with previous occasions when price was adjusted assumes that all other factors are the same, whereas in reality many factors, such as the availability of competitors' services and general macroenvironmental conditions, require some judgment to be made about how a similar price cut might perform this time round.

Tactical pricing can be used to remove unplanned excess supply. An organization may be unable to obtain a strategic price position due to excess supply, both within the organization and within the market generally. A temporary price cut can be used to bring demand and supply back into balance. The excess supply of business hotel rooms that occurred during the recession of the late 1980s resulted in hotels responding tactically with low prices to attract segments that might not otherwise have had the resources to stay in high-quality hotels. Pricing can also be used to capitalize on excess demand relative to supply. In addition to removing discounts and increasing prices, firms can remove low-margin elements from their service mix in order to maximize their returns from high-margin lines.

Short-term tactical pricing can be used to protect markets against new entrants. When a new entrant threatens the existing market of an established supplier, the latter may react with short-term price reductions. If the new entrant is a small opportunist company seeking to make inroads into the larger dominant firm's market, a low price may force the new company to respond with low prices, putting strain on its initial cash flow and possibly resulting in its withdrawal from the market if not a complete cessation of trade. New, market-challenging low-price airlines have often been thwarted by their larger competitors, which have had deeper pockets to wait out any prolonged price war.

Differential pricing with respect to time, which may have been part of the strategic pricing plan, can be implemented by various tactical programs. Off-peak discounts are frequently used in industries such as air travel, telecommunications, and hotels. The converse of peak surcharges can also be employed, for example, the special rates often applied by hotels during vacation periods. Other options include offering added value price bundles at certain periods (e.g., shopping vouchers for off-peak cruise customers) and subtly altering a service offering and making it available only at certain times (a restaurant may slightly differentiate lunch from dinner and charge more for the latter because customers are willing to pay more for an evening social meal).

Similarly, differential pricing with respect to place must be translated from a strategic plan to a tactical program. Implementing differential pricing by area is relatively easy for services on account of the difficulty in transferring service consumption. Hotels and shops, among others, often use different price lists for different locations, depending on the local competitive position. Such lists are often adjusted at short notice to respond to local competitive pressure. Sometimes a common base price is offered at all of an organization's service outlets, and tactical objectives are achieved by means of discounts that are available only at certain locations. Reduced price vouchers offered by a national hotel chain may have their validity restricted to those locations where demand is relatively weak. Local tactical pricing can cause problems where national promotion is price led. In this case, some of a firm's services are often advertised at a nationally uniform rate while related services are priced according to local market conditions.

For differential pricing between different consumer segments, the problem of turning a strategy into a tactical program hinges on the ease with which segments can be isolated and charged different prices. Because services are consumed at the point of production, it is often easy to confine price differences within small segments of a market. In this way, theatres are able to ensure that only students are able to use reduced-price student tickets by asking for identification at the start of the service production process. Sometimes the implementation of a highly segmented pricing program can cause problems for services providers that must compromise between the desire for small, homogeneous segments and the need for segments that are of a worthwhile size to service. As an example, many transportation operators offer low fares to all senior citizens. However, the simplicity of this large homogenous segment is offset by the fact that many people in it are well off and less price sensitive, and may even be traveling on business. Another problem with this form of price segmentation is that goodwill can be harmed when arguments develop over a customer's eligibility for a particular price offer.

Price segmentation can also be implemented by slightly differentiating the service offering in order to make it more attractive to a market segment that is willing to pay a differential price. In this way, first-class accommodation is often provided by airlines as a means of increasing profits from particular segments.

Tactical pricing programs are used to motivate distributors. When a service is provided through an intermediary, the difference between the price that a customer pays and the amount that the service principal receives represents the intermediary's margin. In some cases, price sensitivity of the final consumer is low, but awareness of margins by the intermediary is high, requiring tactical pricing to be directed at maintaining intermediaries' margins relative to those offered by competitors. An example is provided by vacation insurance offered by travel agents. Customers do not typically shop around for this ancillary item of a package vacation, but travel agents themselves decide which policy to recommend to their clients largely on the basis of the commission level they can earn. The price of a service that is charged to the final consumer can also affect an intermediary's motivation to sell a principal's service. An agent who perceives the selling price to be too high may give up trying to promote it in favor of a more realistic and attractive competitor. On the other hand, if the price is too low, intermediaries working on a percentage commission basis may consider that the reward for them is not worth their effort. Airlines such as Southwest Airlines that have promoted low fares have often met a lukewarm response from travel agents who see only a small commission payment in handling their sales.

9.9   PARTICULAR PROBLEMS IN PRICING NOT-FOR-PROFIT SERVICES

It was noted at the beginning of this chapter that price is often a very constrained element of the marketing mix for not-for-profit services, which have much less freedom to implement the strategies and tactics of pricing just described.

The pricing of services that require a high degree of central planning, but that are expected to exhibit some degree of marketing orientation, presents particular challenges for marketers. It may be difficult or undesirable to implement a straightforward price–value relationship with individual service users, for several reasons:

- The social benefits generated by a service may be difficult or impossible for the service provider to appropriate from individual users. For example, users of most roads in the United States are not charged directly for the benefits they receive from the road system. The present methods of charging for roads reflect the technical difficulties in appropriating charges from users and the political problem that access to road space is deemed to be a "birthright" not to be restricted by direct charging. Nevertheless, in some states and overseas countries, the technical and political environment has allowed governments to charge more directly for road space used. In France, for example, many highways are operated by private sector organizations that charge tolls regulated by the government. In order to attract more usage of these highways, effort is put into making them more attractive than the parallel free roads, by such means as the provision of pleasant rest areas. In other cases (e.g., Singapore), attempts have been made to charge for the use of urban roads according to the level of congestion present. It is possible that with improved technology, many social benefits could be internalized by charging users directly for the services they consume.

• When individual consumers of a service can be identified, the benefits to society at large may be as significant as the benefits received by the individual. Education and training courses may be provided at an uneconomic charge in order to add to the level of skills available within an economy generally.

• Pricing can be actively used as a means of social policy. Subsidized prices for training courses can be used to favor skill building among the disabled, unemployed, or other disadvantaged groups. Communication programs are often used by public services to make the public aware of the preferential prices to which they may be eligible. Sometimes, the interests of marketing orientation and social policy can overlap—reduced admission prices to museums for the unemployed may help a disadvantaged group within society while at the same time generating additional overall revenue through segmenting the market in terms of ability to pay.

Problems can occur in public services that have been given a largely financial, market-oriented mission, but in which possibly conflicting social policy objectives are superimposed. Museums, recreation centers, and urban transit systems have frequently been at the center of debate about the relative importance to be attached to economic and social objectives. One solution that has sometimes been adopted is to split a service into two distinct components, one part being an essentially public service for the benefit of society at large, and the other part comprising the elements that are indistinguishable from commercially provided services. In this way, museums have often retained free or nominally priced admission charges for the serious, scholarly elements of their exhibits while offering special exhibitions that match the private sector in the standard of production and the prices charged. Similarly, public libraries have distinguished between basic book lending, which is provided at no charge as public policy, and video and music rental, in which price is used as one element of the marketing mix to gain competitive advantage over private sector competitors.

9.10 INTERNAL MARKET PRICING

The development of matrix-type organization structures (see Chapter 12) can result in significant internal trading within an organization. Services that are commonly traded internally include photocopying, cleaning, transportation, and catering. Very often, the price at which services are traded between a resource-producing department and a resource-consuming department does not reflect a competitive market price. Indeed, a market as such may not exist. Setting transfer prices can raise several issues for an organization, even when external market prices can be readily ascertained. Allowing users of resources to purchase their services from the cheapest source—internal or external—could result in the in-house supplier losing volume to a point where it ceases to be viable, yet its retention may still be required so it can perform specialized jobs that cannot easily be handled by outside contractors. By allowing part of its requirements to be contracted out an organization may increase the loss incurred by its internal supplier while adding to the profits of outside companies. The internal pricing of services therefore needs to balance two possibly conflicting requirements: the in-house production unit's need to make profits and maintain some capacity, and the resource users' need to minimize total expenditure.

Some possible solutions to the problem of setting internal transfer prices can be identified:

- If an external market exists, a "shadow" price can be imputed to the transfer, reflecting what the transaction would have cost if it had been bought from an outside organization.
- Where no external market exists, bargaining between divisional managers can take place, although the final outcome may be a reflection of the relative bargaining strength of each manager.
- Corporate management could instruct all divisions to trade on an agreed full cost pricing basis.
- A system of dual pricing can be adopted whereby selling divisions receive a market price (where this can be identified) while the buying division pays the full cost of production. Any difference is transferred to corporate accounts.
- A proportion of the internal service producer's fixed costs can be spread over all resource users as a standing charge, regardless of whether they actually use the services of the unit. This would enable the internal supplier to compete on price relatively easily and still allow resource users for whom a higher standard of service is worth paying a premium to buy their requirements from outside service providers.

CHAPTER REVIEW QUESTIONS

1. What is the relationship between product life cycle theory and pricing strategy?
2. Give examples to illustrate situations in which price competitiveness may be largely absent in services markets. Is it desirable to restore price competitiveness? If so, how should it be done?
3. Analyze the product mix of a diverse service organization and identify the ways in which price bundling is carried out.
4. Using examples, compare the advantages and disadvantages of "cost plus" and marginal cost pricing.

5. Using a service company of your choice, analyze how price segmentation is practiced between different groups of customers.

6. Examine the role played by pricing for publicly owned recreation centers.

REFERENCES

1. Cyert, R. M., and March., J. G., *A Behavioural Theory of the Firm* (Englewood Cliffs, N.J.: Prentice Hall, 1963).

2. Zeithaml, V. A., Parasuraman, A., and Berry, L. L., "Problems and Strategies in Services Marketing," *Journal of Marketing* 49 (spring 1985): 33–46.

3. Abell, D. F., and Hammond, J. S., *Strategic Market Planning: Problems and Analytical Approaches* (Englewood Cliffs, N.J.: Prentice Hall, 1979): 107.

4. Guiltinan, J. P., "The Price Bundling of Services: A Normative Framework," *Journal of Marketing* 51 (April, 1987): 74–85.

SUGGESTED FURTHER READING

Brooks, D. G. 1975. "Cost Oriented Pricing: A Realistic Solution to a Complicated Problem." *Journal of Marketing* (April): 72–4.

Guiltinan, J. P. 1987. "The Price Bundling of Services: A Normative Framework." *Journal of Marketing* 51 (April): 74–85.

Kamen, J. 1989. "Price Filtering: Restricting Price Deals to Those Least Likely to Buy Without Them." *Journal of Consumer Marketing* (summer): 37–42.

Marks, N. E., and Inlow, N. S. 1988. "Price Discrimination and Its Impact on Small Business." *Journal of Consumer Marketing* (winter): 31–8.

Monroe, K. B. 1973. "Buyers' Subjective Perception of Price." *Journal of Marketing Research* (February): 70–80.

Nagle, T. T. 1987. "*The Strategy and Tactics of Pricing.*" Englewood Cliffs, N.J.: Prentice Hall.

Powers, L. P. 1987. "Breakeven Analysis with Semi-Fixed Costs." *Industrial Marketing Management* 16: 35–41.

Sheffet, M. J., and Scrammon, D. L. 1985. "Resale Price Maintenance: Is it Safe to Suggest Retail Prices?" *Journal of Marketing* (fall): 82–91.

Tellis, G. J. 1986. "Beyond the Many Faces of Price: An Integration of Pricing Strategies." *Journal of Marketing* (October): 146–60.

Zeithaml, V. A. 1987. *Defining and Relating Price, Perceived Quality and Perceived Value.* Cambridge, Mass.: Marketing Science Institute.

Zeithaml, V. A. 1988. "Consumer Perceptions of Price, Quality and Value: A Means-End Model and Synthesis of Evidence." *Journal of Marketing* (July): 2–22.

10

Promoting Services

CHAPTER OBJECTIVES

After reading this chapter, you should be able to understand

- the role played by promotion in the marketing mix for services
- the impact of service attributes on promotional decisions
- the principal elements of the promotion mix and their relationship within the promotional campaign
- methods used to set promotional objectives, develop promotional strategies, implement programs, and monitor results

10.1 INTRODUCTION

Well-developed marketing strategies and tactics should reduce reliance on promotion as a means of generating sales. A well-formulated service offer, distributed through appropriate channels at a price that represents good value to potential customers, places less emphasis on the promotion element of the marketing mix. Nevertheless, few services—especially those provided in competitive markets—can dispense with promotion completely. The purpose of this chapter is to examine the decisions that service organizations must make in formulating this element of the marketing mix. Emphasis is placed on the distinctive promotional needs of services, which flow from some of their distinguishing characteristics, particularly these:

- The intangible nature of the service offer results in consumers perceiving a high level of risk in the buying process.
- Promotion of the service offer cannot generally be isolated from promotion of the service provider.
- Visible production processes—especially the part played by service personnel—become an important element of the promotion process.
- Because services are intangible and have greater possibilities for fraud, their promotion is generally more constrained by legal and voluntary controls than is the case with goods.

The promotional function of any service organization involves the transmission of messages to present, past, and potential customers. At the very least, potential customers need to be made aware of the existence of a service. Eventually, in some way, they should be influenced toward purchase.

10.2 THE COMMUNICATION PROCESS

Promotion involves an ongoing process of communication between an organization and its target markets. The process is defined by the answers to the following questions:

- *Who* is saying the message?
- *To Whom* is the message addressed?
- *How* is the message communicated?
- To *What effect* was the communication made?

The elements of this process are illustrated in Figure 10.1 and described in the following text.

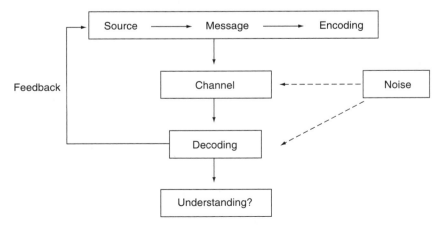

Figure 10.1   The communication process

10.2.1 To Whom Is the Message Addressed?

The audience of a message determines what is to be said, when it is to be said, where it is to be said, and who is to say it. The target audience must be clearly defined. This can be done in several ways:

- The most traditional method of defining audiences is in terms of social, economic, demographic, and geographical characteristics. In this way, audiences are defined according to parameters such as age, gender, social class, and area of residence.
- Audiences can be defined in terms of their stage in the decision making process. For example, a distinction can be made between people who are merely *aware* of the existence of a service, those who are *interested* in possibly purchasing the service, and those who *wish to purchase* the service.
- An audience can be defined on the basis of target customers' usage frequency (e.g., regular users of an airline may respond to communications differently than occasional users do).
- Similarly, audiences can differ in the benefits they seek from a category of service. Airlines aim different messages at vacation travelers, who may seek benefits such as meeting friends and family inexpensively, compared with business users, for whom speed and arrival reliability are most important.
- In services supplied to corporate buyers, audiences can be defined in terms of the type and size of business and its geographical location. More importantly, the key decision makers and influencers must be identified and used in defining the audience. For instance, in many corporate travel services, secretaries can be important in choosing between competing services for the actual service user, and they should therefore be included in a definition of the target audience.

Having defined its target audience, the communicator must then research its important characteristics. One vital aspect to explore is the audience's image of the organization and its services and the degree of image consistency among the audience members. An image tends to persist over time, with people continuing to see what they expect to see rather than what actually exists. The image of a service firm and its service offers can be significantly influenced by how its services are delivered. Therefore, contact personnel play a vital role in the development of this image. Of course, some elements of an organization's image can be derived through channels other than the formal communication process. Studies of industries as diverse as retailing and professional services have found that when differentiating between services, customers prefer to be guided by information from friends and other personal contacts rather by than the usual promotion mix.[1]

A second vital aspect of the audience that justifies research is its degree of perceived risk when considering the purchase of a new service. For highly risky services, customers are likely to use more credible sources of information (e.g., word-of-mouth recommendation) and engage in a prolonged search through information sources. People differ markedly in their readiness to try new products, and attempts have been made to classify the population in terms of their level of risk taking. In each product area, there are likely to be "innovators" or "consumption pioneers" and "early adopters," whereas other individuals adopt new products only much later. A common classification of markets divides consumers into the following adopter categories:

- innovators
- early adopters
- early majority
- late majority
- laggards

The adoption process is represented as a normal distribution when plotted over time. After a slow start, an increasing number of people adopt the innovation. The number then reaches a peak before diminishing as fewer nonadopters remain. A typical adoption distribution pattern is illustrated in Figure 10.2. Innovators are venturesome in that they try new ideas at some risk. Early adopters are opinion leaders in their community and adopt new products early but carefully. The early majority adopt new ideas before the average person does, taking their lead from opinion leaders. The late majority are skeptical, tending to adopt an innovation only after the majority of people have tried it. Finally, laggards are tradition bound and suspicious of changes. They adopt a new service only when it has become sufficiently widespread to take on a measure of tradition in itself.

Although adoption processes for goods and services are in principle similar, services tend to be perceived as more personal than goods and riskier because evaluation of quality and value before purchase is more difficult. Effective promotion of services must therefore start by understanding the state of mind of potential customers and the information they seek in order to reduce their exposure to risk.

10.2.2 Audience Response

In most cases, customers are seen as going through a series of stages before finally deciding to purchase a service. It is therefore critical to know these buyer readiness stages and to assess where the target is at any given time.

The communicator will be seeking any one or more of three audience responses to the communication:

- Cognitive responses—the message should be considered and understood.
- Affective responses—the message should lead to some change in attitude.
- Behavioral responses—finally, the message should achieve some change in behavior: a purchase decision.

Many models have been developed to show how marketing communication has the effect of "pushing" recipients of messages through a number of sequential stages, finally resulting in a purchase decision. The stages defined in three widely used models of communication—"AIDA," the Hierarchy of Effects, and Innovation Adoption—are shown in Table 10.1.

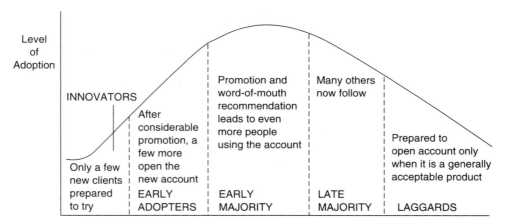

Figure 10.2   Buyer adoption pattern for a new type of bank account. Based on Rogers, E. M., *Diffusion of Information* (New York: Free Press, 1962).

Communication models portray a simple and steady movement through the various stages, although the process should not be seen as ending when a sale is completed. It was noted in Chapter 5 that services organizations increasingly seek to build relationships with their customers, so the behavioral change (the sale) should be seen not as an end but as the starting point for making customers aware of other offers available from the organization.

Smooth progress through these stages is impeded by the presence of "noise" factors which will be discussed later. The probabilities of success in each stage cumulatively decline with "noise," and therefore the probability of a purchase occurring in the final stage is very low.

10.2.3 Communication Source

The source of a message—as distinct from the message itself—can influence the effectiveness of any communication. These are some of the factors that influence the effectiveness of a communication source:

TABLE 10.1   MODELS OF COMMUNICATION

Domain	AIDA model	Hierarchy of effects*	Innovation-adoption model†
Cognitive	Awareness	Awareness Knowledge	Awareness
Affective	Interest Desire	Liking Preference	Interest Evaluation
Behavioral	Action	Conviction Purchase	Trial Adoption

*Based on Lavidge R. J. and Steiner, G. A., "A Model for Predictive Measurements of Advertising Effectiveness," *Journal of Marketing* 25, October (1961): 61–65.
†Based on Rogers, E. M., *Diffusion of Innovation,* (New York: Free Press, 1962).

- If a source is perceived as having power, then the audience response is likely to be compliance.
- If a source is liked, identification with it by the audience is likely. Important factors here include past experience and reputation of the service organization in addition to the personality of the actual source of the communication. A salesperson, any contact personnel, or a TV or radio personality can all be important in creating liking.
- If a source is perceived as credible, the message is more likely to be internalized by the audience. Credibility can be developed by establishing a source as important—high in status, power, and prestige—or by emphasizing reliability and openness.

10.2.4 The Message

A message must be able to move an individual along a path from awareness through to eventual purchase. In order for a message to be received and understood, it must gain attention, use a common language, arouse needs, and suggest how these needs may be met. All of this should take place within the acceptable standards of the target audience. However, the service itself, the channel, and the source of the communication also convey a message; therefore, it is important that these do not conflict.

Three important aspects of a message can be identified: content, structure, and format. The content is most likely to arouse and change attention, attitude, and intention; the appeal of the message is therefore important. The message should include some kind of benefit, motivator, identification, or reason why the audience should think or do something. Appeals can be rational, emotional, or moral.

Messages can be classified according to their dominant theme. These are common focal points for messages:

- The characteristics of the organization and the service on offer—for example, an airline may emphasize the high quality of its inflight service.
- Advantages over the competition—an advertising campaign by Citibank during the early 1990s emphasized the benefits of using its Visa card compared with other Visa cards.
- Adaptability to buyers' needs—many insurance companies emphasize the extent to which their policies have been designed to meet the needs of particular age segments of the population.
- Experience of others—in this way, testimonials of satisfied customers are used to demonstrate the benefits resulting from use and the dependability of the service provider.

Recipients of a message must see it as applying specifically to themselves, and they must see some reason for being interested in it. The actual format of the message will be very much determined by the medium used—the type of print if published material, the type of voice if broadcast media, and so on.

10.2.5 Noise

The creator of a message needs to encode it into some acceptable form for an audience to decode and comprehend. Unfortunately, interference occurs between the stages of encoding and decoding, and although it is difficult to totally eliminate interference in the communication process, an understanding of such "noise" factors should help to minimize their effects. The potential of "noise" to hinder effective communication is usually greater for services than for manufactured goods. Because of the intangible nature of services, expectations of service delivery must be created in peoples' minds without the help of the tangible evidence used to describe manufactured goods.

The nature of "noise" factors can be examined in terms of a simple "black box" model of buyer behavior (Figure 10.3). A communication of some sort (either marketer dominated or non–marketer dominated) is seen as a stimulus to some form of customer response. Response can be expressed in terms of quantity purchased, frequency of purchase, or even nonpurchase. The initial stimulus is distorted within the "black box" process, resulting in different individuals responding in different ways to a similar stimulus. The variables at work within the "black box" are the "noise" factors and can be explained by psychological and sociological factors that are discussed in the following section.

10.2.6 Psychological and Sociological Factors Influencing Message Reception

No two individuals have the same psychological makeup. Each person undergoes different experiences influencing personality, perceptions of the world, motives for action, and attitudes toward people, situations, and objects. Therefore, it is not surprising to find that different people interpret communications differently.

An individual's past experience of a service or organization is an important influence on how messages about that service are interpreted. Both positive and negative experiences predispose an individual to decode messages in a particular way. Also, the personality and motivations of specific members of an audience can significantly influence interpretation of a message.

Analysts have classified motives into those that are biological (such as the need to satisfy hunger or thirst) and those that are psychological and learned. Maslow[2] talks of safety, social, esteem, and self-actualization needs, whereas Bayton[3] distinguishes between ego bolstering, ego defensive, and affective needs. Both agree that

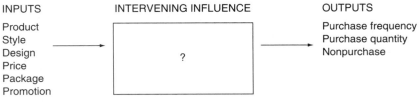

Figure 10.3   "Black box" model of buyer behavior

in different situations, one of these needs becomes dominant over the others and influences perceptions of the outside world. As an example, an individual who has just come home from work hungry, and is about to eat dinner, is unlikely to be interested in how a new life insurance policy could satisfy a higher order need for family security.

In addition to possessing inherent personal characteristics that influence behavior, individuals are influenced by the other people and organizations around them. The conditioning process brought about by the existence of these groups can be analyzed in terms of the attitudes that individuals develop. Attitudes are learned, are extremely enduring, and are very influential in determining how a message is perceived. For example, an individual may have a negative attitude toward a particular bank as a result of having been refused overdraft facilities by that bank. This negative attitude is likely to distort the individual's interpretation of any marketing communication from the bank. In this context, therefore, the bank's communication should involve an attempt to shift attitude as well as merely to inform.

Attitudes are predispositions to act in a particular situation. They involve three elements: cognitive, affective, and conative (Figure 10.4).

- The *cognitive* element of an attitude involves the knowledge and understanding of the object, person, or situation.
- The *affective* element refers to the emotional content of an attitude and is usually expressed in terms of either positive or negative feelings.
- The *conative* element of an attitude refers to the preparedness on the part of the individual holding the attitude to act positively or negatively in a particular situation involving the object or person.

Services marketers have great difficulty in overcoming negative attitudes toward themselves or their services because of the very subjective way in which services are evaluated before, during, and after consumption. There is therefore likely to be a greater chance of attitude change if the service involves tangible aspects that can be produced, offered, or displayed. Such tangible elements need to clearly show that quality has improved.

People develop attitudes from various sources, and great significance is attached to the role of reference groups with which individuals closely identify. These can be groups of which an individual is a member (membership groups) or ones to which membership is aspired (aspirational groups).

Other important sociological influences on behavior include culture and social class. Members of different cultures and classes are likely to interpret messages in different ways. Thus, communications offering credit facilities may be interpreted with suspicion in certain social groups whose members have been conditioned to live within their means, whereas members of other groups may welcome the opportunities represented by the message.

Past experience, personality, motivation, attitudes, and the influence of reference groups can all produce a "noise" effect and thereby distort the audience's interpretation of a message. Individuals are constantly being bombarded by numerous stimuli (visual, auditory, tactile) but are likely to select only the stimuli perceived as being important to them.

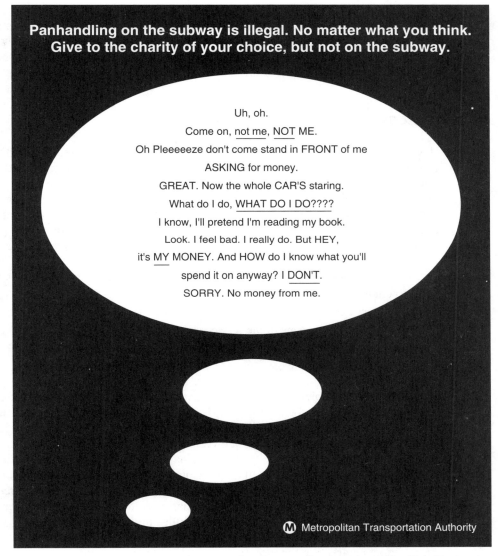

Figure 10.4 In this 1994 campaign, the Metropolitan Transportation Authority of New York City is using transit signs to change commuters' cognitive, affective, and behavioral responses to begging on the subway trains. Source: Copyrighted by the Metropolitan Transportation Authority of New York, used with permission.

- Selective *perception* occurs when communication is perceived in such a way that it merely reinforces existing attitudes and beliefs.
- Selective *reception* occurs when individuals make active decisions as to which stimuli they wish to expose themselves to (for example, a loyal customer of one bank may consciously avoid advertisements from competing banks).
- Selective *retention* occurs when an individual remembers only those aspects of the message perceived as being relevant.

Even if an individual gives attention to a message, understands it, and remembers it, comprehension may still be different from what the communicator expected. This perceptual distortion could be caused by the "noise" factors previously noted, poor encoding on the part of the communicator, or poor understanding by the audience itself. It is therefore important to pretest any marketing communication.

10.3 DEVELOPING THE PROMOTIONAL MIX

Having considered "who says what to whom and for what purpose," the next area of concern is "how." Developing the promotion mix entails selecting and blending different channels of communication in order to achieve the promotional objectives of the marketing mix. Prior specification of communication objectives is important if appropriate messages are to be accurately targeted through the most appropriate channels in the most cost-effective manner possible. Typical promotion objectives might be these:

- to develop an awareness of, and an interest in, the organization and its services
- to communicate the benefits of buying a service
- to influence eventual purchase of the service
- to build a positive image of the service organization
- to differentiate the service from its competitors
- to remind people of the existence of a service and/or the service organization

Ideally, these objectives should be quantified as far as possible. For example, promotional objectives for a new type of auto insurance policy may begin with an objective to obtain awareness of the brand name by 30 percent of the 25- to 55-year-old insurance buying public within one year of launch.

The promotion mix refers to the combination of channels an organization uses to communicate with its target markets. Communication is received by audiences from two principal sources: sources within an organization and external sources. The latter include word-of-mouth communications, or editorials in the press, which, as has already been noted, may have high credibility in the service evaluation process. Sources originating within an organization can be divided into those originating from the traditional marketing function (which can be divided into personal two-way channels such as personal selling and impersonal one-way channels such as advertising) and those originating from front-line production resources. Because services normally involve consumers in the production process, the promotion mix has to be considered more broadly than is the case with manufactured goods. Front-line operations staff and service outlets become a valuable channel of communication. The diversity of the communications channels used for services is illustrated in Figure 10.5.

The combination of communication channels chosen will depend primarily on the characteristics of the target audience, especially its habits in terms of exposure to messages. Other important considerations include the present and potential market size for the service (advertising on television may not be appropriate for a service

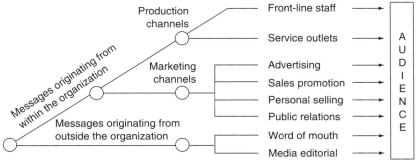

Figure 10.5   Communication channels for services

that has a local niche market, for example), the nature of the service itself (the more personal the service, the more effective the two-way communication channel), and, of course, the costs of the various channels.

A very important consideration is the stage that a service has reached in its life cycle (see Chapter 3). Advertising and publicity are more likely to form important channels of communication during the introductory stage of the life cycle, when the major objective is often to increase overall audience awareness. Sales promotion can be used to stimulate trial, and in some instances, personal selling can be used to acquire distribution coverage. During a service's growth stage, the use of all communication channels can generally be reduced, as demand during this phase tends to produce its own momentum through word-of-mouth communications. However, competition can grow during this stage and on into the maturity stage, calling for an increase in advertising and sales promotion activity. Finally, when the service is seen as going into decline, advertising and public relations are often reduced, although sales promotion can still be quite usefully applied. Sometimes, services in decline are allowed to die quietly with very little promotion. In the case of many long-life financial services that a company would like to delete but cannot for contractual reasons, the service may be kept going with no promotional support at all.

In the following sections, each of the elements of the promotion mix through which communications can be directed is discussed. Before the traditional elements of advertising, sales promotion, personal selling, and public relations are considered, attention is given to the role of operational inputs to the promotion mix of services firms.

10.4 THE PRODUCER–CUSTOMER INTERFACE OF THE SERVICES PROMOTION MIX

Inseparability results in consumers' involvement in a series of encounters with service producers. During each of these encounters, a service organization has an opportunity to communicate with its customers. Without any effort on the part of an organization, customers will pick up messages, whether good or bad. With more planning, an organization can ensure that every encounter is turned into an opportunity to convey positive messages that encourage repeat business from the customer and encourage them to pass on the message to others. Two important sources of non–marketer derived messages are front-line employees and the physical environment of the service encounter.

10.4.1 The Promotional Role of Employees

The important role played by front-line operational personnel as part-time marketers has been previously emphasized in this book. As has also been noted, the activities of such staff can be important in creating an image of an organization that influences target customers' perceptions of the organization.

Staff who have front-line encounters with customers should be trained to treat these encounters as promotional opportunities. Without appropriate training and explanation of what is expected of them, a call for such employees to promote their service more effectively can be little more than rhetoric. Training might be aimed at developing these skills in front-line staff:

- To spot cross-selling possibilities, front-line staff must have empathy for their customers. A bank clerk who sees a customer repeatedly using a service that does not adequately fulfill his or her needs could be trained to try to cross-sell another service that better meets the customer's needs. Training should make such employees aware of the services available and give them skills in effectively approaching customers and referring them to appropriate personnel.
- Many operational staff have quite clearly defined sales responsibilities; for example, restaurant waiters may be expected to encourage customers to spend more on their visit to the restaurant.
- The general manner of staff interactions with customers is important in encouraging customers to return and also to tell their friends about their good experience. Training should emphasize behaviors that have a positive effect on customers' evaluation of their encounter.
- Staff can directly facilitate future business by encouraging customers to book a repeat service or by giving them literature to pass on to friends.

Of course, it is difficult to draw a distinction between operational staff and marketing staff in terms of their contribution to the promotion of an organization. Organizational boundaries should not keep operational staff from being considered an important element of promotion mix planning.

10.4.2 The Promotional Role of Service Outlets

From the outside, service outlets can be seen as billboards capable of conveying messages about the services that take place within them. Service outlets are therefore powerful tools in appealing to both customers and noncustomers. The general appearance of an outlet can promote the image of a service organization. A bright-colored, clean exterior can transmit a message that the organization is fast, efficient, and well run. Outlets can be used to display advertising posters, which in heavily trafficked locations can result in valuable exposure. Many retailers with prominent locations on busy roads consider these opportunities to be so great that they can reduce their expenditure on conventional advertising.

Service outlets can also provide valuable opportunities to show service production processes to potential customers—something that is much more difficult to achieve through conventional media. A fast printing shop displaying sophisticated printing equipment, and a tire retailer's large stocks and the tidy appearance of its employees, all help to promote an organization's processes as much as their outcomes.

Sometimes, the physical environment extends beyond the organization's own premises, widening the reach of messages. A builder undertaking a construction job can promote its name on-site while allowing potential customers to view its production processes. Similarly, transportation companies can use their vehicles as moving communication media, not only as carriers of printed messages but also as demonstrations of important aspects of their service processes (e.g., courteous driving by truck drivers).

CASE STUDY

MCI CALLS UP UNOFFICIAL SALESFORCE

Until a few years ago, long-distance telephone services didn't really need much selling. The Bell system had a virtual monopoly, and promotion was confined to increasing the size of the market rather than trying to gain market share. However, with the breakup of the Bell monopoly and the deregulation of the long-distance telephone market, all that changed. There are now dozens of carriers offering long-distance service. Although most of them have targeted the business market, the fight for residential market share has seen escalating promotional activity by AT&T and its chief rivals, MCI and Sprint.

Promoting a telephone service poses several problems for marketers. The service is highly intangible, and it is very difficult to demonstrate how the product attributes of one operator are superior to those of its competitors. In effect, all operators provide an identical core service, with only minor differences in secondary attributes such as speed dialing, call interception facilities, and payment methods. Conventional advertising is very weak in demonstrating such core product attributes as reliability and the friendliness of contact personnel.

With a basically similar service on offer, promotion had often stressed an operator's price advantage, but here again the companies faced a promotional problem. Tariffs had become very complex, with rates varying by time of day and distance, not to mention the variety of special calling plans that customers could contract into.

For the number-two long-distance carrier, MCI, the high cost of advertising had proved exasperating in its attempts to gain market share within the residential sector. It was difficult to use advertising alone to differentiate its service from that of its competitors, whereas any increase in advertising effort was soon canceled out by an increase by its chief rival, AT&T. Then, in the early 1990s, it began exploiting two important additional communications channels: its employees and its customers.

Although a telecommunications network is highly automated, human operators have to interact with customers on various occasions. The first encounter most people have with MCI is through its sales staff. There may also be subsequent interactions when customers need operator assistance or inquire about their bill. MCI upgraded its training procedures to make all of its staff part-time sales people. As an example, accounting office employees discussing a customer's bill would be expected to empathize with the customer and suggest the benefit of signing up for a particular calling plan, or they might study their needs and suggest that the inquirer take out a calling card.

It was the way in which MCI used its customers as part-time sales people that proved to be its trump card. In 1991, it unveiled a program called Friends and Family, which was designed to encourage customers to recommend MCI to their friends who were not already signed up as MCI customers. The lure was a 20 percent discount on all calls made to up to twelve other numbers that were signed up for MCI service. This incentive proved to be a winner and led to an army of unofficial sales people trying to convince their friends and family to sign up for MCI. A common occurrence was for children to persuade their parents to sign up for MCI. Younger people tended to be more open to new ideas and were prepared to experiment with the relatively new MCI. They also wanted the 20 percent discount every time they called their parents. Their parents were more likely to be set in their ways—they had always been with AT&T and looked to it for security and reliability. Advertisements emphasizing the economic benefits of using MCI often cut little ice—complex arguments seemed to reveal marginal gains, set against a lot of hassle and a possible risk in signing up for a calling service the customer probably did not fully understand. But what if a daughter had checked out MCI and decided it was a good plan? That was different—the daughter was a trusted information source and would be listened to.

The Friends and Family strategy clearly worked for MCI. Within its first year it had signed up 7.5 million customers to the plan, of whom 5 million were completely new customers. Overall, MCI's net revenue increased by half a billion dollars, boosting its share of the $27.5 billion residential market by nearly two percentage points, to 16 percent. Furthermore, it claimed that the customers gained through its Friends and Family strategy were high-value customers, calling 25 percent more than the average for all customers. Newly acquired customers of Friends and Family were also found to be 20 percent less likely to drop MCI than the average for all customers.

In its Friends and Family calling plan, MCI had found a promotional tool that its chief rival, AT&T, was incapable of immediately matching. Because AT&T relied on local phone companies to calculate its residential bills, it didn't have centralized records to show when one AT&T customer had called another. Furthermore, it would not make sense for AT&T to copy the Friends and Family format. Because it held 62 percent of the residential market, it followed that those customers called other AT&T customers about 62 percent of the time. Discounting all of these calls would have meant a huge revenue loss for AT&T. MCI, on the other hand, with its much smaller residential share, could discount calls to other MCI customers without suffering such a big penalty. MCI had spotted a weakness of AT&T and exploited it quite effectively.

CASE STUDY REVIEW QUESTIONS

1. What are the limitations of conventional advertising for increasing the sales of residential telephone services?

2. How would you define the promotional budget for MCI? How should the company decide how much to spend on promotion?

3. Suggest ways in which public relations activity could be employed by MCI in its attempts to increase its residential market share.

10.5 *ADVERTISING AND THE MEDIA*

Advertising is mass, paid communication used to transmit information, develop attitudes, and eventually induce some form of response on the part of the audience. It attempts to bring about a response by providing information to potential customers, by trying to modify their desires, and by supplying reasons why they should prefer that particular company's services.

The planning process for advertising comprises five key stages:

1. "Where are we now?" In the first stage, an organization needs to establish, through marketing research, how its brand or service offer is perceived in peoples' minds.
2. "Why are we there?" An organization should establish how a particular position was reached by examining and identifying causal relationships.
3. "Where could we be?" This reflects an organization's objectives in terms of market share, awareness levels, and so on.
4. "How can we get there?" Advertising strategy and its tactical implementation are planned.
5. "Are we getting there?" An advertising program, having been implemented, must be evaluated for results and control action taken to address any discrepancy.

An essential element of this process is the setting of objectives for an advertising campaign. These should reflect the areas of accountability for those who are responsible for implementing the program. Advertising objectives should contain

- a concise definition of the target audience
- a clear statement of the desired audience response
- an expression of goals in quantitative terms as far as possible
- an expressed understanding of advertising's role in relation to the rest of the promotion program
- an acknowledgment that the goals are demanding but achievable
- a statement of time constraints

Although advertising is commonly thought to increase sales, it is extremely difficult to prove that this alone is responsible for any increase. Sales, after all, can be the result of many intervening variables, some of which are internal to the organization (e.g., public relations activity, pricing policy), while others are external (e.g., the state of the national economy). It is therefore too simplistic to set advertising objectives solely in terms of increasing sales by a specified amount. Given the existence of diverse adopter categories and the many stages in the communication process described earlier, more appropriate objectives can often be specified in terms of levels of awareness or comprehension.

10.5.1 *Media Characteristics*

The choice of media is influenced by the characteristics of each medium and its ability to achieve the specified promotional objectives. The following are some of the most common types of media and their characteristics:

Newspapers. National newspapers, such as the *Wall Street Journal,* tend to have a high degree of reader loyalty, reflecting the fact that each title is targeted to specific socioeconomic segments of the population. This loyalty can lead to readers' perception of a high level of credibility in a message printed in "their" newspaper. Local newspapers offer a much greater degree of geographical segmentation than is possible with national titles. Within their circulation areas, they also achieve much higher levels of readership penetration. Daily newspapers are normally read hurriedly, and therefore lengthy copy is likely to be wasted. Sunday newspapers are generally read at a more leisurely pace and are more likely to be read at home and shared by households, which may be important for appealing to family-based service purchase decisions.

Newspapers can be used for creating general awareness of a product or a brand as well as providing detailed product information. In this way, banks use newspapers both for advertisements designed to create brand awareness and liking for the organization, and for advertisements that give specific details of savings and loan accounts. The latter may include an invitation to action in the form of an account opening form.

Magazines and journals. The United States has a wealth of magazine and journal titles whose advertising rates and circulation details are given in the *Standard Rate and Data Guide.* While some high-circulation magazines (e.g., *TV Guide*) appeal to broad groups of people, most titles are specialized in terms of their content and targeting. In this way, the periodical *Mortgage Banker* can be a highly specific medium in which banks can promote mortgages. Specialist trade titles allow messages to be aimed at service intermediaries. For example, a cruise operator may first gain the confidence and support of travel agents through a magazine such as *Travel Age.*

Although advertising in magazines may seem at first to be relatively expensive compared with newspapers, they represent good value to advertisers in terms of the high number of readers per copy and the highly segmented nature of their audiences.

Outdoor advertising. This is useful for reminder copy and can support other media activities—the effect of an advertisement on television can be prolonged if recipients are exposed to a reminder poster on their way to work the following day. If strategically placed (e.g., at sites located near sports centers or at airports) the posters can appeal to quite specific audiences. Posters can generally be used only to convey a simple communication rather than complex details.

Television. This is an expensive but very powerful medium. Although it is used mainly for the long-term task of creating brand awareness, it can also be used to create a rapid sales response. The very fact that a message has been seen on television can give credibility to the message source, and many smaller service companies add the phrase "as seen on TV" to give additional credibility to their other media communications. The power of the television medium is enhanced by its ability to appeal to the senses of both sight and sound and to use movement and color to develop a sales message.

The major limitation of television advertising is its cost, reflecting high production costs as well as the cost of buying prime air time. Also, it must be determined how many people within the target audience are actually receptive to television advertising. Is the target viewer actually in the room when an advertisement is being broadcast? If the viewer is present, is he or she receptive to the message? The increasing use of video recorders and remote controls could have important implications for the effectiveness of television advertising in the future.

Commercial radio.   Radio advertising has often been seen as the poor relation of television advertising, appealing only to the sense of sound. The threshold cost of radio advertising is much lower than in television. A major advantage over other media is that the audience can be involved in other activities—particularly driving—while being exposed to an advertisement. Another advantage is that commercial radio is a good way for a service to reach a local or regional market. Although there are often doubts about the extent to which a radio audience actually receives and understands a message, radio forms a useful reminder medium when used in conjunction with other media.

10.5.2 Media Selection Criteria

Besides the characteristics of the media themselves, the choice of media mix for an advertising campaign is influenced by other important factors.

- The media habits of the target audience. These must be fully understood through marketing research, and a mix must be developed that maximizes the audience's exposure to a firm's communication.
- The impact that advertising will have on the target audience. Impact is usually more closely related to the message than to the medium. If, however, the medium is the message, then advertising impact should be an important criterion for media selection. Different media vehicles can produce different levels of awareness and comprehension of an identical message. In this way, McDonald's character Ronald McDonald has a much more powerful impact when presented on television than on radio.
- The extent to which the effects of a particular advertising message wear out over time. There is usually a threshold level of advertising beneath which little audience response occurs. Once this threshold has been passed, audience response tends to increase quite rapidly through a generation phase until a saturation level is reached. The power of the message can then be said to wear out in terms of audience response.
- The cost of using each medium. A medium that first appears to be expensive may in fact be good value in terms of achieving promotional objectives. Cost per gross rating point and cost per thousand are commonly used benchmarks for comparing the costs of media.

10.5.3 Determining the Advertising Budget

Advertising expenditure can become a drain on an organization's resources if no conscious attempt is made to determine an appropriate budget and to ensure that expenditure is kept within the budget. Some methods commonly used to determine the level of an advertising budget are these:

What can be afforded.   This is largely a subjective assessment and pays little attention to the long-term promotional needs of a service. It regards advertising as a luxury that can be afforded in good times but cut back during lean times. In reality, this approach is used by many service companies that see advertising spending as an easy way to reduce expenditure in bad times. Because advertising cannot normally produce any guaranteed returns, cutting it can also have the effect of reducing a firm's exposure to risk.

Percentage of sales.   By this method, advertising expenditure rises or falls to reflect changes in sales. In fact, sales are likely to be influenced by advertising rather than vice versa, and this method is likely to accentuate any given situation. If sales are declining during a recession, more advertising may be required to encourage sales; however, the percentage of sales method of determining the budget implies that advertising expenditures go down when sales go down.

Comparative parity.   Advertising expenditure is determined by the amount spent by competitors. Many market sectors see periodic outbursts of promotional expenditure, often accompanying a change in some other element of firms' marketing mix. During the early 1990s, battles for market share in the United States long-distance telephone market saw gradually escalating levels of advertising expenditure as the principal competitors tried to keep up with their rivals' promotional efforts. However, mere increases in advertising expenditure may hide the fact that the other elements of the marketing mix need adjusting in order to gain a competitive market position.

Residual.   This is the least satisfactory approach and merely assigns to the advertising budget what is left after all other costs have been covered. It may bear no relationship whatever to promotional objectives.

Objective and task.   This approach starts by clearly defining promotional objectives. Tasks are then set that relate to specific targets. In this way, advertising is seen as a necessary—even though possibly risky—investment in a particular product or service, ranking in importance with other more obvious costs such as production and salary costs. This is the most rational approach to setting a promotional budget.

10.5.4 Developing the Advertising Campaign

An advertising campaign brings together a wide range of media-related activities so that instead of being unrelated they can be planned and coordinated to achieve promotional objectives. The first stage of campaign planning, as has just been discussed, is to have a clear understanding of promotional objectives. A message can then be developed that is most likely to achieve these objectives. The next step is the production of the media plan. The target audience having been defined in terms of its size, location, and media characteristics, media must be selected that achieve the desired levels of audience exposure. A media plan must be formulated that specifies

- The allocation of expenditure between the different media.
- The selection of specific media components. For example, if print media are used, decisions must be made regarding the type (popular or quality press), size of advertisement, whether use of a Sunday supplement is to be made, and whether there is to be national or local coverage.
- The frequency of insertions.
- The cost of reaching a particular target group for each of the media vehicles specified in the plan.

Finally, the advertising campaign must be coordinated with the overall promotional plan, for example, by ensuring that sales promotion activities reinforce advertising messages.

While the principles of planning a campaign for a services organization are similar to those for a manufacturing company, the intangible, inseparable, and variable nature of services must be kept in mind. Advertisements alone are unlikely to be successful in helping customers make services purchase decisions, but their effectiveness can be increased by following a few guidelines. The following have been proposed by George and Berry.[4]

Use clear and unambiguous messages.   The very intangibility of services can make it difficult to communicate information defining the service offer. This is particularly true of highly complex services, whose advertising copy should emphasize the benefits of a service and how these match the benefits sought—that is, the copy should have a customer orientation rather than a product orientation (Figure 10.6).

Build on word-of-mouth communication.   Recommendations from others influence service customers' decision making. Advertising therefore should be used to enhance this influence. For example, advertising can be used to persuade satisfied customers to let others know of their satisfaction. Organizations can develop material that customers can pass on to noncustomers or that will persuade noncustomers to talk to present customers. Similarly, advertising campaigns can be aimed at opinion leaders who will then "trickle down" information about the service to the rest of their reference group.

Provide tangible cues.   Organizations selling manufactured goods tend to differentiate their products from their competitors' by emphasizing intangible features such as after-sales service and guarantees. Services marketers, however, tend to differentiate their services by emphasizing tangible cues or physical evidence. The use of well-known personalities and objects can act as surrogates for the intangible features of the service. Also, the use of consistent logos, catchphrases, symbols, and themes can help overcome the transitory nature of intangibility and ensure a durable company identity in the customer's mind.

Figure 10.6 This JAL ad uses a clear and unambiguous message to sell skiing tours on Japan Airlines. Source: Printed with permission from New York Festivals, Chappaqua, NY and Dentsu, Young & Rubicam, Hong Kong.

Promise what can be delivered.   The intangible nature of services results in customers having abstract expectations about the standard of service delivery. Customers judge a service to be of poor quality when perceived delivery does not live up to these abstract expectations. Advertising should therefore not promise too much.

Aim advertising at employees, too.   Most services are labor intensive, and advertisers need to encourage both employees to perform and customers to buy. Advertisements that emphasize personal service can motivate contact personnel to perform their duties more effectively and also influence consumer choice.

Remove postpurchase anxiety.   There is little tangible evidence to use in the postpurchase evaluation process for services, and advertising should therefore be used to reinforce positive postpurchase feelings.

10.6 SALES PROMOTION

The aim of sales promotion activities is to stimulate customer purchase and the effectiveness of intermediaries. Although sales promotion can be used to create awareness, it is usually used for the later stages of the buying process—that is, to create interest and desire and in particular to bring about action. Sales promotion can quite successfully complement other tools within the promotion mix, for example, by reinforcing a particular image or identity developed through advertising. It is normally most effective when used in conjunction with advertising.

During recent years there has been a rapid increase in the use of sales promotion within the services sector, for several reasons:

- Internally, there has been a greater acceptance of sales promotion by top management, and more people are now qualified to use it. In addition, there is greater pressure today to obtain a quick sales response, something sales promotion is good at achieving.
- There has been a general proliferation of brands accompanied by increased competitive pressure. As a result of this and the changing economic environment, consumers are more "deal oriented." There is also increased pressure from intermediaries for incentives from service principals.
- It has been argued by many that advertising efficiency is declining because of increasing costs and media clutter.
- New technology in targeting has increased the efficiency and effectiveness of sales promotion.

Sales promotion is no longer confined to traditional private sector services operating in competitive markets. The public and professional services sectors (e.g., recreational centers and opticians) have also accepted sales promotion's role. As a promotional tool, sales promotion is likely to continue to grow in the future.

10.6.1 The Role of Sales Promotion

Sales promotion can contribute in many ways to achieving overall promotional objectives. It is most likely to be used as an incentive incorporating an offer that represents value to the target audience. It can also act as an invitation to engage in a transaction now rather than later. Sales promotion usually attracts brand switchers but is unlikely to turn them into loyal brand users without the use of other elements of the promotion mix. In fact, sales promotion may break down brand loyalty, whereas advertising may build it up. Sales promotion can gain new users or encourage more frequent purchase, but it cannot compensate for inadequate advertising, poor delivery, or poor quality.

10.6.2 Sales Promotion Planning

As with advertising, effective sales promotion involves an ongoing process with distinct stages:

Establishment of objectives.   Sales promotion objectives vary according to the target market. If the target is the customer, objectives could include encouraging increased usage or building trial among nonusers or other brand users. For intermediaries, objectives could be to encourage off-season sales or to offset competitive promotions. Sales promotion activity could also be aimed at internal personnel, making up part of the reward system described in Chapter 7.

Selection of promotional tools.   Promotional objectives form the basis for selecting the most appropriate sales promotion tools. The cost and effectiveness of each tool must be assessed with regard to achieving these objectives in each target market. The tools available to the service marketer will be described later.

Planning the sales promotion program.   The major decisions relate to the timing of the promotion and how long a tool is to be used. Also important are the size of incentive, rules for entry, and, of course, the overall budget.

Pre-testing.   This needs to be undertaken in order to ensure that potentially expensive problems are discovered before the full launch of a promotion. Testing in selected market segments can highlight problems of ambiguity, indicate response rates, and give an indication of cost effectiveness.

Implementation.   The program for implementation must include two important time factors: the "lead time," or the time necessary to bring the program up to the point where the incentive is to be made available to the public, and the "sell in time," or the period of time from the date of release to the date when approximately 90 to 95 percent of incentive material has been received by potential customers.

Evaluation.   The performance of the promotion needs to be assessed against the objectives set. However, even when quantifiable objectives are set, it can be difficult to evaluate the true effectiveness of sales promotion because of extraneous factors. General economic conditions or seasonal variations, for example, may have influenced customers' decision making. It can also be extremely difficult to separate the effects of sales promotion activity from those of other promotional activities—or indeed from other marketing mix changes.

The problem of evaluating the long-term effects of a sales incentive is generally easier for services than for goods. For the latter, incentives could encourage increased sales as consumers build up stockpiles, only to result in lower sales in later periods when customers' stocks are used up. Because services cannot be stored, any short-term increase in sales results in increased immediate consumption with no carryover of stocks.

10.6.3 Sales Promotion Tools

A wide and ever-increasing range of sales promotion tools are employed by services organizations. Some of the more commonly used tools aimed at the final consumer include the following:

Free samples, visits, or consultations.   These encourage trial of a service and can be valuable when consumers are loyal to an existing service supplier. This device, for example, could be used by a video film rental chain to entice potential customers into the branch so they can learn something about the service offer. New services that are incorrectly perceived as being expensive and of poor value to a consumer might encourage consumers to try the service with samples. This has been widely done by cable and satellite television companies, for example, who offer free trial subscriptions. The free offer could include samples of the tangible components of a service, e.g., a sample of fast food. Taken to the extreme, the excessive offering of free samples can demean the value of the service and of the service provider. Customers may become reluctant to pay for a service that they have seen being given away freely.

Money off price incentives.   These are used to stimulate demand during slack periods when price is considered to be a key element in customers' purchase decision. Price incentives can be used tactically to counteract temporary increases in competitor activity. They can also be used to stimulate sales of a new service shortly after launch. Price incentives tend to be expensive to the service provider, as the incentive is given to customers regardless of its motivational effect on individual customers. An amusement park reducing its prices for all customers is unable to extract the full price from those customers who might otherwise have been willing to pay the full price. There is also a danger that price incentives can become built into consumers' expectations so that their removal results in a fall in business.

Coupons or vouchers.   These allow holders to obtain a discount off a future purchase and can be targeted at quite specific groups of users or potential users. To encourage trial by potential new users, vouchers can be distributed to nonusers who fit a specified profile. In this way, the operator of a tanning facility might arrange for vouchers to be given to customers of a cooperating hairdressing salon. To encourage repeat usage, vouchers can be given as a loyalty bonus. Voucher offers tend to be much more cost effective than straight price incentives because of their ability to segment markets. In this way, an amusement park operator is able to recognize that a visitor from overseas might see the full price as being only a small part of the total vacation cost and representing good value, while a local family might need an incentive to make more frequent visits to the park.

Gift offers.   These allow an organization to augment its service offer with an additional gift. The gift can satisfy various objectives. In order to promote initial inquiry and give tangible cues of the service company's offering and image, many firms—especially in the financial services sector—offer a gift for merely inquiring about their service. A gift can also be used to bring about immediate action, for example, a free radio if an insurance policy is taken out within a specified period. For existing customers, gifts can be used to develop and reward loyalty. Vouchers collected at shops can often be used to obtain services provided by another company, thereby satisfying both organizations' sales promotion objectives. Sometimes a company might charge for a gift. Not only could this be self-financing, but it could carry a message that makes the service offer tangible and conveys a repeat message to the user and others. In this way, some gasoline retailers and radio stations, among others, sell ranges of promotional clothing, often partly paid for by a combination of vouchers and cash.

Competitions.   The inclusion of a competition in a service offer adds to the value of the total offer. Instead of simply buying an insurance policy, a customer buys the policy plus a dream of winning a prize to which he or she attaches significance. Competitions can be used both to create trial among nonusers and to retain loyalty among existing users (e.g., a competition for which proofs of purchase are necessary to enter).

Sales promotion activity aimed at intermediaries includes the following:

Short-term increases in sales commission.   These, together with sales bonuses, can be used to stimulate sales during slack periods or to develop loyalty from intermediaries in the face of competitor activity.

Competitions and gifts.   These can be powerful motivators when the individual sales personnel benefit directly from the incentive and use their sales skills to promote the brand with the greatest value of incentive.

Point-of-sale material.   To stimulate additional sales, a service principal can provide a range of incentives to help intermediaries. Examples include cruise operators who agree to send a representative to a travel agency to provide additional information and reassurance for customers or to host a film evening for the agency's clients.

Cooperative advertising.   A service principal may agree to subscribe to local advertising by an intermediary, often in conjunction with a significant event, e.g., the opening of a new outlet by the intermediary, or the launch of a new service.

10.7 PERSONAL SELLING

Personal selling is a powerful two-way form of communication. It allows an interactive relationship to be developed between buyer and seller in which the latter can modify the information presented in response to the needs of the audience. Personal selling allows for the cultivation of a friendship between buyer and seller, which can be an important element of a relationship marketing strategy. It can also be powerful in creating a feeling of obligation by the customer to the salesperson, thereby helping to bring about a desired response.

Although the principles of personal selling are basically similar for goods and services industries, services sales personnel are more likely to combine their sales duties with other functional duties. For example, a travel agent is expected to perform a selling role, as well as to be an expert on travel reservation systems.

10.7.1 The Salesperson's Activities

The actual selling act is only a small part of a salesperson's role. Salespeople invariably also produce reports, service customers, handle complaints, and send in leads. In addition to their specific selling role, two further principal roles can be identified: servicing and intelligence.

The servicing element can be an important contributor to the development of long-term customer relationships when the service in question is perceived as being highly risky. Such relationships need to be regularly attended to, even if there is no short-term prospect of a sale. One study of the life insurance sector found that customers viewed their purchases as being highly risky and unpleasant. Consequently they attached particular importance to the level of support they received from a particular salesperson.[5] There have now been many studies to identify the factors that contribute to relationship satisfaction between buyer and seller.[6]

As well as being the mouthpiece of an organization, sales personnel can also be its ears, thereby filling the intelligence role. They can be extremely useful in marketing research, for example, by reporting customers' comments back to management, or by providing information about competitors' activity. Organizations should develop systems for capturing information collected by sales personnel.

With respect to their selling role, several types of selling situations can be identified:

- Trade selling, where the salesperson's role is to facilitate sales through intermediaries.
- Technical selling, which involves giving advice and technical assistance to customers. This type of salesperson becomes a consultant and assumes importance in many types of business-to-business service sales, e.g., business travel agencies.
- Missionary selling, in which the salesperson is expected not to take orders but to "prepare the ground" by building goodwill.
- New business selling, which involves the acquisition of new accounts and may sometimes involve "cold calling."

The task of selling can be broken down into sequential stages:

- Prospecting—finding new customers. Sales leads can be developed in various ways, for example, records of past customers, past inquiries, or referrals from existing customers and suppliers.
- Preparation and planning—a salesperson should attempt to gain as much information as possible about a prospect before actual contact takes place. For example, a salesperson should know about the prospect's previous buying behavior.
- The sales presentation—this is the focal point for the interaction and will be considered in more detail.
- Handling objections—objections to the sales presentation can be rational (objections to the price or the service itself) or irrational (objections based on resistance to change, apathy, or prejudice). In either case, these objections need to be acknowledged, isolated, and discussed.
- Closing the sale—this is a difficult stage; knowing how and when to close is a skill in itself.
- Follow-up—this stage is often neglected but is essential to develop ongoing relationships. A letter of thanks or a phone call can help reduce postpurchase dissonance, which is especially valuable for services whose benefits are to be delivered in the distant future.

10.7.2 The Sales Presentation

A sales presentation has to achieve several objectives, from initially gaining attention to developing interest, bringing about a desire for the service, and finally inducing action to purchase. If a few guidelines are followed, the effectiveness of a sales presentation as a two-way interactive promotional tool can be increased.[7]

- The salesperson should be recognized as a surrogate for the service. For low-contact services such as life insurance, the salesperson may be perceived as *being* the service. Appearance and demeanor are therefore very important in creating the right impression of the service offer.
- As well as giving information, the salesperson should also ask questions and listen to the customer's answers. One-way communication removes the interactive advantage of personnel selling and may fail to identify a customer's true needs.
- Service features should be linked to benefits, as they will be valued by customers. This is particularly important for highly complex and abstract services.
- Complex information should be used selectively. Too much complication may overwhelm a customer and leave him or her feeling belittled by the salesperson. Such detailed information is more effectively used in response to specific questions.
- The presentation should not be price oriented but should allow a potential customer to balance the overall costs with the overall benefits. Price sensitivity has been suggested to be generally less important for services than for goods.[5]

- The sales presentation should help make tangible an intangible service. Samples of supporting goods, brochures, or audiovisual aids can often give a better and more credible description of a service process than can a salesperson alone. They will also help to keep the client's attention.

- The salesperson should show a deep knowledge of his or her particular area. The training of sales personnel in technical as well as sales skills is therefore important. Without respect for the salesperson's knowledge, customers are less likely to have confidence in the salesperson or the services they are selling.

- The sales presentation should not offer what cannot be delivered. This applies to both goods and services but is particularly important when abstract expectations of service quality are not matched by actual performance. Over-promising may increase short-term sales, but the resulting assessment of poor quality will harm longer-term relationship possibilities. In some circumstances, therefore, it may be more appropriate to under-promise and over-deliver.

- Customers should be given early opportunities to assess service quality, either by seeing evidence of previous outcomes (e.g., previous performance of an investment fund) or by sampling the service process.

- An organization's image and reputation should be used to support sales arguments for high-credence services.

10.8 DIRECT MARKETING

Direct marketing is an interactive system of marketing that uses one or more media to create and exploit a direct relationship between service producers and their customers. In recent years there has been a dramatic increase in the use of direct marketing for promoting services, largely because of the development of new technology that enables organizations to accurately target customers. In the United States, direct marketing has been used extensively by the financial services sector, particularly pension funds and insurance companies. Travel companies, retailers, and hotels have been more recent adopters of direct marketing methods. While direct marketing may include personal selling, the other elements of direct marketing, including telemarketing, direct mail, directories, and videotech, are of more interest here.

The key elements of a direct marketing system are these:

- An accurate record of the names of existing customers, ex-customers, and prospective customers, classified into these different groups.

- A system for recording the results of communications with targets. From this, the effectiveness of particular messages and the responsiveness of different target groups can be assessed.

- A means of measuring and recording actual purchase behavior

- A system to follow up with continuing communication where appropriate.

The two most common forms of direct marketing used by services organizations are telemarketing and direct mail.

10.8.1 Telemarketing

Telemarketing involves two-way communication by telephone. "Outbound" telemarketing occurs where suppliers take the initiative, and "inbound" telemarketing where customers act in response to another stimulus such as a newspaper advertisement. In the United States there has been a rapid increase in the use of inbound telemarketing using toll-free 1-800 numbers. Inbound telemarketing is very powerful when combined with other media action and an incentive for customers to act promptly. Outbound telemarketing has sometimes been used as an alternative to personal selling, especially when some customers are seen as potentially less profitable than others.

It is often possible to measure the cost effectiveness of telemarketing in terms of the value of sales generated, especially where there is little extraneous media advertising that could itself explain sales success. Furthermore, by asking questions of inquirers, companies can identify the source of particularly effective supporting advertisements.

10.8.2 Direct Mail

Direct mail describes the way in which an organization distributes printed material aimed at specifically targeted potential customers. Direct mail's purpose is to bring about a direct interchange between the two parties. Its use is becoming increasingly popular among services industries because of several important advantages.

- It can be used very selectively to target quite specific groups of potential private or business customers.
- The sales message can be personalized to the needs of individual recipients—an important advantage for many tailor-made services such as financial services.
- Direct mail offers a very versatile and creative medium and is flexible in the range of materials that can be used.
- It can be timed effectively to fit in with the overall marketing strategy and is quick to produce.
- It is also quick in terms of producing results.

Direct mail can be employed to achieve several promotional objectives: generating inquiries, keeping prospects interested, keeping customers informed of new developments, and improving the effectiveness of the salesperson (it can be used as a "door opener").

Compared with advertising, the direct mail message can be more detailed. Much more space is available on a direct mail piece, and this allows long and complex messages to be presented—a point that helps to explain its popularity with financial services companies, whose sales messages are typically very complex. The response medium serves a variety of purposes. It can be used to obtain expressions of interest, to obtain sales orders, and to measure the effect of the promotion.

Response from recipients of direct mail is facilitated with the use of reply-paid envelopes and toll-free telephone numbers. The results of individually targeted mailers can be assessed quite easily, and through further refinement of customer profiling and targeting, the cost of contact per person can be reduced to a low level.

10.9 PUBLIC RELATIONS

Public relations is an indirect promotional tool whose role is to establish and enhance the positive image of an organization and its services among its various publics. It involves "the building of good relations with the company's various publics by obtaining favorable publicity, building up a good corporate image, and handling or heading off unfavorable rumors, stories, and events."[8]

Public relations attempts to persuade people that a company is an attractive organization with which to relate or do business. This point is important for services; as has already been noted, services are evaluated very subjectively on the basis of an organization's image and often rely on word-of-mouth recommendation. Public relations facilitates the process of subjective evaluation and recommendation.

An important task of public relations is to avert negative publicity. Because services can be highly variable, it is always possible that the media will pick up one bad incident and leave its audience thinking that this is the norm for a particular organization. This is particularly a problem for highly visible public or quasi-public services about which readers enjoy reading bad news stories that confirm their own prejudices.

External events may also lead to bad publicity, or the negative actions of similar service organizations may lead to a generally poor reputation of the sector as a whole. In all situations, an organization needs to establish contingency plans to minimize any surprise and confusion resulting from the publicity. Bad publicity is more likely to be effectively managed if an organization has invested time and effort in developing mutually supportive good relations with its publics.

Because public relations is involved with more than just customer relationships, it is often handled at a corporate level rather than at the functional level of marketing management, and it can be difficult to integrate public relations fully into the overall promotional plan. As an element within the promotion mix, public relations presents a number of valuable opportunities as well as problems. Some of its more important characteristics are described here:

Low cost.   Public relations tends to be much cheaper in terms of cost per person reached than any other type of promotion. Apart from nominal production costs, much public relations activity can be carried out at almost no cost, in marked contrast to the high cost of buying space or time in the paid-for media.

Audience specificity.   Public relations can be targeted to a small specialized audience if the right media vehicle is used.

Believability.   Public relations messages are seen as credible when they come from an apparently impartial and noncommercial source. When information is presented as news, readers or viewers may be less critical than if it is presented as a biased advertisement.

Difficult to control.   A company can exercise little direct control over how its public relations activity is subsequently handled and interpreted. For example, a press release may be printed in full, although there can be no control over where or when it is printed. At worst, the press release can be misinterpreted and result in very unfavorable news coverage.

Competition for attention.   The fact that many organizations compete for a finite amount of attention puts pressure on the public relations effort to be better than its competitors'.

10.9.1 The Publics of Public Relations

Public relations can be distinguished from customer relations because its concerns go beyond the creation of mutually beneficial relationships with actual or potential customers. The following additional audiences for public relations can be identified:

Intermediaries.   These may share many of the same concerns as customers and may need reassurance about the company's capabilities as a service principal. Service organizations can usually develop this reassurance through the use of company newsletters and trade journal articles.

Suppliers.   These may need assurances that the company is a credible one to deal with and that contractual obligations will be met. Highlighting favorable annual reports and drawing attention to major new developments can help raise the profile and credibility of a company in the eyes of its suppliers.

Employees.   Here, public relations overlaps with the efforts of internal marketing (see Chapter 7). In addressing its internal audiences, public relations uses such tools as in-house publications, newsletters, and employee recognition activities.

Financial community.   This includes financial institutions that have supported or are currently supporting the organization, or who may support it in the future. Shareholders—both private and institutional—form an important element of this community and must be reassured that the organization is going to achieve its stated objectives.

Government.   Actions of government can often significantly affect the fortunes of an organization, and therefore relationships with government departments— at local, state, and federal levels—need to be carefully developed. This can include lobbying of members of Congress, communicating the organization's views to government inquiries and civil servants, and creating a favorable image for the organization by sponsoring public events.

Local communities.   It is sometimes important for an organization to be seen as a good neighbor in the local community. Therefore, the organization can enhance its image through the use of charitable contributions, sponsorship of local events, or being seen to support the local environment.

10.9.2 The Tools of Public Relations

A wide range of public relations tools is available. The suitability of each tool depends on what objectives must be met. In general, the tools of public relations are best suited to creating awareness of an organization or liking for its services and tend to be less effective in directly bringing about action in the form of purchase decisions. While there can be argument as to just what constitutes public relations activity, some of the important elements used within the promotion mix are described here.

Press releases.   The creation and dissemination of press releases is often referred to as publicity, defined as "activity of securing editorial space, as divorced from paid space, in all media read, viewed or heard by a company's customers or prospects, for the specific purpose of assisting in the meeting of sales goals."[8] The aim of publicity is to create over the longer term a feeling of mutual understanding between an organization and the media. This can be developed through press releases, press conferences, and the provision of expert opinion to journalists. For example, a tour operator may be asked by a newspaper to comment on the consequences of a hurricane in an overseas resort. This helps both the reporter and the tour operator, whose representative is described as an expert.

Lobbying.   Professional lobbyists are often employed in an effort to inform and hence influence key decision makers who may be critical in allowing for elements of a marketing plan to be implemented. Lobbying can take place at the local, state, or federal government level.

Education and training.   In an effort to develop a better understanding—and hence liking—of an organization and its services, many services organizations aim education and training programs at important target groups. In this way, banks frequently supply schools and colleges with educational material that will predispose recipients to their brand when they come to open a bank account. Open days are another common method of educating the public by showing them the complex "behind-the-scenes" production processes involved. This tactic is commonly employed by theatres.

Exhibitions.   Most companies attend exhibitions not with the intention of making an immediate sale but to create an awareness of their organization that will result in a sale over the longer term. Exhibitions offer the chance for potential customers to talk face to face with representatives of the organization. The physical layout of the exhibition stand can give valuable tangible evidence about the nature of the service on offer. Exhibitions are used for both consumer services and business-to-business services. As an example of the latter, the annual Hotel and Catering Fair allows a wide range of hotel-related service industries to meet quite narrowly targeted customers and to display tangible cues of their service offering (e.g., brochures and staff).

In-house journals. Many services organizations have developed their own magazines and give them to customers or potential customers. In a news-based magazine format, the message becomes more credible than if it were presented as a pure advertisement. Often, outside advertisers contribute revenue that can make such journals self-financing. This commonly happens with in-house magazines published by banks. Travel operators often publish magazines that are read by captive passengers.

Special events. In order to attract media attention, organizations sometimes arrange an event that is in itself newsworthy and will create awareness of the organization. For example, an airline may gain favorable attention by flying a record-breaking nonstop journey or by agreeing to carry refugees from a war zone at its own expense. Of course, if badly managed, a special event can turn into a public relations disaster.

Sponsorship. There is argument about whether sponsorship strictly forms part of the public relations portfolio of tools. It is, however, increasingly used by services companies and will be described in more detail.

CASE STUDY

NORTHERN IRELAND TRIES TO WOO AMERICAN INVESTORS WITH PUBLIC RELATIONS

Ask most Americans what they associate with Northern Ireland, and they will probably rank it as one of the world's most notorious trouble spots, on a par with Bosnia or Lebanon—not a place where they would want to set up in business. The image perceived by influential developers is inevitably dominated by more than twenty years of "troubles." This has ensured that while the province has regularly remained in the news and has a high recognition factor among the public, it is recognized for the wrong reasons.

Northern Ireland has a desperate need to attract investment to overcome the social problems associated with very high levels of unemployment. In fact, the province has quite a lot going for it that should be very attractive to an American investor. A major task, therefore, is to alter attitudes and remove preconceived prejudices. Unfortunately, bombs and bullets make far more attractive news stories than the beautiful countryside, fishing, and low startup costs for investors.

The Industrial Development Board (IDB) of Northern Ireland is a government service organization that has been charged with stimulating economic development in the province. A vital part of this unenviable task entails promoting a favorable image of the province to overseas investors and trying to counterbalance the negative images that seem to be so deeply ingrained. As well as emphasizing the pleasant countryside and low startup costs, the Board makes the most of the province's cheap, good labor; high educational standards; and lack of labor disputes.

To present a more positive image of the province, public relations is used extensively to communicate with potential investors. Out of an international marketing budget of £5.5 million, advertising in itself only accounts for single-figure percentages. The main reason is that people see advertising as paid-for propaganda, and therefore the messages lack credibility. Public relations accounts for the bulk of its expenditure, and even where advertising is used, it is generally linked to public relations activity—for example, in the form of "advertorial" features. The IDB uses a public relations consultancy that aims to counteract the negative media coverage and to demonstrate to businesses that investing in Northern Ireland can lead to financial success. Success stories are highlighted with companies such as Ford, DuPont, and RJR Nabisco that are prepared to endorse the message. The promotional approach is to cultivate good contacts with influential journalists and decision makers. In an attempt to secure favorable coverage in business journals, site visits are frequently arranged on the principle that actually experiencing the region at first hand is the only true way of overcoming the fears and prejudices produced by the media. The greater part of the IDB public relations budget is spent on hospitality and contact events. Presentations and dinners are regularly organized for professional bodies.

Direct mail is also used, particularly in the European and American markets. Fact sheets describing the positive features of Northern Ireland are sent to the target audiences, and the message is targeted according to the audience. For example, a mailing to the United States emphasized the fact that the high security levels result in a relatively low crime rate.

Personal selling is used to supplement the public relations effort. One of the greatest assets of Northern Ireland is claimed to be its people, so the opportunity to meet a representative of not just the IDB but Northern Ireland as a whole gives an opportunity to evaluate one of the claims made about the province. Indeed, it is often said that northern Irish professionals have the "gift of the gab," and this is put to good effect.

Finally, word-of-mouth recommendation is facilitated through the Northern Ireland Partnership, an international group of senior business people who have links with the region and have agreed to help attract investment into the province. Personal endorsement can help overcome some of the negative images produced by the many years of conflict.

CASE STUDY REVIEW QUESTIONS

1. Summarize the reasons why public relations has assumed such a major role in promoting Northern Ireland
2. Suggest forms of sponsorship activity that may be particularly appropriate to the IDB
3. Identify the ways in which different elements of the promotion mix reinforce each other to produce a coherent campaign.

10.10 SPONSORSHIP

One way that services organizations can make their services appear more tangible is to try to get customers to link the image of their organizations or of specific services with a more tangible event or activity. While publicity can successfully perform this function, sponsorship can also have long-term value.

Sponsorship involves investment in events or causes in order that an organization can achieve objectives such as increased awareness levels and enhanced reputation. Sponsorship activities include restaurant chains' sponsorship of baseball tournaments, banks' sponsorship of faculty and facilities at universities, and the insurance companies' sponsorship of specific television programs.

Sponsorship is attractive to services companies, as it allows the relatively well-known characteristics of an event or activity being sponsored to enhance the image of an organization's own inherently intangible services. As an example, an insurance company wishing to associate itself with high quality may sponsor the activities of a leading arts organization noted for the quality of its productions. A further advantage of sponsorship is that it allows a company to avoid the general media clutter usually associated with advertising. Furthermore, audiences can be segmented and a sponsorship vehicle can be chosen whose audience matches that of the sponsoring company in terms of socioeconomic, demographic, and geographic characteristics. In this way, a regional insurance broker might sponsor a local theatrical group operating solely in its own business area.

It is difficult to evaluate sponsorship activities because of the problem of isolating the effects of sponsorship from other elements of the promotion mix. Direct measurement is likely to be possible only if sponsorship is the predominant tool. Sponsorship should therefore be seen as a tool that complements other elements of the promotion mix.

CHAPTER REVIEW QUESTIONS

1. To what extent do the differences between products and services influence the promotional methods used by a service organization?
2. Are there professional services in which you consider sales promotion activity to be unethical?
3. To what extent can the application of direct marketing be effective in the promotion of a university?
4. Public relations may be a more effective promotional tool for services than other communication methods. Is this true, and if so, why?
5. Identify the problems likely to be faced by an airline in evaluating the effectiveness of its promotion for a newly introduced service
6. A West Coast university sponsors a women's basketball tournament every December. Usually about ten thousand people attend the event. The crowd usually consists of families, Girl Scouts, high school women basketball players, and alumni of the university. Help an independent bookstore located in the community decide whether or not to sponsor the event. If the store sponsors the event, it must pay the athletic department of the university $10 thousand. Sponsorship means that the tournament will be named after the bookstore, so any reference in the local media to the tournament will mean free advertising to the bookstore. Advise the owner of the bookstore by identifying the factors that should influence his or her decision.

REFERENCES

1. Davis, D. L., Guiltinan, J. P., and Jones, W. H., "Service Characteristics, Consumer Search and the Classification of Retail Services," *Journal of Retailing* 55 (1979): 3.
2. Maslow, A., *Motivation and Personality* (New York: Harper and Row, 1954).

3. Bayton, J. A. "Motivation, Cognition, Learning—Basic Factors in Consumer Behavior," *Journal of Marketing* 22 (1958): 282–289.

4. George, W. R., and Berry, L. L., "Guidelines for the Advertising of Services," *Business Horizons* 24 (July/August 1981): 52–56.

5. George, W. R., and Myers, T. A., "Life Underwriters' Perceptions of Differences in Selling Goods and Services," *CLU Journal* (April 1981): 65–70.

6. Crosby, L. A., Evans, K. R., and Cowles, D., "Relationship Quality in Services Selling: An Interpersonal Influence Perspective," *Journal of Marketing* 54 (July 1990): 68–81.

7. George, W. R., Kelly, J. P., and Marshall, C. E., "Personal Selling of Services," in *Emerging Perspectives in Services Marketing,* ed. L. L. Berry, G. L. Shostack, and G. D. Upah (Chicago: American Marketing Association, 1983); and P. Kotler and A. Andreasen, *Strategic Marketing for Non-Profit Organizations* (Englewood Cliffs, N.J.: Prentice Hall, 1991).

8. Kotler, P., *Marketing Management: Analysis, Planning, Implementation and Control* (Englewood Cliffs, N.J.: Prentice Hall, 1994).

SUGGESTED FURTHER READING

CROSBY, L. A., EVANS, K. R., and COWLES, D. 1990. "Relationship Quality in Services Selling: An Interpersonal Influence Perspective." *Journal of Marketing* 54 (July): 68–81.

FIRESTONE, S. H. 1983. "Why Advertising a Service is Different" in *Emerging Perspectives in Services Marketing,* edited by L. L. Berry, G. L. Shostack, and G. D. Upah. Chicago: American Marketing Association.

GEORGE, W. R., and BERRY, L. L. 1981. "Guidelines for the Advertising of Services." *Business Horizons* 24 (July/August): 52–56.

GEORGE, W. R., KELLY, J. P., and MARSHALL, C. E. 1983. "Personal Selling of Services," in *Emerging Perspectives in Services Marketing,* edited by L. L. Berry, G. L. Shostack, and G. D. Upah. Chicago: American Marketing Association.

KEENAN, W. 1990. "The Difference in Selling Services." *Sales and Marketing Management* (March): 48–52.

LOVELOCK, C. H., and QUELCH, J. A. 1983. "Consumer Promotions in Services Marketing." *Business Horizons* (May/June): 66–75.

ONKVISIT, S., and SHAW, J. J. 1989. "Service Marketing: Image, Branding and Competition." *Business Horizons* (January/February): 13–18.

SCHURR, P. H., and OZANNE, J. L. 1985. "Influences on Exchange Processes: Buyers' Preconceptions of a Seller's Trustworthiness and Bargaining Toughness." *Journal of Consumer Research* 11 (March): 939–53.

SINGH, J. 1991. "Voice, Exit and Negative Word-of-Mouth Behaviors: An Investigation Across Three Service Categories." *Journal of the Academy of Marketing Science* (Winter): 1–16.

WEBSTER, C. 1991. "Influences upon Consumer Expectations of Services." *Journal of Services Marketing* 5, no. 1: 5–17.

11

Managing Marketing Information

CHAPTER OBJECTIVES

After reading this chapter, you should be able to understand

- the importance of the effective management of information for giving competitive advantage to services organizations
- the planning and control functions of information
- the concept of a marketing information system
- the purposes for which marketing research is undertaken by services organizations and the reasons for its increasing importance
- methods used to collect and analyze marketing research data

11.1 THE IMPORTANCE OF MARKETING INFORMATION

Imagine how you would react if one morning as you read your newspaper and sipped your coffee you spotted your employer's name in an article about management expert Tom Peters' informal survey of the customer service department of thirteen U.S. firms. Perhaps your employer would be one of the companies like the specialty retailer Nordstrom that gave him great service when he called to file a complaint. Perhaps, though, your employer would be one of the companies that cut him off when he called to register a complaint.[1] In either case, before you acted on the information in the newspaper article, you would want to obtain additional information about your organization's performance.

The management of any service organization requires a constant flow of information for two principal purposes:

- to provide information as an input to the marketing planning process
- to monitor the implementation of marketing programs and allow corrective action to be taken if performance diverges from target

Marketing information has to be seen in the context of the interfunctional dynamics of an organization. A timely supply of appropriate information provides feedback on an organization's performance, allowing actual performance to be compared with target performance. On the basis of this information, control measures can be applied that attempt where necessary to put the organization back on its original targets. Organizations also learn from the past in order to better understand the future. For making longer-term planning decisions, historical information is supplemented by a variety of continuous ad hoc studies, all designed to facilitate better informed decisions. Marketing research cannot in itself produce decisions; it merely provides information, which must be interpreted by marketing managers. As an interfunctional integrator, marketing information draws data from all functional areas of an organization, which in turn use data to perform their functions more effectively. Research involving employees, both as sources of information and as recipients of research findings, becomes important as an integrating device.

The use of information has been identified as a source of a firm's marketing orientation that allows it to obtain a sustainable competitive advantage.[2] It has been argued that processing information should be regarded as the fifth "P" of the marketing mix.[3] Information represents a bridge between the organization and its environment and is the means by which a picture of the changing environment is built up within the organization. Marketing management is responsible for turning information into specific marketing plans.

As information collection, processing, transmission, and storage technologies improve, information is becoming more accessible not just to one particular organization but also to its competitors. Attention is therefore moving away from how information is collected to who is best able to make use of the information. It is too simple to say that marketing managers commission data collection by technical experts and make decisions on the basis of these data. Recent research has focused on the relationship between market researchers and marketing managers, the role of trust between the two, and how that trust helps reduce risk.[4]

Recent technological innovations—for example, Electronic Point of Sale (EPOS) systems—have enabled service companies to greatly enhance the speed, accuracy, and consistency of their core services. In turn, the resulting increase in operational efficiency has allowed service organizations to gain competitive advantage by improving other areas of their service offerings, such as the development of ongoing relationships. At the same time, the increasing ease with which data can be collected and disseminated has made it easier for services companies to manage service quality by setting quantifiable objectives that can be effectively monitored.

New technologies are, of course, only one aspect of an organization's marketing environment that needs to be understood and evaluated. Organizations must also understand the effects of other environmental factors, such as the state of the local or national economy. Without this broader environmental information, routine pieces of marketing research information, such as the market share held by a company's brands over the past year, cannot be interpreted meaningfully. Such environmental factors can arguably be more important for services than for manufacturing industries. These factors are likely to be especially important in sectors such as leisure and travel, where consumers' expenditure reflects national economic performance more closely than is true of many fast-moving consumer goods.

Marketing information allows management to improve its strategic planning, its tactical implementation of programs, and its monitoring and control. A practical problem is that information to meet strategic planning needs is typically much more difficult to obtain than is information to meet operational and control needs. There can be a danger that marketing managers will focus too heavily on easily available information at the expense of needed information.

11.2 MARKETING INFORMATION SYSTEMS

Many analyses of organizations' information collection and dissemination activities take a systems perspective. The collection of marketing information can be seen as one subsystem of a much larger management information system. Other systems typically include production, financial, and personnel systems. In a well-designed management information system, the barriers between these systems should be conceptual rather than real. For example, sales information is of value to all these subsystems to a greater or lesser extent (Figure 11.1).

A marketing information system has been defined by Kotler as a system that:

> consists of people, equipment and procedures to gather, sort, analyze, evaluate and distribute needed, timely and accurate information to marketing decision-makers.[5]

A marketing information subsystem can conceptually be seen as comprising four principal components, although in practice they are operationally interrelated:

- *Internal data* are generated within organizations, particularly in respect to operational and control functions. By careful arrangement of their collection and dissemination, internal data can provide a constant and up-to-date flow of information, useful for both planning and control functions, at relatively little cost.

- *Marketing research* is the part of the system concerned with the structured collection of marketing information. Marketing research can provide both routine information about marketing effectiveness, such as brand awareness levels or delivery performance, and one-time studies, such as changing attitudes toward diet or the pattern of income distribution.

- *Marketing intelligence* comprises the procedures and sources used by marketing management to obtain pertinent information about developments in their marketing environment. Intelligence gathering, which concentrates on picking up relatively intangible ideas and trends, complements the marketing research system, which tends to focus on structured and largely quantifiable data collection procedures.

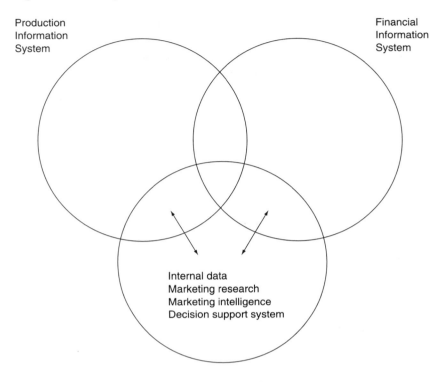

Production
Information
System

Financial
Information
System

Internal data
Marketing research
Marketing intelligence
Decision support system

Marketing Information System

Figure 11.1   A systems approach to managing information

Marketing management can gather this intelligence from a variety of sources, such as newspapers, specialized clipping services, employees who are in regular contact with market developments, intermediaries, suppliers to the company, and specialized consultants.

- *Marketing decision support systems* comprise a set of models that allow forecasts to be made. Information is both an input to such models, in that data is needed to calibrate a model, and an output, in that models provide information on which decisions can be based. Models are frequently used in service outlet location decisions (see Chapter 8), where historical data may have established a relationship between one variable (e.g., the level of sales achieved by a particular service outlet) and other variables (e.g., pedestrian traffic in a street). Predicting the sales level of a proposed new outlet then becomes a matter of measuring pedestrian traffic at a proposed site, feeding this information into the model, and calculating the predicted sales level.

In organizations that have set up marketing information systems, several factors will determine their effectiveness:

The accuracy with which the information needs of the organization have been defined.   Needs can themselves be difficult to identify and it can be very difficult to identify, the boundaries of the firm's environments and to separate relevance from irrelevance. This is a particular problem for large multiservice firms. The mission statement of an organization may give some indication of the boundaries for its environmental search. For example, many banks have mission statements that talk about becoming a dominant provider of financial services in their domestic market. The information needs, therefore, include anything related to the broader environment of financial services rather than to the narrower field of banking.

The extensiveness of the search for information.   A balance has to be struck between the need for information and the cost of collecting it. The most critical elements of the marketing environment must be identified, and the cost of collecting relevant information must be weighed against the cost that would result from an ill-informed forecast.

The speed of communication.   The marketing information system will be effective only if information is communicated quickly and to the appropriate people. Deciding what information to withhold from an individual, and concise reporting of relevant information, can be as important as deciding what information to include if information overload is to be avoided.

11.3 THE SITUATION ANALYSIS

The first stage in the marketing management process is to establish the current position of an organization. If information about this position is inadequate or inaccurate, the value of any subsequent plans must be questioned.

Auditing systems have been used for some time as a means of gathering information to assess the efficiency and effectiveness of an organization's functions. The financial audit is probably the most widely used; because it can be used to assess the financial health of an organization. Personnel and production audits are similarly used to establish the personnel and production strengths and weaknesses of an organization as well as the nature of the environments in which these functions operate. Together, these contribute to the corporate audit—an assessment of an organization's overall strengths and weaknesses relative to its environment. The elements of a corporate audit are diagrammatically represented in Figure 11.2.

A marketing audit is a relatively new concept and has been defined as:

> a systematic, critical and unbiased review and appraisal of the environment and of the company's operations. A marketing audit is part of the larger management audit and is concerned with the marketing environment and marketing operations.[6]

A marketing audit contributes to the corporate audit by addressing three major issues:

- the nature of the environmental threats and opportunities facing the organization
- the strengths and weaknesses of the organization in terms of its ability to cope with the threats and opportunities presented by its environment
- the organization's current market position

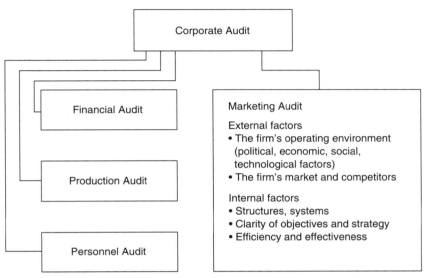

Figure 11.2 The corporate audit

To be effective, a marketing audit needs to be comprehensive, systematic, independent, and periodic. A comprehensive audit covers all the major elements of an organization's activities, including those that are apparently performing well, rather than concentrating solely on problem areas. A systematic audit has a coherent structure and is followed by the development and implementation of plans that are based on the outcome of the audit. The greater the independence of a person undertaking an audit, the more useful it is likely to be, as objectivity may be inhibited when vested interests are at stake.

How frequently should marketing audits be undertaken? At one extreme, it has been argued that marketing audits should be conducted on a continuous but selective basis. At the other extreme, if the process is conducted too frequently, the process itself will demoralize marketing personnel.

11.4 FORWARD PLANNING WITH MARKETING RESEARCH

As a planning tool, marketing research provides management with market and product-specific information, which allows it to minimize the degree of uncertainty in planning its marketing effort. This risk minimization function can apply to the whole of the marketing operation or to any of its constituent parts, such as advertising.

It is impossible to accurately define the exact functions of marketing research within marketing information systems, as organizations differ so widely in size and structure. However, in Figure 11.3, shaded boxes show the areas inside which the marketing research function normally operates.

Information sources can be classified as internal and external. It is in the area of internal data collection that it is most difficult to distinguish marketing research

MARKETING INFORMATION SYSTEM

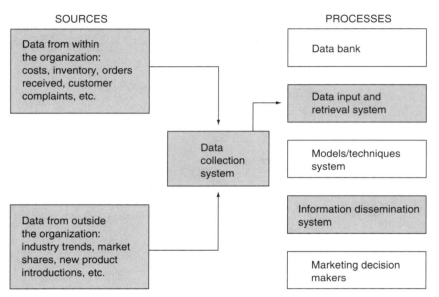

Figure 11.3   The role of marketing research within the sources and processes of a marketing information system
(Adapted from A. Parasuraman, *Marketing Research,* Reading, MA: Addison Wesley, 1991.)

from other marketing information system functions. Much depends on the size, scope, and structure of the marketing information system itself. In many large organizations the collation of regularly generated information, such as costs and sales figures, is not central to the research activity. However, marketing research may well generate new information from within the organization, for example, by collecting information on an ad hoc basis from key groups such as management, the sales staff, and front-line service personnel.

In practice, the main focus of marketing research activity within most service organizations is external data collection. Market researchers become involved with data input and retrieval and with information dissemination systems. In smaller organizations it is possible that the research function also incorporates the setting up and operation of data banks and the development of models and systems that incorporate information gathered by researchers.

11.4.1 Major Uses of Research in Services Marketing

Any distinction between services and goods marketing research is becoming increasingly blurred as goods manufacturers also concentrate on the service and other intangible elements of their offering. One sign of this is the recent considerable increase in research by goods manufacturers into their corporate image. While such companies develop and monitor corporate image programs alongside product branding symbols, services companies seek ways in which they can overcome problems of identification and brand loyalty towards intangibles. Service companies often develop strong, anthropomorphic symbols (nonhuman symbols with which humans nevertheless identify), to help differentiate themselves from competitors. In this context, the fairly recent increase in demand for marketing research from services companies is not surprising.

There is little doubt about the importance of marketing research to service organizations. Christopher Lovelock has identified several factors that tend to characterize successful service businesses.[7] Among them, two factors are particularly pertinent:

Capturing and using customer data.   The significance of information for the planning of marketing activities has already been stated. The implications for services marketers are therefore apparent, and some of their specific needs in this area are outlined here.

Soliciting feedback from customers and employees.   It has already been stated that the gathering of information from customers is vital to marketing success in general. In service industries it is particularly important, as customers do not have a tangible product to assess according to their predetermined criteria. Many predominantly intangible variables contribute to overall satisfaction and may influence the way each experience is perceived. Therefore, the constant or intermittent interaction between customers and the service provider, which occurs as a stream of service encounters, must be evaluated as an ongoing process. Customer satisfaction may fluctuate from one encounter to another. Some aspects of the service may be perceived as good on one occasion and bad on another. For instance, a customer may be satisfied with the time spent waiting in line at a bank one week and dissatisfied the next. Loyalty comes from developing a good long-term relationship with customers, and feedback should be solicited regularly in order to determine the level of satisfaction. There must be some means by which the bank knows when and why a customer is dissatisfied.

The variability of services makes research into them very different in comparison with research into manufactured goods, which may be used over and over again without any variance. In addition, goods marketing does not normally involve any face-to-face interaction with production staff, unlike services, where employees usually perform the service on, or in conjunction with, the customer. Because staff are critically important in making a satisfactory service offer, it is very important to research staff perceptions. One should consider employee views about how well a service is being received by customers and how it may be improved. After all, it is the front-line staff within an organization who have regular and close contact with the users of a service, so the information they provide can be of enormous value.

Organizations should undertake research with employees because they can be seen as internal recipients of marketing efforts. A successful services company should be just as proficient at managing the management/staff interface as it is at managing the staff/customer interface. Feedback from these internal customers should be treated as an important aspect of services marketing research.

Current practice in services marketing research reflects the growing emphasis on the maintenance of quality standards of service. In very simple terms, the essence of service quality is understanding what customers want and ensuring that they are continuously provided with it. It is therefore of utmost importance that services organizations understand their customers' expectations. An appropriate program of marketing research can identify the variance between what customers get as opposed to what they expect. This is a highly subjective matter and requires careful qualitative analysis of customers' expectations of the service and their perceptions of service delivery.

The marketing research process can help identify segments of the population with similar service expectations. Using the principle of benefit segmentation, it is possible to identify the differing requirements of groups of customers in terms of the components of service quality that they perceive as important, and target them with appropriately designed service offerings.

CASE STUDY

FIDELITY BRINGS CUSTOMERS INTO ITS LABORATORY FOR STUDY

Fidelity Investments thought it was doing pretty well. With $113 billion in assets and over eight million customer accounts on its books, the mutual fund giant thought it knew about the needs of its investors inside out. But then came the 1987 stock market crash, bringing with it a slowdown in market growth and an intensification of the competition that Fidelity faced. Top executives worried that Fidelity wasn't distinct enough from its main competitors, and there was a feeling that quality wasn't all it might be. For example, at the beginning of 1989 it was taking an average of eleven days to resolve customer problems.

In the days of plenty, a corporate culture had grown up in which standards were set by managers, not started by analyzing what customers wanted. The culture was geared to speed and volume—where the customer was often seen as something of a nuisance. With the appointment of a vice president for corporate quality management, a new agenda was set for the company's retail business. At the heart of the new approach was finding out just what customers actually wanted out of a mutual fund investment.

One research tool that was rapidly adopted was the use of service labs. In return for lunch, Fidelity invited customers to come and talk about their attitudes toward the company. Using skilled discussion leaders, these focus groups were essentially unstructured and allowed participants to bring to the discussion issues that they considered to be important, rather than confining discussion to a limited agenda of items that management thought customers should consider important. An early series of service labs investigated customers' reactions to Fidelity's automated phone answering service. As a result, Fidelity simplified its automated voice prompts and introduced a softer voice to replace the previous voice, which was considered by the sample of customers to sound too unfriendly. Fidelity also rewrote some of its brochures to clarify the purpose of each toll-free inquiry number, which customers had found confusing. The number of toll-free numbers was also increased from two to five. As a result of these changes, approximately one-third more callers than before got straight through to the function they needed without having to wait for an operator.

The small sample qualitative service labs have been supplemented by a program of more quantitative research. The company now uses questionnaires to undertake annual surveys of its customers. The 1991 survey, which received about 1,500 responses, asked customers to rate Fidelity on seventy different service attributes, from the convenience of branch locations to the politeness of sales personnel. Some results were quite unexpected. Customers were found to value polite treatment even ahead of investment performance and the accuracy of statements. At the top of the list of customers' needs were such items as "people to take responsibility for me" and "people should listen to me".

The marketing information system of Fidelity is also about keeping in touch with its employees. Like many mutual companies, Fidelity had been run with something of a military authoritarian style. The function of employees was seen as implementing instructions and doing so in accordance with clearly specified guidelines. The new approach encouraged employees to submit ideas for ways in which customer service could be improved or operations made more efficient. To back this up, rewards were offered, ranging from mention in the company's newsletters to trophies and lunch with the president.

In the increasingly competitive market, Fidelity recognized that it could gain a lot of ideas by studying how other service organizations operated. Top executives took lessons by studying how McDonald's ensured that its french fries were perfect every time, toured Disney World's training programs to learn how loyalty could be developed, and arranged with the mail order retailer L. L. Bean to see how it handled customer relations by telephone.

CASE STUDY REVIEW QUESTIONS

1. Contrast the uses of Fidelity's focus group and questionnaire-based approaches to gathering information about customer attitudes.
2. For Fidelity, what is the relationship between marketing research and quality?
3. Who should be involved in marketing research at Fidelity?

11.4.2 Major Services Research Activities

The range of tasks that marketing research contributes to the services marketing planning process is growing. Some of the more important specific uses of marketing research, many of which are in fact associated with service quality issues, are listed here.

Research into customer needs.   Research is undertaken to learn what underlying needs individuals attempt to satisfy when they buy services. Identifying needs that are currently unmet by service offerings spurs new service development.

Research into customer expectations.   Needs should be distinguished from expectations. Various qualitative techniques are used to study the standards of service that customers expect when they consume a service, for example, how long a delay are consumers willing to tolerate when they order a pizza at a fast food restaurant?

Customer perception studies.   The most important definition of service quality is what customers consider the quality level to be. Perception studies can be undertaken during or after consumption to test the perceived level of quality. They can also be undertaken before consumers purchase a service. Pre-consumption may reveal the extent to which external factors might have influenced the way an individual perceives an organization or its specific offerings.

Customer surveys.   Ad hoc or regular programs of survey research carried out among customers provide information about their perceptions and expectations (Figure 11.4). These can have the dual functions of providing the service organization with much-needed information and also providing a public relations tool by allowing customers to feel that they have made their feelings known in a way that may allow them to be acted upon.

Similar industry studies.   Many services industries can learn from research undertaken in industries that appear at first sight to be totally unrelated. By learning about operating practices and customer reactions to their service offering, marketing managers in one sector such as shipping can learn a lot from studies carried out within the hotel sector. Through a process sometimes referred to as benchmarking, an organization can set itself targets based on the best practice in its own, or a related, industry.

Research into service intermediaries.   Agents, dealers, and other intermediaries are close to consumers and therefore form a valuable conduit for gathering marketing research. In addition, intermediaries are customers of service principals; therefore, research is undertaken to establish—among other things—their perceptions of the standard of service they receive from the service principal.

Key client studies.   Most organizations see some customers as being more important than others, due to the volume and/or profitability of the business that they generate. When a company derives the majority of its income from one customer, it may make a particular effort to ensure that the customer is totally satisfied with its standards of service and prices. The loss of the business as a result of shortcomings of which it is unaware could be catastrophic for the service organization. In some cases, the relationship with key customers may be of such mutual importance that each partner may spend considerable time jointly researching shared problems. For example, an airport operator with two or three key airline customers may jointly develop a program of research to judge passengers' perception of the total experience that they perceive as they pass through the airport. Sometimes, key clients with whom a sound relationship has been built up can be used as a basis for researching new service ideas before they are released more widely.

Customer panels.   As a means of keeping in regular contact with current and potential customers, panels are often used. These can be used to provide valuable information about proposed new service launches and also to monitor perceptions of current service delivery. For example, Amoco uses a NFO Research, Inc. consumer panel to understand consumer gasoline purchasing, credit card usage patterns, and attitudes toward its brand and product image.[8]

Employee research.   As part of a program of internal marketing, research into employees is often undertaken by service organizations. This research can focus on employees as internal customers of services within an internal market as well as on their thoughts about the methods of service provision. Employee suggestion schemes form an important part of research into employees.

We'd Like Your Opinion.

It'll help us make Arby's even better.

Was this your first visit to Arby's? ☐ **Yes**   ☐ **No**

Time of visit. _____

         date   day   time

What made you select Arby's? _____

_____

Name of employee serving you: _____

What did your meal consist of? _____

_____

What's your favorite radio station? _____ TV Station? _____

Were you coming from ☐ work ☐ home ☐ school ☐ shopping

How far did you travel? ☐ 1 mile ☐ 2 miles ☐ 5+ miles

Are you a coupon saver? ☐ Yes ☐ No

How Do You Rate Us?

Sandwiches _____

French Fries/Potato Cakes _____

Salad _____

Service Speed _____

Beverage _____

Friendliness _____

Order Accuracy _____

Cleanliness of Restaurant _____

Other _____

Will you visit Arby's again? ☐ yes ☐ no

Additional Comments/Suggestions: _____

_____

_____

name _____

address _____

city _____ state _____

phone _____

OFFICE USE ONLY

CAPITOL PARTNERS #1571

UNIT

You can deposit this card in our Suggestion Box, or mail it back to us.

Thank you very much!

© FMS 1991

Figure 11.4 The fast-food company Arby's uses this questionnaire to carry out routine monitoring of customers' attitudes to its restaurants. Source: Reprinted with permission of Arby's, Inc., Iowa City, Iowa.

11.4.3 Setting Services Research Objectives

The research problem almost always results from the incomplete nature of the market information already available to management. For example, a company may have comprehensive and up-to-date information on the market for its current products but may wish to discover what—if any—market needs remain unsatisfied, in order to develop new products.

The marketing researcher could be given one of several types of brief reports:

- defining market characteristics (e.g., defining the services required from travel agents by people who purchase vacations)
- describing market characteristics (e.g., describing to a client the behavior of families with children when purchasing overseas vacations)
- measuring market characteristics (e.g., establishing for a client travel agency the market shares of major United States travel agents)
- analyzing market characteristics—a more thorough investigation of those kinds of information (e.g., analyzing vacation buying behavior according to the age, income, or lifestyle of different segments of the population)

A problem in setting objectives lies in the difficulty of defining just what constitutes the market to be studied. For all products, it can be difficult to identify which near-competitors should be considered to be part of the market that is under analysis. With services, this becomes a problem where service availability is defined in geographical terms. Unlike goods, inseparable services often cannot be brought to the consumer. But how far should the target market of a fixed location service extend, and therefore, what is the achievable market? The market for a proposed new attorney's office may look attractive when defined solely in terms of a small town that is being studied. However, if it is accepted that clients typically are prepared to travel some distance to see an attorney, the market can be sensibly assessed only by including an analysis of the market for attorneys' services in the surrounding region, the boundaries of which are difficult to define.

11.4.4 The Marketing Research Industry and Its Processes

Most definitions of marketing research activity focus on its role as a means by which those who provide goods and services keep themselves in touch with the needs and wants of those who use their goods and services. Within the context of services industries, this could be extended to include the means by which management keeps in touch with the motivation and behavior of its staff. In either case, the key phrase, which encompasses all marketing research activity and differentiates it from the wider scope of marketing information systems, is *keeping in touch*. Data collected should be as up-to-date and relevant to a problem as time and cost constraints allow.

Kotler has described the stages of the marketing research process in a much simpler, linear format than that just offered, beginning with the definition of the research problem and ending with the presentation of the findings (Figure 11.5).

Figure 11.5   The marketing research process

This process follows the same basic pattern as for other forms of research activity, such as scientific or academic research. To be useful, keeping in touch needs to be conducted objectively and accurately. Casual, unstructured research is at best wasteful and at worst misleading.

Market research is itself a service industry, with its own functions and specialists. In order to explain the way in which the process illustrated in Figure 11.5 works, it is useful to briefly describe the structure of the industry. Essentially, market researchers fall into two groups:

- those employed by services companies themselves, for example, banks, retailers, and airlines (often referred to as client companies). These researchers provide information for internal use and generally have specific product and market knowledge of their sector.
- Those employed by marketing research organizations whose specific purpose is the supply of information to other users. These supply companies are often referred to as agencies—something of a misnomer, as they are paid on a fee rather than a commission basis. Staff employed by these companies can generally achieve a high level of expertise in particular research techniques, some of which are described here.

The research process allows for the expertise of both groups to be incorporated at different stages. Client company researchers define a research problem after discussion with marketing and other management. This is usually communicated to potential suppliers in the form of a research brief. The objectives of the study are set by matching management information needs with what can realistically be obtained from the marketplace, particularly in the light of time and budgetary constraints, and may well be defined after initial discussions with possible suppliers.

The area in which marketing research agencies dominate is information collection. The degree to which the client company is involved in developing the research plan and analyzing and presenting the findings varies depending largely on the size and expertise of its research department. Before deciding on the final plan, however, most client companies approach several possible suppliers and ask for their suggestions in the form of a research proposal.

11.4.5   Sources of Information

Data sources are traditionally divided into two categories according to the methods by which they were collected. These are known as secondary and primary data sources—often referred to as desk and field research, respectively. Most organizations would approach a research exercise by examining the available sources of secondary data.

Secondary data refers to information that in some sense is second-hand to the current research project. Data could be second-hand because it has already been collected internally by the organization, although for a different primary purpose. Alternatively, the information could be acquired second-hand from external sources.

Internal information on products, costs, sales, and so on may be accessed through an organization's marketing information system. Where such a system does not exist formally, the information may still be available in relevant departmental records, though it would probably need to be reworked into a form that market researchers can use. Despite modern data processing technology, the manual task of going through stacks of back invoices in order to quantify annual sales by product and customer is still not unknown.

There are numerous external sources of secondary data in both document and electronic formats. These cover government statistics, trade associations, and specialist research reports. A good starting point for a review of them is still the business section of a good library. Some examples of secondary data sources are shown in Table 11.1.

Traditionally, it has been much easier to find external secondary information on goods than on services. However, there has been a considerable increase in services marketing intelligence reports in recent years. Data are also often obtainable from special interest panels; for example, information on attitudes toward airlines is obtainable from a regular airline users' panel.

It is also worth checking whether other organizations, possibly even competitors, have conducted studies similar to the one proposed. Numerous catalogues list sources of external secondary market research data (e.g., Dataquest). Although such information is not as up-to-date or relevant as that obtained by commissioning a new survey, it is normally available at a fraction of the cost.

While secondary, or desk, research, is not the most exciting activity in the world, it is very worthwhile, although the research objectives may not be achieved by this method alone. It can, however, be conducted by company employees and pro-

TABLE 11.1   SOME EXAMPLES OF SECONDARY DATA USED IN SERVICES MARKETING RESEARCH

National media—e.g., *Wall Street Journal* industry surveys

Trade, technical, and professional media—e.g., *Travel Weekly, Bank Management*

Government departments and official publications—e.g., Federal Trade Commission, U.S. Bureau of the Census, Interstate Commerce Commission

Local chambers of commerce

Professional and trade associations—e.g., American Society of Travel Agents, Bank Administration Institute

Yearbooks and directories—e.g., *Dataquest*

Subscription services providing periodic sector reports on market intelligence and financial analyses—e.g., American Demographics, Donnelly Market Information Services, Mintel

Subscription electronic databases—e.g., America Online

vides a useful starting point for further investigation. Undertaking unnecessary primary research that is available through secondary sources is an expensive and time-consuming exercise.

Primary data, generated by field research, is concerned with new information obtained directly from the target population. The phrase *keeping in touch* was highlighted earlier, and marketing research professionals spend most of their time designing and implementing such studies, either on an ad hoc (one-time) or a continuous (monitoring) basis. Primary research in the services sector has expanded rapidly during the 1980s, owing in part to the lack of previously published data.

11.4.6 Research Methods

One important decision to be made when developing a primary research plan is whether to conduct a qualitative or quantitative survey.

Qualitative research.   Qualitative research is the exploration and interpretation of the perceptions and behavior of small samples of target consumers, and the study of the motivators involved in purchasing choices. It is a highly focused, in depth exploration of, for example, the relationship between respondents' motives and their behavior in depth. The techniques used to encourage respondents to speak and behave honestly and unselfconsciously are derived from the social sciences, psychology in particular (Figure 11.6).

When definitions and descriptions are needed—in other words, when no one knows exactly where to start—qualitative research is at its most useful. It can define the parameters for future studies and identify key criteria among consumers that can then be measured by quantitative research. For example, if a bank observed that older consumers were not using automatic teller machines, they might conduct some focus groups with older consumers in order to develop hypotheses about why this particular group was reluctant to use this technology. It is important, however, that the consumers are asked in as objective and sympathetic a form as possible. Qualitative research plans generally incorporate a discussion outline for those collecting the information, but they are essentially unstructured and respondent-led.

Quantitative research.   Quantitative research is used to measure consumer attitudes and choices when the nature of the research has been defined and described. These studies are designed to gather information from statistically representative samples of the target population. In order to achieve total accuracy it would be necessary to take a complete census of everyone in the target group. The scale and cost of the United States census illustrates the impracticality of this in most cases. Therefore, the sample size is related to the size of the total population and the degree of statistical reliability required, balanced against time and cost constraints. In order to achieve margins of error small enough to make the final measurements useful, however, quantitative research is usually conducted among several hundred or several thousand respondents. For this reason, information is generally obtained with standardized structured questionnaires.

"Well you said you wanted small business people."

There's no misunderstanding what the wrong respondents can do to your focus research. To get the right focus group results, it takes *fieldwork*.

fieldwork provides qualified, well screened respondents from a database that's unmatched in the industry. And you'll work in a world class research enviroment--with progressive office facilities and client servjces.

You'll find a *fieldwork* location right where you need us. For the focus group your project deserves, call us today.

fieldwork Atlanta (404) 988-0330	*fieldwork* Chicago (O'Hare) (312) 714-8700	*fieldwork* East (Fort Lee) (201) 585-8200
fieldwork Boston (617) 899-3660	*fieldwork* Denver (303) 825-7788	*fieldwork* East (Westchester) (914) 347-2145
fieldwork Chicago (312) 282-2911		*fieldwork* Phoenix (602) 438-2800

It takes *fieldwork!*

Figure 11.6   This marketing research company specializes in focus group studies. Source: Creative Response Research Services, Inc., Chicago, IL.

11.4.7 Data Collection

Data can be collected either indirectly, by observation, or directly, by interaction with the person being researched.

Observational techniques claim objectivity, being relatively free of respondent bias, but they are limited to descriptions of behavior. They have some uses within the services sector for planning purposes, for example, in site location decisions, which are often based on observation of pedestrian or vehicle flows past a site. They can also be used for routine monitoring of competitor price levels.

A survey—a direct interaction data collection method—normally requests some attitudinal, personal, or historical information about respondents. Questions in a survey can be asked face-to-face or by telephone, or they can be distributed for self-completion. While considerably cheaper than face-to-face interviews, telephone surveys have a refusal rate up to three times higher. The increased use of computer-assisted information collection for telephone (CATI) and personal interviews (CAPI) has speeded up the whole survey process dramatically, with responses being processed as they are received. Immediately prior to the 1992 U.S. presidential election, these systems were used in the next-day publication of survey results from total sample sizes extending into thousands.

In self-completion surveys, respondents obviously self-select, so no matter how carefully the original sample to be contacted is chosen, the possibility of bias is highest. Furthermore, the response rate may be as low as 10 percent, particularly when a mail survey is used. However, some service sector companies, in particular airlines and hotels, have used self-completion questionnaires for many years to obtain customer feedback.

In qualitative research, the open-ended nature of the questions, and the need to establish respondent confidence, preclude the use of telephone and self-completion interviews. Face-to-face (or personal) depth interviews are used particularly in business-to-business research, where confidentiality is especially important, and it is usually most convenient for respondents to be interviewed at their place of work.

In consumer markets, group discussions are most often used. Groups normally consist of about eight people, plus a trained moderator—quite often a psychologist—who leads the discussion. Respondents are recruited by interviewers, who use recruitment questionnaires to filter out unsuitable respondents and to ensure that those invited to attend reflect the demography of the target market. In national markets, groups are arranged at central points throughout the country, the number of groups in each region once more reflecting the regional breakdown of the target population.

It was noted earlier that the collection of market information is the part of the research process most dominated by research agencies rather than client companies. There are two main reasons for this. First, very few client companies can generate sufficient research to justify employing a large staff of full-time interviewers. Second, respondents are more likely to give honest answers to third parties than directly to representatives of the organization providing the service being discussed.

11.4.8 Effects on Research Methods of Service Inseparability

For manufactured goods, it is usually possible within the research process to separate the technical characteristics of a product from the identity and image of the company producing it. For example, in testing a beverage such as tea or beer, it is possible to isolate reactions to the core product by presenting it to respondents in blind format, i.e., in a plain (usually white) container with no clue to the brand or manufacturing company. The respondent is then asked to rate the product along various dimensions, e.g., strength–weakness or light–dark color. The extent to which perceptions are influenced by brand or company connotations can be measured by presenting an identically constructed sample with the same product, fully branded and packaged, and measuring the differences in response along the same dimensions.

It is not always possible to make this kind of neat separation when researching services. Respondents cannot rate the level of satisfaction provided by a financial service, for example, unless they have actually experienced it, which may be difficult to achieve in a laboratory setting. Furthermore, interviewees' responses to proposed new services cannot be isolated from their perceptions of the service provider. An insurance policy cannot be seen in isolation from the reputation of the insurance company that will be responsible for delivering the service benefits in the future. Indeed, some providers of services marketing research argue that attempting such a separation is undesirable and that it is essential to look at all aspects of the company/customer relationship—attitudinal and perceptual, as well as factual and transactional.

11.4.9 Market Segmentation and Marketing Research

Segmentation is a fundamental marketing discipline, but for it to be effective, accurate and timely data must be available. Many services organizations are at the forefront of the development of segmentation methods in the United States. Banks, insurance companies, and the passenger transportation sectors, among others, have well-defined approaches to the segmentation of their markets according to customer type. Among the greatest users of segmentation are retailers. As an example, The Limited group covers the fashion clothing market with a range of highly segmented brands such as Limited Stores, Lerner, Express, and Victoria's Secret.

If the segmentation methods used by services organizations are examined more closely, it becomes apparent that demographic variables tend to be the most widely used segmentation bases. In this respect service industries are no different from goods marketers. Age, sex, and socioeconomic analysis, along with geographic location, provide useful information for building up a profile of users of a service. This can be used for targeting purposes in media planning and for assisting in new service development. It can also contribute to pricing policy and service outlet location. Some indication of the importance of demographic bases for segmentation can be seen in the choice of magazines in which American Express advertises, the range of accounts offered by most of the major banks, the pricing practices of airlines, and the location of restaurants.

Demographic segmentation is useful for designing direct mail campaigns that are an important element of the marketing mix of many financial services companies. Demographic analysis is usually employed in conjunction with a geographic database that enables an organization to identify and locate potential customers with the necessary characteristics. The combination of these two types of segmentation variables is often referred to as geodemographics.

All these applications of segmentation methods rely heavily on the availability of accurate and timely market data. Geodemographic methods of segmentation, for example, require details of customer demographics and their geographic location and can involve secondary data acquisition or primary investigations undertaken on behalf of an organization. However, the degree of sophistication with which segmentation is being approached has moved forward immensely with advances in the capabilities of information technology. From the point of view of services organizations who use segmentation, two relatively recent developments should be mentioned:

- Many firms sell a geodemographic segmentation analysis that allows the identification of small geographical pockets of households according to a combination of their demographic characteristics and their buying behavior. These computerized data systems—such as Infomark, from Equifax Marketing Decision Systems, and Atlas Software, from Strategic Mapping, Inc.—are of considerable value in the planning of direct mail campaigns, store location, and merchandising.
- The wealth of data provided by electronic point of sale systems (EPOS) means that retail services may potentially have access to a most powerful research tool. The applications are numerous, but in this instance it is clear that such a database could enable a firm to identify who its customers are, what they buy, and how often, which can facilitate a whole range of marketing planning activities.

Other approaches to segmentation are seen to be more theoretically sound, such as psychographics (based upon personality, attitudes, opinions, and interests) and self-concept (how customers perceive themselves). Such approaches rely on attitude measurement techniques, including Likert scales and semantic differentials, in order to elicit the necessary information from customers. These segmentation bases provide a useful supplementary set of tools for the subdivision of markets in practice, but they have to be used in conjunction with demographic profiles for targeting purposes.

An alternative qualitative approach to identifying clusters of customers is based on the analysis of the components of a particular service offering. This is effectively a benefit-based technique for distinguishing market segments. A quantitative methodology for undertaking such analysis, called cluster analysis, is commonly applied after the qualitative stage of a study. The segments derived from this type of investigation, based on a combination of factors, may then be targeted by a service firm with specific product offers that have been designed in accordance with the requirements of the segments.

11.5 INFORMATION AND CONTROL SYSTEMS

Many services organizations have plans that have failed, not because of poor planning, but because of poor implementation. It is important, therefore, that a marketing information system recognize the key elements of the plan that need to be monitored and provide information that will allow control action to be taken where a variance from plan is observed. These are some of the things that most services organizations will need information on if they are to adequately monitor implementation:

- financial targets: sales turnover/contribution/profit margin, disaggregated by product/business unit
- market analysis: market share performance
- effectiveness of communication: productivity of sales personnel, effectiveness of advertising, effectiveness of sales promotion
- pricing: level of discounts given, price position
- personnel: level of skills achieved by employees, survey of customer comments on staff performance
- quality levels achieved: reliability, complaint level

Where performance is below target, the reasons may not be immediately obvious. A comprehensive marketing information system can allow an organization to analyze variance. A uniform fall in sales performance across the organization, combined with intelligence gained about the state of the market, would suggest that remedial action aimed at improving the sales performance of individual sales personnel may not be as effective as a reassessment of targets or strategies in light of the changed sales environment.

Successful control mechanisms require three underlying components to be in place:

- the setting of targets or standards of expected performance
- the measurement and evaluation of actual performance
- corrective action taken where necessary

CASE STUDY

FIRST NATIONAL BANK OF CHICAGO ADDS BRANCH SERVICES AS RESPONSE TO CHANGING ENVIRONMENT

First National Bank of Chicago rapidly expanded from five to seventy-seven branches during the late 1980s and early 1990s. This rapid growth has brought the bank into many ethnically diverse neighborhoods in Chicago. As a result, the services offered by the bank are tailored to the diverse needs of each neighborhood. For example, at one branch in a primarily Hispanic neighborhood, the manager has turned her bank into primarily a "currency exchange" that cashes paychecks and issues money orders. Another branch arranged to stamp paid utility bills (receipts) with a large official-looking seal because that was what the particular immigrant community expected. At another branch on the North Side of Chicago, the employees at the bank collectively speak forty-six different languages.

In addition, the bank has been creative in finding ways to loan money to first-time entrepreneurs. A typical bank in the United States would not easily accommodate a request for a small start-up loan. High overhead and transaction costs mean that the same effort is needed to make a $100,000 loan as a $10,000 loan. Furthermore, a $1,000 loan, which is what many grass-roots entrepreneurs would like, is simply too small, unprofitable, and risky for a bank to even consider. To accommodate people with new businesses and no track record, the First National Bank will make personal loans, home equity loans or credit card loans instead of business loans, thus bypassing the traditional business approval process. In another effort to reach small-scale female entrepreneurs, the bank uses an intermediary, the Women's Self-

Employment Project, which is the largest nonprofit entrepreneurial services program targeting low- and moderate-income women in Chicago. Statistics compiled by the National Association of Women Business Owners (NAWBO) in Washington, D.C., indicate that the number of women-owned businesses grew 57 percent from 1982 to 1987 and that women now own 30 percent of all businesses. By the year 2000 women are expected to own 50 percent of all businesses. WSEP not only loans money to women just starting out but offers ongoing technical support and advice.

Another trend that First National Chicago may want to follow is supermarket branch banks. Though limited versions of supermarket bank branches have been around since the 1980s, a new concept of a supermarket bank branch has emerged as a way for banks to capture larger market share at lower costs. This new idea involves establishing in a supermarket a full-scale bank branch that offers the same products and services as a traditional branch with a trained sales staff. The bank gains access to a busy and active client base, and the supermarket customers gain convenience. According to a study from National Bank Services, Inc., the supermarket banking affiliate of National Commerce Bancorp, which is based in Memphis, consumers like the idea. The NCBS president, Douglas W. Ferris, said, "Supermarket banking conforms to consumers' busy life styles—not the other way around."

The NBS survey interviewed more than a thousand customers in sixteen states. It revealed that 72 percent of those surveyed did most of their banking at a supermarket branch. More than 62 percent of those surveyed said that supermarket banking is the most important nonfood service they get at the store. These customers aren't just getting cash from the ATM—the survey indicated that 64 percent said they had taken out a loan at an in-store branch, 47 percent said they had opened investment accounts, 40 percent had opened some type of credit accounts, 14 percent had obtained mortgages at supermarket branches, and 16 percent purchased certificates of deposit. When are consumers using the supermarket branches? Not during traditional banking hours, apparently—the most popular time of day is between 3 P.M. and 8 P.M.[9]

CASE STUDY REVIEW QUESTIONS

1. What methods should a bank such as First National Bank of Chicago employ to search for new business opportunities?
2. What research would you undertake before selecting a supermarket site for an in-store branch of the First National Bank at a Chicago area supermarket?
3. What research would you undertake if you were brought into to rescue a Branch that had recently lost several important long term deposit and loan accounts?

11.5.1 Setting Targets

A clear statement of objectives at the start of the planning process provides a vital foundation for comparing targets with actual performance. In general, the greater the level of disaggregation of targets, the greater the degree of possible control. To be effective in a control process, targets should be specific enough to:

- Give individual managers a clear indication of the standards of performance that are expected of them.
- Distinguish between controllable variables that can be managed by an individual

manager and those that are uncontrollable and should therefore be excluded from their standards for performance.

- Allocate targets to the right person. Ultimately, all costs and revenues are somebody's responsibility and should be monitored and controlled at the appropriate point within an organization. Even a relatively fixed and uncontrollable element such as rent can become controllable over the longer term by senior management.
- Show which targets are to take priority. In any event, targets should not be mutually incompatible.
- Be sufficiently flexible to allow for changes in the organization's environment that were not foreseen when the targets were set.

For control purposes, quantitative targets are generally preferred to qualitative targets. Many apparently qualitative targets, such as customer satisfaction and attentiveness of front-line service personnel, can often be reduced to quantifiable indices, for example, by setting targets for the number of complaints received or the percentage of customers booking a repeat service, or by using an analytic technique such as SERVQUAL (see Chapter 6). The danger, however, in setting purely quantified targets is that they may be a series of relatively simple indicators. Staff attempting to achieve these targets may concentrate their attention on meeting them, possibly at the expense of other more important qualitative aspects of their performance. A customer service office with a target of answering calls within a specified time may lose sight of the quality of information given during the call if its attention is primarily focused on responding within the target time. There is also an argument that marketing managers should not be assessed solely on the basis of their ability to meet quantifiable targets. A more realistic appraisal system might also examine the quality of the decisions that a manager made during the previous period, taking account of the fact that the operating environment posed numerous problems and opportunities that may not have been apparent at the time targets were initially set.

11.5.2 Measuring Performance

Information is needed to measure two aspects of performance: efficiency and effectiveness. Efficiency can be defined in terms of an organization's success in turning inputs into outputs, while effectiveness is the level of success in producing a desired result. An efficient business cannot succeed if it is efficient at doing the wrong things—that is, it is ineffective.

When an organization competes in a market on the basis of its cost leadership, efficiency may be a key measure for evaluating management performance. Within the services sector, important efficiency measures can include the number of services performed per employee, the value of sales achieved per sales person, the cost of advertising per thousand valued impressions, and the level of utilization of assets (e.g., load factors on aircraft).

In contrast to planning information, much of the information needed for control is derived from internal sources and can be collected routinely. Examples include the following:

- Service quality undergoes technical measures, for example, failure rates of ATMs, percentage of flights delayed by more than ten minutes, time taken to answer a telephone.
- Sales figures are routinely analyzed and actual values compared with budget under such headings as regional distribution, customer type, and size of purchase. Invoicing is not seen narrowly as an accounting function but as an opportunity to collate marketing success.
- Routine analysis of invoices indicate whether an organization has been able to maintain its price level.
- Expenditure budgets give an up-to-date summary of actual as against target expenditure under such headings as advertising, sales force cost, and intermediaries' expenses.
- Sales personnels' performance records are routinely maintained.

These regular sources of information may need to be supplemented with external sources of data and ad hoc studies, which are likely to include the following:

- Up-to-date information about the size of a market (collected through syndicated research, trade associations, and government agencies) will allow an organization to monitor its market share.
- While technical quality can often be measured continuously by an organization, the measurement of functional quality frequently calls for marketing research to be commissioned. This can include periodic questionnaire surveys of customers, or less frequent and more in-depth diagnostic research sessions. For control purposes, a service organization may set its managers an objective that at least 90 percent of customers questioned in such surveys should state that their service experience is "good" or better.
- Observational research is becoming increasingly popular as a means of controlling the quality of the service delivery process. Trained "mystery shoppers" are now employed by many restaurants, banks, and transportation companies to check that the service format as specified is actually being delivered. Findings from this form of research are often linked to employees' pay.
- Transaction analysis is used by many organizations to track the progress of services provided to clients, both during and after delivery. This can provide valuable information about customer perceptions of service quality, compared with their expectations. It can also be used to internally monitor the attainment of performance targets.
- Analysis of complaints can be used as a positive source of information from customers. If complaints are communicated to management, it is in a better position to prevent future repeats of the factors that gave rise to the complaints than if the aggrieved customers were to remain silent and quietly take their business elsewhere. For this reason, many service organizations try to make it easy for their customers to communicate grievances to them, and they carefully analyze their customers' responses.

- Research is often commissioned to monitor the effectiveness of an organization's advertising, for example, by monitoring awareness levels.

11.5.3 Using Information for Control

A good marketing information system can generate a lot of information. The key to effective control is to give the right information to the right people at the right time. Providing too much information can be costly in terms of the effort required to assemble and disseminate it and can also reduce effective control when the valuable information is hidden among information of secondary importance. Also, the level of reporting will be determined by the level of tolerance allowed for compliance to goals. An analysis of variance from target should indicate whether the variance is within or beyond the control of the person responsible for meeting the target. If it is beyond that person's control, the issue should become one of revising the target so that it becomes once more achievable. If the variance is the result of factors that are subject to an individual's control, several measures can be taken to try to revise behavior:

- Bureaucratic control can be used. Instructions are sent to subordinates, and disciplinary action or retraining is undertaken if no change occurs.
- Incentive schemes can be used as a control mechanism: Incentives—performance bonuses and sales commission, for example—are often linked directly to performance.
- The allocation of resources (including personnel) offers an important form of organizational control. It has the effect of facilitating some actions and inhibiting others.
- Informal controls can be exercised at different levels. Self-control is essentially based on a system of incentives, which may be financial or psychological (e.g., passing on customer comments about serving staffs' performance). Social control is applied within small groups where violation of a group norm causes other group members to put subtle pressure on the deviating member to perform to standard. Cultural control results from a process of internalizing the cultural norms within each individual so that he or she can be expected to behave in accordance with the norms.

CHAPTER REVIEW QUESTIONS

1. Are there any major distinctions between the processes and practices of marketing research in services and goods markets?
2. To what extent do you agree that the intangibility of services creates a researchability problem?
3. How important is it to have a structured approach to marketing research?
4. Identify the most likely marketing research objectives for a hotel chain.
5. Are any particular difficulties involved in the practice of segmentation policies in the service industries?
6. Explain why a thorough understanding of buyer behavior processes may be important for a cinema chain attempting to enhance its service offer.

REFERENCES

1. Neuborne, E., "Customer Service? What Customer Service?" *USA Today* (Tuesday, May 10, 1994, Section B): 1.

2. Kohli, A. K., and Jaworski, B. J., "Market Orientation: The Construct, Research Propositions and Management Implications," *Journal of Marketing* 54 (April 1990): 1–18; and Porter, M., and Millar, V., "How Information Gives You Competitive Advantage," *Harvard Business Review* 85 (July/August): 149–60.

3. Piercy, N., "Marketing Organisation: An Analysis of Information Processing, Power and Politics," (London: Allen and Unwin, 1985).

4. Moorman, C., Zaltman, G., and Deshpande, R., "Relationships Between Providers and Users of Market Research: The Dynamics of Trust Within and Between Organizations," *Journal of Marketing Research* 29 (August 1992): 314–28.

5. Kotler, P., *Marketing Management: Analysis, Planning, Implementation and Control* (Englewood Cliffs, N.J.: Prentice Hall, 1994): 96.

6. McDonald, M. H. B., *Marketing Plans: How to Prepare Them, How to Use Them* (London: Heinemann, 1984): 14.

7. Lovelock, C. H., *Services Marketing* (Englewood Cliffs, N.J.: Prentice Hall, 1991).

8. Galarza, P., "Providing A Slice of U.S. Life to Test Products," *Investor's Business Daily* (Wednesday, May 11, 1994): A6.

9. Morrall, K., "Banks Lend Support to Women Business Owners," *Bank Marketing* 25, no. 8 (1993): 22–7; Morral, K. "New Frontiers in Supermarket Banking," *Bank Marketing* 25, no. 12 (1993) 9–13. Unsigned, "Banks Rig Up Customers in Supermarket Branches," *Bank Management* 69, no. 2 (1993): 20–2; Welles, E., "Access to Capital: Priming the Pump," *Inc.*16, no. 5 (1994): 92–4.

SUGGESTED FURTHER READING

ANDREASAN, A. A. 1983. "Cost-Conscious Marketing Research." *Harvard Business Review* (July/August): 74–81.

ANTHONY, R. N. 1988. *Planning and Control Systems: A Framework for Analysis.* Cambridge, Mass.: Harvard University Press.

BERRY, L. L., CONANT, J. S., PARASURAMAN, A. 1991. "A Framework for Conducting a Services Marketing Audit." *Journal of the Academy of Marketing Science* (Summer): 255–68.

BOYD, H. W., WESTFALL, R., and STASCH, S. F. 1988. *Marketing Research: Texts and Cases.* Homewood, Ill.: Irwin.

CRIMP, M. 1990. *The Marketing Research Process.* Englewood Cliffs, N.J.: Prentice Hall.

DESHPANDE, R., and ZALTMAN, G. 1984. "A Comparison of Factors Affecting Researcher and Manager Perceptions of Market Research Use." *Journal of Marketing Research* 21 (February): 32–8.

DICKSON, P. R., and GINTER, J. L. 1987. "Market Segmentation, Product Differentiation and Marketing Strategy." *Journal of Marketing* (April): 1–10.

ENGEL, J. F., BLACKWELL, R. D., and MINIARD, P. W. 1990. *Consumer Behavior,* 6th ed. Chicago, Ill.: Dryden.

GARLAND, B. C., and WESTBROOK, R. A. 1989. "An Exploration of Client Satisfaction in a Nonprofit Context." *Journal of the Academy of Marketing Science* (Fall): 297–304.

KINNEAR, T., and TAYLOR, J. 1991. *Marketing Research: An Applied Approach.* New York: McGraw-Hill.

MOORMAN, C., ZALTMAN, G., and DESHPANDE, R. 1992. "Relationships Between Providers and Users of Market Research: The Dynamics of Trust Within and Between Organizations." *Journal of Marketing Research* 29 (August): 314–28.

PARASURAMAN, A. 1991. *Marketing Research.* Reading, Mass.: Addison-Wesley.

PETERSON, R. A. 1982. *Marketing Research.* Plano, Tex.: Business Publications.

PORTER, M., and MILLAR, V. 1985. "How Information Gives You Competitive Advantage." *Harvard Business Review* 85 (July/August): 149–60.

12

Making It Happen: Managing Services Marketing

CHAPTER OBJECTIVES

After reading this chapter, you should be able to understand

- the role of strategic marketing planning in services organizations
- the importance of defining the company mission statement and specifying objectives
- the strategic alternatives open to an organization
- positioning of the service offer
- methods of managing the marketing effort

12.1 STRATEGIC MARKETING PLANNING

Marketing planning is an essential function for services organizations. The idea that they should need to plan strategically over the medium to long term was often not recognized in the comparatively stable markets that many service industries faced before the 1970s. Banks, for example, faced a stable marketing environment and could survive and prosper on the basis of short-term operational planning. During the 1980s, the effects of deregulation of financial markets and the quickening pace of technological change forced banks to pay much more attention to the direction in which they were moving. Faced with competition on many fronts, banks had to choose which fronts they would attack and which would be allowed to fade away.

The importance of strategic marketing planning varies between organizations.

In general, as the size of an organization increases, so too does the scale of risks. Strategic planning can be seen as an attempt to manage the level of risk facing an organization. On the other hand, many smaller service businesses often develop strategic marketing plans unconsciously, without any explicit statement of direction or formally written plan. They may specify a tactical program for the forthcoming year but leave longer-term strategy unstated. Even within small service businesses that appear to manage successfully by "muddling through" without a formal strategic planning process, the introduction of a plan can focus an entrepreneur's attention on long-term rather than short-term aims. Entrepreneurism and strategic planning need not be mutually exclusive processes. An alternative to the accepted principles of disciplined strategic planning is the concept of freewheeling opportunism, whereby opportunities are exploited as they arise and judged on their individual merits within a loosely defined overall strategy.

Giving strategic direction to an organization is not simply a case of analyzing the needs of consumers and gearing resources to earn good short-term profits from meeting these needs. In commercial services organizations, maintaining a balanced portfolio of activities can be just as important as earning adequate short-term profits. In this respect, a bank may both earn an acceptable return and meet a proven need by lending money to fund property purchases. However, a strategic approach to portfolio management may lead the bank to diversify into some other activity with a counterbalancing level of cash flow and risk, and to turn away business that may seem attractive in the short term.

Strategic planning within a service organization can be conceptualized as having two dimensions: horizontal and vertical.

- In the *horizontal* dimension, a corporate strategic plan brings together the plans of the specialized functions necessary to make the organization work. Marketing is just one function of an organization and generates its own planning process. Other functional plans found in most organizations are financial plans, personnel plans, and production plans. The components of these functional plans must recognize interdependencies if they are to be effective. For example, a bank's marketing strategic plan that anticipates a 50 percent growth in sales of mortgages over a five-year planning period should be reflected in a strategic production plan that allows for the necessary processing capacity to be developed and a financial plan that identifies strategies for raising the required level of finance over the same time period.

- In the *vertical* dimension, the corporate planning process provides the framework for strategic decisions to be made at different levels of the corporate hierarchy. Objectives can be specified in progressively more detail, from the global objectives of the corporate plan to the greater detail required to operationalize objectives at the level of individual operational units (or strategic business units) and at the individual service line level.

The precise nature of the corporate planning process varies between organizations. Some put a lot of detail into a corporate plan, which the managers of each strategic business unit are expected to follow closely. Others may view the corporate plan as no more than a general statement of aims that strategic business unit managers are to achieve in a manner they consider most appropriate. Compare, for example, two major American retailers: J. C. Penney and The Limited. The former takes a much more centralized attitude toward corporate planning than the latter, which leaves much more detail to individual unit managers. Similarly, the distinction between corporate planning and marketing planning can be very imprecise. Essentially, it doesn't matter who undertakes marketing planning as long as it gets done.

12.2 STRATEGIC, TACTICAL, AND CONTINGENCY PLANNING

Three levels of marketing planning can be identified. The strategic element of a marketing plan focuses on the overriding direction that an organization's efforts will take in order to meet its objectives. The tactical element is more concerned with plans for implementing the detail of the strategic plan. The difference between the strategic and tactical elements of a marketing plan can sometimes be difficult to define. Typically, a strategic marketing plan is concerned with mapping out direction over a five-year planning period, whereas a tactical marketing plan is concerned with implementation during the next twelve months. Naturally, many service industries view their strategic planning periods somewhat differently. The marketing of large-scale infrastructure projects, such as airports or underground rapid transit systems, requires a much longer strategic planning period to allow for the time delays in developing new capacity and the fact that when capacity does become available, it will have a very long life with few alternative uses. The time taken to build a new airport terminal from the proposal stage to full opening is typically five to ten years. Not only does the technology of airports require a long strategic planning period, the nature of the competitive environment allows an airport operator to take the long view, with little likelihood of unexpected direct competitors coming on to the scene during the plan period. On the other hand, some service industries operate with much shorter strategic planning periods, when new productive capacity can be produced quickly and where the environment is turbulent. An office cleaning contractor using largely casual labor and simple technology will need to respond rapidly to changes in its environment, such as the loss of government contracts or the emergence of lower-cost competition. The organization's strategic marketing plan will probably give only a very general statement of direction beyond a two- or three-year planning period.

A third element of the marketing plan involves the development of contingency plans. These attempt to identify scenarios in which the assumptions of the position analysis on which strategic decisions were based turn out to be false. For example, the planning of a new airport might have assumed that fuel prices would rise by no more than 10 percent annually during the planning period. A contingency plan would be useful to provide an alternative strategic route if, halfway during the plan period, fuel prices suddenly doubled. Such a dramatic increase in fuel prices, if the increase persisted, could cause a fall in the total market for air travel. A contingency plan would identify alternative ways for the airport to respond to such events. For example, management could increase promotional expenditure to preserve the airport's share of a diminishing market. Alternatively, management could identify alternative sources of revenue—such as the development of industrial estates and business centers on airport land—that were not directly related to the level of demand for air travel.

12.3 GIVING DIRECTION TO THE MARKETING EFFORT

Any service organization can drift aimlessly if its managers and employees have no clear idea about where they should be going. At the most general level, all people within an organization should share a sense of purpose about the values of the business and what the business should achieve. This is the role of an organization's mission statement. To give individuals more specific guidance about what they should be achieving, objectives—quantified wherever possible—need to be set.

12.3.1 Defining the Corporate Mission

A corporate mission statement is a means of reminding everybody within an organization of the organization's essential purpose. Peter Drucker has identified several basic questions that management should ask when it perceives itself drifting along with no clear purpose, and which form the basis of a corporate mission statement:[1]

- What is our business?
- Who is the customer?
- What is value to the customer?
- What will our business be?
- What should our business be?

By forcing management to focus on the essential nature of the business they are in and the nature of the customer needs they attempt to satisfy, the problem of "marketing myopia" advanced by Levitt[2] can be avoided. Levitt argued that in order to avoid a narrow, shortsighted view of its business, managers should define their business in terms of the needs that they fulfill rather than the products they produce. In the classic example, railroad operators had lost their way because they defined their service output in terms of the technology of tracked vehicles, rather than in terms of the core benefit of movement that they provided. Accountants learned the lesson of this myopic example during the 1970s by redefining their central purpose away from a narrow preoccupation with providing accounting services to a much broader mission statement, which spoke about providing business solutions.

For a mission statement to be useful, it must be a relevant and up-to-date statement of core corporate values, which allows geographically dispersed personnel within an organization to share a sense of opportunity, direction, significance, and achievement. The mission statement has been likened to an invisible hand, which guides employees to work independently yet collectively toward achieving the organization's goal. Within the marketing planning process, a clear mission statement helps to identify the nature of the market opportunities that the company should be investigating in more detail, while filtering out search activity and proposals that do not fall within its defined mission.

In the services sector, where the interface between consumers and production personnel is often critical, communication of the values contained within the mission statement becomes very important. The statement is frequently repeated by organizations in staff newsletters and in notices at their place of work. Some examples of mission statements are shown in Figure 12.1.

Ameritech: Ameritech will be the world's premier provider of full-service communications for people at work, at home or on the move. Our goal will be to improve the quality of life for individuals and to increase the competitive effectiveness of the business we serve. As we move and manage information for our customers, we will set standards for value and quality. Ameritech's competence will reach worldwide, building on our strength in America's vibrant upper Midwest. Customers can be assured that we will assume no task we cannot do exceedingly well. (Ameritech's Vision Statement is from the American Information Technologies 1993 Annual Report)

Hurricane Island Outward Bound: The mission of Hurricane Island Outward Bound is providing safe, challenging, educational experiences in a wilderness setting, carefully structured to improve self-esteem, self-reliance, concern for others, and care for the environment (Hurricane Island Outward Bound written Mission Statement)

The Limited, Inc.: Our commitment is to offer the absolute best customer shopping experience anywhere—the best store—the best merchandise—the best merchandise presentation—the best customer service—the best of everything that a customer sees and experiences. To achieve this goal:

- We must maintain a restless, bold and daring business spirit noted for innovation and cutting-edge style;

- We must maintain a management culture which is action oriented, always flexible and never bureaucratic;

- We must be tough-minded, disciplined, demanding, self-critical and yet supportive of each other, our team, and our suppliers;

- We must seek and retain Associates with an unquestioned reputation for integrity and respect for all people: customers, suppliers, shareholders and fellow Associates;

- We must continue to make risk acceptable by rewarding the risk-taker who succeeds—that goes without saying—and not penalizing the one who fails;

- And we must utilize our capacity to set qualitative and quantitative standards for our industry.

We are determined to surpass all standards for excellence in retailing by thinking—and thinking small. By staying close to our customer and remaining agile we will continue as a major force in retailing.

Figure 12.1   Example mission statements—Ameritech, Hurricane Island Outward Bound, and The Limited, Inc.

An organization's mission statement reflects several factors:

- The organization's ownership, especially between the private and not-for-profit sectors.
- The previous history of the organization, in particular any distinct competencies that it has acquired or images that it has created in the eyes of potential customers.
- Environmental factors, in particular the major opportunities and threats that are likely to face the organization in the foreseeable future.
- Resources available—without resources available for their accomplishment, a mission statement has little meaning.

Missions define in general terms the direction in which an organization desires to move. They contain no quantifiable information that allows them to be operationalized. For this to happen, objectives need to be set.

12.3.2 Setting Objectives

Having carried out a situation analysis and defined the corporate mission, management can begin the vital task of setting objectives. Objectives have these functions within an organization:

- They add to the sense of purpose within an organization, without which there would be little focus for managers' efforts.
- They help to achieve consistency between decisions made at different points within the organization. For example, it would be inconsistent for a production manager to use a production objective unrelated to the marketing manager's sales objective.
- They are used as motivational devices and can be used in a variety of formal and informal ways to stimulate increased performance by managers.
- They allow for more effective control within an organization. Unless clear objectives have been set at the outset, it is very difficult to know whether the organization has achieved what it set out to achieve and to take any corrective action if its efforts seem to be going adrift during the planning period.

To have most value to marketing management, objectives should possess these important characteristics:

- Objectives should be quantified. In most private sector organizations, the most important objectives can usually be expressed in terms of profitability, sales, or market share. In some public and not-for-profit organizations, these terms may have little meaning, but objectives should nevertheless be quantifiable. For example public libraries may set objectives in terms of the number of books borrowed, or museums the number of people visiting their exhibits. Even an apparently subjective item such as service quality can be quantified by use of a technique such as SERVQUAL.

- Objectives must specify the time period to which they relate. In the case of a new service launch, an objective may be to recover 80 percent of costs during the first year of operation, breaking even by Year 2 and achieving a 25 percent return on capital invested by Year 3.

- To be effective, objectives must be capable of realistic achievement and accepted as such by the people responsible for acting on them. If objectives are set unattainably high, the whole process of planning could be discredited. When objectives are given to a service manager, they should reflect factors over which the manager has some degree of control. As an example, a product manager for mortgages should have some control over the volume of funds available for lending. Restricted resources may otherwise make it impossible for a manager to achieve a specified sales target.

- There must be consistency between objectives. Inconsistency may occur, for example, when a sales objectives can be achieved only by reducing selling prices, thereby making it impossible to achieve a profitability objective. Furthermore, objectives must be ranked in order of priority. Managers of a restaurant chain presented with a list of five key objectives, such as contribution to fixed costs, total sales revenue, number of visits by customers, average spent per visit, and average customer waiting time, may struggle with apparently conflicting objectives. This can be resolved by ranking them in order of importance.

Organizations set a variety of objectives that are acted upon by their staff and that can be classified into several categories:

- Profit objectives feature prominently in the hierarchy of objectives and are communicated vertically through the planning hierarchy, since the ultimate goal of most private companies is to produce an acceptable level of profits for its stockholders.

- Growth objectives may be important to organizations operating in rapidly expanding market sectors where a slow rate of growth effectively means that the organization is falling behind its competitors. In some industries, growth may be an essential objective in order to achieve a critical mass at which significant economies of scale occur.

- Technical objectives are set by organizations when technology is an important element in gaining competitive advantage over competitors.

- Quality-of-service objectives are frequently set for line managers. For example, one of many objectives set for branch bank managers relates to the length of waiting time for customers at their branch. Quality-of-service objectives often assume overriding importance for the not-for-profit sector where financial objectives act more as constraints.

- Sales and market share objectives are set by most private firms. At the corporate level, it can be argued that these represent strategies rather than objectives. For an airline, a specified profit objective could be achieved either by a low-volume, high-price strategy or by a strategy that seeks a greater market share but at the expense of lower prices. However, once the strategy is determined at the corporate level, it is subsequently translated into specific sales objectives for line managers.

12.4 STRATEGY FORMULATION

Having analyzed its business environment and formed a view of the future, an organization must then identify the strategic alternatives that will allow it to achieve its objectives. From these alternatives, a strategy will be selected and implemented.

Competitors within any one industry may each pursue very different strategies, but all may be capable of achievement, given that each organization may be pursuing quite different objectives and may possess differing strengths and weaknesses. Analysts have developed numerous methodologies for classifying the diversity of marketing strategies. While there is no definitive basis for categorizing the strategic alternatives open to an organization, three focal points for strategy development will be considered here:

- strategies that focus on gaining competitive advantage
- strategies that focus on growth options
- strategies that focus on the development of portfolios

It should be noted that this classification device does not represent a strategy typology but just a useful means of describing the literature. In practice, strategy development will bear some relation to each of these three focal points.

12.4.1 Strategies for Competitive Advantage

Firms must be aware of who their competitors are and of their relative strengths and weaknesses. In all competitive markets, the strategic decisions made by one organization are frequently a response to actions—or possible future actions—of competing organizations. One method of identifying and selecting strategies is to identify the activities in which an organization has a competitive advantage over its competitors. Michael Porter has reduced competitive advantage based strategies to three generic types:[3]

Overall cost leadership.   Here, the organization puts a lot of effort into lowering its production and distribution costs so that it can win competitive advantage by charging lower prices. Organizations pursuing this strategy need to be efficient at production.

Cost leadership can result from being able to achieve economies of scale. In services that use high technology, or that require highly trained labor skills, a learning curve effect (also called a cost experience curve) may be apparent. By operating at a larger scale than its competitors, a firm can benefit more from the learning curve and thereby achieve lower unit costs. While this may be true of some service industries (such as telecommunications), others—plumbing and hairdressing, for example—face only a very low critical output at which significant economies of scale occur. Organizations in the latter category may find cost leadership to be a difficult strategy, as many rival firms will also be able to achieve maximum cost efficiency. A cost leadership strategy is more likely to be effective when a high level of output relative to market size is necessary in order to achieve economies of scale. For example, nationwide chains of discount stores require a high minimum level of investment in efficient distribution systems and a high level of turnover to achieve economies of scale in buying. These can prevent small local operators from competing on the basis of lower overhead costs, leaving the major competitors to cut costs and hence offer a lower price for a basically similar service.

Differentiation.   Organizations attempt to achieve superior performance for their service, adding value to their offer that is reflected in a higher price customers are prepared to pay. One way in which firms try to gain advantage over their competitors is to offer greater quality relative to price. Added value can also be provided by offering completely new services that are not yet available from competitors, by modifying existing services, or by making them more easily available. In this way, a bank could seek superior performance in areas such as the greatest number of branches, the highest rates of interest, the greatest number of ATMs, or the most convenient home banking service. An organization can realistically aim to be leader in one of these areas but not in all at the same time. It therefore develops the strengths that will give it a differential performance advantage in one of these benefit areas. A bank with the most comprehensive branch network may build upon it by ensuring that the branches are open at times when customers wish to visit them, that there is no excessive waiting time, and that the branches present a bright and inviting image to customers.

A problem of a differentiation strategy for services is that services can easily be copied, and a company seeking to differentiate by innovation may soon find its new service copied by competitors. Patents cannot protect new services in the way that they can protect new manufactured goods.

Focus.   An organization may focus on one or more small market segments rather than aiming for the whole market. The organization becomes familiar with the needs of these segments and gains competitive advantage by cost leadership, differentiation within its chosen segment, or both.

A cost focus strategy requires an organization to segment its market and to specialize in products for that market. By concentrating on a narrow geographical segment, or by producing specialized services for a very small segment, the organization can gain economies of scale in production. In this way a bus tour operator could focus on physically challenged travelers living in the northeast states. By building up volume of specialized vacations, it may achieve operating economies, e.g., the ability to spread the capital cost of specialized vehicles over a large number of customers. By focusing on the northeast market, it can reduce the costs that may result from attempting to arrange transportation from geographically remote market segments.

A quality differentiation strategy entails selecting a market segment and competing on the basis of the differential quality offering of a service aimed at that segment (Figure 12.2).

A focus strategy may be appropriate for a company that is trying to enter a market for the first time. Mortgage lenders seeking to enter a new national market may focus on small segments by providing specialized products such as foreign currency mortgages or special mortgages for second homes.

Despite the advantages of a focus strategy, there are also dangers. The segments that form the focus may be too small to be economical in themselves.

Figure 12.2   This movie advertisement seeks competitive advantage by differentiating itself from other movies with the all-new songs from Stevie Wonder. Source: Printed with permission from New York Festivals, Chappaqua, NY and Universal Studios, Universal City, CA.

Moreover, an overreliance on narrow segments could leave an organization dangerously exposed if these segments go into decline. Banks that had focused on agricultural markets faced great difficulty during the early 1980s when farming communities in the United States went through a period of depression.

For firms pursuing a similar strategy aimed at similar market segments, Porter contends that the one which pursues that strategy most effectively will be best at meeting its objectives. Of all the car rental companies pursuing a cost leadership strategy, the one that actually achieves the lowest level of costs will be the most successful. Firms that do not pursue a clear strategy are the least effective. Although they try to succeed in all three strategic alternatives, they end up showing no cost leadership, no differential advantage, and no clear focus on one customer group.

It should also be recognized that the ease with which services can be copied can make for very unstable competition in a market. If a market appears attractive to one organization, then it probably appears equally attractive to others, who may possess equal competitive advantage in addressing the market. If all such firms decide to enter the market, oversupply results, profit margins become squeezed, and the market becomes relatively unattractive. An example is the movie rental market, which in the mid-1980s looked highly attractive, given the rapid growth in ownership of videocassette recorders and good margins earned by those operators in the market. This was the signal for many companies to enter the market, with some chains such as Blockbuster being built up very rapidly. The result was that by 1990, the market—whose growth rate had slowed down—had become relatively unattractive, with poor returns and many business failures.

CASE STUDY

STRATEGY SEEMS TO MAKE WAL-MART UNSTOPPABLE

Retailing during the 1980s changed dramatically. Nowhere has this been more true than in the discount store business, a sector that has grown rapidly with increasing value consciousness by consumers. The expansion in this sector has already left some non–discount department store chains badly hurt. For example, Sears lost many of its customers to discounters and was forced to copy some of their tactics. Even among the discounters themselves, a war of attrition has been raging. Of the top ten discounters in 1962, none even existed thirty years later. In the struggle to succeed, the weaker chains inevitably died, often forced out of business by huge takeover debts, recession, and demographic and social change. And as the mid-1990s approached, it looked as though there would be a fight to the death among three of the biggest contenders.

The largest of the three contenders—measured in number of stores—is Kmart, with a 1992 total of 2,200 stores. Ahead of Kmart in sales turnover is Wal-Mart, with 1,590 stores. The third contender is Target, a division of Dayton Hudson, with a chain of 420 stores. In 1990, the three chains between them had 70 percent of the nationwide discount store business. At that time, Wal-Mart directly competed in only about 35% of Kmart's markets. With new store openings, the two chains will be directly competing in more than 75 percent of their markets by 1995. All three will overlap in 40 percent of each other's markets. Wal-Mart opened 165 new stores in 1991, with a strong emphasis on California, which was already a stronghold of Kmart and Target. Further growth will see its network spread from its southern base to the northeast and far west. Target, on the other hand, is setting its sights on Florida as it expands from its strongholds in California and the Midwest.

What is so remarkable is that the three retailers have adopted broadly similar business formats and are trying to pursue similar strategies. All have focused on quite similar product areas. Kmart has focused its efforts on a dozen departments that it considers essential to family life, including clothing, home fashion, home office, fix-it, outdoor, toys, entertainment, and pharmacy. Target aims a range of fashion clothing to the more discerning department store customers who may be looking for better quality, higher-priced apparel while matching other discounters on everyday household items. Wal-Mart has developed a product range broadly similar to that of Kmart. Analysts have speculated that the discount market is large enough for only two of the big three discounters. With similar strategies, success will come to the chain that is best able to execute its strategy.

One of Kmart's big advantages is that it grew before Wal-Mart, allowing it to get hold of the best retail sites in many towns. Research commissioned by the company had indicated that location topped the list of factors influencing customers' choice of discount store, ahead of other factors such as price, product range, and quality. In a decade when convenience will be at a premium, Kmart's store locations could be an extremely valuable asset. However, Kmart is handicapped by the relatively small size of many of its older stores. Too many are 40,000 square feet or less, when 70,000 square feet is considered the minimum to be able to carry the range that customers expect.

All three chains use the offer of low prices to attract customers. The chain that is best able to achieve sustainable low prices will be the one that is most effective in cutting its operating cost levels. All three have invested heavily in checkout scanning systems that give real-time sales data, which are relayed instantaneously to computerized inventory systems. However, the acknowledged industry leader in information distribution is Wal-Mart, whose satellite communication network and computer power allow it instantaneous access to sales information. Wal-Mart has also led in its attempts to cut suppliers' costs. It was the first to insist that suppliers accept orders from computer to computer, and it has dealt with suppliers as partners rather than as adversaries. In this way, both get to share information and new product development, to the advantage of Wal-Mart.

All three have a strategy of achieving customer satisfaction through the performance of its employees, and all have invested heavily in staff training and incentive programs. Again, Wal-Mart seems to be implementing this aspect of strategy more effectively than its rivals. Its training of salespeople (or "associates") and profit-sharing bonuses have inspired legendary loyalty from an otherwise poorly paid workforce.

Overall, Wal-Mart seems to be meeting customers' needs better than its rivals. In a study undertaken by analysts Burnstein & Co., discount shoppers in cities where all three stores operated claimed to be most satisfied with Wal-Mart. They were least satisfied with Kmart.

Wal-Mart's successful pursuit of its strategy on many fronts has resulted in a productivity loop. With higher sales volumes, it can afford to pay for extra bag packers and greeters, which in turn generates more business, making the whole operation achieve even greater economies of scale in buying and distribution, leading to lower prices and still higher sales volume.

The final proof that Wal-Mart had pursued its strategy more effectively than its competitors came on its bottom line. For the year ended January 1991, it earned $2 billion in pre-tax profits, compared to just $1 billion earned by Kmart on just about the same level of sales. As for the future, both Wal-Mart and Kmart have attempted to widen their battlefield beyond the traditional discount stores. Both have been involved in deep discount membership clubs—Wal-Mart with Sam's Club and Kmart with Pace. Both have experimented with having their very large stores sell groceries in addition to the existing lines. Critics have wondered whether Wal-Mart's seemingly unstoppable progress will be slowed down if it enters the very different and competitive grocery sector already inhabited by efficient operators such as Kroger and Safeway.

CASE STUDY REVIEW QUESTIONS

1. Identify strategies by which Kmart and Target could achieve profitable growth. What risks are associated with these strategies? How can these risks be minimized?
2. In what ways could the contenders use positioning strategy to increase their profits?
3. Assume that you have been hired to advise the owners of downtown businesses in a small farming community in Kansas. Wal-Mart is planning to locate on the highway running through town. How could the small downtown business owners compete against Wal-Mart?

12.4.2 Growth Strategies

Most private sector service companies pursue growth in one form or another, whether this is an explicit aim of the organization or an implicit aim of its managers. The thrust for growth can be channelled into one of many directions, and it is therefore useful to develop frameworks for analyzing the growth strategies open to organizations.

Growth can be channelled into new product areas, new markets, or a combination of both. This conceptualization forms the basis of Ansoff's Product/Market Expansion Grid.[4] Products and markets are each analyzed in terms of their degree of novelty to an organization, and growth strategies are identified in terms of these two dimensions. In this way, four possible growth strategies can be identified. An illustration of the framework, with reference to the specific options open to a coastal resort hotel, is shown in Figure 12.3.

The four growth options are associated with differing sets of problems and opportunities for organizations. These relate to the level of resources required to

PRODUCTS

	Existing	New
Existing	Market Penetration Strategy Achieve higher market share among present segment of leisure users	Product Development Strategy Develop health club aimed at present clientele
New	Market Development Strategy Target business customers	Diversification Develop a fast-food restaurant in a nearby town

MARKETS

Figure 12.3   An application of Ansoff's Product Market Expansion Grid to a coastal resort hotel operator

implement a particular strategy, and the level of risk associated with each. It follows, therefore, that what might be a feasible growth strategy for one organization may not be for another. The characteristics of the four strategies are described here.

Market penetration strategies.   This type of strategy focuses growth on the existing product range by encouraging higher levels of service usage among the existing target markets. In this way a specialist tour operator in a growing sector of the vacation market could—all other things being equal—grow naturally, simply by maintaining its current marketing strategy. If it wanted to accelerate this growth, it could do this first by trying to sell more vacations to its existing customers and second by attracting customers from its direct competitors. If the market were in fact in decline, the company could grow only by attracting customers from its competitors through more aggressive marketing policies and/or cost reduction programs. This strategy offers the least level of risk to an organization—the organization is familiar with both its products and its customers.

Market development strategies.   This type of strategy builds on the existing product ranges that an organization has established but seeks new groups of customers for them. In this way a specialist regional ski tour operator that had saturated its current market might seek additional sales in new geographical regions or aim its marketing effort at attracting customers from groups beyond its current age and income groups. While the organization may be familiar with the operational aspects of the service that it provides, it faces risks resulting from possibly poor knowledge of different buyer behavior patterns in the markets that it wants to enter. As an example of the potential problems associated with this strategy, many retailers in the United States have offered their shop formats in overseas markets, only to find that those features which attracted customers at home failed to do so overseas.

Product development strategy.   As an alternative to selling existing products into new markets, an organization may choose to develop new products for its existing markets. A ski tour operator may have built up a good understanding of the vacation needs of a particular market segment—perhaps the 18- to 35-year-old affluent upwardly mobile segment—and offers a wider range of services to them than simply skiing vacations. It might offer additional summer activity vacations. While the company minimizes the risk associated with the uncertainty of new markets, it faces risk resulting from lack of knowledge about its new product area. A common feature of this growth strategy is collaboration with a product specialist, who helps the organization produce the service, leaving it free to market it effectively to its customers. A department store wishing to add a coffee shop to its service offering may not have the skills and resources within its organization to run such a facility but may subcontract an outside catering specialist, leaving it free to determine overall policy. Sometimes growth into new service areas can be most effectively brought about by means of a joint venture. For example, many local telephone companies have set up joint ventures with entertainment companies to provide cable television where regulations allow this to be provided over telephone cables (an example is the agreement announced in 1993 between Pacific Bell and Time-Warner).

Diversification strategy.   In this strategy, an organization expands by developing new products for new markets. Diversification can take several forms. The organization could stay within the same general product/market area but diversify into a new point of the distribution chain. For example, an airline that sets up its own travel agency moves into a type of service provision that is new to it and also deals directly with a segment of the market with which it had had few previous sales transactions. Alternatively, the airline might diversify into completely unrelated service areas aimed at completely different groups of customers—by purchasing a golf course or car dealership, for example. Because the company is moving into both unknown markets and unknown product areas, this form of growth carries the greatest level of risk from a marketing management perspective. Diversification may, however, help to manage the long-term risk of the organization by reducing dependency on a narrow product/market area.

In practice, most growth is a combination of product development and market development (Figure 12.4). In very competitive markets, the service supplier would probably have to slightly adapt its product if it is to become attractive to a new market segment. For the resort hotel looking for new business customers, it may not be

Figure 12.4   The ski resort of Vail, Colorado, is practicing both product and market development by promoting itself as a summer vacation destination. Source: Vail Valley Marketing Board and Reece and Company.

enough to simply promote existing facilities. In order to meet business peoples' needs, it might have to refurbish facilities and offer new services that they desire, e.g., putting in phone lines that handle FAX transmissions.

An organization can grow by two basic means: organic growth and acquisition, although many organizations grow by a combination of the two processes. The manner of growth has important marketing implications, for instance in the speed with which an organization is allowed to expand into new market opportunities. The basis of the two types of growth is analyzed here.

Organic growth.   Organic growth is considered to be the more "natural" pattern of growth for an organization. The initial investment by the organization results in profits, an established customer base, and a well-established technical, personnel, and financial structure. This provides a foundation for future growth. In this sense, success, breeds success because the rate of the organization's growth is influenced by the extent to which it has succeeded in building up internally the means for future expansion.

In terms of marketing, an organization may grow organically by tackling one segment at a time, using the resources, knowledge, and market awareness it has gained in order to tackle further segments. A firm may grow organically into new segments in various ways. Many retail chains have grown organically by developing one region before moving on to another. The Wal-Mart chain, for example, has expanded region by region from its southern base. Other organizations have grown organically by aiming a basically similar product at new segments of the market in the way that the retailer The Limited has developed new shop formats aimed at new segments of the market.

There is evidence that service firms may find organic growth difficult when new market opportunities suddenly arise. Within the financial services sector, one study found that many of the assets of companies, such as specialized staff and distribution networks, were quite specific to their existing markets and couldn't easily be adapted to exploit new markets. Growth by acquisition was in many cases considered to be a better method of expansion.[5]

Growth by acquisition.   The rate of organic growth is constrained by—among other things—the rate at which a firm's market is itself growing. An organization attempting to grow organically in a slowly developing sector such as household insurance will find organic growth more difficult than an organization serving a rapidly growing sector such as computer maintenance. Also, companies with relatively high capital requirements will find organic growth relatively slow.

In such cases, growth by acquisition may appear attractive. In some cases it may be almost essential in order to achieve the critical mass that is necessary for survival. The grocery retail sector in the United States is one in which chains have needed to achieve a critical mass in order to pass on lower prices resulting from economies in buying, distribution, and promotion. Small chains have not been able to grow organically fast enough to achieve this size, resulting in their takeover or merger to form larger chains.

Growth by acquisition may occur when an organization sees its existing market sector contracting and tries to diversify into other areas. The time and risk associated with starting a new venture in an alien market sector may be considered too great, and acquiring an established business could be less risky, allowing access to an established client base and technical skills.

A major problem for firms seeking to grow by acquisition within the service sector lies in the high price often paid for very intangible assets, especially the skills and knowledge of the acquired firm's employees. Unlike physical assets, key personnel may disappear following the acquisition, reducing the earning ability of the business. Worse still, key staff could defect to the acquiring company's competitors, taking with them their lists of client contacts.

12.4.3 Portfolio Planning

Services organizations operating in a market environment face increasingly turbulent patterns of demand. For a company to put all of its efforts into supplying a very limited range of services to a narrow market segment is potentially dangerous. Overreliance on this one segment can make the survival of the organization dependent on the fortunes of this one segment and the segment's liking for the company's product. In any event, the fact that most markets change to some extent over time implies that its products will eventually move out of line with customers' requirements. For these reasons, organizations try to manage their growth in a manner that maintains a portfolio of activities.

Risk spreading is an important element of portfolio management which goes beyond marketing planning. Some service providers deliberately provide a range of services that—quite apart from their potential for cross selling—act in contrasting manners during the business cycle. For this reason, accountancy firms have become potentially more stable units as they have amalgamated, by allowing pro-cyclical activities such as management buy-out expertise and venture capital investment to be counterbalanced by contra-cyclical activities such as insolvency work. Services organizations often take on a base load of relatively unattractive but predictable work to counter balance highly cyclical work—attorneys may undertake criminal defense work to cushion them against over reliance on relatively lucrative but cyclical property transferring work. Sometimes, statutory requirements may require a balanced portfolio of output—the Federal and State Bank Examiners' regulation of the U.S. banking system, for example, imposes constraints on banks' freedom to be market led in the pattern of their lending decisions.

Organizations should also maintain a portfolio of activities that are differentiated in terms of their cash generation abilities. An organization that has a predominance of mature service lines may eventually go into decline when its service range goes into decline. An organization that ties its fate to a small number of rapidly expanding service lines may find its own corporate growth slow down when these services reach maturity. It is important for most organizations to maintain a balanced portfolio of activities at different stages in their life cycle. This forms the basis of the BCG matrix, which conceptualizes a portfolio made up of "Stars" (services with a high market share and high market growth rate); "Problem Children" (services with a low market share but with a high rate of market growth); "Cash Cows" (services with a high market share in a low growth market); and "Dogs" (services with a low market share in a market which is not growing).

12.5 POSITIONING STRATEGY

Positioning strategy is an organization's attempt to distinguish its offerings from those of its competitors and to create a competitive advantage within a market. Positioning puts a firm in a subsegment of its chosen market; therefore, a firm that adopts a product positioning based on "high reliability/high cost" will appeal to a subsegment that desires reliability and is willing to pay for it. Some analysts see positioning as essentially a communications issue: the nature of a service is given and the objective is to manipulate consumer perceptions of it. Others, such as Lovelock,[6] point out that positioning is more than merely advertising and promotion but involves considerations of pricing, distribution, and the nature of the service offer itself, the core around which all positioning strategies revolve.

Organizations must examine their opportunities and take a position within a marketplace. A position can be defined by reference to certain scales. Service quality and price are two very basic scales along which a firm can position a service. A high price position combined with a high quality position may represent a sustainable market position for a service that appeals to a quality seeking, wealthy segment. A low price/low quality position, targeted at a more price-conscious segment, may be equally sustainable. Some combinations of positioning elements may be unsustainable over the longer term. For example, a high price/low quality position can be described as a "cowboy" strategy and generally is not sustainable, although it may sometimes be attractive—for example, in some tourism-related activities where tourists are unlikely to return to the area again. A high quality/low price position, by contrast, indicates that an organization is failing to achieve a fair exchange of value. Price and quality are very basic determinants of positioning strategy. In practice, firms position themselves using a variety of criteria based on features, promotional impact, customers' attitudes, and so on. In Figure 12.5, a product positioning map plots restaurants' positions with respect to two important service characteristics: customers' reasons for eating at the restaurant and the speed of service. Again, some positions are more sustainable than others. For example, a relaxed pace of serving may be compatible with positioning as a restaurant that friends or family visit for a social meal. A relaxed pace would be less appropriate in a functional restaurant satisfying hunger needs, where fast service is more appropriate.

The value of positioning maps comes from being able to identify positions

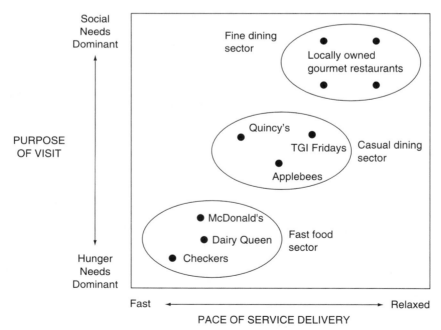

Figure 12.5   A product positioning map for restaurants in the United States

where latent demand is high, but that few operators have adopted. It became clear during the 1980s that the relaxed pace/social eating position and the fast service/hunger satisfaction position were adequately served (by fine dining and fast-food restaurants, respectively), relative to the demand for them (see Figure 12.5). At the same time, there was considerable latent demand for a middling position of semi-relaxed pace and semisocial eating, which was not adequately catered for. This position has since been vigorously adopted by casual dining chains such as Applebees, Bennigans, and TGI Fridays.

These are six generic scales along which a recreational center could be positioned, based on the general positioning definitions defined by Wind:[7]

- Positioning based on specific product features. The recreational center can promote the fact that it has the largest swimming pool in the area or the most advanced solarium.
- Positioning on benefits or needs satisfied (Figure 12.6). The recreational center could position itself somewhere between meeting pure physical recreation needs and pure social needs. In practice, positioning will combine the two sets of needs, for example, by giving up gym space to allow the construction of a bar.
- Positioning on the basis of usage occasions. The center could be positioned primarily for the occasional visitor, or the service offering could be adapted to aim at the more serious user who wishes to enter a long-term program of recreational activities.
- Positioning for user category. A choice could be made between a position aimed at satisfying the needs of individual users and one aimed at meeting the needs of institutional users such as sports clubs and schools.
- Positioning against another product. The recreational center could promote the fact that it has more facilities than its neighboring competitors.
- Positioning by product class. Management could position the center as an educational facility rather than a sports facility, thereby positioning it in a different product class.

Selecting a position for a service involves three basic steps:

- Identifying the organization's strengths and the opportunities in the marketplace to be exploited. An organization that is already established in a particular product position will normally have the advantage of customer familiarity to support any new service launch. A vacation tour operator that has positioned itself as a high-quality/high-price operator can use this as a strength to persuade customers to pay relatively high prices for a new range of value-added vacations. Sometimes a weakness can be turned into a strength for positioning purposes. The Avis car rental chain emphasizes that by being the number two operator, it has to try harder. Against internal strengths must be considered the attractiveness of a subsegment. For the tour operator seeking to build on its strong reputation for offering high-qual-

British Columbia vacations play very well for those looking for a serene getaway. This year however we've changed our tune (moderately, of course). You'll find musical events, performances and concerts everywhere, all part of our music '91 celebration. Toe-tapping, "hey look at that" fun. You can still take in the usual sounds. A blue lake rippling from the stroke of your paddle, mountain meadows rustling with a parade of scarlet widflowers, or the throaty gurgles of a cappuccino machine at a bay-side café. The countryside is within whistling distance of the city around these parts. For the whole score on travel here call **1-800-663-6000.** Tourism British Columbia, Parliament Buildings, Victoria, British Columbia, V8W 1X4. Now back to our regular show.

Super, Natural British Columbia

Figure 12.6   British Columbia is positioned as a serene getaway. Source: Tourism British Columbia, art director Bill Cozens, writer Alvin Wasserman, agency Melcim Vane Ouver.

ity/high-cost vacations, an analysis of the market may reveal greater opportunities in a segment that seeks a basic budget range of vacations. Should the organization decide to enter this market, it must avoid tarnishing its established brand values by association with a lower-quality product. One solution is to adopt a separate identity for a new service that assumes a different position (something the retailer The Limited has done by using the Lerner's name for the lower-quality chain of stores it acquired).

- Evaluating the position possibilities and selecting the most appropriate. An organization may discover several potential positions, but many may have to be discarded if they result in uneconomically small market segments or are too costly to develop. Other positions may be rejected as being inconsistent with an organization's image. Selection of the remaining possibilities should be on the basis of the organization's greatest differential advantage in areas that are most valued by target customers.

- Developing the marketing mix and establishing in the eyes of target customers the position that has been adopted. Organizations must develop programs to implement and promote the position they have adopted. In this way an airline that positions itself as providing superior flight attendant services must develop a program for recruiting, training, motivating, and retaining appropriate attendants who can deliver the desired service. It must also develop a creative platform for its promotional program that makes clear in the minds of target customers and employees just what a brand stands for. Positioning for a service industry differs from manufacturing industry in that the method of producing the service is an important element of the positioning process.

Services can be positioned either on a stand-alone basis or as part of a service organization's total service range—in effect, the service organization adopts a position, rather than the individual service. The fact that consumer decision processes are likely to evaluate the service producer at least as much as a particular service makes this approach to position analysis valuable. Shostack has suggested that within a range of services provided by an organization (or "service family"), a marketer can consider positioning strategies based on structural complexity and structural diversity.[8] Structural complexity comprises the number of steps that make up a service production process; diversity represents the extent to which service output is variable. In this way, a doctor's service is highly complex in terms of the number of processes involved in a consultation or operation. It is also highly variable, for service outcomes can be diverse in terms of both planned and unplanned deviations in outcome. Some processes can be high in complexity but low in diversity. Hotels, for example, offer a complete range of processes but are able to establish relatively low levels of diversity. An example of a service that is low in complexity but high in diversity is the service provided by a singer.

Positioning is seen by Shostack as a process of deciding how the service provider wishes to position its total range of services in relation to its customers. Complexity and diversity are two key dimensions by which an organization can be positioned. Positioning decisions have implications for the overall image of the provider and hence of individual services within its range. As an example, a dentist could take a more divergent position by adding general counseling on health matters, or reduce it by undertaking only diagnostic work. Complexity could be increased by adding retailing of supplies, or reduced by offering only a limited range of dental treatments. Some of the positioning options facing a dentist are shown diagrammatically in Figure 12.7. The position adopted by an organization will be influenced by its strengths and weaknesses relative to the market it addresses. A large dental practice may be better placed to position itself as a provider of complex services but needs to ensure that diversity in outcomes is minimized in order not to adversely affect its image. A small dental practice may find the most appropriate service position to be the provision of relatively simple services with divergent outcomes.

Many services organizations have found a low-complexity/low-diversity position to offer great opportunities for exploiting niche markets. For example, some attorneys specialize in the will-writing business, offering one standardized product line with little scope for variability. By developing expertise and reducing overheads, such companies can satisfy customers who do not need the more complex, or more divergent services of full-service attorneys.

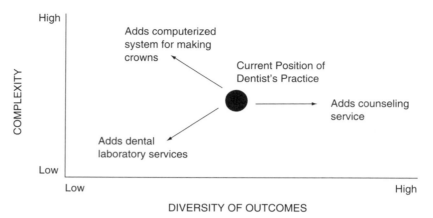

Figure 12.7   Service positioning strategies based on service structure
(Based on G. L. Shostack, "Service Positioning Through Structural Change," *Journal of Marketing* (1987) 51: 34–43)

12.5.1 Repositioning

Over time, organizations may seek to reposition their service offering for various reasons:

- The original positioning strategy may have been inappropriate. Overestimation of an organization's competitive advantage or over-estimation of the size of the subsegment to whom the positioning was intended to appeal could force a reevaluation of positioning strategy.
- The nature of customer demand may have changed. For example, it is argued that many grocery shoppers' preferences have changed away from an emphasis on low prices toward higher levels of service. Many grocery retailers have therefore repositioned their stores to keep pace with changing customer expectations.
- Service providers try to build upon their growing strengths to reposition toward meeting the needs of more profitable subsegments. In many service industries, organizations start life as simple, no-frills, low-price operations, subsequently gaining a favorable image, which they use to "trade up" to relatively high-quality/high-price positions. This phenomenon is well established in the field of retailing, in which McNair identified what has become known as the wheel of retailing.[9] This contends that retail businesses start life as cut-price, low-cost, narrow-margin operations, which subsequently "trade up" with improvements in display, more prestigious premises, increased advertising, delivery, and the provision of many other customer services that serve to drive up expenses, prices, and margins. Eventually, retailers mature as high-cost, conservative, top-heavy institutions with a sales policy based on quality goods and services rather than price appeal. This in turn opens the way for the next generation of low-cost innovatory retailers to find a position the maturing firms have vacated.

12.6 MARKETING MANAGEMENT FRAMEWORKS

The planning and implementation of marketing programs requires management, whether within a formal marketing department or elsewhere in the corporate structure. The importance that a marketing department assumes within any organization is a reflection on the nature of its operating environment. An organization operating in a fiercely competitive environment typically attaches great importance to its marketing department as a means of producing a focused marketing mix strategy by which it can gain competitive advantage over its competitors. By contrast, an organization operating in a relatively stable environment is more likely to allow strategic decisions to be made by personnel who are not marketing strategists. For example, pricing decisions may be made by accountants with less need to understand the marketing implications of price decisions.

In fact, the existence of a marketing department in an organization may be a barrier to the development of a true customer-centered marketing orientation. By placing all marketing activity in a marketing department, nonmarketing staff may consider themselves to be absolved of responsibility for the development of customer relationships. In service industries where production personnel are in frequent contact with the consumers of their service, a narrow definition of marketing responsibility can be potentially very harmful. But, a marketing department is usually required to coordinate and implement functions that cannot sensibly be delegated to operational personnel—advertising, sales management, and pricing decisions, for example.

12.7 THE INTERNAL ORGANIZATION OF A MARKETING DEPARTMENT

Responsibilities given to marketing departments within service organizations vary from one organization to another, reflecting the competitive nature of their business environments and also their traditions and organizational inertia. Where a formal marketing department does exist, responsibilities for marketing activities need to be allocated. Responsibilities are allocated by these four commonly used starting points:

- functions performed
- geographical area covered
- products or groups of products managed
- market segments managed

In practice, most marketing departments show more than one of these approaches to structure, for example, by integrating them into matrix-type structures, which will be described.

12.7.1 Functional Organization

A traditional and common basis of organizing a marketing department is to divide responsibilities into identifiable marketing functions (Figure 12.8). Typically, these functions may be advertising, sales, research and development, marketing research, and customer services. The precise division of the functional responsibilities depends on the nature of an organization. Buying and merchandising are likely to be an important feature in a retailing organization, whereas research and development assume greater importance in a technology-based service such as telecommunications.

The main advantage of a functional organization is its administrative simplicity. A disadvantage of this organization is that responsibility for specific services or markets can tend to become lost among numerous functional specialists. Without a manager championing specific products, weak and low-prestige products could easily become neglected. Destructive rivalry between functional specialists for their share of marketing budgets is also possible—for example, rivalry between an advertising manager and a sales manager for a larger share of the promotional budget.

12.7.2 Geographical Organization

Organizations providing a nationwide service frequently organize many marketing functions on a geographical basis. This particularly applies to the sales function, although it could also include geographically designated responsibilities for service development (e.g., opening new outlets) and some local responsibility for promotion. Service organizations operating internationally usually have a geographical basis to organization in the manner in which marketing activities are organized in individual national markets.

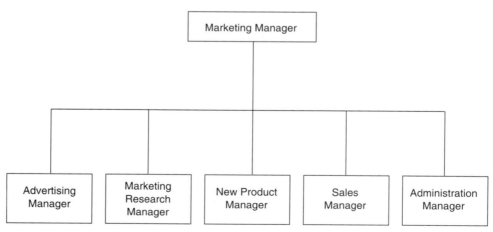

Figure 12.8   Functional organization of a marketing department

12.7.3 *Product Management Organization*

Multi-output organizations frequently appoint a product manager to manage a particular service or group of services (Figure 12.9). This form of organization does not replace the functional organization, but it provides an additional layer of management that coordinates the functions' activities. The product manager's role includes several key tasks:

- developing a long-range, competitive strategy for a service or group of services
- preparing a budgeted annual plan
- working with internal and external functional specialists to develop and implement marketing programs, for example, in relation to advertising and sales promotion
- monitoring the product's performance and changes occurring in its business environment
- identifying new opportunities and initiating product improvements to meet changing market needs

A product management organization structure has these potential advantages:

- A service benefits from an integrated cost-effective approach to planning. This particularly benefits minor products that might otherwise be neglected.
- The product manager can in theory react more quickly to changes in the product's

Figure 12.9 Product management organization

marketing environment than if no one had specific responsibility for it. Within a bank, a mortgage manager is able to devote a lot of time and expertise to monitoring trends in the mortgage market. He or she could become a focal point for initiating change and seeing it through when the environment changes.

- Control within this type of organization can be exercised by linking product managers' salaries to performance.

Despite these advantages, product management structures are frequently associated with problems:

- The most serious problem occurs in the common situation when a product manager is given a lot of responsibility for ensuring that objectives are met but is given relatively little control over resource inputs at his or her disposal. Product managers must usually rely on persuasion to get the cooperation of advertising, sales, and other functional specialist departments. Sometimes this can result in conflict, for example, when a product manager seeks to position his or her service in one direction while the advertising manager seeks to position it in another in order to meet broader promotional objectives.

- Confusion can arise in the minds of staff within an organization as to whom they are accountable for their day-to-day actions. Staff involved in selling insurance policies in a branch bank may become confused at possibly conflicting messages from an operations manager and a product marketing manager.

- A further problem, particularly relevant to many service industries, lies in product marketing managers' tendency to be in their job for only a few years before moving on to another position. The knowledge gained of a market and the confidence gained from key customers is therefore partially lost and must be rebuilt by the successor.

- Product marketing management structures lead to larger numbers of people being employed, resulting in a higher cost structure, which may put the organization at a competitive disadvantage in price-sensitive markets.

- Research has suggested that the existence of the optimal product management form is rare and that it is typically associated with an unwillingness of senior management to delegate authority to product managers.[10] Furthermore, research in the services industries suggests that the interdependencies of many services make product management structures difficult to implement and control.[11] As an example, one study of the insurance industry, an industry with a product marketing structure, found a high level of intra-organization transactions and a lack of profit center status enjoyed by divisions. This, together with inappropriate internal transfer pricing and poor incentive and control systems, severely curtailed the benefits of this type of structure, resulting in a hybrid structure that showed some degree of centralization.[12]

Finally, an interesting application of product management structures can be found in several service industries where ethical considerations may call for separation of functions. This can occur when a relationship developed between an organization and a customer in one product area can result in unethical marketing practices in another product area. A good example is provided by commercial banks that offer portfolio management and capital raising services. In a proposed takeover bid, it is often necessary for those involved in raising the capital required by a client to work very discreetly for fear of prematurely raising the share price of the target company. If this information were available to those staff working in portfolio management, it would give them an unfair advantage over the market, allowing them to build up a stockholding in the target company ahead of the announcement of a takeover bid. Commercial banks have attempted to build "Chinese walls" around their operations where this risk is present, and the adoption of a functional marketing management structure allows greater effective separation of functions. Numerous other service industries can be identified in which similar ethical problems can be lessened by the adoption of a product management structure. Accountants selling both auditing services and management consultancy services to a company may be tempted to gain business in the latter area at the expense of integrity in the former.

12.7.4 Market Management Organization

Many organizations provide services to a diverse range of customers with widely varying needs. As an example, an international airline provides the basically similar service of transportation for the private consumer market, the business travel market, and the tour operator market. However, the specific needs of each group of users vary significantly. Business passengers are likely to differ from vacation travelers in the importance they attach to service attributes such as flexibility, ease of reservations, and speed. In such situations, market managers can be appointed to oversee the development of particular markets, in much the same way as a product manager oversees particular products. Instead of being given specific financial targets for their products, market managers are usually given growth or market share targets. The main advantage of this form of organization is that it allows marketing activity to be focused on meeting the needs of distinct and identified groups of customers— something that should be at the heart of all truly marketing-oriented organizations. New innovative services are more likely to emerge within this structure than when an organization's response is confined within traditional product management boundaries. Market management structures are also arguably more conducive to the important task of developing relationships with customers, especially for business-to-business services. When an organization has many very important customers, it is common to find the appointment of key account managers to handle relationships with those clients in order to exploit marketing opportunities that are of mutual benefit to both.

Many of the disadvantages of product management organization are also shared by market-based structures. Again, there can be a conflict between responsibility and authority, and this form of structure can also become expensive to operate.

12.7.5 Matrix Organization

Organizations that produce many different services for many different markets may experience difficulties if they adopt a purely product-based or market-based structure. If a product management structure is adopted, product managers require detailed knowledge of very diverse markets. Likewise, in a market management structure, market managers require detailed knowledge of possibly very diverse product lines. An alternative is to introduce a matrix type of organization, which combines market managers with product managers. Product managers concentrate on developing new products and promoting their own particular product, whereas market managers focus on meeting consumer needs without any preference for a particular product. An example of matrix structures can be found in many car dealers, where market managers can be appointed to identify and formulate a market strategy with respect to the distinct needs of private customers and business lease customers as well as being appointed to manage key customers. Market managers work alongside product managers who can develop and promote specialized activities—such as servicing, bodywork repairs, and auto rental—that can be made available to final customers through the market managers. An example of a matrix structure applied to a financial services organization is shown in Figure 12.10.

The most important advantages of matrix structures are that they can allow organizations to respond rapidly to environmental change. Short-term project teams can be assembled and disbanded at short notice to meet changed needs. Project teams can bring together a wide variety of disciplines and can be used to evaluate new services before full-scale development is undertaken. A bank exploring the possibility of developing a banking system linked to personal customers' home computers might establish a team drawn from staff involved in marketing personal banking services and also from staff responsible for technology-based research and development. The former may include market researchers and the latter computer development engineers. Matrix structures need not necessarily be confined within the boundaries of a traditional marketing department. Indeed, matrix organizations normally embrace all of an organization's functions. In this wider context, the flexibility of matrix structures can be increased by bringing temporary workers into the structure on a contract basis as and when they are needed. During the 1990s there has been a trend for many services organizations to lay off significant numbers of workers—including management—and to buy them back when needed. Besides cutting fixed costs, such "modular" organizations have the potential to respond very rapidly to environmental change.

Where matrix structures exist, great motivation can be present in effectively managed teams. However, matrix-type structures can also be associated with problems, most seriously, the confused lines of authority that often result. Staff may not be clear about which superior to report to for a particular aspect of their duties, resulting in possible stress and demotivation. When a matrix structure is introduced into an organization with a history and culture of functional specialization, it can be very difficult to implement effectively. Staff may be reluctant to act outside a role they have traditionally defined narrowly and guarded jealously. Finally, matrix struc-

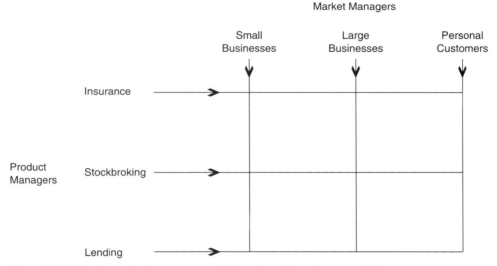

Figure 12.10   Matrix organization structure applied to a financial services organization

tures invariably result in more managers being employed within an organization. At best, this can result in a costly addition to the salary bill. At worst, the existence of additional managers can also actually slow down decision making processes when the managers show a reluctance to act outside a narrow functional role.

The great diversity of organizational structures highlights the fact that there is not one unique structure that is appropriate to all firms, even within the same service sector. Overall, the organization of a marketing department must allow for a flexible and adaptable response to customers' needs within a changing environment, while aiming to reduce the level of confusion, ambiguity, and cost inherent in some structures.

12.8 THE RELATIONSHIP BETWEEN MARKETING AND OTHER ORGANIZATIONAL FUNCTIONS

It was noted earlier that the business environment of a firm could favor a production or a sales orientation rather than a marketing orientation. In a truly production-oriented firm, a marketing department has little role to play other than processing orders. In this way, gas and electricity companies enjoying monopolistic and stable markets have been able to attach minimal importance to marketing, compared with the relative importance attached to the exploration of new energy sources and more efficient methods of distribution.

In a truly marketing-oriented service organization, marketing responsibilities cannot be confined to something called a marketing department. In the words of Peter Drucker, "Marketing is so basic that it cannot be considered to be a separate function. It is the whole business seen from the point of view of its final result, that is, from the customer's point of view."[13]

In marketing-oriented organizations, the customer is at the center of all the organization's activities. The customer is the concern not simply of the marketing department but also of the production and administrative personnel whose actions may directly or indirectly impinge upon the customers' enjoyment of the service. In a typical service organization, the activities of several functional departments impinge on the service outcome received by customers:

- Personnel plans can have a crucial bearing on marketing plans. The selection, training, motivation, and control of staff cannot be considered in isolation from marketing objectives and strategies. Possible conflict between the personnel and marketing functions may arise when—for example—marketing demands highly trained, flexible, and motivated front-line staff but the personnel function pursues a policy that places cost reduction and standardized recruitment policies above all else.

- Production managers may have a different outlook than that of marketing managers. A marketing manager may try to respond as closely as possible to customers' needs, only to find opposition from production managers who argue that a service of the required standard cannot be achieved. A marketing manager of an airline may seek to segment markets with fares tailored to meet the needs of small groups of customers. However, operations managers who are responsible for actually issuing travel tickets on a day-to-day basis may have misgivings about the confusion that finely segmented fares might cause.

- The actions of finance managers frequently have direct or indirect impact on marketing plans. Ultimately, finance managers assume responsibility for the allocation of the funds needed to implement a marketing plan. At a more operational level, finance managers' actions in respect of the level of credit offered to customers, or toward stockholdings when these are an important element of the service offering, can also significantly affect the quality of service and the volume of customers that the organization is able to serve.

Marketing requires all these departments to think about the customer and to work together to satisfy customers' needs and expectations. There is argument as to what authority the traditional marketing department should have in bringing about this customer orientation. In a truly mature marketing-oriented service company, marketing is an implicit part of everybody's job. In such a scenario, marketing becomes responsible for a narrow range of specialist functions such as advertising and marketing research. Responsibility for the relationship between the organization and its customers is spread more diffusely through a range of "part-time marketers," who may not have any direct line management responsibility for marketing but whose activities may indirectly impinge on the quality of service received by customers.[14]

It can be argued that the introduction of a traditional marketing department to a service organization can bring problems as well as benefits. In a survey of 219 executives representing public and private sector services organizations in Sweden, Gronroos tested the idea that a separate marketing department may widen the gap between marketing and operations staff. The results of a survey indicated that respondents in a wide range of services organizations considered that there were dangers in the creation of a marketing department. An average of 66 percent agreed with the notion, with higher than average agreement being found among nonmarketing executives and those working in the hotel, restaurant, professional services, and insurance sectors.[15]

12.9 IMPROVING ORGANIZATIONAL EFFECTIVENESS FOR MARKETING

Several studies have attempted to identify methods by which organizations can introduce a greater marketing orientation. These are some of the most frequently cited methods that are applicable to services organizations:

- The appointment of senior management who have a good understanding of the philosophies and practices of marketing.
- The introduction of in-house educational programs that aim to train nonmarketing management to empathize with customers' expectations.
- The introduction of outside consultants who can, from an impartial perspective, apply their previous experience of introducing a marketing culture to an organization.
- The installation of a formal market-oriented planning system. This can have the effect of forcing managers to work through a list of marketing related headings, such as an analysis of the competitive environment and identification of market opportunities, when they develop their annual plans.

There has been debate on the relationship between marketing strategy and the organizational structure within which such strategy is developed and implemented. The traditional view is that structures adapt to fit the chosen strategy, although more recent thought has focused on the idea that strategy is very much dependent on the structure adopted by an organization. One approach is to create a cross-functional team of managers for the purpose of designing a marketing plan for a market or market segment selected by top management for attention. The managers' initial view of their target market is challenged and refined through a focused marketing audit that requires continual iteration, forcing participants to go backward and forward through the process. The resulting marketing plan is likely to represent a high degree of commitment and ownership by those involved in creating it. The attraction of this type of approach is that it challenges managers to design better ways of addressing their markets by allowing things to be said that in a conventional planning process may be politically unacceptable. The marketing problem defines the agenda, rather than letting it be determined by the structure and political ideology of the organization. The process is designed to bring about marketing-led strategic change within the organization.[16]

CASE STUDY

GTE USES RE-ENGINEERING TO FIX ITS STRUCTURES AND PROCESSES

Management fads come and go, but during the early 1990s, one new management tool received a lot of attention from the services sector. It was called re-engineering, and although the basic ideas had been around for a long time, unprecedented enthusiasm for implementation was being shown by many services organizations.

What, then, is re-engineering? Essentially, it is about *radically* redesigning the *processes* by which an organization does business to achieve major savings in cost or improvements in service levels. It is about the operations of a business, rather than its strategy, and it starts the design of processes and structures with a clean sheet of paper. This is in contrast to most organizational change, which starts with an analysis of existing structures and attempts to tinker with it. Re-engineering starts by asking "If we were a new company, how would we organize ourselves?" It follows that re-engineering can stand for a total sudden change, inevitably challenging vested interests within an organization that are comfortable within their own departmental boundary.

Increasingly competitive markets have often been the spur for a company to re-engineer itself. Structures and processes that might have worked in less turbulent times can become a handicap to a business. This was the case at the telecommunications company GTE. Its telephone division, accounting for 80 percent of the group's $20 billion turnover in 1992, had been battered by increasingly ferocious competition on cost and service levels. Rather than continue the process of getting continuous marginal improvements in its repair, billing, and marketing departments, the company examined its operations from the outside in by looking at what customers wanted from the organization. The starting point was the company's belief that its customers wanted one central person to contact who could be responsible for seeing an inquiry through, whether it was to fix a faulty phone, question a bill, sign up for additional services, or any combination of services offered by GTE. The company wanted to avoid the all-too-common situation in which customers are bounced from one office to another and sometimes disappear in the cracks between departmental responsibilities.

During 1992, GTE set up a pilot customer care center in Garland, Texas, to see how things could be done. The company started with repair clerks, who had traditionally taken down information from a customer, filled out a report card, and sent it on to other employees who would check out the problem and fix it. GTE wanted the whole process to happen while the customer was still on the line—something that was currently happening just once for every two hundred calls. The first step in re-engineering was to move testing and switching equipment to the desks of the repair clerks, who were re-named front-end technicians. The aim was to increase the proportion of calls that the clerks could pass on without further referral.

The second step was to link the repair service with sales and billing. To do this, GTE has given its telephone operators new computer software that gives them access to databases that allow them to handle almost any problem a customer may have.

So far, GTE's results have been typical for a firm undertaking re-engineering. It has improved productivity by 20 to 30 percent, it has required hefty investment in training and information technology, and inevitably many employees have been laid off.

In the process of radically changing the structure and processes of its business, GTE challenged many vested interests. To be effective, re-engineering needs to be led by strong individuals who have authority to oversee implementation from beginning to end. They will need a lot of clout because fear, resistance, and cynicism will inevitably slow the task down. At first sight, though, this approach to re-organization appears to be in conflict with the principles of total quality management and other participative schemes that emphasize employee involvement in change. In fact, re-engineering works effectively only if it takes place in an environment of continuous improvement based on TQM principles. GTE, like many companies, tried to involve its employees in the details of implementation, even though the radical nature of the agenda was not negotiable. The employees who had to live with the new operating processes at least felt they had a hand in designing the new system.

GTE claimed to be satisfied with its pilot exercise in re-engineering. A painful and expensive process had delivered significant improvements in customer service at a lower cost. The process has since been applied to other customer service centers.

CASE STUDY REVIEW QUESTIONS

1. What should be the role of marketing at GTE?
2. What are the principal problems associated with a major re-engineering exercise?
3. What is the link between service quality and re-engineering?

12.10 MARKETING MANAGEMENT WITHIN THE NOT-FOR-PROFIT SECTOR

Marketing management is increasingly being introduced to the not-for-profit sector. However, attempts to introduce marketing management structures must recognize the great diversity of marketing tasks facing the sector. While some not-for-profit organizations function in competitive markets just like any private sector organization, others provide very complex services which by their nature can be distributed only by centrally planned allocation. The role played by marketing management in these instances may therefore be very limited. Nevertheless, it is recognized that many services provided by the not-for-profit sector—especially the public sector—would benefit from the introduction of some form of marketing management structure. Many of the comments noted earlier about introducing a marketing culture to an organization apply to not-for-profit organizations.

Another response to the desire for greater marketing orientation of public services has been the creation of single service agencies and social partnerships, which have been given duties previously carried out within government itself.[17] The number of such organizations has grown during the 1980s, for various reasons:

- Agencies and social partnerships can bridge the cultural gap between the bureaucracy of large public sector structures and the potential dynamism of small, semiautonomous, quasi–private sector organizations.
- In many social partnerships (e.g., urban renewal programs), the private and public sectors may have overlapping marketing responsibilities. A partnership allows for the reduction of duplication and for the entrepreneurial skills of the private sector to be combined with the resources of the public sector.
- By creating a semiautonomous body at arms length, it is sometimes possible for the body to gain access to additional funds from the private sector.

CHAPTER REVIEW QUESTIONS

1. What is meant by a matrix organization structure? Suggest services industries for which this type of structure might be appropriate, and discuss its possible strengths and weaknesses.

2. Do you agree with the idea that a marketing department can actually be a barrier to the successful development of a marketing orientation within service organizations? Give examples.

3. What are the main differences between implementing a market-oriented management structure within the public sector and implementing such a structure in the private service sector?

4. Suggest steps that could be taken by a telecommunications company to make its marketing management more responsive to customers' needs.

5. In what ways does the setting of marketing objectives differ between the private and not-for-profit services sectors? Give examples.

6. What is the value of contingency planning within the service sector? Identify one sector where the production of contingency plans is likely to be important and the factors that must be taken into account.

7. What factors should be taken into consideration by a travel agency in positioning its chain of outlets?

REFERENCES

1. Drucker, P. F., *Management: Tasks, Responsibilities and Practices* (New York: Harper & Row, 1973): ch. 7.

2. Levitt, T. "Marketing Myopia," *Harvard Business Review* (July/August 1960): 45–56.

3. Porter, M. E., *Competitive Strategy: Techniques for Analyzing Industries and Competitors* (New York: Free Press, 1980): ch. 1.

4. Ansoff, I. H., "Strategies for Diversification," *Harvard Business Review* (September/October 1957): 113–24.

5. Ennew, C., Wong, P., and Wright, M., "Organisational Structures and the Boundaries of the Firm: Acquisitions and Divestments in Financial Services," *The Services Industries Journal* 12 (1992): no. 4, 478–97.

6. Lovelock, C. H., *Services Marketing, Text, Cases and Readings* (Englewood Cliffs, N.J.: Prentice Hall, 1991): ch. 4.

7. Wind, Y. J., *Product Policy: Concepts, Methods and Strategy* (Reading, Mass.: Addison-Wesley, 1982): 79–81.

8. Shostack, G. L., "Service Positioning Through Structural Change," *Journal of Marketing* 51 (1987): 34–43.

9. McNair, M. P., "Significant Trends and Developments in the Post-War Period," in A. B. Smith, ed., *Competitive Distribution in a Free High Level Economy and Its Implications for the University* (Pittsburgh: University of Pittsburgh Press, 1958): 1–25.

10. Hill, C. W. L., Pickering, J. F., "Divisionalization, Decentralization and Performance of Large United Kingdom Companies," *Journal of Management Studies,* 23 (January): 26–50.

11. Channon, D. F., *The Service Industries* (London: Macmillan, 1978): ch. 1.

12. Ingham, H., "Organisational Structure and Internal Control in the UK Insurance Industry," *The Services Industries Journal* 11, no. 4, (October 1991): 425–38.

13. Drucker, P. F., *Management: Tasks, Responsibilities and Practices* (New York: Harper & Row, 1973): ch. 1.

14. Gummesson, E., "Marketing-Orientation Revisited: The Crucial Role of the Part-time Marketer," *European Journal of Marketing* 25, no. 2 (1991): 60–75.

15. Gronroos, C., *Strategic Management and Marketing in the Service Sector* (Cambridge, Mass.: Marketing Science Institute, 1983): ch. 1.

16. Piercy, N., "Marketing Concepts and Actions: Implementing Marketing-led Strategic Change," *European Journal of Marketing* 24, no. 2 (1990): 24–39.

17. Waddock, S. A., "Understanding Social Partnerships: An Evolutionary Model of Partnership Organizations," *Administration and Society* 21, no. 1 (1989): 78–100.

SUGGESTED FURTHER READING

ANSOFF, H. I., 1984. *Implementing Strategic Management.* Englewood Cliffs, N.J.: Prentice Hall.

BERRY, L. L., CONANT, J. S., and PARASURAMAN, A. 1991. "A Framework for Conducting a Services Marketing Audit." *Journal of the Academy of Marketing Science* (Summer): 255–68.

BOOMS, B. H. and BITNER, M. J. 1981. "Marketing Strategies and Organization Structures for Service Firms" in *Marketing of Services,* edited by J. Donnelly and W. R. George. Chicago: American Marketing Association, 51–67.

BOWEN, D. E. and SCHNEIDER, B. 1988. "Services Marketing Management: Implications for Organizational Behavior." *Research in Organizational Behavior* (10): 43–80.

ENNEW, C., WONG, P., and WRIGHT, M. 1992. "Organizational Structures and the Boundaries of the Firm: Acquisitions and Divestments in Financial Services," *The Services Industries Journal* (12, no. 4): 478–97.

GRONROOS, C. 1983. "Innovative Marketing Strategies and Organization Structures for Service Firms" in *Emerging Perspectives in Services Marketing,* edited by L. L. Berry, et al. Chicago, Ill.: American Marketing Association.

GUMMESSON, E. 1990. "Organizing for Marketing and Marketing Organizations" in *Handbook of Services Marketing,* edited by C. A. Congram and M. L. Friedman. New York: AMA-CON.

KOTLER, P. and ANDREASEN, A. 1991. *Strategic Marketing for Non-profit Organizations.* Englewood Cliffs, N.J.: Prentice Hall.

LOVELOCK, C. H. 1988. *Managing Services: Marketing, Operations and Human Resources.* Englewood Cliffs, N.J.: Prentice Hall.

LOVELOCK, C. H., LANGEARD, E., BATESON, J., and EIGLIER, P. 1981. "Some Organizational Problems Facing Marketing in the Service Sector," in *Marketing of Services,* edited by J. H. Donnelly and W. R. George. Chicago, Ill.: American Marketing Association.

MILLS, P. K. 1986. *Managing Service Industries: Organizational Practices in a Post-Industrial Economy.* Cambridge, Mass.: Ballinger.

PETERS, T. J., and WATERMAN, R. H. 1982. *In Search of Excellence: Lessons from America's Best Run Companies.* New York: Harper & Row.

SANDY, W. 1991. "Avoid the Breakdowns Between Planning and Implementation." *The Journal of Business Strategy* (September/October): 30–3.

Shostack, G. L., 1987. "Service Positioning Through Structural Change." *Journal of Marketing* (51): 34–43.

Thomas, D. R. E., 1978. "Strategy is Different in Service Businesses." *Harvard Business Review* (July/August): 158–165.

Waddock, S. A., 1989. "Understanding Social Partnerships: An Evolutionary Model of Partnership Organizations." *Administration and Society* (21, no. 1): 78–100.

13

International Marketing of Services

CHAPTER OBJECTIVES

After reading this chapter, you should be able to understand

- the nature of international trade in services and the reasons for its development
- methods used by services organizations to assess the attractiveness of overseas market opportunities
- the development of marketing mix strategies that are sympathetic to local market needs
- strategies for entering and developing overseas service markets

13.1 INTRODUCTION

At some point, many services organizations recognize that their growth can continue only if they exploit overseas markets. A company that has successfully developed its marketing strategy at home should be well placed to extend this development into overseas markets. Many of the fundamental principles of marketing management that have been applied to the domestic market will be relevant in an international setting. The processes of identifying market opportunities, selecting strategies, implementing those strategies, and monitoring performance, for instance, are basically similar. The major challenge to services companies planning to expand overseas lies in sensitively adapting marketing strategies that have worked at home to the needs of overseas markets whose environments may be totally different from anything previously experienced.

The purpose of this chapter is to identify the main differences facing the task of marketing management when services are provided in an international rather than a purely domestic environment. Some of the key differences between trade in goods and trade in services are emphasized, in particular, the diverse nature of buyer–seller interactions that cause international trade in services to take different forms.

13.2 THE IMPORTANCE OF INTERNATIONAL TRADE IN SERVICES

International trade in services is becoming increasingly important, representing not only opportunities for domestic service producers to earn revenue from overseas but also a threat to domestic producers from overseas competition. Some indication of the importance of international trade in services for the United States can be seen in the trade statistics. In 1992, the United States had an overall trade deficit of $62.5 billion. However, the trade deficit in manufactured goods was much worse—$96.2 billion—and has been steadily deteriorating. The impact of the trade deficit in manufactured goods is significantly offset by services, which generated a surplus of $57.6 billion. Travel-related and financial services have been particularly important "exports" of the United States.

13.3 DEFINING INTERNATIONAL TRADE IN SERVICES

Conceptual difficulties can occur in the attempt to analyze international trade in services. While trade in manufactured goods can be represented by stocks of goods moving in one direction and payment (in cash or in goods) in the other, the intangible nature of most services makes it difficult to measure a physical flow—trade statistics cannot rely on records of goods passing through customs. Any analysis of international trade in services is complicated by the diverse nature of producer/supplier interaction, stemming from the inseparability of the service production/consumption processes.

International trade statistics for services hide the fact that trade can take many forms. Sometimes, credits are earned by foreigners traveling to an organization's domestic market in order to consume a service (for example, an overseas tourist visiting the United States). On other occasions, credits are earned by domestic producers taking their production processes to customers in overseas markets. A further category of services can be identified that allow production and consumption to be separated. In these services, producers and consumers do not need to meet in order for international trade to occur. The form that international trade takes can be seen as dependent on the mobility of both producer and consumer and the separability of the production/consumption processes (Figure 13.1).

Immobility in service production processes occurs when it is either not possible or not sensible to produce a service in an overseas market, and customers in these markets must travel if they are to receive the service. This is typical of many tourism-

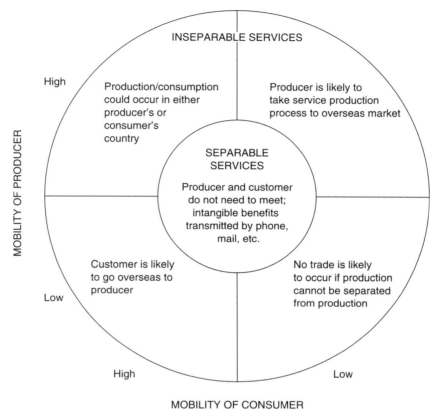

Figure 13.1   Producer-consumer interaction in overseas trade

related services that are based on a unique historic site. In other cases, it is customers who are inflexible, requiring the production process to be taken overseas to wherever they are located (e.g., building contractors must travel to a building site).

Because of the diverse ways in which international trade takes place, estimates of the total value of international trade in services are much more unreliable than for manufactured goods and are frequently subject to revision.

From the diversity of producer/consumer interaction, three important patterns of trade can be identified:

Production of a service in one country for consumption in another country.   While manufactured goods are commonly traded on this basis, this pattern can occur only in services whose production and consumption can be separated. This has often been achieved with mail and telephone communications. In this way, an insurance policy for a ship can be produced at Lloyds of London but the benefits of the policy relayed to the policyholder at any point in the world. Similarly, many information services can be traded between countries by modern telecommunications. It can be difficult for official statistics to accurately record both the outward flow of services and the inward flow of money for this type of trade.

Production of a service by a domestic company in an overseas market for overseas consumption. When the problem of inseparability cannot be overcome, a domestic service producer may be able to access an overseas market only by setting up production facilities in that market. Examples of services in this category include catering and cleaning services, which must deliver a tangible outcome at a point of the customer's choice. The various methods by which a company can set up overseas service outlets are discussed in more detail later in this chapter. While this type of international trade can be of great importance to services organizations, it appears in a country's balance of payments only in the form of capital movements, remitted profits, and trade in the tangible components of a service offer.

Production of a service at home for sale to overseas customers for consumption in the domestic market. It is often expensive or impossible to take a service production process to overseas customers; therefore, customers travel overseas to consume a service. This can occur for several reasons:

- Demand for a highly specialized service may be very thinly dispersed, making it uneconomic to take highly specialized staff and equipment to the market. As an example, it is common for patients to travel long distances to visit specialized medical facilities (Figure 13.2). Affluent consumers in overseas countries may find that while their own market does not support complex body scanning equipment, it is available if they travel to the United States.
- The laws of an overseas country may make the provision of a service in that market illegal, forcing those seeking the service to travel overseas. Countries that forbid abortion operations often do so to the benefit of abortion clinics in countries such as Britain, where a more liberal regime applies.
- Production costs may be lower in an organization's own country, making it attractive for overseas customers to travel in order to obtain a service. As an example, the lower price of labor in many less developed countries makes it attractive for shipowners to send their ships away for major overhaul work.
- A country may possess unique geographical features that form an important element of a service offer, and in order to receive the benefits of related services, customers must travel to that country. This is particularly important in tourism-related industries, in which the benefits of services associated with heritage sites or climatic differences cannot be taken to consumers. If European tourists wish to see the Grand Canyon, they must travel to the United States—the service provided by sightseeing and hotel services located at the Grand Canyon cannot be taken to customers overseas.

13.4 REASONS FOR OCCURRENCE OF INTERNATIONAL TRADE IN SERVICES

However it is measured, international trade in services has been increasing. From the perspective of national economies, several reasons can be identified for its increasing importance:

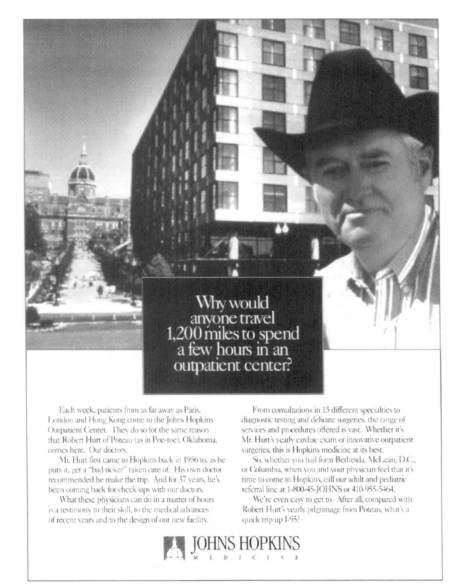

Figure 13.2 Johns Hopkins Outpatient Center is an example of a service that is produced in the United States and sold to overseas customers. In this ad, the Center is trying to persuade local consumers to use its facilities by highlighting its international reputation. Source: Johns Hopkins University.

- Services are traded between economies in order to exploit the concept of comparative cost advantage, which holds that an economy will export those services that it is particularly well suited to producing and import those services in which another country has an advantage. The concept of comparative cost advantage was developed to explain the benefits to total world wealth resulting from each country exploiting its comparative cost advantages with regard to access to raw materials and energy supplies. However, it can also be applied to the services sector. In this way, a favorable climate or outstanding scenery can give a country an advantage in selling tourism services to overseas customers, a point that has not been lost on tourism operators in the Bahamas. Another basis for comparative cost advantage can be found in the availability of low-cost or highly trained personnel (cheap labor for the shipping industry and trained computer software experts for computer consultancy, respectively). Sometimes the government of a country can itself directly create comparative cost advantages for a service sector, as when it reduces regulations and controls on an industry, allowing that industry to produce services for export at a lower cost than its more regulated competitors. For example, many "offshore" financial services centers, such as those on the Cayman Islands, impose lower standards of disclosure and taxation than do their mainstream competitors.

- The removal of many restrictions on international trade in services (for example, through negotiations of the General Agreement on Tariffs and Trade [GATT]) has allowed countries to exploit their comparative cost advantages. Nevertheless, restrictions on trade in services generally remain more significant than those on manufactured goods.

- Increasing disposable household incomes result in greater consumption of the categories of services that can be provided only by overseas suppliers, especially overseas travel and tourism. However, economic development within an economy can result in local provision of many specialized services that were previously bought from overseas organizations. Many developing countries, for example, are trying to reduce their dependence on overseas banking and insurance organizations.

- Cultural convergence, which has resulted from improved communications and increasing levels of overseas travel, has led to a homogenization of international market segments. Combined with the decline in trade barriers, convergence of cultural attitudes toward services allows many service providers to regard parts of their overseas markets as though they were part of their domestic market. For an individual company, development of overseas markets can be a combination of "pull" factors, which derive from the attractiveness of a potential overseas market, and "push" factors, which derive from the increasing unattractiveness of an organization's domestic market.

- For firms seeking growth, overseas markets represent new market segments that they may be able to serve with their existing range of products. In this way, a company can stick to producing services that it is good at. Finding new overseas markets for existing or slightly modified services does not expose a company to the risks of expanding both its product range and its market coverage simultaneously.

- Saturation of its domestic market can force a service organization to seek overseas markets. Saturation can come about when a service reaches the maturity stage of its life cycle in the domestic market while being at a much earlier stage of the cycle in less developed overseas markets. While the market for fast-food restaurants may be approaching saturation in the United States, fast food operators have new opportunities in many eastern European countries where few fast-food restaurant chains have yet been developed.

- Environmental factors may make it difficult for a company to fully exploit its service concept in its domestic market, forcing it to look overseas for opportunities. As an example, earlier regulations preventing banks from expanding across state borders led many banks to channel their growth into overseas expansion.

- As part of its portfolio management, an organization may wish to reduce its dependence on one geographical market. The attractiveness of individual national markets can change in a manner unrelated to other national markets. For example, costly competition can develop in one national market but not in others; world economic cycles show lagged effects between different economies; and government policies—through specific regulation or general economic management—can have counterbalancing effects on market prospects.

- The nature of a service may require an organization to become active in an overseas market. This particularly affects transportation services, such as scheduled airline services and courier services. A United States–based airline flying between Los Angeles and Sydney would most likely try to exploit the nondomestic market at the Australian end of its route.

- Industrial companies operating in overseas countries may require that their services suppliers cater to their needs across national boundaries. A company may wish to engage accountants who are able to provide auditing and management accounting services in its overseas subsidiaries. For this, the firm of accountants would probably need to have created an operational base overseas. Similarly, firms selling in overseas markets may wish to engage an advertising agency that can organize a global campaign in those markets.

- In many cases, private consumers demand a service that is internationally available. An example is the car rental business, whose customers frequently need to be able to book a rental car in one country for collection and use in another. To succeed in attracting these customers, car rental companies need to operate internationally.

- Some services are highly specialized, and the domestic market is too small to allow economies of scale to be exploited. Overseas markets must be exploited in order to achieve a critical mass that allows a competitive price to be reached. Specialized aircraft engineering services and oil exploration services fall into this category.

- Economies of scale also result from extending the use of service brands in overseas markets. Expenditure by a fast-food company on promoting its brand image to U.S. residents is wasted when those people travel abroad and cannot find the brand they have come to value. Newly created overseas outlets will enjoy the benefit of promotion to overseas visitors at little additional cost.

13.5 ANALYZING OPPORTUNITIES FOR OVERSEAS DEVELOPMENT OF SERVICES

Overseas markets can represent very different opportunities and threats compared with those an organization has experienced in its domestic market. Before a detailed market analysis is undertaken, an organization should consider in general terms whether the environment of a market is likely to be attractive. By considering in general terms such matters as political stability or cultural attitudes, an organization may screen out potential markets for which it believes further analysis cannot be justified by the likelihood of success. When an exploratory analysis of an overseas marketing environment appears to indicate some opportunities, more thorough analysis may suggest that important modifications to a service format would need to be made before the service can be successfully offered to the market.

This section first identifies some general questions that need to be asked in assessing the marketing environment of overseas countries and then considers specific aspects of researching such markets.

13.6 THE OVERSEAS MARKETING ENVIRONMENT

The combination of environmental factors that contribute to success in an organization's domestic market may be absent in an overseas market, resulting in the failure of attempts to export a service format. In this section, questions to be asked in analyzing an overseas marketing environment are examined under the overlapping headings of the political, economic, social, demographic, and technological environments.

13.6.1 The Political Environment

Government and quasigovernment organizations influence the legislative and economic frameworks within which organizations operate. Although the most important political influences originate from national governments, intergovernment agreements can also be important in shaping a national market.

National government framework.   At a national level, individual governments can influence trade in services in several ways:

- At the most general level, the stability of the political system affects the attractiveness of a particular national market. While radical change rarely results from political upheaval in most Western countries, the instability of many Eastern European and South American governments leads to uncertainty about the economic and legislative framework in which services will be provided.
- Licensing systems may be applied by governments in an attempt to protect domestic producers. Licenses can be used to restrict individuals practicing a particular profession (e.g., licensing requirements for accountants or lawyers may not recognize experience and licenses obtained in the United States), or licenses can be used to restrict foreign owners setting up a service operation (e.g., many overseas governments do not allow overseas investors to own majority interests in domestic airlines).
- Regulations governing service standards may require expensive reconfiguration of the service offer to meet local regulations or may prohibit its provision completely. Gambling-related and medical services often fall into this category.

- Import controls can be used to restrict the supply of the goods that form an integral part of a service. A restaurant seeking overseas outlets may be forced to purchase its materials locally, leading to possible problems in maintaining consistent quality standards and also possibly losing economies of scale.
- Service production possibilities can be influenced by government policies. Minimum wage levels and conditions of service can be important in determining the viability of a service. For example, many countries restrict the manner in which temporary seasonal staff can be employed, and this could make the operation of a seasonal resort hotel inflexible and uneconomic.
- Restrictions on currency movements may make it difficult to repatriate profits earned from an overseas service operation.
- Governments are major procurers of services and may formally or informally give preference in awarding contracts to locally owned services organizations.
- Legislation protecting trade marks varies between countries. In some countries, such as Thailand or Greece, the owner may find it relatively hard to legally protect itself from imitators.

Beyond the national level, international institutions can have important consequences for the international marketing of services. Some of the more important are described here:

North Atlantic Free Trade Agreement (NAFTA).   Negotiations for a free trade area comprising the United States, Canada, and Mexico have had a bumpy ride. When the agreement finally passed the United States Congress in November 1993, the world's largest free trade area moved closer to becoming a reality. While the United States has had bilateral agreements with both countries (for example, the 1988 free trade agreement with Canada), NAFTA opens up a wide range of service industries to unrestricted international trade, such as financial services, civil aviation, and cross-border trucking. Its passage will have an effect on how companies do business. For example, Canadian Fracmaster, LTC, announced it would create two new divisions in a reorganization aimed at expanding the company's global presence. The NAFTA division will focus on North America, Central America, the Caribbean basin, and South America; the other, the International Division, will focus on Europe, Russia, Southeast Asia, and Southern Asia.[2]

The European Union (EU).   NAFTA is in many ways a reflection of the European Union, a twelve-nation trading area with a population of more than 340 million in which internal trade barriers have gradually been removed. Although trade barrier removal initially benefited manufactured goods, the service sector is now increasingly benefiting from increased cross-border trade. As a result of the Single European Act of 1987, service firms licensed to operate in one of the EU's member states are increasingly able to use those licenses to operate in any other member state. An American bank or financial services company wishing to expand in Europe is increasingly able to view Europe as one market rather than as twelve separate markets. Although major internal differences will continue, Americans—as outsiders—have often been better able to spot the potential of Europe-wide marketing programs than their domestic European competitors.

The General Agreement on Tariffs and Trade (GATT). The origins of GATT lie in the early post-World War II period, when the signatories to the agreement attempted to achieve greater international economic prosperity by reducing the barriers that inhibited international trade. All the signatories agreed not to increase tariffs on imported goods beyond their existing levels and to work toward the abolition of quotas that restricted the volume of imports.

GATT has proceeded to reduce tariffs and quotas through several rounds, the most recent of which—the Uruguay round—has attempted to reduce barriers to international trade in services. Because of the multilateral nature of the GATT negotiations, attempts to liberalize trade in services can be impeded by arguments in completely unrelated areas of trade. For example, attempts to liberalize trade in financial services have been linked to demands to reduce agricultural subsidies given by some countries.

Friendship, commerce, and navigation treaties. These are agreements with other countries that define the rights of companies doing business between the two countries. At their simplest, they include bilateral agreements between two countries—for example, the Bermuda agreement, which governs the allocation of transatlantic air rights between the United States and Britain. Even here, change can be slow when there are many items on a hidden agenda. More complex multilateral agreements between governments can create policies and institutions that directly affect the marketing environment of firms. Examples include the International Civil Aviation Organization and the Universal Postal Union.

13.6.2 The Economic Environment

A generally accepted measure of the economic attractiveness of an overseas market is the level of GNP per capita. The demand for most services increases as this figure increases. However, organizations that wish to sell services overseas should also consider the distribution of income within a country, which may identify valuable niche markets. For example, the relatively low GNP per head of South Korea still allows a small and relatively affluent group to create a market for high-value overseas vacations.

An organization assessing an overseas market should place great emphasis on future economic performance and the stage a country has reached in its economic development. While many Western developed economies face saturated markets for many services, less developed economies may be just moving on to that part of their growth curve where services begin to appeal to large groups of people.

A crucial part of the analysis of an overseas market focuses on the level of competition within that market. This can be related to the level of economic development achieved within a country—in general, as an economy develops, its markets become more saturated. This is true of the market for most financial services, which is mature and highly competitive in North America and most Western European countries but relatively new and less competitive in many developing economies of the Pacific Rim.

The level of competitive pressure within a market is also a reflection of government policy toward the regulation of monopolies and the ease with which it allows new entrants to enter a market. As an example, while the European telecommunications market continues to be highly regulated in Belgium and Italy, deregulation in Britain has sent many U.S. companies seeking growth in that market.

13.6.3 The Social and Cultural Environments

Together, the social and cultural environments represent the values of a society. An understanding of culture and, in particular, an appreciation of cultural differences is clearly important for marketers. Individuals from different cultures not only buy different services but may also respond in different ways to the same service offer. These are some examples of differing cultural attitudes and their effects on international trade in services:

- Buying processes vary between different cultures. For example, the role of women in selecting a service may be different in an overseas market than in the domestic market, thereby possibly requiring a different approach to service design and promotion.
- Some categories of services may be rendered obsolete by certain types of social structure. For example, the extended family structures common in some countries have the ability to produce a wide range of services within the family unit, including caring for children and elderly members. Extended families also often reduce the need for external financial services by circulating funds within a very closed system.
- A service that is taken for granted in the domestic market may be seen as socially unacceptable in an overseas market. Interest charged on bank loans may be regarded as a form of usury in some Muslim cultures.
- Attitudes toward promotional programs differ between cultures. The choice of colors in advertising or sales outlets needs to be made with care because of symbolic associations (e.g., the color associated with mourning and bereavement varies across cultures).
- What is deemed to be acceptable activity in procuring sales varies between cultures. In Middle Eastern markets for example, a bribe to a public official may be considered essential, whereas it is unacceptable in most Western countries.

In short, culture not only conditions an individual's response to products and influences the nature of the purchase process, but also exercises considerable influence on the structure of consumption within a given society. It should also be remembered that no society is totally homogeneous. Every culture contains smaller subcultures, or groups of people with shared value systems that are based on common experiences and situations. These identifiable subgroups share attitudes and behaviors that reflect subcultural influences. They may be distinguished by race, nationality, religion, age, geographical location or some other factor.

13.6.4 The Demographic Environment

An analysis of the population of an overseas market will reveal, first of all, whether it is increasing in terms of the total number of people available to purchase services. Within the European market, the total population grew by 1.6 percent during the period 1985–1990, but this figure hides differences—the former West Germany, although it had a high level of GNP per capita, grew in numerical terms by only 1.04 percent, whereas Belgium actually contracted during the same period (by 1 percent). The strongest growth was shown by Italy and Ireland (3.5 and 5.7 percent, respectively). Much greater growth still was experienced in other parts of the world, especially Latin America (11.8 percent) and Oceania (7.9 percent). Of most importance is the projected population growth rate during the planning period.

Within these population totals, structures can differ significantly, for example, in the proportion of the population that is either young or elderly. As an example, within Europe during that same time, the proportion of the population aged 60 and above ranged from 15 percent in the Irish Republic to 21 percent in the United Kingdom. By contrast, the Irish Republic had the greatest proportion of under 15s (30 percent), compared with the former West Germany, which had the lowest (15 percent). This type of demographic information is crucial to services firms seeking overseas markets for highly targeted services. In addition to age differences, population structures can differ in ways that have implications for marketing planning:

- Very significant differences occur in home ownership patterns, with implications for demand for a wide range of home-related services. Within the European market, the proportion of households living in rented accommodation ranges from 21 percent in Spain to 53 percent in West Germany, while the proportion with a mortgage ranges from 8 percent in Spain to 44 percent in the United Kingdom.
- The proportion of the population living within metropolitan areas can have implications for services as diverse as car repair services, entertainment, and retailing. Within Europe, the proportion living in metropolitan areas varies from 13 percent in Italy to 44 percent in France.
- For some services (such as personal pension schemes), it may be important to identify markets where a high proportion of the population is self-employed (within Europe, this ranges from 45 percent in the Netherlands to 17 percent in Italy).

13.6.5 The Technological Environment

An analysis of the technological environment is important for services organizations that require a well-developed technical infrastructure and a workforce that is able to use technology. Communications are an important element of the technological infrastructure; poorly developed telephone and postal communications may inhibit attempts to develop an overseas market, for credit cards, for instance.

13.7 *SOURCES OF INFORMATION ON OVERSEAS MARKETS*

The methods used to research a potential overseas market are in principle similar to those used to research a domestic market. Companies normally begin by using secondary data about a potential overseas market that are available to them at home. Sources that are readily available through specialized libraries and government organizations include Federal Trade Commission briefings, reports of international agencies such as the Organization for Economic Cooperation and Development (OECD) and chambers of commerce. Use can also be made of specialist research reports commissioned by private organizations such as A. C. Nielsen and the Economist Intelligence Unit.

Initial desk research at home will identify the markets that show greatest potential for development. A company then often follows this up with further desk research of materials available locally within the short-listed markets, often carried out by a local research agency. This research may include a review of reports published by the target market's own government and by specialized market research agencies.

Just as in home markets, secondary data have limitations in assessing market attractiveness. Problems in overseas markets are compounded by the greater difficulty in gaining access to data, possible language differences, and problems of definition, which may differ from those with which an organization is familiar. In the case of services which are a new concept in an overseas market, information on current usage and attitudes to the service may be completely lacking. For this reason, it would be difficult to use secondary data to assess how consumers in many Eastern European countries would respond to large out-of-town superstores.

Primary research is used to overcome shortcomings in secondary data. Its most important use is to identify cultural factors that may require a service format to be modified or abandoned altogether. A company undertaking primary research in a new proposed overseas market would almost certainly use a local specialist research agency. Apart from overcoming possible language barriers, a local agency would better understand attitudes toward privacy and the level of literacy that might affect response rates for different forms of research. However, the problem of comparability between markets remains. For example, when a Japanese respondent claims to "really like" a product, the attitude may be comparable to that of a German consumer who claims to "quite like" the product. It would be wrong to assume on the basis of this research that the product is better liked by Japanese consumers than by German consumers.

Primary research is generally undertaken overseas when a company has become happy about the general potential of a market but is unsure of some factors that would be critical for success. For example, companies might ask if intermediaries would be willing and able to handle their new service, or if traditional cultural attitudes would present an insurmountable obstacle for a service not previously available in that market. Prior to commissioning its own specific research, a company may go for the lower-cost, but less specific route of undertaking research through an omnibus survey. These surveys, regularly undertaken among a panel of consumers in overseas markets (for example, the Gallup European Omnibus), carry questions on behalf of several organizations at once.

13.8 INTERNATIONAL SERVICES MARKETING MANAGEMENT

Many of the issues raised in Chapter 12 with respect to domestic operations apply equally to the management of overseas services marketing. The process of defining the organization's mission, analyzing opportunities, setting quantifiable goals, and implementing and monitoring results is just as important in overseas operations as in domestic operations.

The mission statement has a valuable function in communicating the central purpose of the organization. A simple, straightforward mission statement is a vital element in creating a common sense of purpose among diverse international groups of workers who may be expected to produce a globally uniform service output.

Objectives must be clearly stated for each overseas market, preferably in a quantified form. Objectives must be set, with due regard to local conditions, so as to be achievable. A global return on investment objective may be inappropriate in locally competitive markets where a service firm wants a presence in order to secure international coverage. For this reason, a hotel chain might develop in a popular area to satisfy the needs of its regular users and retain their international loyalty, even though the hotel will not be able to achieve its normal profit objective.

As in any new venture, objectives are essential if performance is to be monitored and any corrective action taken. Because overseas markets are generally much less certain than domestic markets, it is important that any variance from target is rapidly analyzed and corrective action taken. There must be a clearly defined process by which failing services can be assessed for their prospects of long-term viability. It may be, for instance, that assumptions on which a market entry decision was based have proved to be false and that no amount of local reformulation of a service will allow it to break even.

A major issue in the international management of services marketing concerns the extent to which an organization's headquarters should intervene in the management of overseas subsidiaries. A commonly heard complaint from marketing managers of overseas subsidiaries is that they are given insufficient freedom to respond to local market conditions. However, an argument can be made that intervention from headquarters is vital in order to secure the development of a consistent standard of service output in a planned way. Where a service is quite specialized to a national market and international brand building is relatively unimportant (e.g., municipal contract cleaning services), there is strong argument for delegation of management responsibilities on a geographical basis. On the other hand, where the service appeals to an international audience, there is a stronger case for introducing global product or market management structures to which overseas managers are answerable.

13.9 REFINING THE MARKETING MIX FOR OVERSEAS MARKETS

Having analyzed an overseas market and decided to enter it, an organization must make marketing mix decisions that will allow it to successfully penetrate that market.

Marketing mix decisions focus on the extent to which the organization will adapt its service offering to the needs of the local market, as opposed to the development of a uniform marketing mix that is globally applicable in all of its markets.

The process of globalizing a service offer can be different than with tangible goods because of the greater variability of services. In addition to being highly variable, services can be extremely flexible—they are more likely than goods to be designed around the specific requirements of small groups of consumers using a basically common formula. The extent to which services firms are either able or willing to adapt their service offerings to the needs of local markets depends partly on the nature of the service. Some fast-food restaurants, for example, have adapted their menus, architectural designs, and staff training methods to suit local needs while retaining a common process formula worldwide. Compared with manufactured goods, services can enjoy the best of both worlds, retaining their competitive advantage by remaining true to their basic managerial approach while changing their product to meet local needs.

One approach to globalizing services is the process of industrializing the service through the replacement of people with machines and through a systems approach to management. Theodore Levitt has attributed the worldwide success of McDonald's restaurants to the "same systematic modes of analysis, design, organization and control that are commonplace in manufacturing."[1] This process has occurred not just within the restaurant sector but also in the construction, hotel, professional, and technical service sectors. Standardization is often accompanied by a high degree of centralization, sometimes creating further management problems when local managers are instructed to sacrifice their local autonomy in order to benefit the organization globally.

13.9.1 Product and Promotion Decisions

Product and promotion decisions are at the heart of international marketing mix strategy. Five possible strategies can be identified for adapting the product offering and promotional effort in overseas markets, based on the extent to which each of them varies from the global norm.

Maintain a uniform product and promotion worldwide.   This approach effectively develops a global marketing strategy as though the world were a single entity. The benefits of this approach are numerous. Customers traveling from one market to another can immediately recognize a service provider and the values that its global brand stands for. If, on the other hand, the service formulation is different in an overseas market, a traveler visiting an overseas outlet may come away confused about the values of the brand. As an example, a car rental company with an established position in its home market as the operator of a very modern fleet of cars can harm its domestic image if it pursues a strategy of operating older cars in an overseas market. Standardization of the service offer can also yield benefits of economies of scale, which include economies in market research and the design of buildings and uniforms, although the greater adaptability of services renders these benefits less important than in the case of manufactured goods. The use of a common brand name in overseas markets, either for the service provider or for specific services, also benefits from economies of scale. Travelers to overseas markets will already be familiar with the brand's values as a result of promotion in the domestic market. However, care must be taken in selecting a brand name that will have no unfortunate connotations in overseas markets. The "Big Mac," for example, translates in French as the "big pimp." There can also be problems where legislation prevents an international slogan from being used. In France, for example, legislation limits the use of foreign languages that can be made in advertising, brand names, and the packaging associated with many services.

In the case of transportation services that operate between different markets, it may not be feasible to adapt the service offering to each of the local markets served. Either a compromise must be reached or the needs of the most important market must be given precedence. Airlines flying between two countries may find that the pricing of inflight services, the decor of the aircraft, and the catering must satisfy very different market needs at either end of the route.

Retain a uniform service formulation, but adapt promotion.   This strategy produces an essentially uniform global service but adapts promotional effort to meet the sensitivities of local markets (Figure 13.3). The manner in which brand values are communicated in advertisements reflects the cultural values of a society. For this reason, an airline may use a straightforward, brash, hard-sell approach in its American market, a humorous approach in its British market, and a seductive approach in its French market, even though the service offer is identical in each market. Similarly, certain objects and symbols used to promote a service abroad might have an effect opposite to that at home. Animals are often used in the United States to promote a range of home-based goods and services and present a caring and comfortable image, but in some markets, such as Japan, animals are seen as unclean and disgusting.

Adapt the service offering only.   This may be done in order to meet specific local needs or legislation while retaining the benefits of a global image. For this reason, a car rental company that offers nothing smaller than a compact car in its domestic market may offer a range of predominantly subcompact cars in areas where average journeys are short (e.g., islands of the Bahamas).

Adapt both product and promotion.   In practice, a combination of slight service and promotion modification is usually needed in order to meet both differing local needs and differences in local sensitivity to advertising.

Develop new services.   Markets may emerge overseas for which a domestic company has no product offering which can be easily adapted. For financial services companies, the social and economic structure of a country can be so different that none of a company's products can be easily adapted to it. As an example, the pattern of property ownership in Malaysia has given rise to a novel two generation property mortgage not generally found in the United States.

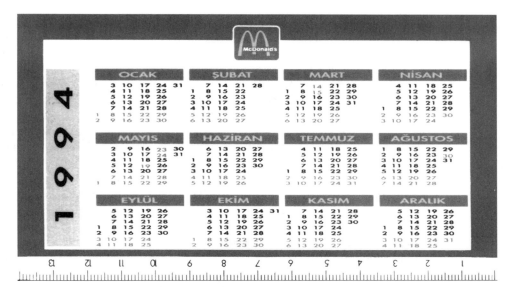

Figure 13.3   This handout is used by McDonald's in Turkey. This side shows a Turkish calendar and ruler and the McDonald's logo. At least in Turkey, McDonald's has followed a uniform service formulation but adapted promotion. Source: McDonald's.

13.9.2 Pricing Decisions

The issue of whether to globalize or localize the service offer arises again in respect to pricing decisions. On the one hand, it might be attractive for an organization to be able to offer a standard charge for a service regardless of where in the world the service is consumed—consumers will immediately have an idea of how much a service will cost and this helps to develop a long term relationship between client and company. A common pricing policy will help to project that company as a global brand. However, the reality is that a variety of factors cause global service operators to charge different prices in the different markets in which they operate. There is usually no reason to assume that the pricing policies adopted in the domestic market will prove to be equally effective in an overseas market. Furthermore, it may not be important to charge comparable prices for the same service in different markets if the local populations mainly produce and consume the services.

There are a number of factors that affect price decisions overseas:

- Competitive pressure varies between markets, reflecting the stage of market development that a service has reached and the impact of regulations against anti-competitive practices.
- The cost of producing a service may be significantly different in overseas markets. For services that employ people-intensive production methods, variations in wage levels between countries will have a significant effect on total costs. Personnel costs may also be affected by differences in the welfare provisions for which employers

are required to pay. Other significant cost elements that often vary between markets include the level of property prices or rental costs—the cost of acquiring space for a service outlet in the United States for example, is usually significantly lower than in most west European countries.

- Taxes vary between different markets; for example, sales taxes can be as high as 38 percent in Italy, compared to the 3.8 percent level that is more typical of the United States. There are also differences between markets in the manner in which sales taxes are expressed. While it is common practice in America to quote prices exclusive of sales tax, in most European countries, inclusive prices are normally quoted.

- Local customs influence customers' expectations of the way in which they are charged for a service. While customers in the domestic market might expect to pay for bundles of services, in an overseas market consumers might expect to pay a separate price for each component of the bundle. Also, while it is common for customers in the United States to expect to pay a tip to the person providing a service, other cultures expect to pay an all inclusive price without the need to subsequently add a tip. Formal price lists for a service may be expected in some markets, but in others, the prevalence of bartering may put an operator who sticks to a fixed price list at a competitive disadvantage.

- Government regulations can limit price freedom in overseas markets. In addition to controls over prices charged by public utilities, many governments require "fair" prices to be charged in a wide range of services, for example, tourism related services, and for the prices charged to be clearly publicized.

Exporters of manufactured goods are generally more able to sustain discriminatory pricing policies between countries than are service organizations. If wide differences in the pre-tax price of goods emerge between countries, entrepreneurs may buy goods in the lower priced market and sell them in the higher priced market. The inseparability of production and consumption generally prevents this happening with services—a low priced hotel room cannot be taken from the relatively cheap American market and offered for sale in the more expensive Bahamian market.

13.9.3 Accessibility Decisions

When a service organization is launching a service into a new overseas market, intermediaries can play a vital role in making the service available to consumers. The selection of intermediaries to facilitate the introduction of a service to a new overseas market is considered in more detail later. Consideration is given briefly here to the place and manner in which a service is made available.

The analysis of location decisions presented in Chapter 8 can be applied equally to overseas markets. However, a service provider must avoid assuming that a locational strategy that has worked in the domestic market will work just as effectively in an overseas market. A revised strategy may be required due to differences in the geography of the overseas market, consumer expectations, current methods of making that type of service available, and legislative constraints.

- Geographical differences can be important where land use patterns differ greatly in the target overseas market. As an example, fashion retailing in most European countries is still concentrated in downtown areas and an American fashion retailer might find difficulties in simply copying its suburban format in the European market.
- Consumer behavior may differ significantly in overseas markets. What is a widely accepted outlet in one country may be regarded with suspicion in another. The idea of consuming refreshments in a snack bar located within a clothing store may appear quite ordinary within the United States, but may encounter resistance in more traditional markets. Also, the extensiveness of outlet networks will be influenced by customers' expectations about ease of access, for example, in relation to the availability of car parking facilities or the distance that they are prepared to travel.
- Differences in the social, economic, and technical environments of a market can be manifested in the existence of different patterns of intermediaries. As an example, the inter-relatedness of wholesalers and retailers in Japan can make it much more difficult for an overseas retailer to break into that market compared to other overseas opportunities. In some markets, there may be no direct equivalent of a type of intermediary found in the domestic market; real estate agents on the U.S. model are often not found in many markets where the work of transferring property is handled entirely by a lawyer. The technological environment can also affect accessibility decisions. The relatively underdeveloped postal and telecommunications services of many eastern European countries makes direct availability of services to consumers relatively difficult.
- A method of distributing a service that is legal in the domestic market may be against the law in another country. Many countries restrict the selling of financial, travel, and gambling services to different agents than the domestic market.

13.9.4 People Decisions

It has already been noted that the people element of the marketing mix is more important for services than for goods, therefore it is important that this element is appropriately formulated for an overseas market. Where overseas service delivery involves direct producer-consumer interaction, a decision must be made on whether to employ local or expatriate staff. The latter may be preferable in those cases in which a service is highly specialized and may be useful in adding to the global uniformity of the service offering. In some circumstances, the presence of front-line expatriate serving staff can add to the appeal of a service; for example, a chain of American style steak houses established in Britain may add to their appeal by employing authentic American staff.

For relatively straight forward services, a large proportion of staff would be recruited locally, leaving just senior management posts filled by expatriates. Sometimes, an extensive staff development program may be required to ensure that locally recruited staff perform in a manner that is consistent with the company's global image. This can sometimes be quite a difficult task. A fast food operator may have difficulty developing values of speed and efficiency among its staff in countries where the pace of life is relatively slow.

Where staff are recruited locally, employment legislation can affect the short and long term flexibility of service provision. This can have an impact on the ease with which staff can be laid off or dismissed should demand fall. In Germany, the Dismissals Protection Law (Kundigungsschutzgesetz) gives considerable protection to salaried staff who have been in their job for more than six months, allowing dismissal only for a "socially justified" reason. Countries' laws also differ regarding the extent to which an employer can prevent a former employee with knowledge of valuable trade secrets from working for a competitor.

CASE STUDY

CHOICE OF INTERNATIONAL MARKET ENTRY OPTIONS

In the hotel industry, global brands can become valuable assets. Customers booking hotel accommodations are often traveling overseas where a plethora of unknown brand names only serves to increase the perceived riskiness of hotel decisions. Just what standards should travelers expect when they book into an unknown hotel in Rio de Janeiro? And how does an American get to hear about it in the first place? Clearly, an international chain has many potential marketing advantages over independent stand-alone hotels. For international travelers, international hotel brands allow rapid recognition of the standards of service that a hotel is likely to offer. A chain is also better able to support a worldwide sales operation than is a single hotel, making reservations of accommodation relatively easy for travelers. Hotel chains have achieved such significance that by the early 1990s, it has been estimated that about 70 percent of 50-plus bedroom hotels in the United States belonged to some form of chain, the majority as franchise operations. The comparable figure for most European countries was in the range of 10 to 25 percent. The United Kingdom was just 15 percent.

The U.S.-based Choice Hotels International owned a series of hot brand names that were widely recognized and respected in its domestic market. Over time, it had built up a series of highly segmented chains, with—among others—Econo Lodge and Friendship Inns providing basic facilities at the lower end of the market and its Clarion and Quality brands providing more upscale chains. Choice had grown to be the largest hotel operator in the world (when measured by hotel numbers rather than rooms), with a total of 250,000 bedrooms in 2,300 hotels in 29 countries. All but 5,000 of its bedrooms are operated on a franchise basis, the latter being located in a small number of company-operated or -managed hotels. The challenge for Choice was to increase its representation in Europe to satisfy not only domestic European customers but also the increasing number of Americans visiting Europe to whom Choice brands had acquired high recognition. With a lot of experience of franchising in its domestic market behind it, Choice chose this route for its European expansion. However, an analysis of its implementation illustrates some of the possible pitfalls as well as the opportunities of international services franchising.

The Choice strategic plan for Europe, developed during the late 1980s, envisaged having 300 hotels operating under the Choice umbrella by 1997 and 500 by the year 2000. One of its first moves into the British market was to sign a franchise agreement with Scandic Crown Hotels U.K., a small chain of five hotels. In return for paying franchise fees, the owners of Scandic Crown Hotels were able to benefit from the worldwide marketing effort of Choice Hotels. The chain was to operate under the brand name of Clarion—one of Choice Hotels' more upscale brands. However, this initial venture into British franchising encountered several problems. While Choice attempted to develop a strong brand that would stand for internationally consistent attributes, it came up against the loyalty of franchisees to their existing names. The latter insisted on giving primary emphasis to their own names and only secondary emphasis to the Clarion brand name, to the point where one typical hotel became known confusingly as the "Clarion Scandic Crown Nelson Dock." Choice Hotels also became only too aware of the variable efforts made by its franchisees in implementing the service quality standards that the Clarion brand stood for.

Faced with the problem of establishing values for its franchisees to follow, the company resorted to developing its own small chain of branded hotels to hold up as an example of the standards expected of the brand. In this way, Quality Hotels Europe was founded with the aim of creating a chain of thirty Quality Hotel or Comfort Inn branded hotels throughout Europe, using $200 million of capital provided by the parent company in the United States.

In expanding into Europe, the company was careful not to Americanize the European hotel scene, but incorporated the local character and operating style of hotels to suit the needs of both domestic and international customers. For this reason, it decided not to take the American-style Econo Lodge, Rodeway, and Friendship brands to Europe, opting instead to develop the Clarion, Quality, Comfort, and Sleep Inn brands. Of the latter, Quality and Comfort Inns formed the focus of the company's effort.

In the case of the Sleep Inn brand, Choice sold a franchise for exclusive development rights in the United Kingdom to an organization called Budgotel. Its first hotel opened at Nottingham in 1990, with planned openings soon following on new sites at Hull and Chesterfield. Meanwhile, the European subsidiary established by Choice continued to sell franchises for the Quality and Comfort brands. Unlike the completely new buildings that characterized new Sleep Inn openings, 75 percent of Quality and Comfort franchises were conversions from existing hotels. Franchise fees typically worked out at an initial one-time fee of £120 per bedroom, a 1 percent payment on sales turnover, and reservation fees of £3.50 per booking paid to Choice. Franchise agreements were normally for an initial term of twenty years, with mutual rights to terminate after three, six, ten, and fifteen years.

The initial poor performance of its European operations led Choice to impose much stricter controls over its franchisees. Existing franchisees were no longer allowed to use the corporate brand as secondary to its own name, while new franchisees were required to be fully branded from the outset. Any hotel owners who failed to brand their hotels in this manner would lose their franchise. Plans to extend the range of Choice brands available in Europe for franchise were limited in the short term to the four core brands of Comfort, Quality, Sleep, and Clarion.

For the longer term, the company recognized that opportunities existed in the more up-market luxury hotel sector, which it currently did not adequately serve. In addition to the possibility of developing franchise links with existing well-respected hotel names, it has also investigated the possibility of acquiring an upscale European brand with an already strong position in the luxury hotel sector. Such a move might make a lot of sense for Choice, allowing its bed space to be sold through its worldwide sales network. The development of a new brand for the European market in addition to its highly segmented range of American brands can be seen as a recognition of the need to adapt brands to meet the needs of overseas markets.

CASE STUDY REVIEW QUESTIONS

1. For Choice Hotels International, compare the advantages and disadvantages of franchising with those of managing its own hotels in Europe.

2. How important do you think it is for a hotel to belong to an international chain?

3. What alternative strategies for overseas development are open to Choice Hotels?

13.10 MARKET ENTRY STRATEGIES

A new overseas market represents both a potential opportunity and a risk to an organization. A company's market entry strategy should aim to balance these two elements.

The least risky method of developing an overseas service market is to supply that market from a domestic base, something that is often possible in separable service offerings. A wide variety of financial and information services can be provided to overseas markets by mail or telephone, avoiding much of the cost and risk of setting up local service outlets.

When inseparability of service production and consumption occurs and the producer must go to the consumer, local outlets must be established. Risk can be minimized by gradually committing more resources to a market, based on experience to date. Temporary facilities could be established that have low start-up and close-down costs and where the principal physical and human assets can be transferred to another location. A good example of risk reduction through the use of temporary facilities is found in the pattern of retail development in eastern Germany following reunification. West German retailers who initially entered eastern Germany in large numbers were reluctant to commit themselves to building stores in specific locations in a part of the country that was still economically unstable and where patterns of land use were rapidly changing. The solution adopted by many retailers was to offer branches of their chain in temporary tents or from mobile vehicles, which could move in response to the changing pattern of demand. While the location of retail outlets remained risky, this did not prevent retailers from establishing their networks of distribution warehouses, which were considered to be more flexible in their manner of responding to changing consumer spending patterns.

Market entry risk reduction strategies also have a time dimension. While long-term benefits may accrue to the first company to develop a new category of service in an overseas market, there are also risks. If development is hurried and the service is launched before quality can be guaranteed to live up to an organization's international standards, the company's long-term image can be damaged, both in the new overseas market and in its wider world market. In the turbulent marketing environment of Eastern Europe in the late 1980s, two of the world's principal fast-food retailers—McDonald's and Burger King—pursued quite different strategies. The former waited until political, economic, social, and technological conditions were capable of allowing it to launch a restaurant that met its global standards. Burger King's desire to be first in the market led it to offer a very substandard service, giving it an image that it will probably take a long while to recover from.

When the inseparability of a service offer makes it impossible for an organization to supply the service to an overseas market from its home base, an assessment of risk is required in deciding whether an organization should enter an overseas market on its own, or in association with another organization. The former maximizes the strategic and operational control that the organization has over its overseas operations but exposes it to the greatest risk where the overseas market is relatively poorly understood. A range of entry possibilities are considered here:

13.10.1 *Direct Investment in Overseas Subsidiary*

This option gives a service organization maximum control over its overseas operations but can expose it to a high level of risk because of a poor understanding that it may have of the overseas market. A company can either set up its own overseas subsidiary from scratch (as many American retailers have done to develop outlets in overseas markets), or it can acquire control of a company that is already trading (such as the acquisition by AT&T of the Istel computer services company, based in the United Kingdom).

When the nature of a service offer differs relatively little between national markets, or when it appeals to an international market (as with hotels), the risks arising from creating a new subsidiary are reduced. Where there are barriers to entry and the service is aimed at an essentially local market with a culture different from that of the domestic market, the acquisition of an established subsidiary may be the preferred course of action. Even this course of action is not risk free, as was illustrated by the problems encountered by the United Kingdom's Midland Bank following its acquisition of a substantial interest in the U.S.-based Crocker Bank during the 1980s.

Direct investment in an overseas subsidiary may also be made difficult by legislation restricting ownership of certain services by foreigners. Civil aviation is a good example: many countries prevent foreigners from owning a controlling interest in a domestic airline.

13.10.2 *Management Contracting*

Rather than setting up its own service organization overseas, a company with a proven track record in a service area may pursue the option of running other companies' businesses for them. For a fee, an overseas organization that wishes to develop a new service would contract a team to set up and run the facility. In some cases, the intention may be that the management team should get the project started and gradually hand over the running of the facility to a local management team. This type of arrangement is useful for an expanding overseas organization where the required management and technical skills are difficult to obtain locally. In countries where the educational infrastructure offers less opportunity for management and technical training, a company (or, in many cases, overseas governments) can buy in state-of-the-art management skills.

For the company supplying management skills under such contracts, the benefits are numerous. Risks are kept to a minimum, as the company generally does not need to invest its own capital in the project. The company gathers overseas market knowledge, which it may be able to use to its own advantage if it plans similar ventures of its own in other countries. Staff employed by the company can benefit from the challenge of working on an overseas project and from career opportunities outside the mainstream domestic management route.

Management contracting has found many applications in the service sector. Within the hotel, civil aviation, and retailing sectors, many American companies have sold their management skills in developing countries, most recently in Eastern Europe. A number of American universities have contracted with overseas universities to build American style programs overseas.

13.10.3 Licensing / Franchising

Rather than setting up its own operations in an overseas market, a company can license a local company to provide a service. A license allows an overseas company to sell a service on behalf of the principal. In the service sector, it can be difficult to distinguish between a licensee and a franchisee. Licensing is more commonly associated with manufactured goods, where the identity of the overseas licensee who manufactures the goods is not usually important to the customer as long as quality control is adequate. The inseparability of service offers makes service producers an integral part of a service, requiring greater control over the whole process by which an overseas business operates. Therefore, while exporters of manufactured goods frequently license an overseas producer to manufacture and sell their products, a company developing a service overseas is more likely to establish a franchise relationship with its overseas producers.

Franchising in an overseas market can take several forms. Some companies attempt to enter into a direct franchising relationship with each individual overseas franchisee. The problem with this approach is the difficulty in monitoring and controlling a possibly large number of franchisees in a country far from home. To alleviate some of these problems, the franchisor would normally establish its own subsidiary in the overseas territory, which would negotiate and monitor franchisees locally. Alternatively, it would grant a master franchise for an area to a franchisee so that the latter effectively becomes the franchisor in the overseas country. In between these options are several strategic permutations. For example, a subsidiary could be set up as a joint venture with a local company in order to develop a franchise network.

As with the development of a domestic franchise service network, franchising can allow an organization to expand rapidly overseas with relatively low capital requirements. While a clearly defined business format and method of conducting business is critical to the success of an overseas franchise, things can still go wrong, for many reasons. The service format could be poorly proven in the home market, making overseas expansion particularly difficult. Unrealistic expectations may be held about the amount of human and financial resources that need to be devoted to the operation of an overseas franchise. Problems in interpreting the spirit and letter of contractual agreements between the franchisor and franchisee can result in acrimonious misunderstanding. A good example of an overseas franchise failure is the breakdown of the agreement made in the 1970s between McDonald's and its Paris franchisee, which resulted in McDonald's successfully pursuing legal proceedings against the latter for failing to maintain standards as specified.

13.10.4 Joint Ventures

An international joint venture is a partnership between a domestic company and an overseas company or government. Joint ventures take various forms and can be attractive to domestic firms seeking entry to an overseas market for many reasons:

- The initial capital requirement threshold may be too high for one firm to stand alone, resulting in a high level of risk.
- Overseas governments often restrict the rights of foreign companies to set up business on their account, making a partnership with a local company—possibly involving a minority stockholding—the only means of entering the market.
- There may be significant barriers to entry that a company already based in the overseas market could help to overcome. Barriers to entry could include the availability of intermediaries and licenses to operate.
- Consumers may be reluctant to deal with what appears to be a foreign company. A joint venture can allow the operation to be fronted by a domestic producer with whom customers are familiar while allowing the overseas partner to provide capital and management expertise.
- A good understanding of local market conditions is essential for success in an overseas market. It was noted earlier that the task of obtaining marketing research information can be significantly more difficult abroad than in an organization's domestic market. A joint venture with an organization already based in the proposed overseas market makes the task of collecting information about a market, and responding sensitively to it, relatively easy.
- Taxation of company profits may favor a joint venture rather than outright ownership of an overseas subsidiary.

A distinction can be made between equity and nonequity joint ventures. The former involves two or more organizations joining together to invest in a "child" organization, which has its own separate identity. A nonequity joint venture involves agreement between partners on such matters as marketing research, new service development, promotion, and distribution, without any agreement to jointly provide capital for a new organization. Joint ventures are an important feature of many services sectors where the benefits listed above can be achieved. They have assumed particular importance in the hotels, airlines, and financial services sectors.

Strategic alliances—whether or not involving joint equity—are becoming increasingly important within the service sector. These are agreements between two or more organizations whereby each partner seeks to add to its competencies by combining its resources with those of a partner. A strategic alliance generally involves cooperation between partners rather than joint ownership of a subsidiary set up for a specific purpose, although it may include agreement for collaborators to purchase shares in the businesses of other members of the alliance.

Strategic alliances can be very powerful within the service sector. They are frequently used to allow individual companies to build on the relationship they have developed with their clients by allowing them to re-sell services that they do not produce themselves but are produced by another member of the alliance. This arrangement is reciprocated between members of the alliance. Strategic alliances have assumed great importance within the airline industry, where a domestic operator and an international operator can join together to offer new travel possibilities for their respective customers (see the following case study).

International strategic alliances can involve a principal nominating a supplier in related service fields as a preferred supplier at its worldwide outlets. This strategy has been used by car rental companies to secure a linkup with other transport principals, to offer what the latter sees as a value-added service. An example is the agreement whereby Hertz Car Rental was appointed by British Airways as a preferred worldwide supplier for a five-year period beginning in 1988. Under the arrangement, passengers could reserve a Hertz car at the same time as their air ticket and in some instances (e.g., for shuttle passengers), Hertz guaranteed that a car would be waiting for passengers at their destination airport even if no prior reservation had been made. Hertz gained additional customers for its car rental business, while British Airways was able to add value to its service offer.

CASE STUDY

BRITISH AIRWAYS AND USAIR SET TO FORM WORLD'S LARGEST AIRLINE ALLIANCE

It is not economically feasible for airlines to operate direct flights between all the airports they serve, just as a telephone company doesn't run cable from each telephone to every other telephone in its network. So, during the 1970s and 1980s, airlines developed a series of "hubs"—airports where passengers could fly in on one route (a "spoke") and make a connection to another route. The development of hub and spoke systems potentially allows an enormous range of origin–destination possibilities.

Despite the improved journey possibilities brought by the development of a hub and spoke system, problems may arise for transferring passengers making connections at a hub airport. If the two connecting services are operated by completely independent carriers, it may be necessary to purchase two separate tickets, and the passenger may have to transfer his or her own baggage rather than checking it through to the final destination. Should the incoming flight be delayed, the second carrier may show little sympathy in rescheduling a ticket on account of delay caused by another airline.

Because of these operational problems, competitive advantage at hub airports is gained by airlines that can offer the most comprehensive and integrated network of services. This can be achieved either by being very large or by forming strategic alliances with other airlines. The latter approach can make sense where a domestic operator with an intensive network of local routes from its hub and an overseas carrier operating into that hub come to an agreement for the through ticketing of passengers between national and international routes. The benefit for passengers would be a seamless journey, free of the dual ticketing and transfer problems just described. For the airlines, a strategic alliance brings mutual benefits: the domestic operator feeds passengers into its partner's international services, while the latter provides its partner with additional domestic business.

During the late 1980s, British Airways had been watching with concern the growth of very large American carriers, such as American, United, and Delta, which were capable of offering a very comprehensive network of services. These airlines were putting British Airways at a competitive disadvantage. For several years, British Airways had been seeking a strategic alliance with an American airline that would allow it to compete with these large carriers by being able to provide "seamless" transatlantic travel from Europe to a comprehensive range of American destinations. Discussions had been taking place with United Airlines to form a strategic alliance, but these broke down following the failure of a proposed management buyout for United. British Airways then pursued an alliance with the Dutch airline KLM, hoping that the alliance might have included the Dutch airline's stake in Northwest Airlines. Again, discussions broke down.

In July 1992, British Airways announced that it had reached agreement to buy 21 percent of the voting shares in USAir for $750 million, creating an airline with a combined annual turnover of $16 billion. Because of statutory restrictions on the level of voting power that could be held by non-American citizens in United States airlines, British Airways would be able to only cast 21 percent of the votes at USAir shareholders' meetings, despite agreeing to purchase 44 percent of the total shares. Nevertheless, its American competitors pointed out that the structure of the deal would give British Airways effective control over several crucial management decisions. As a result of strong lobbying by the large American airlines, who wanted permission for the takeover to be made conditional upon American carriers gaining greater access to the British market, the proposed strategic alliance was initially blocked by the United States government.

Both partners were anxious to not let the proposed alliance be lost. They lobbied hard to win approval, both directly to the federal government and indirectly through the British government. Eventually, in March 1993, a modified strategic alliance was approved by the new Clinton administration, with a number of awkward caveats that prevented British Airways from taking too much control too quickly. Crucial to the deal was approval of a "code sharing" agreement that allowed international flights to appear in USAir schedules as USAir operated flights but in British Airways's schedules as British Airways flights. The agreement with USAir meant that British Airways would be able to feed passengers from its transatlantic route network into USAir's hub airports for onward movement by the latter's network. Similarly, USAir's loyal clientele would be fed into the combined British Airways/USAir network of transatlantic services and then on to connecting flights via British Airway's European hub airports. Both airlines would be able to significantly increase the range of "seamless" journeys possible within their networks.

British Airways claimed that the alliance with USAir was a major step toward achieving its policy of globalization, paving the way for a comprehensive global airline group. Progress toward globalization had already been made by an agreement in 1990 with the Russian airline Aeroflot to form a new international airline "Air Russia" and with a German regional airline to form Deutsch BA.

CASE STUDY REVIEW QUESTIONS

1. Why have international strategic alliances become so important in the marketing of airline services?
2. What possible problems might have been envisaged for British Airways or USAir as a result of their proposed alliance?
3. What public policy issues are raised by this alliance?

CHAPTER REVIEW QUESTIONS

1. Examine the reasons why a United States–based financial services company might attempt to expand into the European market
2. What cultural differences might cause problems for a hotel chain developing a location in India?
3. How might a bank go about researching market potential for business development loans in an overseas country?
4. In what circumstances is a global rather than a localized marketing strategy likely to be successful?
5. Suggest methods by which a firm of consulting engineers can minimize the risk of proposed overseas expansion.
6. What is meant by a strategic alliance, and why are they important to the services sector? Give examples of strategic alliances.

REFERENCES

1. Levitt, T., "Addendum on Marketing and the Post-industrial Society," *The Public Interest* no. 44 (Summer, 1976): 69–103.
2. "Business News," *The Financial Post* (May 26, 1994, Section 1): 45.

SUGGESTED FURTHER READING

ANDERSON, E., and COUGHLAN, A. T. 1987. "International Market Entry and Expansion via Independent or Integrated Channels of Distribution." *Journal of Marketing* 51 (January): 71–82.

AYAL, I. 1981. "International Product Life Cycle: A Reassessment and Product Policy Implications." *Journal of Marketing* (Fall): 91–96.

BAKER, M. J. 1985. "Globalization Versus Differentiation as International Marketing Strategies." *Journal of Marketing Management* (1): 145–55.

BARTOS, R. 1989. "International; Demographic Data? Incomparable!" *Marketing and Research Today* (November): 205–12.

CATEORA, P. R. 1987. *International Marketing.* Homewood, Ill.: Irwin.

COWELL, D. 1983. "International Marketing of Services." *Services Industries Journal* (November): 478–97.

EDVINSSON, L. 1986. "Organizational Development for International Services Marketing" in *Creativity in Services Marketing,* edited by M. Venkatesan et al. Chicago, Ill.: American Marketing Association.

EDVINSSON, L., and NANDORF, T. 1983. "The Exporting of Services: An Overview and Presentation of a Case Study Approach" in *Emerging Perspectives in Services Marketing,* edited by L. L. Berry et al. Chicago, Ill.: American Marketing Association.

KASHANI, K. 1989. "Beware the Pitfalls of Global Marketing." *Harvard Business Review* (September/October): 91–8.

KEEGAN, W. J. 1989. *Global Marketing Management,* 4th ed. Englewood Cliffs, N.J.: Prentice Hall.

LEVITT, T. 1983. "The Globalization of Markets." *Harvard Business Review* (May/June): 92–102.

PALMER, J. D. 1985. "Consumer Service Industry Exports: New Attitudes and Concepts Needed for a Neglected Sector." *Columbia Journal of World Business* (20, no. 1, Spring): 69–74.

PORTER, M. E. 1990. "The Competitive Advantage of Nations." *Harvard Business Review* (March/April): 73–93.

VANDERMERWE, S., and CHADWICK, M. 1989. "The Internationalization of Services." *The Services Industries Journal* (1): 74–87.

Glossary

Blueprint a method of visually portraying the processes and participants involved in the production of a service

Branding the process of creating a distinctive identity for a service or service organization

Competitive advantage benefits conferred by a firm's marketing mix that the target market sees as better meeting its needs than the competitors'

Consumer services services that are finally used up in consumption by individuals and give rise to no further economic benefit

Co-production of service contribution of more than one party to a service benefit that can be realized only in that way (e.g., customer–producer co-production implies that customers take a role in producing service benefits)

Core service the essential nature of a service, expressed in terms of the underlying need it is designed to satisfy

Critical incidents encounters between customers and service producers that can be especially satisfying or dissatisfying

Customer charter a statement by a service organization to its customers of the standards of service that it pledges to achieve

Customer expectations the standard of service against which actual service delivery is assessed

Customer needs the underlying forces that drive an individual to make a purchase and thereby satisfy those needs

Customization the deliberate and planned adaptation of a service to meet the specific requirements of individual customers

Culture the whole set of beliefs, attitudes, and ways of doing things shared by a group of people

Direct marketing direct communication between a seller and individual customers using a promotion method other than face-to-face selling

Discriminatory pricing selling a service at two or more prices when the difference in prices is not based on differences in costs

External benefits service benefits for which the producer cannot appropriate value from recipients

Franchise an agreement whereby a franchisor develops a good service format and marketing strategy and sells the right for other individuals or organizations (franchisees) to use that format

Functional quality customers' subjective judgments of the quality of service delivery

High-contact services services in which the production process involves a high level of contact between an organization's employees and its customers

Industrialization of services the process of deskilling and simplifying service production processes with the aim of reducing variability in outcomes and processes

Inseparability the fact that production of most services cannot be spatially or temporally separated from their consumption

Intangibility the inability of pure services to present tangible cues that allow them to be assessed by the senses of sight, smell, sound, taste, or touch

Intermediaries individuals or organizations who are involved in transferring service benefits from the producer to the final consumer; in services usually requiring the intermediary to become a co-producer of the service

Internal marketing the application of the principles and practices of marketing to an organization's dealings with its employees

Just-in-time delivery reliably getting products to customers just before they need them—an essential aspect of perishable service production processes

Key clients customers who are particularly important to an organization

Management contracting selling an organization's management expertise to manage another organization's facility on its behalf

Marginal cost the addition to total cost resulting from the production of one additional unit of output

Market a group of potential customers with similar needs who are willing and able to exchange something of value with sellers offering products that satisfy their needs

Market segmentation a process of identifying groups of customers within a broad product market who share similar needs and respond similarly to a given marketing mix formulation

Marketing audit a systematic review of a company's marketing activities and its marketing environment

Marketing mix the aspects of marketing strategy and tactics that marketing management use to gain a competitive advantage over its competitors; a conceptual framework which—for services—usually includes elements labeled the service offer, price, promotion, accessibility, people, physical evidence, and processes

Mission statement a means of reminding everyone within an organization of the essential purpose of the organization

Multiplier effect the addition to total income and expenditure within an area resulting from an initial injection of expenditure

Mystery shopper a person employed by an organization to systematically record the standard of its service delivery

Organizational image the way consumers see the organization providing a service, based on their set of beliefs and previous exposure to the organization

Perishability the inability of service capacity to be stored for sale in a future period—if capacity is not sold when it is produced, the chance to sell it is lost forever

Positioning developing a marketing mix to influence consumers' perceptions of the service and to give the organization a competitive advantage with its chosen target market

Producer services services that are sold to other businesses in order to assist them in producing something else of value; often referred to as business-to-business services

Product line a range of service offers that are related to each other

Product mix the total range of services offered by an organization

Productivity the efficiency with which inputs are turned into outputs; difficult to measure for services, as inseparability means that changes in production inputs often affect consumers' perceptions of the value of service outcomes

Pure services services that have none of the characteristics associated with goods, i.e., they are intangible, inseparable, instantly perishable, and incapable of ownership

Quality of service the standard of service delivery, expressed in terms of the extent to which it meets customers' expectations

Quality circles groups of employees formed to discuss methods of better meeting customers' expectations of quality

Queuing system a system for handling temporal excesses of demand relative to capacity

Relationship marketing a means by which an organization attempts to maintain an ongoing relationship between itself and its customers, based on continuous patterns of service delivery rather than on isolated and discrete transactions

Roles behavior of an individual that results from his or her social conditioning rather than from innate predispositions

Scripting pursuing a pattern of behavior that is tightly specified by another party

Service agents intermediaries who assist a service principal in making service benefits available to consumers; an agent is usually a co-producer of a service and acts on behalf of the service principal, with whom customers enter into legal relations

Service encounter the period during which an organization's human and physical resources interact with a customer in order to create service benefits

Service image the way consumers picture a service offer, based on their set of beliefs and previous experience of the service

Service offer the complexity of tangible and intangible benefits that make up the total functional, psychological, and social benefits of a service

Service principal a relational term describing an organization that produces a service but makes some or all of the benefits available through intermediaries

Service process the activities involved in producing a service which can be specified in the form of a blueprint

SERVQUAL a method of researching service quality and the gaps between customers' expectations and perceptions of actual service delivery

Substantive service the essential function of a service

Tangible cues physical elements of the service offer: brochures and advertisements, which provide tangible stimuli in the buying decision making process

Technical quality objective measures of quality, not necessarily the measures that consumers consider to be important

Variability the extent to which service processes or outcomes vary from a norm

Index